UPRIVER Families

Acadian Roots and Creole Heritage

Leonide Martin
Katherine Bonnabel
Corinne Martin
2022

Made for Success Publishing
P.O. Box 1775
Issaquah, WA 98027
www.MadeForSuccessPublishing.com

Copyright © 2022 Leonide Martin, Katherine Bonnabel, Corinne Martin

All rights reserved.

This book is based upon extensive research on the history of the Acadian people and genealogical studies of the Vial and Martin family lineages. Sources are documented in the text. Any errors or misinterpretations are entirely the responsibility of the authors.

In accordance with the U.S. Copyright Act of 1976, the scanning, uploading, and electronic sharing of any part of this book without the permission of the publisher constitutes unlawful piracy and theft of the author's intellectual property. If you would like to use material from the book (other than for review purposes), prior written permission must be obtained by contacting the publisher at service@madeforsuccess.net. Thank you for your support of the author's rights.

Library of Congress Cataloging-in-Publication data
Martin, Leonide, Bonnabel, Katherine, Martin, Corinne
UPRIVER FAMILIES: Acadian Roots and Creole Heritage
p. cm.

LCCN: 2022905612

ISBN: 978-1-64146-728-5 (*Paperback*)
ISBN: 978-1-64146-729-2 (*eBook*)

Printed in the United States of America

For further information contact Made for Success Publishing
+14255266480 or email service@madeforsuccess.net

Photo Credits:

Most of the photos of family members, houses, and places are from the personal collections of the authors. When obtained from other sources, these are acknowledged and the photos are used with permission.

Historic drawings are public domain, obtained from Wikimedia Commons, and attributed as requested. Links:
https://commons.wikimedia.org/wiki/File:Port_Royal,_Nova_Scotia_-_circa_1612_-_Project_Gutenberg_etext_20110.jpg
https://commons.wikimedia.org/wiki/File:Meeting_of_Francoise_Marie_Jacquelin_and_Charles_de_la_Tour.jpg
https://commons.wikimedia.org/wiki/File:Joseph_Broussard_en_Acadia_HRoe_2009.jpg

Paintings by Claude T. Picard of early Acadians are used by permission of the artists' family and Parks Canada, current owner, attributed as requested.

Historic photos of the Martin-Triche house and Leon C. Vial I are used by permission of Henry E. Yoes III, attributed to his publications.

Cover Photo:

The home of J.B. Martin Sr. and Celeste Triche Martin, Hahnville, LA c.1910.

On the front porch left to right: Celeste Irma Martin (m. Leon Charles Vial I), Celeste Triche Martin, Marie Emilie "Keet" Martin (m. Laurent Labry).

Photo from family collection.

Praise for *Upriver Families*

With this fascinating book, the authors take a 400-year genealogical journey to discover their Acadian roots. Along the way, the triumphs, struggles, and perseverance of their ancestors are interwoven with their own memories of the Martin and Vial families. Their personal accounts create a fuller understanding of these families that are well known for their political and educational contributions to the growth of the area known as the river parishes in Louisiana.

Rachel J. Allemand,
Educator and Author of *From Humble Beginnings:
St. Charles Parish Public Schools 1803-1980.*

Upriver Families is an origin story—different branches of a Louisiana family tracing their lineage to French Acadia almost 400 years ago. Yet it also serves as a rich historical lens, a trenchant study of the dynamic between Creole, Acadian and American cultures that have defined the River Parishes since the Purchase of 1803.

Howard Hunter,
co-author with James Gill, *Tearing Down the Lost Cause:
The Removal of New Orleans's Confederate Statues.*

Upriver Families: Acadian Roots and Creole Heritage reflects a tremendous amount of research on one specific line of the author's family; however, what unfolds is a very thorough explanation of Louisiana and St. Charles Parish history and culture, as that line expands collaterally. The story of this Acadian to Creole transformation is the genealogy of so many families in Louisiana.

Jay Schexnaydre,
President, German-Acadian Coast
Historical & Genealogical Society

I loved this book! It would have been so helpful when we were involved with Education Through Historical Preservation (ETHP), which included students from St. Charles Parish Schools… It follows my favorite way to learn—a great story being told with impeccable research to back it up.

Rita Carlson,
Board Member St. Charles Museum & Historical Association,
Co-chair Virtual Museum of St. Charles Parish History (SCPHistory.org),
leader of Education Through Historical Preservation (ETHP)

CONTENTS

Acadian Genealogy of Leonide Mary Vial..vii

Preface – Are We Cajuns?..ix

Ch. 1 – Discoveries and Reconnections..1

Ch. 2 – Of Place and Past: Leonide (Lennie) Martin Remembers Hahnville.........17

Ch. 3 – You Can Go Home: Corinne Martin Remembers Hahnville...................35

Ch. 4 – Beginnings in Acadia...43

    Charles Amador de St. Étienne de La Tour—Marguerite Membertou......43

    Jeanne de La Tour—Martin D'Aprendestique dit Martignon..............71

Ch. 5 – Acadian Generations..77

    Marianne D'Aprendestique—Guillaume Bourgeois.........................77

    Jeanne Anne Bourgeois—Jean LeBlanc....................................81

Ch. 6 – The Acadia Expulsion: Le Grand Dérangement..............................91

    Marie-Anne LeBlanc—Joseph Bujol......................................91

Ch. 7 – From Maryland to Louisiana...131

    Marguerite Bujol—Juan Francisco Vicente Chevalier Vives............131

    Jean Landry Chevalier Vives—Marguerite Marie Bourgeois.............158

Ch. 8 – Statehood and Secession 167
    Marie Malvina Vives—Martin Songy Reynaud 167
    Louise Marie Malvina Reynaud—Joseph Albert Bossier 181

Ch. 9 – A New Century in a Changing World. 207
    Louise Clothilde Malvina Bossier—Louis Adolphe Vial 207

Ch. 10 – Vial and Martin Families in St. Charles Parish. 235
    Leonide Mary Vial—Jean Baptiste Martin Jr. 235

Epilogue – Acadian to Cajun 277

Descendants of J.B. Martin Jr. and Leonide Mary Vial. 289

Appendix – Family Trees 291

Acknowledgements 297

About the Authors 299

References 301

Acadian Genealogy of Leonide Mary Vial

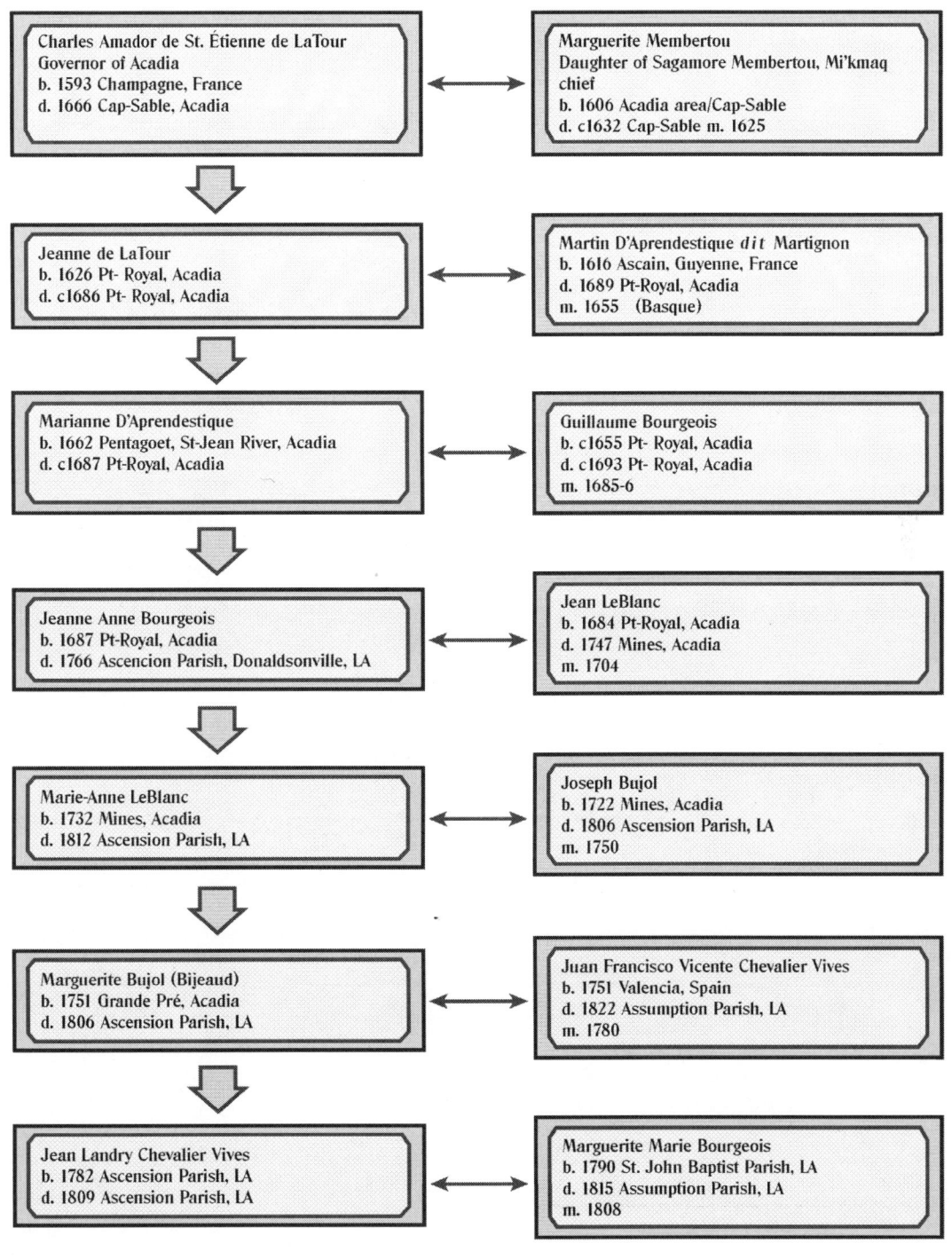

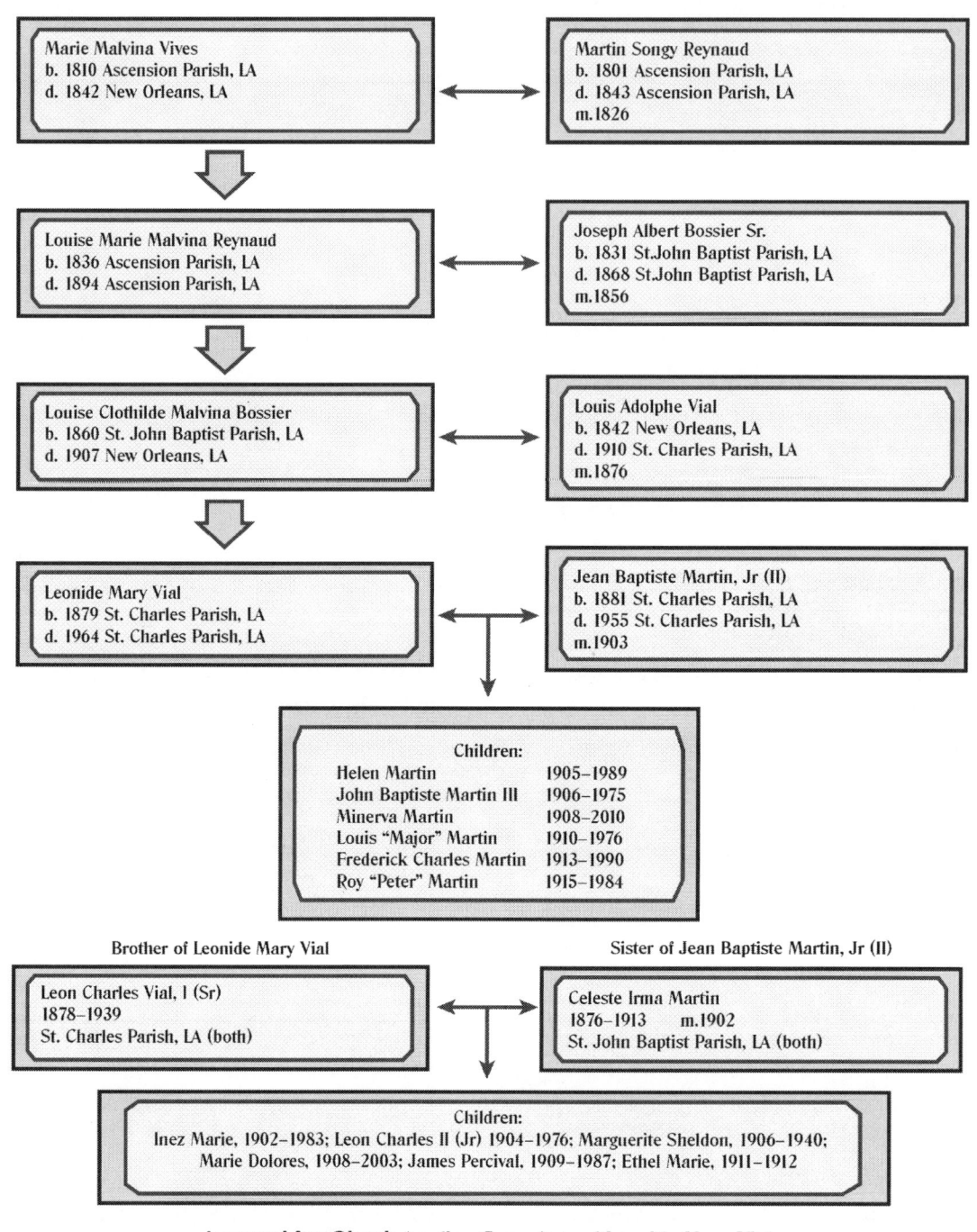

Legend for Chart: Acadian Genealogy of Leonide Mary Vial

Left column with large arrows—direct line of descent from Charles Amador de St. Étienne de LaTour to Leonide Mary Vial.

Right column—married into the line of descent.
b. born
d. died
m. married

PREFACE

Are We Cajuns?

The quest for self-knowledge is inherently human. Life is a journey of self-discovery as people seek answers to basic questions: Who am I? Where did I come from? Can knowing my family history give insight into my present life? How have my background and heritage shaped me? The search for answers often leads to genealogical research. We strive to know about our ancestors, to get a sense of the places and cultures where they lived, and to learn about their experiences. Perhaps in these discoveries will be cues, if not revelations, about forces shaping our families and the legacy they left.

Such curiosity about those who came before was a key factor in launching us—my daughter and myself—on the path of research and writing this book. It has taken the better part of a decade to bring the project to completion. It has required travel to places and countries where our ancestors lived, searching old records and documents in a wide variety of locations. We wanted to assemble a coherent account of the generations leading to our current family. We hope that other family members will find this both informative and enjoyable; they might even learn things they never suspected about their heritage. It will become part of our family's legacy to future generations.

If history is interpretation, as was famously said, then genealogy is perspective. What viewpoint do you take to trace the family lineage? Each generation offers several points of departure: the two parents, and their two parents, and the parents' sets of parents. Which line of descent will you follow? Go back five generations and you have 16 points of departure. The numbers of choice points accelerate rapidly into the hundreds. Some genealogists decide to follow the paternal line, which is easier to trace. The maternal line often gets lost with name changes following marriage.

As the family tree keeps branching, there are so many choice points that it's easy to get lost in the tangle, the abundance of data, names, and dates. The situation cries out for perspective, for taking a viewpoint and pursuing it. Perspective gives focus and reasons for choosing to inquire along certain branches, and not others. This is precisely what we've done in compiling this book about the Martin and Vial family genealogy.

The original idea was seeded many years ago by my mother's response to this question: "Do we have any Cajun blood in our family?" My mother was among the blue-blood Bonnabels of Metairie, a suburb of New Orleans saturated with places, streets, and institutions named after her prestigious family. Her shocked and disdainful response was: "Certainly not!" My mother's unusual emphasis in asserting the family had no Cajun connections stuck in my mind, especially as southeastern Louisiana is full of them. Cajuns are descendants of the Acadians of Nova Scotia and New Brunswick, originally known as Acadia when colonized by France in the early 1600s.

With many French names in the family, I always wondered about Cajun connections. My paternal grandparents, their siblings, and several of their children spoke French. My father, however, did not learn French and consequently I missed the opportunity to be bilingual from childhood. There was less French heritage on my mother's side, whose ancestry is mainly Dutch, Welsh, German, and Irish. Though my interest in the Cajun connection waned over the years, I was aware of a pervasive bias against Cajuns among my family's social circles.

When my daughter Katherine Bonnabel became interested in genealogy and created our family tree in MyHeritage, this re-awakened my curiosity about family origins. Through her research, we found that ancestors on my father's side had indeed come from Acadia, the line descending through his mother, primarily on maternal sides. Our trip to Nova Scotia and New Brunswick in 2011 opened a floodgate of discoveries, as we found ancestors in graveyards, historic sites, museums, and civil records. We determined to track this heritage through the generations to my paternal grandmother, Leonide Mary Vial Martin. We thought there might be Acadian infusions through my grandfather J.B. Martin's side, but this does not appear to be the case.

Leonide Mary Vial Martin became the point of departure. We have pursued this genealogical study from the perspective of tracing her Acadian lineage. It has led us back and forth between maternal and paternal descent, although primarily maternal. Such pathways are not simple to trace among family trees, and we owe a huge acknowledgement to our cousin, Wayne Vial, for the extensive genealogy site he has developed. This rich resource gave numerous insights not easy to come by. Wayne Vial and I share a common great-grandfather, although we have different great-grandmothers. Thus we are half second cousins.

To understand genealogical heritage, context is key—seeing ancestors within the time periods and geographic regions that shaped their lives. The chapters of this book are organized according to the ancestral couples whose offspring eventually led to Leonide Mary Vial Martin. Thus, each chapter provides descriptions of the regions in which they lived, and some history of what was happening politically and culturally in their societies. The Vial-Martin ancestors experienced turbulent times in nearly every generation, beginning with the founders and early settlers of Acadia. The account begins in 1610 with Charles Amador de St. Étienne de La Tour arriving in Acadia from Champagne, France. He became a leader and governor of this region of "New France" and married the daughter of a First Nations Mi'kmaq chief. It is possible to go back a few more generations in France, but this seemed a good place to start. From there, the account follows the son or daughter who transmitted this lineage, through five generations living in Acadia and then six generations in Louisiana. La Tour's first daughter, half-Mi'kmaq, married a Basque trader. Otherwise, all blood lines were Acadian until arrival in Louisiana.

There were many remarkable women in our lineage, although discovering them is difficult due to limited options for female leadership. Immense courage and resilience were required to handle their life challenges, especially the major disruption of *Le Grand Dérangement* when the Acadians were forcefully expelled from their homeland. Two women in the family leap from the pages of history, however. Antoinette La Tour, the second daughter of Charles Amador, had a heavenly voice and sang before the Royal Court in Paris at the Queen's request in 1644. Shortly after, she took vows as a nun at a French convent. Two centuries later, Herminie Vial was a piano virtuoso and studied with Franz Liszt in Paris. Liszt dedicated a piano fantasia to her in 1834, and they performed together in 1835.

Acadia was a highly contested land from the beginning, caught between imperial European powers and changing hands among them eight times over 109 years (1604-1713).

France and Britain were the main contenders, although divisions within French factions led to a short "civil war." The Dutch briefly conquered Acadia and named it New Holland. After an incursion by Scottish settlers, it became a Scottish colony for three years, giving the name Nova Scotia, "New Scotland." The Acadians tried to remain neutral through protracted colonial wars of the 17th and 18th Centuries, but after the British took over in 1713 relations deteriorated. Britain wanted to establish English-speaking, Protestant settlers on the rich farmlands of these French-speaking, Catholic Acadians. Ultimately Britain decided to deport a large portion of the Acadian population to its Atlantic coast colonies, or return them to France.

The devastation of the Acadian expulsion from their homeland, starting in 1755, is described through experiences of our ancestors. Some migrated to French-held regions and fought in the Acadian resistance with Beausoleil Broussard. Others were deported to Maryland, and subsequently journeyed to south Louisiana and settled above the German Coast of the Mississippi River (St. Charles and St. John the Baptist Parishes). The area they settled became known as the Acadian Coast (St. James and Ascension Parishes). The German/Acadian Coast is located 30-50 miles above New Orleans. Our ancestors who emigrated there were the last purely Acadian generation. Their children married into local Creole families of both French and Spanish origin. As far as our research shows, there was no more infusion of Acadian lineages after this. The next three generations further diluted Acadian roots by intermingling with Creoles and recent arrivals from France.

Creole is one of the least understood words applied to South Louisiana peoples. The original meaning of Creole is simply "one who is native or indigenous to an area." The word Creole is a French corruption of the Spanish term *criollo*, which meant a descendant of a European who was born in an Hispanic region of the new world. Initially, common usage of Creole applied only to whites, but in French regions of the Caribbean, particularly Saint-Domingue (Haiti), Creole was used for colony-born people regardless of color, differentiating them from indigenous natives. In early Louisiana the term meant descendants of settlers—French, Spanish, German, Irish, Italian, and African—who were born in the region. My ancestor six generations back, Jean Landry Chevalier Vives, was a Spanish Creole born in 1782. His father emigrated from Valencia, Spain; a Chevalier (knighted noble) who was granted a plantation near Donaldsonville, where he built Belle Alliance Plantation House.

Belle Alliance Plantation House

Over time, the white Creoles coalesced into a caste that considered itself superior to other French-speaking groups, especially the Acadians. White Creoles distinguished themselves from Creoles of color, and the term became synonymous with aristocrat. Louisiana-born Acadians, although technically classified as Creoles, recoiled from the local gentry's social pretensions. Many preferred their traditionally simple lifestyle and refused to use the term. But, upwardly mobile Acadians and members of the Acadian elite publically assumed Creole identity, marrying French and Spanish Creoles, and using this for political advancement.

During the 1900s, traditional Acadians were commonly called Cajuns, a corruption of "Cadien" which is the shortened version of the French spelling Acadien. The divergence between Cajuns and Creoles became more sharply drawn during the economic turmoil following the Civil War. Many planter class Creoles managed to preserve much of their land and wealth, while the Cajuns became more impoverished and less able to remain landholders. This social and economic divide widened until Creole classes regarded Cajuns as lower class, uneducated, and generally lazy and hedonistic.

Any simplistic division fails to recognize the complexity of South Louisiana's French-speaking population, however. The great cultural, racial, and ethnic diversity among Francophone groups was only recently acknowledged. Over time, interaction and intermarriage among these groups has blurred many distinctions, with divisions occurring mainly along socioeconomic lines. The Cajuns maintained a cohesive identity until two world wars and their desires to enter the economic mainstream pushed them in the process of Americanization. In the late 1900s a cultural revival of Cajun food, music, and folklore caught the public's attention, making South Louisiana's "Acadiana" region a prime tourist attraction. Still, erosion of French language among most families and loss of simple lifestyles continued to alter Cajun identity. This transition is discussed fully in the Epilogue.

The Vial-Martin family entered the 20th Century as Creole professionals and merchants in St. John the Baptist Parish, and then as large-scale sugar planters in St. Charles Parish. The generations in the first half of the century provided numerous government leaders and educators. Leonide Mary Vial Martin, her older brother Leon Charles Vial Sr. (I), and their siblings are the ancestors who carried Acadian lineage into current generations of our family. Even though by now Acadian genes have become a very small proportion, we can indeed say that we have Acadian heritage. But, my mother was conceptually if not technically correct—we don't have Cajun blood, because it turned Creole.

Leonide Luella Martin (Lennie)

Katherine Lee Bonnabel (Kathi)

CHAPTER 1

Discoveries and Reconnections

*"Two households, both alike in dignity,
In fair Verona, where we lay our scene,
From ancient grudge break to new mutiny...
Where be these enemies?—Capulet—Montague,
What a scourge is laid upon your hate,
That heaven finds means to kill your joys with love!
And I, for winking at your discords too,
Have lost a brace of kinsmen..."*

—Shakespeare, **Romeo and Juliet**

Feuds among families make for rich story material. While this was not the impetus for our book about family heritage, it became an underlying theme. The primary motivation was learning about our Acadian roots, from the Louisiana generations back to those originally from Nova Scotia—the area settled by French immigrants in the early 1600s, first called Acadia. Three women of the Martin family launched this quest, but soon discovered that the genealogical pathway we needed to follow went through the Vial family. But, we had few connections with our Vial relatives. It seemed strange, since the two families had lived on properties next to each other for several generations. The reason for the disconnection, we learned, was because of the Vial-Martin feud.

It was not as dramatic as the feuds between the Capulets and Montagues, or even the Hatfields and McCoys. But it did have a significant impact on our family relationships. Our generation of Martin cousins hardly knew anything about those Vial cousins of Hahnville, a large and locally prominent group. By now, several of our Martin generation had moved away from Louisiana, scattered to both coasts, rarely visiting after our grandparents died in the mid-1950s to mid-1960s. Those who remembered, our aunts and uncles, were similarly scattered and never spoke to us about these things.

As in Shakespeare's tragedy, it took a death to begin to reunite the families. Not a heart-rending double-death of young lovers, but the anticipated passing of the oldest living aunt, Minerva Martin. Aunt Min was 102 years old when she departed in 2010. In her later years, she was close to her niece, Corinne Martin, who oversaw her estate and provided for her final years. It was the duty of returning Aunt Min's ashes to Hahnville, to be interred beside the rest of her Martin family, which brought Corinne in contact with our Vial relatives. Corinne was drawn to her Louisiana roots, bought a house in Hahnville, and gradually rebuilt relationships with the Vials. This has been a major pathway for the Vial-Martin cousins to reconnect.

In the later years of her life, Aunt Min also reached out to her grandniece, my daughter Katherine Bonnabel. They exchanged many letters and phone calls, beginning when Kathi was in high school, which included family trees and information. These spurred Kathi's interest in genealogy, and she created a website. Aunt Min put her in touch with Sunny Vial (Leon C. Vial III), Min's first cousin, still living with his family in Hahnville. He sent a big envelope of family history documents; in these was information about Wayne Vial's genealogy website. Kathi connected with Wayne, her second cousin once removed, and found his website an outstanding source of information.

Through studying the Vial family lineage on Wayne's website, Kathi discovered and became intrigued with the Acadian roots of the family. This led to our trip to Nova Scotia in 2013, which sowed the seeds for writing this book. What we deduced, by researching Acadian roots and ferreting out the descent through 11 generations, was that this Acadian blood passed down into the Vial family in 1876. In that year, Louise Clothilde Malvina Bossier married Louis Adolphe Vial; they established their family in St. Charles Parish in the town of Hahnville. The Acadian blood, now quite diluted by French and Spanish Creole marriages, was carried by Louise.

Louise and Louis had 12 children; all but two survived childhood, so the Vials became a large family. Two of their children married into the Martin family. Leon C. Vial Sr. (I) married Celeste Irma Martin. His sister, Leonide Mary Vial, married Jean Baptiste (J.B.) Martin Jr. (II). Irma Martin and J.B. Martin were sister and brother. This "double marriage" made their children double first cousins. The Vials and Martins were intricately interconnected. They grew up living on adjacent properties bordering the Mississippi River, parcels from the old Fashion Plantation. They became leaders in St. Charles Parish, holding numerous government, civic, and education system positions.

But, the Vial and Martin families had a falling out in the mid-1940s. They were vying for political power, leading to confrontations that ruptured family relations. From that time until recently, there was limited communication between branches of the family. The cousins who remained in the river parishes had more contact, with Aunt Min and her brother Uncle Major (Louis Bebé) reaching out to Vial relatives in the 1960-1970s. Our grandmother, Leonide Vial Martin, had her lawyer nephew, Leon C. Vial III (Sunny), draw up her will; he also did the will her son, Uncle Major.

This accord, however, did not filter down at once to our generation (their nieces and nephews). Many of us were widely dispersed by then. We knew almost nothing of our relatives in the Hahnville area.

Once Corinne bought a home in Hahnville, and Kathi began celebrating her birthday with annual trips to New Orleans, we made a gradual reconnection with the Louisiana Vial-Martin relatives. There were several gatherings at homes of cousins in Hahnville, Ama, and New Orleans. We started exchanging historic documents and genealogical information as work on this book progressed. It is truly a family collaborative project, a wonderful reuniting of the Vial and Martin branches of the family.

Like the Capulets and Montagues, we had "... lost a brace of kinsmen..." but were now re-discovering each other. In the chapters of this book, the story of our Acadian descent is told. Each generation is framed within the historic events, socioeconomic conditions, and geography of their time and place, to give better appreciation of what their lives were like and what challenges they faced. The background and events of the feud are described in detail in Chapter 10. Stories of our Hahnville memories and present reflections follow, both below and in the next two chapters.

— **Leonide (Lennie) Martin**

Katherine Bonnabel Instigates the Acadian Roots Quest

My earliest memories of my family in Hahnville are shrouded by the mists of time. My great-grandmother's house seemed enormous to me. The back entrance had stairs leading up to a screened porch that wrapped around the side of house. There were the pecan trees in the back, and I remember spending autumn afternoons picking them up from the moist, fragrant soil, watching for the myriad collection of creatures beneath the leaf litter under the trees. I was only 5 years old when Leonide Vial Martin died, but my faint memory of her is one of quiet dignity and kindness.

The house next door belonged to Tante Keet who was sister to my great-grandfather, Jean Baptiste Martin Sr. (J.B. Martin was the second of three to have that name. He changed from Jr. to Sr. after his father died.) He died four years before I was born. Tante Keet's house was a wonder, a magical place full of adventures waiting to happen. She had a greenhouse that was like a magnet to me. I couldn't resist the pull of its mossy entrance beckoning me to come and explore all of its secrets. The green frogs, centipedes, anole lizards, and salamanders were living their best lives in that moist cavern full of lush foliage, and I was delighted any time I could pay them a visit.

There was an enormous cast-iron sugar cane kettle in the yard near the greenhouse. It was another place of mystery and delight. It was filled with rainwater and green algae, a habitat of abundant aquatic life. I would stand on my toes and peer over the lip of the kettle, which was about chest high on me. There were tadpoles galore, diving beetles, and once in a while I would catch a flash of shimmering orange goldfish swimming through the veils of the deep green algae. Transfixed, I would gaze into the depths of the water for what seemed like an eternity.

Though Hahnville was not the place that I spent most of my childhood, it always felt like coming home. It was the place where my roots ran deep into the earth. The scents of the river, the feel of the air, the big oaks with their veils of Spanish moss. All of it felt like family.

As the years went by, my relationship with my Great-Aunt Minerva Martin developed into something of a mentorship. She was a steady source of wisdom and encouragement. We exchanged many letters and phone calls. My letters to her always returned with a response, including spelling and grammar corrections in red pencil. I was exploring creative writing in high school and would send her some of the pieces I had written. She submitted one of my pieces to her English class at the University of Maryland for critique. I was both honored and terrified by this, and it turned out to be a great learning experience on constructive criticism.

She also sparked my interest in the history of the Martin and Vial families. We had so much information about the Bonnabels, my grandmother's prominent New Orleans family, but not a lot about my grandfather's. Aunt Min began sending me family trees and other historical information. I dabbled in it a bit here and there, but it wasn't until 2010 that I really started working on it in earnest. Aunt Min had her 102nd birthday that year and left this world to join our ancestors on September 4, 2010.

During the course of my research, I was able to connect with Wayne Vial who was a treasure trove of historical information about the Vial family. It was through my correspondences with him that I first discovered the Acadian roots of our family. To be fair, they were somewhat distant. But still, it was fascinating to me, as I had been repeatedly told that we had no such connections. This came from my grandmother, Dorothy Bonnabel Martin. It was absolutely true from her side of the family tree, being mostly Parisian French and Irish.

I continued working on our genealogy website, putting all the pieces together and gathering the stories as best I could. When so many of the names of people and places led back to Nova Scotia, I began to feel the call to go there and see for myself where these hardy, resilient Acadians had made their home. In 2013, my mother and I were able to make the pilgrimage to the very spot where our Acadian ancestors had settled in Grand Pré and Beaubassin. Beaubassin was designated a Canadian National Historic Site in 2005. I was able to put my hands in the soil where my ancestors built one of the first settlements in Acadia.

On August 15, 2013, my mother and I found ourselves in the small town of Bouctouche, New Brunswick. It happens to be the celebration of National Acadian Day. Part of the celebration is a "Tintamarre," an Acadian tradition of marching through one's community making noise with improvised instruments and other noisemakers. We met some of the local people who asked us what Acadian family we came from. We told them that we were descendants of the Bourgeois line, and they were overjoyed to hear that, welcoming us into the festivities with much enthusiasm. Joseph Bourgeois was considered a hero of the Acadian resistance, alongside the famous Joseph Broussard *dit* Beausoleil.

We joined the parade as it went through the streets and over a long wooden bridge which finished at the Island (Île-aux-Puces) at "Le Pays de la Sagouine." This is an

Acadian heritage center where we joined several hundred others that were waiting. Together everyone began singing and spent the afternoon dancing and celebrating their Acadian heritage. (See photo in Afterword)

Our trip to Nova Scotia was also a miniature family reunion of sorts, as our cousin Corinne Martin was not very far away, living in Maine. She was able to join us for part of the journey, and so began the reconnection of our lives to each other, to our family in Hahnville, and our distant ancestors in the lands of the Acadians.

— **Katherine (Kathi) Bonnabel**

Corinne Martin Returns Aunt Min's Ashes to Hahnville

Sometimes a place lays claim to you and there's nothing you can do but heed the call. I've thought about why that happens; maybe like magnetic forces in minerals and soils, our bodies are drawn to the elements that formed us. It makes sense that we can be drawn to a place, that our bodies know where they belong. I never thought that I'd go home to Louisiana, and I didn't exactly volunteer. But after almost a decade of helping my Aunt Min manage her older years, she finally let go and I brought her ashes back to Hahnville for a final rest.

I took Aunt Min's ashes back in November 2010, two months after her death. And the strangest thing happened. I stood at the door of the church where her service was held and saw—after decades—familiar faces, heard well-known names, and was swept up in the arms of our large extended family. I was flooded with sweetness and longing and gratitude. I was welcomed back, suddenly fed something I didn't even know I was hungry for. I felt so full and sustained, so happy. After the service, we went to the Taft cemetery and found the family tomb with many of Min's siblings, and then we searched around looking for Grandma and Papa. We found their graves and those of other Vial and Martin relatives, and shared family stories. It was a sunny and warm day, made surreal by the chemical plants with huge belching equipment and smoke that surrounds the cemetery. Not exactly a contemplative space!

My second cousin Leon (Sunny) Vial, his wife Mary Janet, and his daughter Nanette Vial hosted a reception after the service and burial, and I met so many cousins that it took me about two years to figure out who everyone was and how we were all related. It was a lovely gathering; lots of great food, some folks I remembered hearing about from Aunt Min, a few I knew. It felt like a great homecoming—there's something about blood relations that just grabbed me up and made me feel at home.

For the next few years, whenever I went back I spent time with my cousins: Sunny and Nanette, Dede Vial Schneider, Jara Roux, Mary Ann Vial Lemmon and her daughter. Nanette often took me fishing, photo shooting, and exploring bayous and lakes, and I learned more about the history of the Vial and Martin families. My body remembered these people and this place. I remembered how the air smelled when the river was high, the drone of cicadas, fierce mosquitoes, trains hooting in the night, ancient moss-bearded trees with limbs touching the ground so little children could climb right up into their hearts. I remembered cherry bounce and crawfish and alligators, and herons rising over the levee, the only hill we knew.

I wrote in my journal later how odd and sweet it felt, how unexpected that sinking into family soup. And I couldn't get enough. I went back, again and again, to my welcoming cousins who have lived there most of their lives. A fierce and hungry body-love for these, the flesh of my flesh, and for the land my own roots had known since my feet could walk that heavy soil, made me want to go home. And so I have.

I bought my Hahnville house on a whim about eight years ago. One day in Maine (where I lived), I off-handedly googled houses for sale in Hahnville and found one that looked sweet and affordable. I called Nanette (who is a realtor) and asked her about it; she had just shown it the day before! It was only a couple of houses away from the Lemmon law firm, where Mary Ann and some of her kids practice law. Turns out that Mary Ann's grandfather kept his horses in the back field for decades. Nanette said if I was interested, I better let her know soon because the Dollar Store next door was trying to buy it.

The house needed some work, and I was worried about making an offer on a house I hadn't even seen. My daughter Lara was flying just then to New Orleans to visit my sister Celeste, so I called Celeste at the airport and asked her to drive by the house on her way back to Houma, where she lives. Nanette met Celeste and Lara at the house, and soon afterwards I got the thumbs-up from them and made an offer. Buying the house was a minor miracle. I needed to sign papers and fax them back to the seller's firm by the end of the day; a Friday around 4:00 pm. I had no fax at home, and a major blizzard was descending on Portland, Maine. I decided to drive to the University of Southern Maine campus (where I work) and use their fax. The roads were terrible and I was sliding all over, but made it to work just in time to figure out that the school had closed due to the storm.

In tears, I returned home, called the seller and explained the situation. They said they could wait until Monday. Two weeks later, the sale went through! Considering how house sales normally go, it was kind of a miracle. So, lots of repair work later, I had the house. Now I spend most of the winter in my sweet house in Hahnville, with the levee rising from my back yard, and my loving extended family nearby.

— Corinne Martin

Vial-Martin Family Gatherings

There were many members of the Vial-Martin family living in South Louisiana into the 21st century. We have relatives in New Orleans, Hahnville, Ama, Metairie, Kenner, Houma, Lake Charles, and others. Corinne bought a vintage cottage in Hahnville in 2014, living there during the winter to escape harsh Maine weather. Her land extends to the base of the levee, from which the vast expanse of the Mississippi River can be seen. Kathi started the "NOLA invasion" tradition, inviting friends and relatives to join her in New Orleans almost yearly to celebrate her January birthday. Since Corinne had initiated reconnections with our Vial relatives, we gathered together during this time to get to know each other after years of separation. For many of us, these were our initial meetings as cousins.

January 2012. Kathi organized a big birthday luncheon at a downtown New Orleans hotel. Many out-of-town guests stayed at a colorful bed-and-breakfast near the French Quarter. It was once a bordello, and the decor was apt testimony to its previous occupation. Martins from Lake Charles, San Francisco, Oregon, Maine, and Baton Rouge came (see photo in Afterword). Some of us later gathered with Vial relatives in Kenner to watch the playoff game between the New Orleans Saints and San Francisco 49ers. We met second and third cousins from the Hahnville Vial family for the first time at Francesca (Dede) Vial's house. Naturally, all the Louisiana folks were passionate Saints fans. But David Gortner (Lennie's husband) was a 49ers fan from his Bay Area days. He managed to keep quiet almost through the entire game, but the spectacular nail-biting ending demolished his resolve. For football fans, the final two minutes is famous. The lead changed three times, and when a Saints' victory seemed guaranteed, 49ers quarterback Alex Smith ran with the ball from scrimmage and squeaked across the goal line with nanoseconds to go. In a stunned silence among Saints fans, David let out a few whoops. The looks he got were enough to kill. We probably didn't endear ourselves to our newfound cousins, sad to say.

Lennie Martin, Lara Anderson (Martin), Corinne Martin, Nanette Vial, Dede Vial
Kenner, LA (2012)

January 2015. On this trip we (Kathi and Lennie) stayed for a while at Corinne's house in Hahnville. We had opportunity to meet several Vial-Martin relatives for the first time. Our cousin Jara Roux arranged a family gathering at her home in Ama, just downriver from Hahnville. We had a wonderful time learning about each other and shared a delicious potluck and libations. The genealogically-minded congregated in Jara and husband Jeff's office to look at family trees and historic documents. As Jara pointed out, we are all in the combined Vial-Martin family because of the double marriage. We discussed the book about our family's Acadian heritage and agreed to share information. The relatives there were:

Descendants of Leonide Mary Vial and John Baptiste Martin Jr.: Leonide (Lennie) Martin, Corinne Martin, Helen Celeste Martin, and Katherine (Kathi) Bonnabel.

Descendants of Leon Charles Vial Sr. and Irma Celeste Martin: Irma Tinney Dubroca, Stanley Dubroca, Jara Roux, Mary Ann Vial Lemmon.

Spouse: Jeff Roux (took picture). Friend: David Arata.

Mary Ann Lemmon, Stanley Dubroca, Jara Roux, Lennie Martin, David Arata, Kathi Bonnabel Helen Celeste Martin, Irma Tinney Dubroca, Corinne Martin
Ama, LA (2015)

January 2019. This was a memorable trip for several reasons: We had a number of gatherings with various combinations of relatives and made a pilgrimage to Whitney Plantation to experience their museum and shrines for enslaved people. Kathi had her birthday luncheon at Truck Farm Tavern in St. Rose, across the river from Ama and Hahnville. This diner of local fame has an alligator suspended from the ceiling, animal wall art, curly ceiling lights, old cars and trucks in a garage museum, and iconic Cajun dishes. At the luncheon were:

Kathi Bonnabel, Lennie Martin, Corinne Martin, Doug Martin, Cary Martin, Jara Roux, Jeff Roux.

Kathi Bonnabel, Lennie Martin, Jara Roux, Jeff Roux, Cary Martin, Doug Martin.
Truck Farm Tavern, St. Rose, LA (2019)

Three of us (Kathi, Corinne, Lennie) went to Whitney Plantation, located upriver from Hahnville in Wallace. Built around 1790 by Jean Jacques Haydel (our relative), it first grew indigo but switched to sugarcane in the early 1800s. By 1860, the plantation produced over 400,000 pounds of sugar and had over 100 enslaved people. After the Civil War, it decreased in size and production, was bought by a New York businessman in 1867 and named after his children. After passing through several owners, Whitney was restored and opened as a museum in 2014 by John Cummings, a New Orleans attorney.

In 2019, he donated it to a nonprofit to operate, with the purpose of educating the public about the history of slavery and its legacies.

Visiting Whitney Plantation is a powerful and sobering experience. They have preserved buildings and implements, created shrines and memorials, and developed media programs that depict the cruelty of slavery and the suffering of enslaved people. Guided tours are given by their descendants; stories and lists of numerous enslaved people from the region have been collected and preserved. It offers one step toward atonement for slavery.

In 1795, there were 19,926 enslaved Africans and 16,304 free people of color in Louisiana. The German Coast, where Whitney Plantation is located, had 2,797 enslaved workers. The U.S. outlawed the Atlantic slave trade in 1807, but thousands were smuggled in illegally. Just before the Civil War in 1860, Louisiana had 331,726 enslaved people; the German Coast had increased to 8,776. Enslaved people led a grueling life, working from sunup to sundown, doing hard field work and providing domestic services, often as wet nurses to their owners' children, to the detriment of their own. Punishment was frequently administered by whipping, and families were callously separated. Enslaved people resisted, tried to escape by running away, and formed maroon colonies in the swamps. Those caught suffered severe retribution and faced death.

We all felt enormous remorse that our family history includes several sugarcane plantation owners who used enslaved workers from the early 1800s until the Civil War.

January 2020. This year's trip focused on visiting relatives and graveyards. We were well into writing this book, had collected a huge amount of genealogical and historic data, and were trying to verify connections. We went on an ancestor grave quest, spending hours in cemeteries where our research indicated there were relatives' graves. Our results were a bit disappointing; some key ancestors who should have been there could not be found. In some instances, headstones were eroded or graves unmarked; in others we found distant relatives but not those in our direct family line. It was easier for the Martins; our grandparents and most aunts and uncles are buried in the surrealistic Our Lady of the Most Holy Rosary Church Cemetery in Taft, surrounded by petrochemical plants. Some Vials are buried there, but this large clan is also distributed among St. John the Baptist Cemetery in Edgard and Ascension of Our Lord Cemetery in Donaldsonville. Some may also be at St. Peter Catholic Church Cemetery across the river in Reserve.

Our Lady of the Most Holy Rosary Church Cemetery
Martin graves in foreground, petrochemical plant in background.
Taft, LA (2020)

Gatherings with Vial-Martin relatives were both enjoyable and provided important information about the relations between our families in the mid-1900s. We went to the home of our second/third cousin, Leon C. Vial III (Sunny). He lives in the big Vial house built by his father, Leon C. Vial, Jr. (II). Three generations of Vials have lived there, including Sunny and his wife, Mary Janet, and their children. Sunny's father was St. Charles Parish sheriff during most of the time that J.B. Martin (Lennie's grandfather) was Superintendent of Schools. In the early 1900s, J.B. Martin's house and that of his sister, Marie "Keet" Martin Labry, were on properties just upriver from the Vial home. When we (Lennie and Corinne) were children visiting our grandparents, we were forbidden to venture past Tante Keet's house onto the adjoining Vial property. Our generation grew up never getting to know our nearby Vial cousins.

The reason, of course, was the Vial-Martin feud. Now we were visiting our Vial cousins, in their home, discussing what happened to cause the animosity that divided our families. Sunny had old documents and letters that he generously shared, as well as his recollections, so we could piece things together.

Lennie Martin, Kathi Bonnabel,
Corinne Martin, Leon C. (Sunny) Vial III
Hahnville, LA (2020)

We visited with Jara and Jeff Roux during this trip, delving more into family genealogy and sharing a great dinner with others in their family. It was impressive to meet our distinguished cousins, including Mary Anne Vial Lemmon, the first woman appointed as a federal judge in the parish, and Manina Dubroca, Jara's sister, a parish attorney. They told us of others holding administrative and legal positions in the parish. Both Jara and Jeff have contributed immensely to local historic and civic groups.

Discoveries and reconnections among the Vial-Martin relatives have been key to finishing this book. Our deepest gratitude to all those who have contributed. Indeed, in untold ways this is a family effort!

Discoveries and Reconnections 15

Jara Roux, Jeff Roux, Lennie Martin, Mary Ann Vial Lemmon,
Kathi Bonnabel Corinne Martin, Justice Harry Lemmon
Ama, LA (2020)

CHAPTER 2

Of Place and Past

Remembering Hahnville
by Leonide (Lennie) Martin

Sometimes, you are immersed in the power of place and past. The flood of memories makes those places of the past more real than current life. The cardinal's song high on cedar branches, misty sunlight dappling damp forest floors, pounding rain splattering the porch, chickens clucking and scratching, humming insects, delicious smells wafting from the kitchen. There is an ache that cannot be quelled for welcoming arms and safe havens and promises of endless adventures in that most exciting of places, my grandparents' home in Hahnville.

Thinking of it now brings a mixture of sadness and joy. It was a place that permeated my childhood; that now is no more. The big house is gone, the property sold, no resemblance remains that matches my memories except the long driveway from River Road. Next door, Tante Keet's house stands, still a semblance of what I remember. In that spacious lawn with tall pecan and oak trees, house with creaky porches and eaves, rickety greenhouse, and neglected sugar cauldron, I still feel the essence of people and places past, my family roots along the Mississippi River. The musty smell of swamps, the graceful sway of moss on limbs, the gracious and tradition-steeped, loving and smothering people of my family still persevere.

"*I see the Hahnville trees! I see the Hahnville trees!*" My brother Freddie and I chanted in unison, bouncing on the back seat of our family's 1940s vintage Ford, when we caught sight of the tall cypress trees lining our grandparents' property. Our dad drove upriver on River Road, with the levee on the right and houses set far back on the left. We were delighted to be visiting Poopsie and Grandma. Their big two-story home and immense (to us) property promised many adventures. We knew the place well, spending a good part of each year staying with our grandparents while our father was away fighting in World War II, and our mother was working as a Registered Nurse in New Orleans.

Our excitement grew as the car turned onto the long gravel driveway that cut straight through the center of the property, leading to a cluster of buildings. One side of the driveway had bright orange daylilies; the other was an open lawn with several stately oak and pecan trees surrounded by hedges. The lawn by the daylilies had a raised, grassy ridge running from the road to the front entrance of the house. I never understood why, because there was no gate at the road; it was bordered by a deep ditch. Near the house, an arbor covered with climbing roses and row of hedges defined a small front yard. From the arch to the front stairs, a paved walkway led to the elevated porch and branched right to meet the driveway. I guess this was the "formal entrance," although everyone seemed to arrive by the back entrance.

As our car passed the arbor, we saw the driveway make a big loop in the back yard, circling two tall pecan trees. The parking area was near the back porch. Continuing straight, the driveway led to a garage that seemed really far back on the property to us kids. A building for the washroom and servants' quarters was between the garage and house. When the car stopped, Fred and I jumped out and rushed toward the house where Poopsie and Grandma were coming down the stairs to greet us. Amid lots of hugs and kisses, we rejoined our beloved grandparents who doted on us and put up—mostly—with our escapades.

My brother, Frederick Charles Martin Jr., was born in 1941, and I was born 14 months earlier, in 1940. Named Leonide Luella Martin after my two grandmothers, in childhood I was called "Lennie Lou" and Fred was called "Freddie." Our father, Frederick Charles Martin, Sr., was born and raised in Hahnville along with his two sisters and three brothers. Our mother, Dorothy Bonnabel Martin, was from New Orleans.

I was the first grandchild in a family remarkably averse to marriage. Three of Daddy's siblings never married; one sister married late and did not have children. Only Daddy's youngest brother Peter married and had two daughters. My cousin Corinne was born seven years after I was, and Helen Celeste a little later. Thus, I had special significance

Home of J.B. Martin Jr. (II) and Leonide Mary Vial Martin
Hahnville, LA c.1930

for the family, and so did Fred as the first and only grandson. We were tight as ticks with Poopsie and Grandma. Our sister Sylvia was born when I was six, after Daddy returned from World War II. Fred and I considered her a nuisance, and the age difference kept her from being a playmate. As she got older, we played toy games with plastic horses in our Lafayette home. Being a tomboy, when I got dolls as gifts I promptly passed them on to Sylvia. My memories of Sylvia in Hahnville are very meager.

The big Hahnville house was a wonder and delight for us. We spent months at a time there during the war years. The back porch was L-shaped along the dining room and kitchen. As with nearly all porches, it had floor-to-ceiling screens. In South Louisiana, if porches were not completely screened, they became unbearable due to swarms of blood-thirsty mosquitoes all year round. At one end of the porch was the only bathroom, with a tub, sink, flush toilet, and hot water heater closet. I remember this closet distinctly, because Poopsie used it for punishment when I became entirely insufferable. I don't recall him ever spanking me, but when I was wailing due to "unreasonable" discipline, he would put me in that closet saying, "If you keep that crying up, you'll fill the closet and drown in your own tears." I'm pretty sure I didn't believe him, but just being locked in was bad enough.

The water supply to the house came from a huge cistern, located just outside the bathroom with a screen on top to keep leaves and debris out. Using cisterns for water was common in this region with its plentiful rain. There was a well behind the wash shed providing water for washing but not for drinking. Underground water levels were really high and probably contaminated. Cisterns had to be cleaned out from time to time, a nasty job involving emptying the water then climbing inside to shovel up the goop that collected at the bottom. There was a smaller cistern supplying water to the kitchen.

From the back porch a hallway went to the side porch and kitchen, with a separate entrance into Grandma's pantry. The kitchen seemed very large and full of fond memories. In the center was a big table; along the walls were the sink, counters, stove, refrigerator, and many cabinets. Inside the cabinets were all manner of delicious things, in particular canned condensed milk. I remember making raids on the condensed milk, savoring the incredible sweetness of its caramelized flavor. Grandma was a wonderful cook and put up food by canning and smoking. The pantry shelves were lined with jars of tomatoes, green beans, fruit, pickles, preserves, and other vegetables and meats.

Fred and I played games at breakfast that must have amused Grandma. When she made soft fried eggs and grits, of course with bacon, we played the levee-breaking game. We would pierce the yolk and watch the yellow liquid slowly creep downward toward pockets formed in the white part. We selected a certain pocket as our "home" and watched with trepidation to see if the "levee break" would flood it. Our squeals as the "flood" approached caught Grandma's attention, and she admonished us to put up barricades with crusts of bread. This quickly led to gobbling the yolk-soaked bread and all the rest of the hearty breakfast.

Down the hallway was the side porch, a favorite place during long summer evenings spent in Hahnville. This porch also had floor-to-ceiling screens and rocking chairs, big ones for Poopsie and Grandma and little ones for Fred and me. We played games while our grandparents read or talked. Grandma did mending, and Poopsie smoked his cigar. I remember the sweet smell of freshly lit tobacco; when cigars got old and cold, they smelled pretty awful. But I've always been fond of freshly lit cigar smell since it holds strong associations with Poopsie. His fingernails and fingers were darkened and his teeth yellowed by the tobacco residue.

In those times no one considered smoking a bad thing. Both my parents smoked cigarettes for most of their lives, quitting in later years. Everyone smoked then; just watch some 1940-1950 vintage movies. Fred and I stole their cigarettes and experimented with chewing as well as smoking. It all tasted disgusting and neither of us ever smoked.

Poopsie played special games with me. It was clear that I was his favorite, and we had this strong bond. One game involved a tiny colorful spider that lived on the side porch. Poopsie would put his hand next to the spider as it crawled along the arm of his chair, allowing it to climb onto his fingers. He called me over to watch as he gently prodded the spider, causing it to rear on its hind legs and wave its beady eyes at him. I was fascinated at the spider's visual apparatus and quick-footed agility, able to scoot in every direction. The spider did not seem afraid and even appeared to enjoy the game. Soon I had the spider climb on my hand and play with me. From this, I've always been partial to spiders, at least little ones.

Developmental specialists say that during the early years you are "scripted" by important people in your life. They create the pattern through which you engage with life and set the story line for where you are headed. Poopsie "scripted" my life and gave me a pattern for success, a story line that said anything was possible. Being the consummate educator, he read stories and told tales of overcoming adversity and doing great things. When I could read, he sent me books including *Reader's Digest Condensed Books* of great classics, launching a lifelong love of reading and historical literature. It opened my eyes to different worldviews and faraway places, giving me a vicarious experience of many cultures. Reading space fiction brought a universe of possibilities beyond the usual, creating a "what if" mentality where worlds unknown could be imagined. It was through this genre that my first awareness of black people as co-equals was launched. My grandfather cultivated my creativity, praising my early efforts at drawing and modeling clay animals. He encouraged my writing, and we exchanged many letters over the years. For all these priceless gifts from Poopsie, I am eternally grateful.

The big house at Hahnville had a formal dining room, seldomly used except for family occasions and holidays. A long, dark wood table and matching china cabinets were offset by lacey drapes on windows to the back porch. From the dining room doors opened into

Grandma's bedroom and the living room; a stairway led to the second story. There was a seldom used, double-sided fireplace shared with the living room. Grandma's bedroom was nearest the bathroom and had a four-post bed, armoire, cabinets, and fireplace. Usually Fred slept with Grandma when we were little.

A door opened between Grandma's and Poopsie's bedrooms. There was a *prie-dieu* ("pray to God") in one corner of his where they said prayers. This kneeling bench with armrest is used by Catholics for devotions at home. Grandma said the rosary there every evening. At bedtime, I usually slept with Poopsie when I was little. We spent evenings in Grandma's bedroom with the fire burning during cold weather. I remember a picture above her cabinet of two children, a boy and girl, crossing a rickety wooden bridge high above a ravine. They looked scared, but I knew they would get across fine because their guardian angel was hovering over them with arms outstretched. I have a smaller version of that picture even today.

Poopsie's bedroom opened into the living room, actually two rooms with a partial dividing wall. The closer side served as his office with desk and bookshelves. The front entrance door led into this room. The second side was larger, with couches and chairs, piano and fireplace. The family gathered here for visits and holidays, and Grandma played the piano until her arthritic joints became too swollen. There was an ancient record player with an arm that folded back on itself. I remember Christmas gatherings with brightly decorated tree, lots of presents, animated chatter, and numerous aunts, uncles, and cousins.

When Fred and I got older, we slept in bedrooms upstairs. There was a creepy painting on the wall by the stairs, a dark-haired woman holding a lyre with one hand, the other pressed to her throat. Her expression was vaguely frightened, probably because a large black bug was perched beside her. Were it me, I'd be sprinting away from that bug. Once getting past the picture, we entered a central room with a creaky wooden floor that budged upward in the middle. The boys' bedroom was at one end of the central room. Though there was a window, it always seemed dark and musty to me. I wondered what it was like for the four brothers growing up in this room; probably it was fine since they went downstairs as soon as they smelled bacon frying.

On either side were two eaves with the girls' bedrooms, large windows bringing brightness. These were simply furnished with a bed, armoire, and table holding the water pitcher and basin. Beneath the bed was the slop pot for use during the night. The upstairs had no plumbing, so such things were necessary.

One of my favorite memories of Hahnville is waking up in the eastern bedroom, sun streaming through the curtains and birds chirping vociferously at daybreak. I loved the many birds that lived among the trees. Their cheery songs and the bright sunshine promised a day full of fun and exciting discoveries. I was seldom disappointed.

My memories of the Hahnville property are magical. The wonderful yard offered endless possibilities for an adventurous little girl to climb trees, explore thickets, or venture into mysterious back pastures. I loved the row of cypress trees along the fence extending from River Road to the side porch. Tree branches overlapped, and I would often climb up the farthest tree and make my way to the last one, scrambling from branch to branch. Although I got some scrapes and splinters, this challenging journey at dizzying heights was among my favorites.

Birds were always a fascination; among my first words were "da boids" according to family lore. Hahnville abounded with blue jays, cardinals, mocking birds, sparrows, doves, hummingbirds, and others. Early on I became somewhat of a "chicken whisperer" and had pets among the flock. One special rooster was a colorful fighting cock with large spurs on his legs. He was quite aggressive with a reputation for spurring anyone who annoyed him. Somehow I won over this fighter; he followed me sedately with a string tied to one of his legs, sat in my lap, and allowed his shiny red and black feathers to be stroked. This tale became a family favorite for years.

One chicken escapade did not turn out well. I saw a hen inside the chicken house sitting on a bunch of eggs. The wooden nests were built along a wall, about 2-3 feet above the ground. Since I loved the fluffy yellow chicks, I wanted her to remain there to hatch the eggs. So, I tied a piece of string around her neck and attached it to a nail on the wooden nest. When I returned a few hours later, the poor hen was hanging below the nest, suspended by the string around her neck. It had scraped back some feathers, too, but she was still alive. I removed the string and took her outside to the compost pile, where I left her in a heap. She wasn't looking too good, but I was scared so I never told anybody. To this day I don't know if she recovered and feel really badly about harming the hen.

Insects provided an endless stream of entertainment. The subtropical climate encouraged an immense insect population, everything from ants to beetles to grasshoppers. I remember the sound of cicadas rising as the temperature ascended. At times it became a roar, making conversation difficult. I still love the sound of cicadas. There was a unique type of grasshopper that we called "Devil's horses." Their bodies were black with thin red lines along back and legs. When they spread their wings to fly, these were a startling crimson color. When touched, they emanated a strong tobacco-like odor. Fred and I would tie strings that were attached to a matchbox bottom around the grasshopper's body. The Devil's horses then pulled our tiny wagon down the sidewalk. I guess we were the Devil!

In summer twilight, the air would twinkle with tiny lights, a fairyland made by lightning bugs. Walking among the swarm felt like being in a magical forest where fairies, dragons, or unicorns might appear at any time. Of course, we couldn't stay out at dusk for too long, or we'd get "eaten alive" by mosquitoes.

There were snakes, mostly harmless garter or grass snakes whose slender dark bodies slithered among the bushes. When venturing into swampy areas, we might encounter a water moccasin. We learned to recognize and avoid them by the cottony white membranes inside their mouths. Farther back in the swamps were coral snakes and green tree snakes, but we seldom went there. Beyond the back pasture were marshes; just going to the barn and among the cows was a big adventure. It seemed an enormous distance from the house. If you were brave enough to continue through the marsh, you'd arrive at the railroad tracks which marked the western border of the property.

It rained a lot during the summer. Sometimes Freddie and I sat on the side porch and watched rain pummeling down, spraying through the screen, making puddles on the porch. Then we played flooding games, moving our toys around and building levees. Mud did not deter us; a photo shows us covered with mud using a garden hose to create even more mud puddles. Standing next to us is a skinny black girl, our nanny just a few years older, holding the hose. Probably we needed to be washed up more than once daily.

On one occasion we played a game with very unpleasant outcomes. We pretended our home was in hedges surrounding a pecan tree in the side yard. Nice soft-leaved vines grew inside the rough-leaved hedges, so these we used as washrags. Picking off the soft leaves, we wiped our faces, arms, and legs with them. A few hours later, red itchy welts appeared everywhere we used the leaves. Our washrags were poison ivy, a common plant in the region. Several days of furious itching followed, only relieved when Grandma swathed us in calamine lotion, making us look like bumpy pink crustaceans. To this day, I have no trouble identifying poison ivy.

Learning to fish and hunt was typical for children of South Louisiana families. Both Fred and I were taught from early childhood to fish, crab, collect crawfish, operate an outboard motor boat, and swim. Later we were taught to shoot and hunt; I had a small .410 shotgun at one point. I really didn't like hunting because I could not stand to kill birds. My brother was more accomplished in hunting, a lifelong practice. Going out before dawn to hunt ducks and geese and sit in cold, wet blinds way back in dreary lakes and marshes held no appeal for me.

However, I did for many years enjoy eating game, until my vegetarian days. One specialty of Grandma's was turtle soup; if you've never had this delicacy you have missed a unique, piquant flavor. Poopsie warned us to be careful around turtles, especially snapping turtles whose jaws had such pressure they could break off your fingers. It was reputed that once they clamped on, they would not let go unless killed. Crabs and crawfish were seasonal; these crustaceans were turned into justifiably famous gumbos and Creole etouffée.

One fond memory involves accompanying Poopsie to hunt mushrooms. We walked to nearby forested areas on adjoining properties. He knew how to recognize edible mushrooms and avoid poisonous ones. I can almost smell the dank humus of the forest floor covered with rotting branches, ferns, and mosses. The stillness was enchanting, broken only by our footsteps and random bird calls. Sunlight filtered through moss-draped trees and patterned the ground, giving a glow to the misty forest world. Skinks and lizards darted away as we approached, and we might occasionally disturb a sleepy owl, who hooted irritably at us.

Land on the other side of River Road gradually rose toward the levee. Originally this land was part of the Hahnville property, but it was partitioned off and sold when I was a child. Still, we had access to the levee and would take walks along the top. Between the levee and the river was a no-man's-land called the batture, often filled with overflow water. When the river was running high, the batture would be completely flooded halfway up the levee. Straggling tree branches hanging from twisted trunks trailed in swirling currents as the muddy Mississippi had its way.

The Mississippi River was an ever-present force in life along its banks. It provided an avenue for transportation and commerce, but also presented threat of flooding that could devastate the landscape nearby. There were multiple floods affecting river parishes, with "great floods" about every 10 years that destroyed crops and displaced people and animals. The story of the Hymelia Crevasse is among the most renowned. On May 14, 1912, a "crawfish hole" weakened the levee at Hymelia Plantation upriver from present-day Killona, just above Hahnville. Soon it opened a 500-foot-wide gap, spilling water across a huge area as far as Donaldsonville, Thibodaux, and Gretna. Hymelia Crevasse waters rushed hundreds of miles, severely impacting the west bank of St. Charles Parish. Late that night, water was three feet deep in the streets of Killona, reaching four to five feet in Paradis and Des Allemands in the days following. Fields were flooded for miles and crops ruined. Hundreds of state convicts were drafted to work on levee repairs. The gap widened to 1500 feet; it took the U.S. Corps of Engineers around 25 days to repair the levee using pile drivers, putting in posts to shore up a barricade.

River floods continue regularly. Spillways were built in the 1930s to divert rising waters. The Bonnet Carré spillway just upriver from Hahnville was first opened in 1937 and has protected river parishes from serious flooding in subsequent years.

When I visit Louisiana, my body knows this place—the accents and voice inflections, pungent spices, heavy atmosphere pressing against my skin. I relish watching dark bayous slipping silently past drooping willows, brackish marshes honeycombed with waterways among tall swaying grasses, the surprising expanse and power of the Mississippi River high between its levees. All this water teems with herons and cranes, ducks and geese, snakes and alligators, fish and crabs. I love the cuisine, this vibrant multicultural blend known as Creole and Cajun. A sense of belonging surges, to the land and people, my reuniting family, and I'm happy. Even though I escaped Southern constrictions for the open horizons of California, now my home, these neural connections, tendrils, and entangled roots are part of me still.

Background of the Vial-Martin Family

My grandfather Poopsie was Jean Baptiste Martin, Jr. (called Sr. after his father's death). J.B. was born in 1881 in St. Charles Parish. How his nickname became "Poopsie" I cannot remember; it's likely Fred and I gave it to him. Our cousins called him "Papa," which is typical for Southern grandfathers. His birthday was August 13 and mine is August 14, probably no coincidence astrologically since we always had a very strong bond. Poopsie was my father figure in early childhood since my dad was sent to the Army's Pacific theater when I was 1 year old. I have no memory of Daddy until he returned when I was 6 years old. Everyone was worried about how our relationship would go, and for good cause. My bond with Poopsie was too deep to be displaced.

My grandmother was Leonide Mary Vial, of the well-established and politically prominent Vial family of St. Charles Parish. She was born in 1879 and was two years older than her husband. They married in 1903 at Our Lady of the Holy Rosary Church in Taft, St. Charles Parish. Grandma was from a very large family, one of 13 children; all but two lived to adulthood. Leonide Mary was the third child born to Louis Adolphe Vial (born 1842 in New Orleans) and Louise Clothilde Malvina Bossier (born 1860 in St. John the Baptist Parish). The first child died in infancy; next came Leon Charles Vial I (born 1878), with Leonide Mary born a year later. Among this huge Vial clan were many local luminaries, including sheriffs, clerks of court, assessors, police jurymen, judges, school superintendents, and teachers.

Poopsie was a prominent figure in the parish. He served as clerk of court and school superintendent for many years. Some siblings and their spouses were also public figures. Poopsie and Leon C. Vial I and their wives were "double in-laws." The men married each other's sister: J.B. Martin married Leon's sister Leonide Mary Vial, and Leon C. Vial married J.B.'s sister Irma Martin. That makes my father's generation double first cousins with the Vials, and my generation double second cousins. But while I was growing up, I did not know my Vial relatives.

Relationships between the Martin and Vial families became strained due to political differences and rivalries in the 1940s. I was only vaguely aware of this, though it prevented getting to know my Vial relatives. My brother Fred and I recall that we were only allowed to venture from our grandparents' home to one adjoining property. The house across the fence was where Poopsie's sister Tante Keet and husband "Unkie" lived (Marie Andre Emilie Martin, Laurent Joseph Labry). Stepping-stones led from our side porch to the fence gate, inviting us to open it and wander onto Tante Keet and Unkie's land. We'd climb the stairs into her large two-story house, get treats in her kitchen, and explore the green house and sugar cauldrons in her back yard.

But we were forbidden to keep going downriver onto the next adjoining properties, which belonged to the Vials. During this time, the Vials and Martins were not talking to each other.

My mother told an interesting story about Poopsie and me around this time. His conflicts with the Vial faction about membership on the school board and setting school policy were coming to a head in 1944 when Poopsie resigned as superintendent of schools. I was 4 years old and have no recollection of these difficulties. Poopsie and I used to take walks from the house along the driveway with his German Shepherd Rex. He walked on one side of Rex, and I was on the other, my arm resting upon the dog's back, which was at shoulder height for me. He talked to me during these walks, but I don't remember what about. My mother was reputed to say, in effect: "Look at that selfish old man, unburdening his troubles on that poor little girl."

I would have happily listened to Poopsie's troubles and helped if I could. Maybe in a way, I did help unknowingly.

French was the primary language in both my grandparents' childhood homes. Poopsie's sister Tante Keet (Marie) remarked that they couldn't even speak English until they went to school. This was common at the turn of the 20th century in Louisiana Creole households. People spoke a dialect similar to mainland French; it was called "Paris French." Local newspapers used this form of French, as did government and civil administrators, until English gradually took over. The Cajuns spoke a patois French that was derived from 17th-century versions of the language. Their ancestors had emigrated from France in the early 1600s to settle in Nova Scotia, becoming the Acadians. Over time their dialect blended in Caribbean and indigenous words for a distinctive, colorful, and lyrical language. Those who spoke these different dialects of French could understand each other for the most part.

When my grandparents wanted to converse privately, they used French. My father's older siblings spoke French fluently, but he never learned. That has always frustrated me, since I missed the opportunity to be bilingual. Society in Louisiana when Daddy grew up was moving away from bilingualism. People who wanted to get ahead knew they had to speak good English, the language of education, government, and enterprise.

Fred C. Martin, my father, was the fifth child in this order: Helen, J.B. Jr. (Johnny, actually J.B. III), Minerva, Louis (Major, Bébé), Fred, and Roy (Peter). It's a Southern thing to have nicknames, though it creates confusion in figuring out who's who. All siblings were born and grew up in Hahnville in the big house along River Road. I have memories of them all, jumbled together over time and space.

While none was clearly my favorite, Aunt Min was the most exotic because she traveled and lived abroad. With a doctorate from University of Maryland and career as an English professor, she spent years at the Munich branch and lived for a time in Paris. I recall her telling me she could speak Paris French so perfectly that people took her for a native. Aunt Min was witty and full of information with a "cat swallowed the canary" smile hinting at juicy secrets. A bit of a tease, she called me "butterfly," though later I found out she used it for all her nieces and grandnieces. When around 13 years old, I took my first flight to visit Aunt Min in Maryland, where she took me to many historic sites and museums in the U.S. capital.

Aunt Helen was the oldest sibling, a tall and quiet woman whom I never knew well and did not see often. She also had a college degree; Poopsie was dedicated to education and encouraged college for all his children. She married Roscoe Cole, and they lived in Virginia. Aunt Helen never had children herself, but became a step-mother to Roscoe's children.

Uncle Johnny (J.B. Jr.-III) was a dermatologist who lived most of his adult life in Lake Charles. I got to know him better after my family moved to Lake Charles when I was 12 years old. I stayed in his house through my final year of college. He was quiet, kindly, never married, and committed suicide.

Uncle Major (Louis, Bébé) lived at the big house in Hahnville essentially his whole life. He never married but had a close female relationship later in life. He was the shortest of the sons, with a square face with receding hair, and wore glasses. Once he took me to visit the sugarcane factory where he worked and showed me the process of turning raw cane into pure white sugar granules. The factory was on the river to take advantage of barges for transport of sugar barrels along this main commercial route. I was awed by the huge vats that collected cane juice, the cauldrons where it was boiled down, molasses drained off, and the clear syrup dried into granules. Tall chimneys spouted white smoke, loud machines clanked, pipes curled everywhere, and a pervasive sweet-sour smell hovered in the air. Uncle Major gave me samples of cane at each step, from stringy, crushed raw cane to the various steps of syrups leading to purified sugar. I liked molasses best of all.

Uncle Peter (Roy) seemed a quiet person with a sweet smile. He was the youngest and married Ellen Purcell Wilson from New Orleans. They had two daughters, Corinne and Helen Celeste, the only Martin-Vial cousins that I knew well. My memories of Uncle Peter and Aunt Nell are mainly during holidays at the big house in Hahnville when we all gathered around the Christmas tree or Thanksgiving table for festivities.

Although I had nine great-aunts and uncles in my grandmother's Vial family, I don't remember meeting any of them. Although Poopsie's sister Celeste Irma was married to Grandma's brother, Leon Charles, I have no memory of them. I've learned about Leon from historical records and family documents, since he held important positions in St. Charles Parish, including sheriff and tax collector. There are many cousins on the Vial side whom I don't know, although I've met several since reconnecting with Vial relatives.

My Grandparents in Perspective

Poopsie and Grandma were anchors during my childhood and through adolescence. Poopsie died when I was 15 years old; that loss required years and therapy to resolve. Their continual love and support helped shape me into the person I am today. The sound foundation they provided, affirming my worth and ability, is priceless. As a health professional, I've witnessed too often the indelible scars caused by a childhood without such affirmation.

When I remember Poopsie, bringing him to my mind's eye, here is what I see: a man of light frame, not tall, with high forehead and bald crown, a small rim of hair curving at the nape of his neck. His eyes were dark and twinkling, smile charming, nose arched and prominent. In certain pictures he looks quite the rascal; in learning about his professional and political activities, it's clear he had strong opinions and expressed them freely. He was a great storyteller and loved to read, keeping me enthralled for hours. Younger photos of him reveal an intense expression that conveys determination and power. He was reputed to have immense willpower; once he set his mind to something, it was as good as accomplished.

My mother told a story about his willpower that was striking. He was out drinking the night Grandma had her last baby, Peter, and it was a difficult birth. Legend has it that she nearly died. Friends were sent out to find him; once they brought him home and he learned how serious things were, he declared that he would never touch another drop of liquor. This was quite a vow given the susceptibility to alcoholism in the Martin family. But Poopsie kept his word and discontinued drinking. At a party sometime later, my mother watched him interacting with increasingly inebriated guests. She said he appeared to be getting just as high as all the rest, but she was sure he never took any alcohol. Poopsie was able to match the mood of the guests but remain sober.

Poopsie's realm was the world of ideas, learning, education, and envisioning a better future for schools. He left a legacy for the parish school system and education in the region. The J.B. Martin Middle School in Paradis is named in his honor, and he is called the "Father of St. Charles Parish Schools." Most of the advances in parish education have been attributed to him.

J.B. Martin Jr. (Poopsie) and Leonide Mary Vial Martin (Grandma)
Hahnville, LA c.1940

Thinking of Grandma and bringing her to my mind's eye, this is the picture: a rather tall woman of solid build and regal bearing, with deep-set black eyes under naturally arched brows. Her forehead was high and accentuated by upswept black hair styled with a bun on top. As she got older, the bouffant of hair sat atop her head like a white crown with a black cap. Her nose was aquiline and straight, lips full, cheekbones high, and chin strong, creating a lovely face with harmonious balance. In her youth, one could say she was beautiful.

Even as a grandmother, she was shapely and dressed well, wearing sensible shoes with thick heels that made her stand half-a-head taller than Poopsie. Her abilities included running a household of six children and servants, keeping a garden and chickens, canning and putting up food, smoothing communications among the family, and comforting us when needed. In the kitchen her skills were legendary. The smell of fresh-roasted Creole coffee with chicory never fails to evoke vivid images of Grandma filling demi-tasse cups from a white enamel French drip coffee pot. This antique pot now resides with me as a treasure from childhood.

Grandma possessed innate nobility with her striking face and upright stance. Many people have remarked on this; in fact she was descended from Spanish and French nobles. It is through her line that we traced the many twining branches back to the Acadian roots of our family. Primarily the lineage was passed on the maternal side, which is quite a challenge when researching genealogy. Two notable ancestors in her line were noblemen: Charles Amador de St. Étienne de La Tour from Champagne, France, an early settler and governor of Acadia (Nova Scotia); and Juan Francisco Vicente Vives, Spanish chevalier from Valencia, Spain, a prominent planter in Ascension Parish who built the Belle Alliance Plantation house near Donaldsonville.

To me, Grandma had a Spanish appearance, so I was not surprised to discover the Valencian infusion. In addition, many French ancestors were from southern provinces bordering the Pyrenees, with Iberian bloodlines. We have Basque ancestors on this side of the family. Of interest, the first wife of Charles de La Tour was a Mi'kmaq "princess," daughter of Sagamore (Chief) Membertou.

The Acadian roots of our family spread through many offshoots that mingled with Louisiana Creoles. Eventually the Acadian connection was forgotten, and the family saw no resemblance to the Cajuns who lived around us. As you follow the tortuous genealogical path through 11 generations, you will see how the Acadian and Creole lines merged and separated.

This journey takes us to the Vial-Martin Acadian connection: **Leonide Mary Vial Martin**, my grandmother and namesake.

Graveyards are places where the living can be with the dead. I'm drawn to their serenity and mystery. The cemetery at Our Lady of the Most Holy Rosary Church in Taft has a row of Martins and several Vials. I visit them whenever

I'm in Hahnville. It's an odd feeling to see my name carved in script on a simple granite headstone: Leonide V. Martin. My grandmother's bones lie there beside her husband's and children's; I thank them and remind them of my love. Crouched on damp grass beside their minimal mounds, the view to the horizon is surrealistic. Surrounding the small graveyard is a towering petrochemical plant—tanks and smokestacks, tubes and catwalks, steaming columns and eternal flames discolor the sky.

This is Louisiana. This contrast of family embedded in the soil, in blood and awareness and the ravaging of the land. The inevitable cycle of becoming and deceasing. My—our—origins, to honor where we can, accept as we must, grow through and often away from. We are all this... and much more.

CHAPTER 3

On Home Ground

Remembering Hahnville

by Corinne Martin

⚜

Sometimes, you really can go home. A decade ago, I never would have imagined that anything about Louisiana would pull on me. Not the hellfire heat, not the motley mess of history and values and quirks and flatland and murky waters. Not what I saw as the small-minded, overly polite, racially tense, slightly dangerous morass of drinking and overeating and blustery gun-toting and codependence and rigid religiosity.

I had broken free.

But after the death of a beloved 102-year-old aunt (who had, herself, escaped), I brought her ashes home. I stood at the door of the church and saw faces I hadn't seen for 50 years. Or had never seen at all, just heard bits about from Aunt Min. And I was so happy.

My body remembered these people, and this place. All those long-lost faces and names flooded back—Tante Fafitte and Uncle Bizou; Tine, and Tante Ella, and Tante Loule; Sunny Jim, and Mamere Martin, and Bebé, on and on. At the sweet family gathering hosted by my newfound cousins, the food was familiar and irresistible, and the greetings were warm.

Childhood memories swamped over me. I remembered the way the air smelled when the river was high and water rolled over the land; the high-pitched drone of cicadas in the trees; the fierce mosquitos and the low, flat fields; trains hooting in the night; the ancient, moss-bearded trees whose limbs scooped down to the ground so little children could climb right up into their hearts. And cherry bounce, crawfish, alligators, herons rising up over the levees, and the levees themselves, the only hills we could ever find to climb.

I wrote in my journal later how odd and sweet it felt—how unexpected, that sinking into family soup. And I couldn't get enough; I wanted to go back, again and again. A fierce and hungry body-love for these, the flesh of my flesh, and for the land my own roots had known since my feet could walk that heavy soil, kept calling to me. I wanted to go home. And so, I have.

When I was growing up, Hahnville was a haven for me. Away from the larger town of Houma where my parents had settled, the tiny town and its inhabitants were always welcoming, and a little mysterious. The old Martin family house where I'd go to visit my grandparents held the leftover childhood of my dad and aunts and uncles and the history of my grandparents and their people for so many generations.

It was a comforting place to be. My sister and I could explore the big old house and play games and act out stories we made up. We could trek across the big, rambling yard or pick blackberries in Tante Fafitte's field, as long as the bull wasn't out. Or we might cross the side yard and drop in at Tante Keet's house. There, we could sit in the little cubby under the upstairs steps to play, or plink away at piano keys, or read to each other while lying in the big hammock on the front porch.

Or I might "help" Grandma with her chores or sit with the older folks in the early afternoon on the front gallery. If it was very hot, Grandma would pull out a hankie from her pocket and pat at beads of perspiration. Uncle Major might sit with us for a while, or we might be joined by Tante Loule or Tante Ella, or Bizou or Tante Keet. The grown-ups would chat and gaze out at the road. They knew who was passing by and where everyone was probably going. They also knew that if one of them needed a ride somewhere, they could just stand on the side of the road and someone they knew would stop and pick them up. Grandma and Uncle Major might fill the visitors in on what was happening lately: who had been by to check in, who was having a hard time, who was struggling with health issues, what was going on in the town, how the dog was doing, which of the grandkids had visited lately. And they told stories I soaked up.

Several years after my Aunt Min died, I began to understand how you can love a place so much that it becomes part of your bones. And even though I had no intention of moving down South, I followed a visceral longing for our family's "home ground" and bought a small house in Hahnville, a five-minute walk from where my dad and seven generations of his family had been born and raised. There, I fell into the old mystery of that "family soup" and couldn't get enough.

Now that I'm back, I trek out to the river most mornings. At the river's edge, water rushes and curls into the space between the sandbar and the batture, pushed by passing ships. A few wild hibiscuses stand in the tangled brush. Across the river, the sky is often dark, streaked with rain falling far away. Some thunder might rumble overhead. But still, it's hard to leave. The scent of water, the hundred green things in the knotted woods, the teeming insect sounds, the stagnant, alligator-hiding pond are so familiar. I want to breathe it all up and hold it close.

Time is a funny thing. I know the past happened and is gone. But really, I see right through it when I look around. Here, I can stand on the river beach I came to after my Aunt Min had died and I tried to sink down into her past and my dad's, and my own, and the land's, and the river's. My feet that stepped around mucky puddles, around raccoon tracks pressed into soft mud, remembered following traces of my aunt when she was first gone.

Now, I am here on my own. Things are quieter. The river that was free and roiling when I was a child has been calmed, at least in this one spot, by the bulky line of barges. Sun glints through the trees. Somewhere in the messy batture woods, an alligator probably waits for the air to warm. Snakes could be stirring. Somewhere in these sodden grains of gray river sand, tiny flakes of my aunt's skin, and my dad's, and his mother's, and brothers', and seven generations of our relatives have probably settled into the land's memory of itself. So, in being here now, I can walk over and through the past.

And I love the river as if it were my blood. My body knows where it belongs.

―⋈―

The stories were rich. There was the time Aunt Helen almost drowned in a swimming hole when they were kids, and Tante Keet's future husband, whom we all called "Unkie," jumped in and saved her.

And the time my dad and his brothers went out at night in a pirogue on a swamp pond, trying to catch frogs. They ended up beaning a sizeable alligator and pulling it into the boat, thinking it would make a tasty stew. But then it awakened and started thrashing around, and the boys scrambled frantically to get it back into the water.

There were stories about Papa, who relished his cigars, wore a green "shade" as he read, and let me climb into his lap when he was reading the paper. One favorite family tale was about the time he was sitting on the side gallery reading his Bible during a thunderstorm, and lightning struck so close to his chair that his Bible burst into flames, and he raced back into the house.

And there was the story, often told with some variations, about how he stopped drinking. Apparently, when Grandma was in labor with my dad (after having had a couple of miscarriages), Papa was off somewhere drinking with friends, and the doctor had to send someone to get him to come home in case she died in labor. When he finally made it back, the doctor gave him a stern lecture about indulging in alcohol. On the spot, Papa decided he'd never drink again. He had the hired man lock him in a shed and not let him out for two weeks. He'd get food and water in through a small opening in the shed wall. And once he emerged, he never drank again.

As my Aunt Min aged, she'd shared some of her own stories, too. There were so many that she wanted to write a memoir of those early childhood days. She would have called it "yellow cotton underpants" because that's what they all wore—underwear sewn by their mother from the cheapest unbleached cloth. When the kids were climbing trees and looked up, that's what they saw.

Each morning as I walk along River Road, I pass Mary Janet and Sunny's house, and Nanette's, and Keet's, and then Tante Fafitte's field. I pass this little nest of family where our bones have pressed into mucky soil for decades, our skin has stitched itself to the skin of the land. And all the single sweet grains of us have cooked up together to become something smooth and rich and nourishing. Irresistible.

I suppose it's a failure to want that again, to go to such lengths to reclaim it at this age, and not want to move on. But it feels like a great grace, a nectar of belonging my cells can drink right up.

I had my own stories, too. At my grandparents' house, people would show up at the back door, standing to chat or bringing cream from their cow (so thick you had to spoon it out of the jar) or eggs (with double yolks). Uncle Bizou, Tante Ella, Tante Loule, Uncle Dick, and others whose names I've forgotten might drop by. As a child, I didn't get to know them well, but together they all seemed like a comfortable cloak that wrapped around us little ones, keeping an eye on us as we wandered and explored.

Some days, I'd stand in the old wash shed with Grandma as she scooped the newly washed clothes out of the wringer washing machine and slapped them free of wrinkles, then hung them on the line. As water gurgled through the thick black hose and pumped onto the ground, she'd wipe at perspiration that collected on her brow, and I tried to imagine her as a young bride, shy and smitten with her educated husband. I'd seen photos of the passel of her young ones who came along, one after another, the youngest one of them my dad. They were all a little ragged, half-wild, laughing and playacting, barefoot and busy with adventures.

Or Grandma might stand in the pantry early in the day, humming while she ironed before the heat swamped us all. There are so many sweet and visceral memories I have of her—her yummy fig preserves; her turtle soup; throwing breakfast leftovers out the kitchen door to the dogs; the sticky sugar bowl; and Grandma's story of how the kids once had a pet raccoon that was able to lift the sugar bowl lid and scoop out crusted sugar by the paw-full. I still remember that she smelled like Tangee lipstick and Lady Esther face powder, that her hugs were soft, and that there was always a kiss on both cheeks when we arrived.

One day, I helped her lug my dad's old army trunk out to air in the sun. As we opened it up and sorted through the contents, I tried to catch little bits of what his life had been like. I wondered how much of him had been changed by the battles during the war and by being away from home. I didn't know how to think of him as a soldier—my dad, the man who was so protective of me and my sister had certainly killed people. That was hard for me to understand.

And there were other memories of my dad in that place, too. As a young child, I'd accompany him to Vial's Bar (owned by one of his cousins). I would sit on a stool next to my dad as he drank a chilled beer while more cousins and a few school friends, all noisy and chatting, crowded around. I could watch my dad in this familiar element and imagine him as a young man.

A special treat was any ride down the bayou with my dad. We both loved those drives—there was, and still is, something about being in the low, waterlogged bayou country that just made us feel at home and free. Even though I sometimes didn't understand the Cajun patois, the people were nothing but welcoming. On fishing or crabbing trips down to Bayou Gauche or Bayou Terrebonne, or farther afield to Cocodrie or Robinson Canal or Isle de Jean Charles, my dad was happy. I think those rides took him back to his childhood years of wandering around the sodden land, into thickets, out in boats at night, or swimming at the edge of the Mississippi even though it was forbidden.

To this day, I love trips down to any bayou. I think my dad would be glad to know that I've come back, and that on any afternoon, I might suddenly pile the dog into the car, and head on out to that brown water under the big skies. I think Grandma and Papa might like that too, that someone in the "future" would love it as much as they did and be willing to come back, to take on the current-day problems in exchange for that particular grace and beauty and family.

Bayou Terrebonne near Montegut, LA

Walking home, I am swamped again—almost brought to tears—by an overwhelming homage and gratitude for this place; for the heavy impossible soil, the damp air, green tangles and wild throbbing that presses into whatever small bit of order we try to make. And for the long and wide and not-quite-tamed river of our people—their talents, and joys and struggles, and their courage to take it all on: the unpredictable skies, corruption that lurks at the edges of honor, the river that rises and threatens and nourishes and rolls on and on. Our family that sank roots, deep and faithful, here.

Early on in our discussions about family, I didn't know what to think of Lennie's claim that we are, at least a little bit, descended from the Acadians in Nova Scotia who were displaced by the *Grand Dérangement*. As a child, I'd been told that absolutely we were not Cajuns; we might be Creoles somewhere along the family line, but we were definitely from France, not anywhere else. Now, of course, I can imagine that, with such a large family, it makes sense that there might have been some rambling, some branching out.

And why not settle here, where the language and the land were similar to what they'd been forced to leave behind?

Today, despite the continuing mystery of our people's origins, there is something so special to me about this family and the land that shaped and supported and challenged them. Maybe there was something unique to the areas their ancestors had come from that informed and influenced how they settled into this new place. Their ability to learn and adapt and their willingness to persist, experiment, commit, explore, talk things through, or take a stand fit right in with the resiliency of the land and its early inhabitants. And their dignity, feistiness, and unique and particular challenges and graces continue on. Seven generations later, they're still thriving, still working, still willing to learn and always ready to share—a tribe, in a way, whole unto itself, but generous, and fun, and welcoming, taking care of each other and committed to the place they call Home.

I often wonder why I need these things, why my body is so ridiculously happy just to be walking that back field even though my feet are sopping wet with heavy dew before I've gotten through the yard. Or why I can't pass by the little colony of lyre leaf sage, tall and rough-leaved and blue-flowered, without stopping to pick some. Or how I know the red-shouldered hawk is coming before she sails into the tallest tree and where to look for her mate. Or when new fruit will be ready in the blackberry tangles along the batture.

This is what I'm made of, I guess. And not just me, but Sunny and Nanette and Jara, and Dede, and Mary Ann and Lennie, and Kathi and Wayne and Keet, and on and on. Decades, a hundred-plus years after our people worked the soil and planted their own roots, we still follow their muddy trail.

Standing on this ground my body knows so well, I still wonder about our relatives—all those people who came before me. I can see them in my mind's eye. I wonder if they ever imagined a child of the future, a hundred years, two hundred years ahead, coming home. I wonder if they'd be surprised, or care. If time were a mist I could walk right through, it would be fun to stop by and say hello. To walk up to one of those porches and introduce myself. We could peer at each other, look for something familiar, swap names and degrees of relatedness. But then, how would we say goodbye? How would I ever say goodbye and walk away?

That's something I still don't know.

CHAPTER 4

Beginnings in Acadia

Charles Amador de St. Étienne de La Tour (1593-1666) – Marguerite Membertou (c.1606-c.1630)

⚜

Slate waves rolled endlessly toward the horizon, where they blended into the ashen sky. Alone in vast grayness, the schooner rose and fell with the waves, leaving a wake of white froth. The young man stood by the ship's railing, scanning the distance for land. They had sailed across the Atlantic for two months and should see coastline any day. He was eager to leave rolling decks to step upon solid ground. That ground would be one of France's early settlements in the New World, called Acadia. Their first destination was Cap-Sable, the southernmost tip of a large peninsula, now called Nova Scotia. They planned to sail around the cape into Baie Française and arrive at Port-Royal, a French outpost.

Young Charles, born in 1593, was 17 years old when he accompanied his father Claude on his second grand adventure. Charles and Claude de St. Étienne de La Tour had been among the adventurous Frenchmen who accompanied Jean de Biencourt de Poutrincourt on a venture in 1606 to establish a permanent colony at Port-Royal. The settlement was abandoned two years later due to financial troubles. The party, including Poutrincourt's 19-year-old son (also named Charles), sailed from Dieppe, France, in 1610.

Claude de St. Étienne de La Tour was born around 1570 in Champagne, France. His birth name was Claude Turgis *dit* Nicolas, son of a master mason of Paris. Ambitious and charming, Claude secured a fortunate marriage to Marie de Salazar, widow of Paul de

Verrines de Vouraches, allied to the French noble House of Bouillon. The Salazars were Basques from the Spanish Pyrenees, heirs to the Barony of St. Just and several *seigneuries* (estates) near Paris. This marriage made Claude related to Poutrincourt's mother, granted him landed estates, and added two noble *de's* to his name. He was a Huguenot (French Protestant Calvinist) and lost most of his estates in the Wars of Religion. Claude made the second trip to Acadia in hopes of advancing his fortunes through finding mineral wealth. By then a widower, he sold some of his wife's property in Champagne to finance the voyage.

The Acadian land had been explored for more than 100 years when the La Tours arrived. The name "Acadia" derived from Portuguese explorer Verrazano, who called the region "Arcadia" because it reminded him of the classical "Land of Content." Early cartographers used a variety of spellings—L'arcadie, La Cady, La Cadie. The Mi'kmaq used a similar sounding word, *akade*, meaning a good place to live. This shaped the final spelling.

English, Spanish, Portuguese, Breton, and Basque fishing ships plied the cod-rich shores of present-day Newfoundland. Several voyages by Spanish and French explorers sought the elusive passage that would take them to the spice-rich East Indies. Spain had established its hegemony from the Carolina and Florida coasts to the Caribbean, but the northern coasts were quite contested. Britain, France, and Portugal entered the fray, pursuing lucrative fur trading as well as a foothold in the New World. Only a few tenuous settlements existed in 1610. Pierre de Mons, first "Governor of Acadia" with monopoly of the fur trade in New France, joined Samuel de Champlain and 77 men to build the first settlement at Île St.-Croix in 1604. A brutal winter and lack of fresh fruit and vegetables caused 35 deaths from scurvy. They relocated to Port-Royal where they anticipated milder winters. This became the first permanent settlement in 1605.

Port-Royal was a favorable site for a settlement. Samuel de Champlain described "La Cadie" as a land rich with promise of minerals, its high mountains full of verdigris which came from copper veins. The area situated on a protected cove at the head of a basin (now Annapolis Basin) offered reliable sources of water, good farmland, and wood. Champlain named it Port-Royal because it provided such a suitable and pleasant site for a settlement.[1]

After the losses at Île St.-Croix, de Mons settled in this lovely basin across the Baie Française (present Bay of Fundy), which he promised to Poutrincourt. During the summer of 1605, his men built structures resembling the fortified farm hamlets common in France at that time, laid out in a rectangle. Included were homes, storage and work areas, and ramparts with overlooking cannons. Called *l'habitation*, it was surrounded by vegetable gardens, a fish pond, and a water-powered mill on the nearby Allains River. Their ship brought seeds, fruit trees, and domestic animals, including cattle, swine, sheep, pigeons, and poultry. This allowed them to set up an agricultural base in Poutrincourt's new settlement. Inevitably, rats also arrived on the ship and escaped to the countryside, infesting *l'habitation* and the nearby Mi'kmaq village, threatening meager food supplies. Fifty men joined the small group that remained from Île St.-Croix. There were no women or children.

L'habitation at Port-Royal c.1612   Samuel de Champlain
Wikimedia Commons, Project Gutenberg

Claude de La Tour assisted in overseeing construction of buildings, tilling of the soil, and planting crops. His men were instructed to plant wheat on a natural meadow upriver from the settlement. They built a mill, the first gristmill in Acadia and the entire land. Claude learned about the lucrative fur trade and how trading was carried out with the Indians. The two noble teenage boys were also put to work. Charles Biencourt and Charles de La Tour were encouraged to spend time with the local Mi'kmaq, learning hunting skills and navigating rivers and waterways. They took "... easily to Indian ways" ...paddling bark canoes "...for hours along the water highways, growing strong and hardy. In winter, they would master the wide-swinging snowshoe stride, tracking moose through deep snows, learning to keep all senses alert..." The boys also "... teased the Indian girls, freer and more independent than the girls back home, and learned the language of their new friends."[2] Biencourt became so proficient in Mi'kmaq that he served as his father's interpreter.

Fortunately, the winter of 1606-07 was mild. Poutrincourt kept his men well fed to avoid scurvy (only four died), and Champlain founded the "Order of Good Times" (*L'Ordre de Bon-Temps*) to stave off boredom. The Order included not only French nobles and advisors, but also Mi'kmaq *sagamore* (chief) Membertou and some of his tribesmen, their wives, and children. Poutrincourt wrote music, secular and religious; Marc Lescarbot, his lawyer, literary companion, and family friend, wrote plays; Louis Hébert, his in-law, was a master pharmacist and amateur horticulturist who learned native remedies for scurvy; and argumentative free spirit Robert Gravé du Pont, son of their navigator, added friction. Other members of the settlement were a surgeon, firelock repairer, journeymen carpenters and woodcutters, but no priests or ministers. They passed a good winter, and started sowing seeds the end of March. Soon the food supply was abundant enough to share with the Mi'kmaq; according to Lescarbot, they "came to the French to beg beans, peas, biscuits, and other edibles."[3]

Just as the budding colony was doing well, a series of misfortunes befell de Mons, who was in France. Court politics and volatile French colonial policy led to cancellation of his 10-year trade rights and concessions by the king. Behind this were fur trade competitors and court schemers, who alleged that de Mons had not converted a single "savage" and had been defrauding the company that employed him. Up against too many odds, de Mons gave up, notified Poutrincourt, and sent a ship to bring back the settlers.

Poutrincourt, Champlain, and the La Tours waited to harvest the grain before leaving. They also waited to say farewell to Membertou, who had been away leading a war party against a rival tribe, the Almouchiquois. After the great chief returned in triumph, the grain was harvested in fall 1607, and the Frenchmen departed. Champlain reported that "Membertou and the Indians were sorry to see them go. There were tears and lamentations. The Indians promised to protect the settlement, which they did with complete fidelity."[4]

These early settlers learned a great deal in the three years spent in Acadia. They made immense progress in mapping the region, expanding geographic understanding of the relation between Acadian lands and the continent. These years allowed them to establish lasting relationships with the Indians and gain understanding of their governing system of regional chiefs with well-defined groups. Their experiences in St. Croix and Port-Royal prepared them for Acadian winters, and the French never again abandoned a colony due to climate. Acadia was still a land of great promise.

Poutrincourt and de Mons were given a second chance in 1608. They argued that English and Dutch incursions into the territory were a growing threat, reminding the king and merchants that France needed monopoly over the fur trade and fisheries to maintain a permanent presence in America. They praised the new land's fertility and marvelous wheat crops. King Henri IV was convinced and granted de Mons a one-year extension on his monopoly. After that, the region would revert to free trade, prompting Champlain to declare the new concession was worthless. He broke away to focus on Canada.

As second in command, Poutrincourt was to further develop the *seigneurie* at Port-Royal. However, French Queen Marie di Medici wanted Jesuits at the colony to convert the natives. Poutrincourt disliked Italian-based Jesuits, as did many devout French Catholics, so he pulled strings to obtain services of a secular priest, *Abbé* Jessé Fléché. Cobbling together financial backing for another Acadian venture, he outfitted a ship with furniture, food, and munitions in early 1610. Young Charles de La Tour returned to Port-Royal on this ship for his second Acadian adventure, along with 40 passengers and *Abbé* Jessé Fléché. As before, there were no women or children.

Upon arriving at *l'habitation* at Port-Royal, they found it in good condition despite years of neglect, thanks to Membertou's care. The buildings required roof repairs, and the mill needed work, and they dug a well inside the fort since the spring was a distance away. One of the first things Poutrincourt did was to summon the local Mi'kmaqs, who were overjoyed to see the Frenchmen return. Mindful of the Queen's mandate, Poutrincourt had *Abbé* Fléché begin converting the natives. The young Biencourt, who had become fluent in Algonquin during his earlier stay, instructed the Indians in tenets of the faith. *Abbé* Fléché preached to Membertou's band of Mi'kmaq, baptizing the bearded *sagamore* and 20 others on June 24, 1610; the first converts in New France. Within a year, the secular priest had "saved" over a hundred Algonquin, including some Etchemin from a village on Rivière St.-Jean.

The Frenchmen then focused on fur trading and making the colony agriculturally self-sustaining. They planted wheat in the meadows and vegetables on the rocky slope behind *l'habitation*. Poutrincourt parceled out farms in his *seigneurie,* creating grants with signed deeds for his colonists, initiating wider settlement in Acadia. Things were going well for the colony, but within a few years discord returned in the guise of black-robed Jesuits.

To secure more financial support, young Biencourt returned to France in 1611, meeting a new king, Louis XIII, with his devout mother in a powerful position. She demanded that Jesuits be taken to Acadia, making Biencourt's Huguenot supporters withdraw. Funds from Catholic nobility were contingent on taking Jesuits, so Fathers Biard and Massé arrived in Acadia in 1612. Further conflicts with French nobility led to Poutrincourt's financial ruin. Acadia was further destabilized by conflicts between Biencourt and the Jesuits, while other French opportunists competed in the fur trade.

The British had eyed Acadian lands for some time with intent to acquire their natural resources. In 1613 the newly founded Virginia colony sent English captain Samuel Argall up the coast to Acadia, his orders to remove rival powers. He was "to raze every French fort or settlement as far as Cape Breton... to sack all French ships and to send the prisoners back home."[5] Argall made a sneak attack on Port-Royal while Biencourt and most of his men were hunting with the Indians. Argall gathered livestock, looted and burned *l'habitation*, and set fire to crops, though he failed to find the gristmill. Argall captured one of the Jesuits, Father Biard, who supposedly informed him about Port-Royal. When Biencourt returned, he met with Argall and demanded the Jesuit so he could hang him, but was refused. Argall left with booty and prisoners but was lost at sea in perhaps an act of poetic justice.

Winter was approaching and Port-Royal had been decimated. Biencourt and his men, including Charles de La Tour, lived among the Mi'kmaq (some sources say the two leaders spent the winter in the gristmill). They would not have survived without the Indians' help. Since no resources arrived from France, they could not rebuild the settlement and abandoned it, giving up farming. The Frenchmen spent the next 10 years pursuing the lucrative fur trade. Here began the next significant chapter in Charles de La Tour's life.

The Mi'kmaq Princess—Daughter of Chief Membertou

Relationships between the French and the Indians were unique in annals of European and Native American contacts. French explorers, fur traders, fishermen, and colonists established congenial relations, mingled easily with natives, accepted their customs, and frequently intermarried. This was especially true of the Acadian settlers and the Mi'kmaq who inhabited the lands of Nova Scotia, New Brunswick, Prince Edward Island, and Newfoundland. Survival of Acadian settlements depended on cooperation with the indigenous people, who had lived and adapted there for 13,000 years. Their lives followed an annual cycle of seasonal movement, living during the winter in scattered camps in the interior, and gathering in larger coastal communities in the summer. Theirs was a hunter-gatherer lifestyle, subsisting mostly on fishing and hunting. These semi-nomadic bands were made up of several matrilineal-related families.

In the early 1500s the Mi'kmaq nation, called Mi'kma'ki, was divided into seven districts each led by a district chief titled *Nikanus*. They met periodically in a Grand Council with its leader, war chief, and recorder. Each of the seven districts had its *Nikanus* and a council of *sagamore* (Sagamaw, local band chiefs), elders, and other community leaders. The district councils enacted laws, dispensed justice, apportioned fishing and hunting grounds, made war and peace. Local bands of extended families were led by a *sagamore* and council of elders. The Mi'kmaq Nation was well-governed, strong, knowledgeable, and successful.

Their language was part of the Algonquin group which stretched from lands east of the St. Lawrence River to the Adirondacks and Appalachians. The Mi'kmaq belonged to a larger tribal group called the "Wabanaki Confederacy" which also included the Maliseet, Passamaquoddy, Penobscot, and Abanaki tribes of Eastern North America. Before European contact, the Mi'kmaq population was an estimated 35,000. This was reduced largely by disease to 3,000 by the time Acadia was settled by the French 100 years later. Although many coastal Indians became wary or hostile after years of dealing with Europeans, the Mi'kmaq of Acadia remained friendly and helpful.

Charles de La Tour and Charles Biencourt spent considerable time with the Mi'kmaq. These hardy young men "... lived much like an Indian, roaming the woods with a few followers, and subsisting on fish, game, roots, and lichens." Their experiences engendered an abiding respect for the natives; instead of calling them *sauvages* (forest-dwellers), they referred to their native friends as "people of the country." The Frenchmen went bare-chested in summer and fur-clad in winter, as did the Mi'kmaq, and "... endured the smoky warmth of flea-ridden bark wigwams, slept on furs laid over spruce boughs, ate strips of half-roasted meat and potluck stew. In small... Mi'kmaq canoes they explored the coasts and inland river systems as far south as the Kennebec and learned... to speak the tongues of the different tribes."[6]

It is likely that Charles de La Tour spent time with the Mi'kmaq girl who became his first wife, a daughter of *sagamore* Anli-Maopeltoog Membertou, during these sojourns. Many Frenchmen married native women, a practice called *métissage*. With no European women there during the early colony years, it seemed natural to pair with native women, though how many considered themselves married is open to question. In Charles' case, his union with Membertou's daughter was considered a marriage, possibly because of her high standing in the tribe.

Chief Membertou (1507-1611) was *sagamore* of a Mi'kmaq band living near Port-Royal and became close friends with Jean de Biencourt de Poutrincourt. He was an *autmoin* (shaman or medicine man) and warrior leader. Reputed to be over 100 years old in 1605, he met Jacques Cartier in 1534 and acquired a French ship decorated with his own totems, which augmented his status in trading. Both Lescarbot and Champlain witnessed him conducting a funeral in 1606 for a fellow *sagamore* killed in battle. He led some 400 warriors in revenge, killing 20 men himself and wounding 10-12 more. The French held Membertou in great esteem, Father Biard writing: "This was the greatest, most renowned and most formidable savage within the memory of man, of splendid physique, taller and larger-limbed than is usual among them; bearded like a Frenchman... grave and reserved, feeling a proper sense of dignity for his position as commander."[7]

When Membertou was baptized Catholic, he was given the name of the French King Henri; his wife was named Marie for the Queen; his eldest son given the dauphin's name Louis; and his daughter who later married La Tour was named Marguerite. Desiring to be a devout Catholic, Membertou gave up polygamy and shamanism. He urged the priests to learn his language to better teach his people. When he fell ill of dysentery in 1611, he asked Biencourt to have him buried with his ancestors, after receiving last rites by the Jesuit priest. This sparked conflict between Biencourt and Father Biard. The Jesuit priest objected, because this meant burial in unhallowed ground. Biencourt suggested the burial place could be blessed, but the priest refused since heathens would also be buried in consecrated ground. Membertou then relented since the priest would not say prayers over his grave, and was buried at the French cemetery upon his death on September 18, 1611. The ceremony had vespers and a solemn funeral fitting for the commandant himself.

Congenial French-Mi'kmaq relations began through the fur trade. The Indians traded their pelts for prized goods only Europeans could provide, such as colorful beads, copper goods, and steel knives. The French initially came and went instead of making permanent settlements; when they did settle, their population grew very slowly. They chose to be near Indian villages, were comfortable with natives, and did not try to push them off their lands. In the late 1630s, when the French built settlements near the Bay of Fundy marshes and started agriculture, it did not affect the natives' traditional way of life. Acadian farmers reclaimed land from salt marshes with their clever dam system called *aboiteaux*. The Mi'kmaq had used these lands only tangentially, and the crops grown were suitable for sharing, including grains, peas, cabbages, and vegetables. This was vastly different than English colonists along southern coasts who grew tobacco, a nutrient-depleting cash crop, and who forced natives off the land to expand lucrative cultivation.

While the population of colonists in New England, New York, Chesapeake Bay, and Virginia exploded, and many died in conflicts with Indians, the Acadians knew peace with the natives until their last few years in the colony.

La Tour Takes Over Port-Royal and Starts a Family

The raid by Samuel Argall foreshadowed a pattern that plagued French Acadia for nearly a century. Because of its geographic position, Acadia was a buffer zone between rival empires, with different ones prevailing. The French government was unwilling to make substantial investments to sustain its Acadian colony, while the shifting political environment added instability.

In 1615, Jean de Bienville de Poutrincourt, who was still in France, was killed at age 58 while fighting an anti-monarchical uprising near his Champagne estates. Charles de Biencourt inherited his father's title and claims in Acadia. Despite difficulties, Charles was determined to continue the fur trade, since pelts could only be acquired in large quantities in the North American wilderness. But fur trading in Acadia decreased between 1618 and 1623, Port-Royal was crumbling through neglect, and few new settlers arrived. Biencourt lived increasingly with the Indians in his last years, accompanied by his "lieutenant," Charles de La Tour. When Biencourt died in 1623, held in the arms of his longtime companion, he bequeathed his holdings to a cousin. La Tour formed a partnership with the cousin's younger brother, Jacques de Salazar of Saint-Just, who inherited family estates in France. De Salazar had no interest in the Acadian enterprises, precarious as they were, and happily left these to La Tour.

La Tour took charge of Port-Royal and made improvements, but decided to build another stronger post at Cap-Sable, located around the tip of the peninsula facing the

Atlantic Ocean. Soon it was called Port-La Tour. Shortly afterwards, in 1625, he married a Mi'kmaq woman. Her native name is not known, but she was baptized Marguerite, along with her father Chief Membertou. There were no priests left in Acadia, so Charles had his union "blessed" by the Récollets after they returned in 1630. The first daughter, born in 1626, was named Jeanne de La Tour. Charles was 30 years old, and Marguerite was 19 (1606 birth date) or 33 (1593 birth date). They had two additional daughters: Antoinette, baptized as a young child in 1632, and a younger girl whose name is unknown. La Tour treated his girls as legitimate: "He seems to have been a devoted father, taking considerable trouble over their upbringing."[8]

By 1627, most of the Acadian colonists had settled down, some in their older location at Port-Royal, but most with La Tour at Cap-Sable. During that time 70 Scottish settlers sent by Sir William Alexander took up residence in Port-Royal and called it Scots Fort. That year, war broke out between France and England, and La Tour was worried about the future of the Acadian colonies. The past 20 years of French neglect had left them without defense and economic aid. The British took over Port-Royal, leaving La Tour's fort as France's only remaining Acadian outpost. He wrote letters to King Louis XIII and Cardinal Richelieu requesting assistance, explaining that he was the acting administrator in Acadia and heir of Biencourt. Pointing out that he had maintained France's hold in Acadia, he asked for a proper commission authorizing him to defend the area.

Charles' father, Claude de La Tour, who had remained in France, presented the letters and gave full account of conditions in Acadia. The king sent this request for men and supplies to the new trading association, *Compagnie de la Nouvelle-France.* Charged with encouraging further settlement, the company had powers to grant *seigneuries* and held rights to trade with the Indians. The next spring, it sent four ships laden with supplies to Cap-Sable; Claude was also on board. But the ships were captured by Sir David Kirke and his brothers, privateers working for the British. Claude was taken prisoner and brought to England.

A resourceful man, Claude put his charming personality to work finding a solution to his troubles. He was quickly on excellent terms with Sir David Kirke, who introduced him to the English court. The gregarious Frenchman formed friendships with palace gentlewomen and Scottish poet Sir William Alexander, another colonizer enticed by Acadian riches. King James I of Scotland and England had granted Alexander all of Acadia in 1621, where he had already taken over Port-Royal, and planned to form multiple settlements of industrious Lowland Scots. But he had few takers among the Scots he approached for money and men to settle New Scotland (Nova Scotia). Claude, on the other hand, found this an attractive offer. Alexander was happy to avail himself of the elder La Tour's knowledge of the region.

Claude espoused the English cause and promised to win over his son Charles, in exchange for them both becoming baronets and receiving large land grants in Acadia. Many Frenchmen considered this treason; for Claude it was expediency. Since Kirke's raids had devastated all of France's posts (Port-Royal, Quebec) except Cap-Sable, Claude felt there was no hope that France would regain its territory. To further consolidate his position, Claude married one of British Queen Henrietta Maria's maids of honor. It was his third marriage. Claude and his new wife set sail for Nova Scotia in early 1629, with Alexander's son in charge. They established a Scottish settlement, Charlesfort, near the ruins of Port-Royal with 70 men, women, and children.

Father and Son La Tour Feud

There was no doubt in Claude's mind that he would readily convince his son of the wisdom of turning over Fort-La Tour to the British. But such was not the case.

Waiting at Cap-Sable with his band of French, Mi'kmaq, and Métis, Charles heard reports of the Kirkes' attacks and worried for months about what had happened to his father. In 1630, three years after Claude carried appeals to France, two ships unexpectedly entered the bay at Cap-Sable and dropped anchor in the sheltered cove. From one ship Claude came ashore, much to the relief of his son Charles, who desperately needed supplies. But the assistance being offered was from the wrong country.

Their encounter was surprising to both: "We can easily imagine the frustration, the emotion, the surprise which overwhelmed the son when his own father urged him to cede his territory. The father must have been just as much surprised when he was faced with complete refusal on the part of his son. Neither his advances, nor his exhortations, nor his offers, nor his threats had any effect on this son; he was simply running his head against a cement wall."[9]

Even the offer of a title and generous land grant by the English did not sway Charles, who remained loyal to the French king. Accounts vary about the standoff, but it seems Claude resorted to force and attacked his son's fort. One version says the battle lasted one whole day and one whole night; another relates troops led by Claude attacked for over 24 hours, but without success. Whether Charles experienced any casualties is not known, but it appears that the attackers lost some men. The unsuccessful, and no doubt greatly discomforted, father was obliged to retreat back to Port-Royal.

A few weeks later, two ships of the *Compagnie de la Nouvelle-France* arrived at Fort La Tour filled with supplies and a relief party including workers, artisans, and three Récollet priests (one of whom blessed Charles' marriage to the Mi'kmaq Marguerite). They were sent in answer to Charles' plea three years earlier. The workers soon enlarged and strengthened the post, renaming it Port-La Tour. Charles was charged to build another fort where he thought it most useful. He chose the mouth of the Saint John River, a rich source of furs, strategically located on a stone promontory rising 50 feet above water level. Named Fort Saint Louis (later Fort Sainte-Marie), it had an excellent view of the bay entrance and both sides of Cap-Sable Island.

Claude meanwhile was having a miserable time in Port-Royal. The English leaders and Scottish colonists were displeased and ostracized him and his wife. He dared not return to England, as his life might be forfeit, and his courtly wife was "a great embarrassment to him." Though offered a return to England, she would not abandon her husband, desiring to stay with him. Claude decided to inform his son about their life in disgrace and request sanctuary at Cap-Sable. In his letter, Claude begged Charles to "...permit his wife and himself to remain in the country, since after what had passed, he did not dare return to England because he would there lose his head."[10]

Charles was of noble enough character to provide his father and wife sanctuary. Prudently he built them a small dwelling outside the walls and forbade them to enter the fort. Arriving with luggage, two men servants and two maids for the wife, the couple was supported by Charles and lived comfortably, being quite amply provided for. Claude was still around to give his consent to his son's second marriage in 1639.

Governor of Acadia and Lieutenant General of the King

On February 8, 1631, King Louis XIII signed a royal commission naming Charles de La Tour governor of Acadia and lieutenant general of the king. The ship that brought the commission also carried additional materials for the new fort at Saint John River. A year later Scots from Port-Royal attacked the new fort, damaging structures and pillaging supplies. La Tour retaliated after a few months, captured the English fort at Machias, and plundered it as a warning. Within a year, France and England reached concord, signing the Treaty of Saint-Germain-en-Laye (1632), which returned Acadia and Canada to the French.

More troubling to La Tour than the Scottish incursion was news that Cardinal Richelieu, acting for the French king, had appointed highly placed and respected Chevalier Isaac de Razilly as "Lieutenant General in all the country of New France, known as Canada, neighbourlands and coasts in all their extent." This in effect made Razilly supreme governor of all France's northern colonies, including Acadia. Razilly's fleet, supported by the *Compagnie de la Nouvelle-France,* included 300 people bound for Acadia to augment settlements. He arrived at La Hève in fall 1632, accompanied by young naval officer Menou d'Aulnay, cousin to Richelieu, in command of the largest ship. Within a few months they ousted the Scots from Port-Royal, though many Scottish settlers chose to remain in the region.

La Tour sailed to France in 1632, since Acadia was now securely under French control, to clarify the limits of his and Razilly's authority, deal with company business, and attend to personal affairs. He brought his daughters, intending to secure for them a good French education. Also on the voyage were his staff and two Mi'kmaq men, one a chief. The Indians were important for court action he was taking against a Basque captain who was poaching in the fur trade in Acadia.

The Three Métis Daughters. It is not certain that La Tour's oldest daughter, Jeanne, who was 6 or 7 years old, came on the trip. If she did, she did not remain in France. His next daughter Antoinette was around 5 years old, and the youngest must have been a toddler; both her name and birth date are lost. Bringing these young children on a risky voyage suggests that his Mi'kmaq wife must have died. Children this young would normally be left in their mother's care. His wife Marguerite's death is thought to have occurred around 1629.

It was common practice for girls of good families to be educated in convents. If there was insufficient money for a dowry, they frequently entered religious life, taking vows as nuns. Antoinette first lived with her father's relatives in La Rochelle, who were Huguenots. After three years, relatives of Razilly with connections to Richelieu intervened to have her sent to the rich and ancient Beaumont-les-Tours Abbey in Touraine in 1642. Perhaps the competing Acadian governor, whose family lived in La Rochelle, was acting out of kindness to assist La Tour's daughters. His relative Mère Louise de Razilly was in charge of novices. She discovered that Antoinette had an exceptionally beautiful voice and gave her training with the best voice teachers. News of her singing, called "out of this world," traveled quickly in circles of nobility; many people of rank attended her novitiate vows in 1644. One Franciscan friar, after hearing her sing three times, carried such enthusiastic accounts to the Queen of France (Anne of Austria) that an audience was arranged. Queen Anne brought Antoinette by private coach to Paris, lodged her in the most select convent there, and came often to hear her sing. All the high dignitaries of the Royal Court gathered to listen to the Acadian girl's remarkable voice.

After staying in the Paris convent for half a year, Antoinette "begged humbly to return to her former convent." She was returned to the Beaumont Abby, where she took her final vows in 1646 in the presence of a number of high-ranking persons. Her story is preserved in convent records. As summarized by d'Etremont: "Sister Antoinette, this Port La Tour born child, this first child born in North America to become a nun, after having captivated the people of high rank with her beautiful young voice, preferred in her modesty, to the splendour of a convent that the queen had just built, the less dazzling cloister of the Benedictine nuns of Tourraine, where she, in its obscurity, shut herself up from the rest of the world so completely that she was not heard of afterward."[11]

Sister Antoinette is mentioned once more, when she became godmother at the baptism of her niece. In 1660 at La Rochelle, the daughter of her sister Jeanne was baptized and given the name Antoinette. La Tour's youngest daughter, whose name is not known, was placed by her father in the care of Razilly's relatives soon after arriving in La Rochelle. First taken to the abbey at Tourraine, she was moved to the convent of the Ursuline Sisters due to an agreement that had been made. She died within a few years in the Ursuline convent.

The first daughter, Jeanne, married a rich Basque merchant, Martin d'Aprendestique *dit* Martignon, in what is now Castine, Maine. They had five children and are the ancestors of many Acadians, including the Bourgeois, LeBlanc, Bourdreau, Dugas, and other families. Their lives are covered later.

Charles de La Tour had a profitable visit to France in 1632-1633. He forged strong links with directors of the *Compagnie de la Nouvelle-France* and obtained permission from Richelieu to load a ship with emergency supplies for his Saint John River fort. He went to Paris with a colorful retinue of colonial officers and Indians at Christmastime, stayed with a high court advocate, and became firm friends with Jean de Lauzon, king's councilor and future governor of Canada. He renewed acquaintance with the elderly Samuel Champlain, who was in Paris publishing a book. La Tour negotiated agreements with the Company giving fair and equal division of the fur trade between him and Razilly, with privileges of checking each other's storehouses for enforcement. Essentially, they were watchdogs over each other. Such an arrangement could only work among men of goodwill; fortunately, Isaac de Razilly was respected by all as fair-minded and a model Christian gentleman. His successor, however, was not so inclined.

La Tour must have reveled in the winter season in Paris, full of pleasure-seekers and parties. He was presented at the Royal Court and designated *"chevalier de l'ordre du roy"* for his appearance before King Louis XIII. Having led an active life, a self-assured and bold man, 39-year-old La Tour undoubtedly cut a fine appearance in stylish clothes, bringing an exotic touch through having lived among *sauvages*. He probably met the woman who would become his next wife, Françoise-Marie Jacquelin, during his stay in Paris. She was the daughter of a doctor from the Loire district, a man of stature in the upper reaches of his profession. Dr. Jacquelin's daughters were better educated than most women, and Françoise-Marie was skilled in mathematics, bookkeeping, and maneuvering in the world of business. She was an assertive and smart woman. These qualities would serve her in good stead during the tumultuous years as Charles' wife.

Before returning to Acadia, La Tour put advertisements in the widely circulated *Gazette* inviting colonists to join him in New France. He promised rich and fertile land, rivers full of fish, birds and game animals, and abundant beaver. Settlers' spiritual needs would be provided for through services by Capucin priests. He was not dismayed by the sparse response, for his primary interest was fur trading, and supporting a large colony would be a needless expense. He set sail with a few much-needed tradesmen, including masons, a baker, surgeon, locksmith, and trumpeter. The two Mi'kmaqs returned, along with La Tour's officers Captain Étienne de Mourron and Guillaume Desjardins, as well as his kinsman François Godard.

Back in Acadia by 1635, La Tour restored his fort on the Saint John River, named it Fort Sainte-Marie, and settled his small group of colonists. By all indications, La Tour and Razilly got along well, amicably dividing the region: Razilly controlled La Hève, Port-Royal, and the Sainte-Croix area; La Tour was in charge of Cap-Sable and the Saint John River region. Both could anticipate mutual cooperation and an untroubled time of peace.

But such welcome reprieve was short-lived. Isaac de Razilly died suddenly, later in 1635. His brother Claude nominally succeeded but stayed in France and delegated the family interests in Acadia to his cousin, Charles de Menou d'Aulnay. It seems that d'Aulnay was already antagonistic toward La Tour, bridling because such a colonial backwoods inferior had more influence with high officials than did he, a member of the establishment. Jealousy over La Tour's status as a king's governor and lieutenant general in Acadia spurred d'Aulnay to embark on a campaign to wrest away control of the region. La Tour's descendants later remarked: "This jealousy caused a great disagreement between them, which went so far that they waged open warfare."[12] The history of Acadia over the following six years is largely a record of their strife.

Acadian Civil War

In 1635, d'Aulnay retook the trading post at Pentagouet, originally built by Claude de La Tour but captured by the New Englanders in 1626. When the Company gave back the post to La Tour in 1636, d'Aulnay became outraged. Using his connections at the French court, he eventually convinced the king to give Pentagouet to him, resulting in an untenable division of land. In their ignorance of Acadian geography and history, Louis XIII's ministers granted d'Aulnay the land lying north of the Bay of Fundy except Fort Sainte-Marie, and La Tour the peninsular region but not Port-Royal. La Tour considered Port-Royal part of his inheritance from Biencourt.

Colonists brought by d'Aulnay went to Port-Royal to establish agriculture. In the meadowlands used previously to grow wheat, the new colonists drained the flatlands and built dikes, turning rich tidal flats into grain fields and grasslands for cattle. The system they used to drain lands was called *aboiteaux*, a dike with a sluice that was forced shut as the tide rose on the seaward side, then pushed open from the other side as the tide fell, thus draining water from the fields. The colonists, mostly natives of marshy regions of the lower Loire valley and western Poitou, were familiar with this system. After a few years, the *aboiteaux* would leech sea salt from the soil behind the dike and convert tidal marshes into fertile fields that would support many crops. While waiting for salt to clear out, the fields served as pasture for sheep and cattle, as well as a source of salt.

Creating colonies was expensive; the Company sought more government money and was refused, but Cardinal Richelieu personally lent them 17,000 livres. New shareholders were recruited; one came with his family to Acadia to see his new investment. He had an eligible daughter, Jeanne Motin. Governor d'Aulnay, now in his early 30s and unmarried, lost no time snatching up the French girl, a rarity in these parts. In addition, Jeanne had a nice dowry that included shares in the Company. They married in 1636 when Jeanne was 21 years old, immediately starting a family that would produce four boys and four girls. These were apparently not d'Aulnay's first progeny; a

New England family named Doney claimed to be his descendants—Métis children who later took part in Indian uprisings.[13]

The two governors argued over competing claims, and a letter to d'Aulnay from the king in 1638 deplored their deteriorating relations and ordered them to overcome their differences. They also were charged to divide the fur revenues equally between them, as in the days of Razilly. The king demanded more information on the situation in the colonies. This royal directive probably made La Tour furious and d'Aulnay frustrated.

In August, 1639, La Tour and his men Desjardins and de Mourron met at Cap-Sable to consider their next moves. Since Razilly's death four years ago, difficulties had increased, and they felt certain that d'Aulnay meant to establish a dynasty in Acadia. His wife Jeanne had already borne several children. La Tour was age 46 and a widower, without a son to become his heir and successor. He sent Desjardins and de Mourron to France to secure a wife and negotiate the marriage contract. Although the document he gave his envoys did not contain the bride's name, he probably had Françoise-Marie Jacquelin in mind. The envoys found her still eligible, made arrangements, and the marriage contract was endorsed in Paris on New Year's Eve, 1639. It was exceptionally generous; La Tour believed a French woman of good standing needed incentive to make the difficult journey and live in the colonies. She received money for jewelry, an inheritance fund, and a half-share in all holdings acquired during the marriage, thus becoming a full partner in her husband's concerns.

In June 1640, Françoise-Marie Jacquelin and Charles de La Tour were married by priests at the fort of Saint-Louis at Cap-Sable. The Acadian lands must have seemed foreboding to the French woman, the wedding party sailing along rocky coastlines past fog-shrouded islands. Passing through the Bay of Fundy, they arrived at Fort Sainte-Marie greeted by cannon fire and a fleet of Indian canoes. Perhaps Françoise-Marie admired the bright-beaded robes and headdresses of natives from the nearby village.

The fort was set atop the steep-sided knoll. Newly peeled logs of the enlarged stockade surrounded a square complex that could house 90 people, roofed with yellow tiles. The complex included a cookhouse and larder, trading room, workshops, living quarters with two great-rooms and several bedrooms, a chapel, and rooms for the Récollet priests. Two huge fireplaces warmed the great-rooms, one for leaders and officers, the other for workers and soldiers. Cabinet makers at the fort had built most of the plain, sturdy furniture, but there were a few chairs and chests from France.

In a woman's manner, Françoise-Marie likely made her quarters as bright and comfortable as possible. She would find difficult the bitterly cold winter, with ice floes on the bay, snow covering the hills, and chilling fog. By spring she was probably with child; she had at least one son. No other children are known. Her women companions were two waiting women and 14-year-old Jeanne La Tour, who lived with her father.

Charles de La Tour meets Françoise-Marie Jacquelin 1640
Wikimedia Commons, CW Jefferys

A few weeks after Françoise-Marie settled in at Fort Sainte-Marie, the conflict between her husband and d'Aulnay intensified. La Tour suspected his rival of taking more than his share of furs and determined to check for himself. Under the royal edict and by prior agreements, he had a right to examine d'Aulnay's fur stores. He also thought a plausible excuse for a visit to Port-Royal was to introduce his wife and have her meet d'Aulnay's spouse, Jeanne Motin, with her growing family.

La Tour sailed across the bay with two armed ships, his wife, and Desjardins, soon entering the harbor of Port-Royal. The fort sat on rocky shores below the looming cliff, with cannons menacing the wide river approaches. His request for permission to land was brusquely refused, since d'Aulnay was away taking supplies to Pentagouet, and his officer in charge had specific instructions not to admit La Tour. Humiliated by this rebuff, which he felt was an insult to his wife, La Tour remained fuming in the harbor overnight. The next morning he sailed back toward Fort Sainte-Marie but encountered d'Aulnay's returning ships just outside the river's mouth. Hostilities erupted at once; both men claimed the other fired the first shot, but each was in a fighting mood.

La Tour's gunners shot down the mast of d'Aulnay's first vessel and killed several men, while d'Aulnay's shots killed La Tour's captain and a few others. He drove La Tour's ships into the shallows where they foundered. La Tour, Françoise-Marie, Desjardins, and surviving men were captured and taken to the Port-Royal prison. Although d'Aulnay asserted self-righteously that La Tour and his "mistress" were humanely treated, the lightless dungeon must have been unpleasant and humiliating. By calling La Tour's wife his "mistress," d'Aulnay showed that he viewed her as unworthy of respect. Capucin friars who were with d'Aulnay drew up an agreement referring the quarrel to the French king and admonished both men to keep the peace. After La Tour signed it, he and his people were released and returned to their fort across the bay. The Capucins wrote a long report, mostly favorable to d'Aulnay.

Never one to meekly accept defeat, La Tour sent Desjardins to La Rochelle, setting in motion a counterstrategy in France. He filed a suit against d'Aulnay's ship captain for murder. Though the captain was arrested, the case dragged on for years with negligible immediate effects, although it ultimately revealed d'Aulnay's fraud against the Company. The Capucins' report, along with influence by d'Aulnay's well-connected father, led to a devastating outcome for his rival. The king ordered La Tour to come immediately to France and explain himself and charged d'Aulnay to take over in Acadia. Richelieu revoked La Tour's commission as governor due to "bad behavior." As part of this action, Desjardins was arrested and all his goods seized.

With brewing rebellion at home, French leaders did not send representatives to Acadia to check the facts. When these royal edicts reached La Tour in the summer of 1642, he refused to return to France, contending that the orders were obtained through lies and misrepresentation. Realizing his dire situation, he withdrew men from Cap-Sable, which was difficult to defend. At once d'Aulnay took over and burned the fort, church, and Récollet monastery despite the king's orders to preserve La Tour's assets. The monks and La Tour were dismayed; this early settlement meant a great deal to them.

La Tour seeks assistance in Boston. Realizing that he could no longer turn to allies in France, La Tour sought assistance in New England, offering free commerce between their colonies while requesting help with his war against d'Aulnay. Boston Governor John Winthrop favored free trade but was reluctant to give military aid. When d'Aulnay learned of these negotiations, he hastened to France and charged La Tour with treason. The king issued another summons and gave d'Aulnay control of all Acadian posts. Learning that Desjardins was sending a ship to La Tour with supplies, d'Aulnay set up a three-ship blockade in the entrance to Fort Sainte-Marie.

By the fall of 1642, the blockade seriously affected La Tour's fort. He could not get furs out for trade, and no supplies could be brought into the fort. They began to lack essentials for survival and defense, running short on flour, sugar, wine, clothing, tools, and ammunition. La Tour requested help again from Boston, but was offered only trade. La Tour was desperate but knew he could not go to France. So, he sent his wife Françoise-Marie to plead his cause.

Her endeavors in France made clear how smart, capable, and devoted she was. Cardinal Richelieu died in December 1642; his successor was his nephew, Armand de Maillé, who was overseer of the Company. Françoise-Marie garnered support from Company directors who always considered d'Aulnay a usurper, thrust on them by the king. The young woman with no experience of high-level negotiation rose to the challenge; her modest self-opinion, discernment, and confidence made her imminently believable. "Completely convinced of the justice of her husband's cause, she apparently had, besides, an intuitive quality which allowed her to sense what to say and when to say it."[14]

She presented supporting documents for allegations of d'Aulnay's bad faith and distortion of the facts. One example was the destruction of La Tour's Cap-Sable fort and mission, which the king had ordered be preserved. The Récollet friars who lived in Cap-Sable had also lodged complaints about their mission being burned. Armand de Maillé was sympathetic and ignored the orders and revocations of power the King had set against La Tour. Had Richelieu been alive, this would not have happened. Françoise-Marie received permission for the Company to send a warship with men and supplies to La Tour and an order from de Maillé describing him as lieutenant general and governor for the king on the coasts of Acadia.

It was a great victory by Françoise-Marie, but the ship was prevented from reaching Fort Sainte-Marie by d'Aulnay's blockade. La Tour managed to slip past the blockade under cover of darkness and reach the Company ship. His reunion with Françoise-Marie must have been very emotional. They quickly set sail for Boston, where the authorization order from de Maillé helped secure aid. La Tour and Françoise-Marie made solid friendships during their stay, including Governor Winthrop and Major-General Edward Gibbons, a leader and businessman. Françoise-Marie developed amiable relationships in the Puritan city by going regularly to church with the leaders' wives, even implying she might convert. With her Huguenot background, comfort with Protestantism came naturally. Although the Boston city council did not reach agreement about official support, La Tour was given permission to obtain private assistance. He arranged this with Major-General Gibbons by mortgaging his Acadian properties.

The five warships hired by La Tour encountered d'Aulnay's blockade, drove the ships ashore at Port-Royal, and demanded reparations for d'Aulnay's destruction of Cap-Sable. When refused, La Tour attacked the fort, killed several defenders, and burned the structures and fields. On return to Fort Sainte-Marie, he captured d'Aulnay's fur ship and confiscated the pelts. Immediately after, d'Aulnay complained again to the French king, accusing La Tour of open rebellion and being a heretic because he fraternized with Protestants in Boston.

La Tour again sent Françoise-Marie to France in the fall of 1643, but she was unsuccessful in pleading his cause this time. Most offensive were his alliance with Protestants and repeated disobedience of the king. Nearly all the information about the Acadian conflict came from d'Aulnay; La Tour was once more ordered to appear and answer charges or face arrest. Although Françoise-Marie was forbidden to leave France, she slipped past port authorities and escaped to England after sending an urgent message to her husband warning of his enemy's victory. She alerted him that d'Aulnay was returning with formidable forces.

In England, Françoise-Marie chartered an English ship to take her to La Tour's fort; delayed by foul weather, they encountered d'Aulnay's warship. The English captain hid Françoise-Marie deep in the hold, said they were en route to Boston, and was allowed to proceed. Meanwhile, La Tour had been in Boston seeking more assistance but was denied. He left Boston only eight days before his wife arrived. Major-General Gibbons gave her refuge, while the Boston council lamented "… that they had ever allowed themselves to be drawn into the quarrel."[15]

Françoise-Marie filed and won a lawsuit against the English captain who failed to deliver her to La Tour's fort, using the gains to hire three ships to take her back with supplies. Sailing through buffeting December seas along the rocky coastline, her ships evaded d'Aulnay's blockade, and she returned home after 16 months. But there was little time to relish the reunion. The supplies would not last through the winter, so La Tour sailed again to Boston in early 1645 for essential reinforcements.

Françoise-Marie Defends Fort La Tour. Morale within the fort was running low. The men had received no wages for some time, ammunition was low, and they were nearly starving. Their loyalty was astonishing, for they knew the risk: dungeons, torture, or execution for following a declared traitor. Emotional disputes erupted inside the fort, however. Françoise-Marie and the Récollet priests got into a violent dispute over her adherence to Protestantism, resulting in excommunication of any men who remained loyal to her. The priests and nine men left the fort, going across the bay to d'Aulnay and finding a sympathetic ear.

They told d'Aulnay that La Tour was away in Boston. Springing into action, he sailed his warship for another assault, planning a deception to get inside the enemy fort. Mooring the warship out of sight, he sent a boat with the Récollets and their men, giving the appearance that they were returning. Françoise-Marie was ready to forgive and welcome them back and ordered the main gate opened. Amid excited greetings, she heard the returnees inciting her men to abandon the fort and come over to d'Aulnay's side. Françoise-Marie had her soldiers push them back through the gatehouse, forcing them onto the small boat. Though the invasion was repelled, the seeds of discontent had been sowed.

As the bitter winter dropped heavy snows, d'Aulnay's warships lay in wait at the harbor's mouth. In early April, they captured the relief ship sent from Boston with badly needed food and munitions, and letters of encouragement from La Tour. The ship's captain and men were put on an island deep in snow, with only a tattered wigwam for shelter. Later they were returned to Boston. Taking advantage of La Tour's absence, d'Aulnay determined to take the fort quickly. His first attack was soundly repelled with heavy losses; next he called up every man from his settlements capable of fighting, several hundred men. The fort's handful of guns battled the warships' 16 cannons and numerous other guns. Cannon siege was set up behind the fort; the roar of cannons, crashing cannonballs, splitting wooden beams, smashing windows, and whistling shots of muskets and pistols filled the air. The battle raged for three days and nights, according to one report, but d'Aulnay said it lasted one long day from morning to sunset.

Françoise-Marie led the defense and proved herself a determined and capable warrior. Through many hours, the fort's two surgeons and one pharmacist cared for the wounded as best they could. The defenders fought bravely, although heavily outnumbered and outgunned. In the late afternoon of April 16, 1645, Easter Day, d'Aulnay withdrew beyond artillery range. In the sudden quiet, Françoise-Marie ordered her men to rest as much as possible, inside the fort full of sulfurous fumes, smoke from burning timbers, and the reek of blood and sweat.

At sunset, as shadows lengthened and the sky darkened, d'Aulnay's men advanced stealthily on the fort. The fort watchman, Hans Vandre, was a Swiss mercenary, probably Catholic. When he saw how outnumbered the defenders were, he kept silent and allowed the attackers to advance. They streamed over the shattered palisades, battling fort defenders once inside. Françoise-Marie led the charge, a feat depicted in famous drawings of the event. After a short battle, her forces were nearly overwhelmed. She surrendered on the condition that her men be spared, to which d'Aulnay agreed.

However, d'Aulnay did not keep his word. Furious when he saw the few defenders in dire straits, he felt too many of his men were lost to their obstinacy, and they must be punished. Never would he have agreed to surrender terms had he known. He ordered all defenders hanged except Vandre and the man who carried out the executions. In an act of exceptional cruelty, he put a rope around Françoise-Marie's neck and forced her to watch as her men were killed. It was unimaginably agonizing for this woman, standing in the burning shambles of her husband's fort, surrounded by shattered bodies of the dead and dying. She knew every one of her companions and loyal supporters who died of slow strangulation; many were long-time friends. Perhaps she wished to be hanged with them.

After d'Aulnay's men buried the dead and made rough repairs on the fort, Françoise-Marie, her two women, and her son were initially given some freedom. This ended quickly when she attempted to send her husband a letter using Mi'kmaqs from the village nearby. Put under restraint, she was taken to the fort dungeon and told she would be sent back to France to stand trial for treason. There she suffered in the cold darkness for weeks, full of despair and sorrow, feeling hopeless. Her future held only imprisonment, punishment for rebellion, possible torture, and execution. With her strength already drained by starvation and trauma, she fell ill, perhaps from an infection her body would normally overcome. According to her servants, she became sick from sadness and resentment. The Capucins wrote that she fell sick from rage. Most accounts say she died three weeks after Fort La Tour fell.

The Capucins claimed that Françoise-Marie repented before her death and refuted the heresy she had professed among the English. She was buried behind Fort La Tour near her soldiers' graves, interred with solemn ceremony. Even d'Aulnay acknowledged her stature during funeral rituals; noting her courage, resourcefulness, and strength of purpose far beyond ordinary.[16]

Her son was sent back to France in the care of her waiting woman, arranged by d'Aulnay. It is not known where they went, and no further record of the boy has been found. Françoise-Marie has gained the stature of a heroine in Acadian history.

La Tour's Later Years

Charles La Tour was in Boston when he learned of his wife's death and his fort's destruction in late June 1645. He had lost everything and was destitute at age 52 years, well into middle age at that time. A lesser man would have been crushed; two generations of effort to establish estates in Acadia had come to nothing. He had just mortgaged his lost fort and lands along the Saint John River, and all his ships were lost. Gibbons must have sorely regretted the huge sums he had invested in this Acadian mirage. La Tour was forced to rely on the charity of his friends, who advanced him money.

Never one to accept defeat, La Tour rallied and set upon his next ventures. He visited Sir David Kirke in Newfoundland, his father's old friend, securing a pinnacle for a 3-month fur trading voyage. But once at Cap-Sable, La Tour and his men seized the ship and cast away the crew to the mercy of local Indians. When word got back to Boston, Winthrop called La Tour a pirate. La Tour probably considered it his just due from the New Englanders, who caused him untold grief with their self-righteous fence-sitting. He sailed to Quebec, where he had several friends, in spring of 1646.

La Tour spent four years as an honored, respected citizen of Quebec, welcomed by Governor Huault de Montmagny, Champlain's successor. He attended and took part in various public ceremonies and was present at marriages of important families, signing one marriage contract as former lieutenant governor of Acadia. Records say he became active in Catholic Church affairs and defense of the colony. Jesuits related that he fought in the Iroquois war for two years, assisting the French and their Huron allies. Returning to the fur trade, he amassed enough funds to make generous gifts to the church, where he was assigned honored roles in church ceremonies, and was in demand for baptisms. He was the godfather of a number of children, which gave him connections within Quebec society.

One interesting rumor, though not substantiated, is that La Tour traveled as far north as Hudson Bay pursuing fur trading. He had reconciled with his old friend Gibbons in Boston, who provided assistance. La Tour is credited with inspiring young Médard Chouart, Sieur des Groseilliers, to pursue interest there, which eventually became the Hudson's Bay Company. Previously, La Tour had been a witness at this young man's marriage in Quebec.

Meanwhile, Charles Menou d'Aulnay consolidated his gains in Acadia. He tracked down rival fur trade ships, capturing at least 10 vessels: Basque, Flemish, and some belonging to the Company. In 1647, he seized Company posts on Cape Breton and Miscou Islands, scattering colonists and missionaries. The Company protested to the French royal council, accusing d'Aulnay of gross usurpation of power and false practices, and requested he be dismissed as governor. But earlier that year the Queen's orders confirmed d'Aulnay as governor of Acadia with far-reaching powers, extending from the St. Lawrence River to Virginia.

The Company could not prevail against the French court favorite. But just as d'Aulnay seemed invincible, the tides of fortune turned.

Despite d'Aulnay's ambition and greed that created chaos throughout Acadia, he did the most to build settlements and support his struggling colonists. He encouraged families to put down roots in the Port-Royal basin and helped them develop agriculture, including *aboiteaux* to reclaim swampy land. These farms grew into enduring commercial enterprises. The Capucin superior at Port-Royal noted that d'Aulnay worked side by side with his colonists. On May 21, 1650, he saw d'Aulnay return by canoe from the marshes "... soaked with rain and mud-stained up to his belt and elbows..." after doing a hard day's work with his colonists "... planting stakes, tracing lines, and marking off with cords another plot of land to be drained."[17]

Only three days later, d'Aulnay was in a canoe paddling from Port-Royal, probably to continue work on the new *aboiteau*. The day was stormy, and his canoe capsized in the tidal basin, throwing him and a servant into the water. The river was cold and the swirling current strong; d'Aulnay struggled to swim ashore for an hour and a half. Although he did make it to shore, all his energy and determination had been consumed. Well into middle age at 45 years old, the ordeal was too much for him. After dragging himself onto the bank, he died of cold and exhaustion. The servant reached shore and found his master dead, lying across the overturned canoe. (Another version says a party of Mi'kmaq found his body.) The Capucin superior conducted a solemn requiem mass and buried his body beneath the steps of the chapel, attended by his wife, soldiers, and colonists.

Perhaps d'Aulnay had a premonition of his death. The Capucin said that during the last six months of his life, the man changed completely. He became pious, attending mass and reciting litanies daily on his knees with his head covered. To keep his conscience clear, he confessed every other day. He devoted all his attention and energies toward improving his settlement. The priest rebuked rumors circulating about d'Aulnay's pursuits of women, saying these were absolutely false. But the will left by the governor one year before his death raises questions, for it reads like a plea for forgiveness, particularly from his wife, for earlier transgressions. He wanted to be buried under the church steps so all who passed would have pity for someone "... who merits only the thunderbolts and chastisement of a justly angry God."[18]

Charles de Menou, Lord of Aulnay, intended to establish an Acadian barony with substantial wealth and lands going to his heirs. Perhaps he might have succeeded, had fate not intervened. What he left instead was heavy debt and a young family, many enemies and rivals, an embroiled legal situation, and a burgeoning but struggling colony. An estimated 300 people, perhaps 50 families, lived in Port-Royal basin when he died in 1650. His young widow, Jeanne Motin, found herself in a serious situation, with her husband's chief creditor, Emmanuel Leborgne of La Rochelle, claiming he was owed well over 300,000 livres.

Charles de La Tour sprang into action upon learning of his rival's death. He promptly returned to France and argued his case at the royal court. Silver-tongued as usual, the intrepid adventurer regained royal favor and was completely reinstated within a few months. In February 1651, the Queen Regent confirmed all his powers and rights and charged him to maintain Acadia as he would have if d'Aulnay had not prevented him. Such are the whims and fickleness of royalty—though credit must be given to Charles's powers of persuasion.

La Tour returned to Acadia in 1653 as the reinstated governor, bringing several colonist families, including his friend Philippe Mius d'Entremont, to whom he gave the *seigneurie* of Pobomcoup. As part of the agreement, d'Entremont rebuilt the trading post at Cap-Sable, and it reverted to La Tour's control. La Tour demanded that d'Aulnay's widow return his old Fort Sainte-Marie on the Saint John River. She was powerless to prevent it. Nicolas Denys also reclaimed his holdings in Acadia; he and La Tour were old friends and joined forces. This left only Port-Royal and its basin lands to Jeanne Motin.

Emmanuel Leborgne came to Acadia after obtaining legal papers making him d'Aulnay's successor and claimed the rights to the whole of Acadia. He began harassing the reinstated governor, other landowners such as Denys and d'Entremont, and Jeanne Motin. A few months before La Tour returned, he had seized Port-Royal and returned Jeanne's loyal supporters to France. The widow and her children now had only d'Aulnay's fort at Port-Royal.

Charles La Tour made another amazing move. He persuaded Jeanne Motin to marry him. Although this persuasion emphasized promoting peace between their families, he must have wanted to bolster his claim to Port-Royal. Jeanne was beleaguered on all sides, deeply in debt, trying to raise four children on her own, and cut off from priests and settlers who supported her. She accepted his proposal, and they were married during the summer of 1653. Witnesses were Germain Doucet de La Verdure and Jacques Bourgeois *dit* Jacob, surgeon of d'Aulnay. Charles was 60 at the time of his third marriage; Jeanne was in her mid-30s. They had five children, three girls and two boys. All these children married, and all but one had issue, leaving such a wide-reaching family lineage that virtually all Acadian descendants can claim ancestry tracing back to Charles de La Tour.

In contrast, the dynasty that Charles d'Aulnay hoped to create came to naught. His four sons returned to France and died in its wars, none leaving children. His four daughters, also sent to France, were unable to marry because they lacked dowries large enough to attract suitable husbands. All entered convents and finished their lives in the cloister. The d'Aulnay line ended with his children. Yet his widow, Jeanne, gave La Tour the sons he needed to continue his name and daughters who added to his descendants. Although one might conclude that justice was served, both men had their faults and gifts. For d'Aulnay, his enduring legacy continued through the Acadian settlers he nurtured, many migrating to the Beaubassin region and north into New Brunswick.

The British Take Over Acadia. While La Tour and Leborgne tussled over debt and holdings, everything changed abruptly in 1654. England had mounted an expedition under direction of Oliver Cromwell to attack the Dutch, when peace was declared. Loathe to allow fine forces to go waste, Commander Major Robert Sedgwick decided to move against French settlements to the north. The large force of 500 men in well-equipped warships moved swiftly up the coast and captured the French posts in rapid succession: Pentagouet, Saint John (Fort Sainte-Marie), and Port-Royal. With few cannon, almost no ammunition, and only 70 men at his fort, La Tour was compelled to surrender. He was taken prisoner and sent to London, where he waited two years before obtaining an audience to see Cromwell. La Tour resurrected his Scottish title, obtained by his father years ago, and asked for return of his property on the grounds that England and

France had been at peace when the capture took place. Cromwell recognized La Tour's title and rights as a baronet of Nova Scotia, provided he accept English allegiance, pay off his debt to Boston merchants, and pay for the English garrison in Fort Saint John. Cromwell refused to return all La Tour's Acadian holdings. With little choice, La Tour accepted these conditions but had to sell his rights to two Englishmen, William Crowne and Thomas Temple, to raise the 15,000 pounds he owed. He retained a small percentage of the revenues they acquired from Acadian commerce.

The last decade of La Tour's life was spent in retirement, living at settlements in Port-Royal and Cap-Sable with his wife Jeanne and growing family. Their five children were born between 1654 and 1663. Jeanne Motin died following the birth of their last child, probably related to childbirth; by then she had borne 13 children. Perhaps these years of quiet life were satisfying for the ambitious and inventive Acadian pioneer—now devoted to raising his family and ensuring that his descendants would set strong roots in the land he had helped shape for 56 years. Most accounts say that Charles de La Tour died in 1666 at age 73. Most likely, he was buried at Port-Royal, perhaps not far from his old enemy d'Aulnay's grave.

Legacy of Charles de La Tour

Ambitious, confident, full of determination, and possessing great natural ability for persuasion, Charles Amador St. Étienne de La Tour is a controversial figure. As a born leader, he inspired loyalty and garnered many friends and supporters, often on both sides of issues. It is said that both Charles and his father Claude put La Tour concerns ahead of any other obligations, which created conflicts and enemies. Charles seems an ultimate survivor, managing to rise again after great adversity, often using novel solutions. He was not a great settler, remaining mostly interested in fur trade and commerce. His nemesis, Charles Menou d'Aulnay, deserves recognition for doing more to promote settlements and aid the French colonists who became the Acadians.

Mainly through his daughters, the lineage of Charles de La Tour continues strongly today. Many of his descendants intermarried with the colonists supported by d'Aulnay. These descendants spread throughout Canada, into New England and Louisiana, other regions of the United States, and to France. The expulsion of Acadians in the mid-18th century caused most of this dispersal. Acadian communities were strategically placed between English and French holdings and served as buffer zones and battlegrounds in the struggles between these countries. The history of Acadia might have been different had the vast resources expended by La Tour and d'Aulnay in their "civil war" been put instead to developing and strengthening their settlements.

The Vial-Martin family tree descends through La Tour's oldest daughter, Jeanne de La Tour, by his Mi'kmaq wife called Marguerite Membertou. Most of the early families of Acadia are able to claim kinship with Charles La Tour.[19]

Jeanne de La Tour (1626-c.1686) – Martin d'Aprendestique *dit* Martignon (1616-1689)

Jeanne de La Tour. Born in 1626 when her father Charles de La Tour was engaged in fur trading, living a partly native lifestyle among the Mi'kmaq Indians, Jeanne was half-Mi'kmaq and must have learned many of their traditions. Her mother, baptized with the name Marguerite, was daughter of *sagamore* Anli-Maopeltoog (Henri) Membertou, one of the most honored and legendary Mi'kmaq leaders. Marguerite had at least five siblings, and probably more, since polygamy was practiced among the natives. Jeanne grew up associating with the Mi'kmaq, close to the pristine wilderness, traveling by canoe through winding rivers, learning women's crafts of harvesting berries and curing fish. She probably spoke the Algonquin language and participated in native rituals. Her father Charles had inherited his close friend Charles Biencourt's holdings after his friend died with no heirs. Charles was in a leadership position as acting governor of Acadia when he married Jeanne's mother in 1625.

Jeanne's early years were spent between Port-Royal, the main Acadian settlement, and Cap-Sable, an outpost built by her father on the southern tip of what is now the peninsula of Nova Scotia. Cap-Sable was a distance from the main French settlement at Port-Royal, but there were seasonal Mi'kmaq villages in the area. A few years later, Charles de La Tour received a formal commission as lieutenant general and governor of Acadia from the French king. He then relocated to the mouth of the Saint John River, which gave better access to interior rivers where fur trapping took place. There he built a strong bastion on a high cliff, called Fort Sainte-Marie (later Fort La Tour). Jeanne was 5 or 6 years old when her family moved to the new fort. Just down the shoreline was a Mi'kmaq village where she could continue her ties with her mother's people.

In the bright days of summer, Jeanne would have scrambled down the steep footpath from the fort to the Mi'kmaq village. She hurried toward the rough-log stockade of the village, watching smoke spiraling up from bark wigwams. On the shore, bare-limbed

Indians repaired birch canoes or adjusted the poles and nets of their large fish weir, while men in canoes hauled in silvery-sided salmon during an abundant summer run. She might sit with her mother's family, braiding sinews for moccasins or sewing softened hides into shirts or leggings. Later the women followed forested trails to gather local peas, herbs, and berries, ripening red and orange in the summer sun. Often the Mi'kmaq and French families shared meals, either at the village or in the fort.

Two younger sisters were born before her mother died some time before the fall of 1632. That autumn Charles sailed to France with at least two, if not all three, of his daughters. It is not certain that Jeanne went on the voyage. The other two daughters were placed in convents and remained there the rest of their lives. Why Jeanne remained in or returned to Acadia is uncertain, though one could speculate that she was more attached to her Mi'kmaq relatives. Or perhaps her father intended for her to marry an Acadian settler and become his heir, since by French law women could inherit. In any event, Jeanne was residing at Fort Sainte-Marie when her father brought his second wife there in 1640.

Françoise-Marie Jacquelin was 36 years old, and Jeanne was 14 when her stepmother arrived with two serving women. Outside the Mi'kmaq villages, women were rare in the Acadian posts, and Jeanne must have welcomed their company. Françoise-Marie was bright, highly educated, and well-traveled for her time. She regaled Jeanne with exciting stories of her life in Paris among artists and courtly society, and how different her life was living in Loire with its old castle towns such as Chateau Saint-Jean and the village where she grew up, Nogent-le-Rotrou, with its cobbled streets.

Jeanne, in turn, could teach Françoise-Marie the skills of frontier living. Behind the back palisade of the fort were several outbuildings and garden plots. There men and women worked the rows of vegetables, peas, and wheat while the farm animals foraged at the edges. There were sheep, cows, pigs, chickens, and the fort cats, who prowled grain stores keeping mice in line. Though the governor's wife and daughter were not expected to tend garden and wheat fields, they certainly would be involved in putting up food and preserving meat. Françoise-Marie would oversee the cooking and kitchen, Jeanne showing her the best herbs and spices to use with local foods, taking her along trails to show where to pick them. In a small shallop with rowers, the women would take excursions up the Saint John River, going through the reversing falls, a strange phenomenon created by the immense tides of Fundy Bay. When tides were coming in, the low falls dropped away from the bay; when tides reversed so did the falls, now flowing back the opposite direction. Boats could cross over the falls at slack tide, when flows were in balance.

The fort community would be buzzing with activity during the warmer seasons. There was a blacksmith shop, cookhouse, trading room, storage area, and woodworking shop, all contributing their sounds and odors. Trading was the major function, and the courtyard would be filled with tradesmen, fur clerks, workmen, soldiers, and an assortment of Indians including Mi'kmaq, Maliseet, and Passamaquoddies who came far distances to trade. At the south corner of the courtyard was a flagstone well room, where a deep shaft going down to bedrock provided a constant supply of fresh water.

Winters were mainly spent inside due to snow and bitter cold. Plentiful furs for coats and bedding kept the women warm, used also to cushion the benches and chairs in the great-room. Fireplaces kept constantly burning provided some warmth and most of the light during long winter evenings, though they also had a few lanterns. Sitting around the hearth, the women would sew clothing and repair shoes and leggings. By spring it is likely that Françoise-Marie was pregnant, her son born in the fall. Typical of adolescent girls, Jeanne would be delighted with the baby, fussing over her little brother and helping her stepmother with his care.

For the years between 1640 and 1655, when Jeanne was married, no record has been found of her life. If she was at Fort Sainte-Marie when Charles Menou d'Aulnay made his final, brutal assault in 1645, evidence is missing. Françoise-Marie bravely led her men during this attack and then was forced to watch them hanged. No mention is made of Jeanne being in Port-Royal in the aftermath of her stepmother's death. Perhaps she took off into the woods with her Mi'kmaq relatives to avoid the disastrous attack. Father d'Entremont, in his story about her sister Antoinette becoming the first North American nun, mentions that Jeanne was married in what is now Castine, Maine. In Jeanne's time, this was Fort Pentagouet, situated on Penobscot Bay. It served from 1670 to 1674 as the capital of Acadia and is called the battle line of four nations. Castine is considered the oldest permanent settlement in New England.

In 1655, when she was 29 years old, Jeanne married Martin d'Aprendestique (also spelled Aprendestiguy or Arpentigny), a rich Basque merchant from southwest France.[20] How and when they met is not known, but Martin was a close associate of Jeanne's father Charles de La Tour.

Martin d'Aprendestique *dit* Martignon. Born around 1616 at Ascain, Guyenne, France, Martin was a Basque. The Basques are an indigenous ethnic group who stayed relatively isolated in Europe, which enabled them to retain a unique language (*Euskara*), common culture, and shared genetic ancestry. Their genetic pattern is distinct from nearby regions in France and Spain, descended from early farming groups 5,500 years ago, who became isolated and largely unaffected by subsequent migrations that shaped genetic patterns elsewhere in Europe. This group primarily lives in the mountainous region of the western Pyrenees on the Bay of Biscay coast. The Basque region straddles parts of north-central Spain and southwestern France. Their culture includes close home and family ties, inheritance and leadership patterns giving women near equality, and typical cuisine and ceremonies. Basques migrated to many regions, where they usually worked in shepherding and ranching, maritime fisheries, and as merchants. Basque fishermen sailed the coasts of Newfoundland and Acadia, and some became involved in fur trading.

Martin was in partnership with merchants of Saint-Jean-de-Luz on the Basque coast, captain of a vessel that came annually to the Acadian coasts for fishing and trading during the 1650s. At the time he had permission from Guillaume Lebel, guardian of late governor d'Aulnay's children. During his regular voyages to Acadia, he met Charles de La Tour and formed a friendship. In 1655, Martin married Jeanne La Tour, and lent his father-in-law considerable sums of money. Probably the loan was to help Charles repay debts he owed Boston merchants, since he was negotiating with Cromwell to restore his Acadian barony around this time. Martin and Jeanne were not married long before he ran afoul of Nicolas Denys.

On a voyage in 1656, Martin was captured and taken prisoner by Denys, who had purchased fishing rights to that part of the Acadian coast in 1653 and was now lieutenant general of the area. Martin was taken to Denys' headquarters at Saint-Pierre, Cape Breton, and then sent to France where he faced legal proceedings. Two men in Martin's crew managed to escape on a Basque fishing vessel and went to Saint-Jean-de-Luz to seek help. Martin's business associates successfully took legal action to secure his release and regain their ship, with its cargo of furs and cod. They argued successfully that notice of Denys' monopoly on that coast had not yet been posted in their port.

Martin returned to Acadia in 1660, reunited with his wife Jeanne, and settled near Charles de La Tour, either at Cap-Sable or on the Saint John River. In 1672, Martin was granted a *seigneurie* by the *intendendant* of New France, Jean Talon, at the mouth of the Saint John River, gaining the title Sieur de Martignon. Martin and Jeanne lived in a fort originally built by d'Aulnay, on the opposite bank from her father's old fort. After Martin repaired d'Aulnay's fort, it was called Fort Martignon, and a town by that name exists there today. Although the land grant was extensive, it provided only a modest living through the fur trade, hunting, and fishing.

Jeanne probably felt comfortable and content with this lifestyle. She had always lived among people, both natives and Europeans, who had adapted to modest ways and enjoyed being close to wilderness. Although Governor Perrot noted in 1686 that there were only three people in the Saint John region who "lived miserably by the fur trade," an agreeable but *fainéant* (do-nothing) life, it suited Martin and Jeanne. Martin also would receive a *seigneurie* at Jemseg, farther up the Saint John River, along with the title Sieur de Jemseg.

Jeanne de La Tour and Martin d'Aprendestique had five children, a son and four daughters. Their son, Jean, died at La Rochelle in 1668 at age 12. Only one daughter married; what became of the other three is unknown. Marianne d'Aprendestique, born in Pentagouet around 1662, married Guillaume Bourgeois in 1686. Marianne was 24 years old when they married in Port-Royal, where Guillaume was a merchant, the son of Jacques Bourgeois *dit* Jacob.[21]

The exact dates of death for Jeanne and Martin are not known. When the first Acadian census was taken in 1686, Martin was 70 years old; he did not appear in the next census in 1689. Jeanne was not included in the 1686 census, so she must have died before then.

CHAPTER 5

Acadian Generations

Marianne d'Aprendestique (1662-1687) –
Guillaume Bourgeois (1655-1693)

Marianne d'Aprendestique was born in Pentagouet in 1662. Her parents, Martin d'Aprendestique *dit* Martignon and Jeanne de La Tour, had been married for seven years but were separated by Martin's capture by Nicolas Denys that kept him in France until 1660. Her older brother, Jean, was born in 1656, the year after their parents were married. Jean must have been sent to La Rochelle, France, around age 12 to further his education. There were no schools in Acadia suitable for educating the sons of *seigneurs*; Martin was granted two *seigneuries* on the Saint John River. Unfortunately, Jean died in La Rochelle; no details of this have been found, nor of the lives of the three other girls.

By the time Marianne was married to Guillaume Bourgeois in 1686, the English were no longer in control of Port-Royal and most of Acadia. These settlements were returned to France in 1670 following the Treaty of Breda (1667). During the 16 years of British rule, the Acadian settlers had largely been left on their own. Their interactions with the British were mostly to sell supplies of wheat, vegetables, and meat to Port-Royal. Despite foreign rule, they expected Acadia to revert to France sooner or later, and most refused to leave their farms in the Port-Royal valley. The fertile valley had become their home, and they were forming an Acadian identity. These farming families had close ties originating in France; many were from the same districts, and they had intermarried for generations already. Now their children were born and grew up in Acadia, found mates among neighbors, and began spreading farther up the valley. Using their *aboiteaux* technique, they wrested new agricultural land from the salt marshes and created farms to raise food for their expanding families. Older folks enjoyed their grandchildren and extended family activities.

"A spirit of independence and self-sufficiency had taken hold of these French farmers. France, in spite of herself, had planted sturdy roots in the troubled soil of Acadia."[1] Their expansion from Port-Royal was a natural progression as Acadian population grew. Written records between 1671 and 1686 are few, as the British officials had no interest in registering land ownership. Some settlers had received permission to farm portions of *seigneuries,* but many had no recorded title of settlement. In their small and closely related society, claims of land ownership were matters of communal memory and mutual agreement. They would worry about registering with civil officials when the time came. Those settling on land without an obvious and recorded title were understandably wary of attempts to introduce formal registration practices to confirm their holdings. But this was coming with return of French control.

Guillaume Bourgeois was a Port-Royal merchant, the son of Jacques Bourgeois *dit* Jacob, who had been the surgeon of Charles de Menou d'Aulnay. Jacques Bourgeois *dit* Jacob (1621-1701) had an interesting background. He was born in La Ferté-Gaucher, a commune in the Seine-et-Marne department, Île-de-France region of north-central France. He was the son of Marguerite Bourgeois of the same region (1585-1620). His father was said to be Nicholas Grandjehan of the Champagne region (1586-1620), but he did not use that name. Instead, he used his mother's name, suggesting that he was probably her "natural" son. Another source gives his father's name as Nicholas-Jacques Bourgeois *dit* Grandjehan (1570-1621), who married Marguerite Bourgeois, making Jacques legitimate.[2] Jacques was recruited by the brother of Isaac de Razilly, and came to Acadia in 1641. He was the first to practice medicine in the colony. In 1653, Jacques witnessed the signing of the marriage contract between Governor Charles de La Tour and Jeanne Motin, widow of former governor d'Aulnay. Also, he was a merchant trading with New England and learned English, becoming "king's interpreter."

In 1643, Jacques married Jeanne Trahan, who had come to Port-Royal in 1636 with her family.[3] Jeanne's father, Guillaume Trahan, headed a syndic (representatives or delegates) that governed Port-Royal 1667-1670 during the interim between English and

French possession. Father Molin called him a *maréchal*, or marshal. Jeanne's mother, Françoise Corbineau, died young, and in 1666, at age 65, Guillaume remarried to 19-year-old Madeleine Brun. They had seven children, the last born in 1678.

Jacques Bourgeois *dit* Jacob had become a prosperous farmer in the Port-Royal valley but decided to move around 1671 to settle along the lower Missaguash River near an arm of the Bay of Chignecto, which connects to the Bay of Fundy. The Mi'kmaq had long been familiar with this place, and early French settler Jean de Biencourt de Poutrincourt traveled there in 1612, accompanied by Jesuit Father Biard, who described it as having "many large and beautiful meadows, extending further than the eye can reach… the country… would be very fertile if it were cultivated."[4]

Six decades later Jacques was doing just that. He had visited the area in his fur-trading days, and was probably seeking better access to Mi'kmaq trading as well as more farming lands. He persuaded five other families to accompany him, including his two oldest sons (Charles and Germain), and two of his sons-in-law. This area was a large continuous expanse of marshlands amenable to building *aboiteaux;* they called it the *Tintamarre* (uproar, din, clangor—the French word referred to a tradition of marching through one's community making noise in celebration). Even without building dikes, there were great meadows of salt-marsh hay for grazing cattle and sheep. Jacques built a flour mill and sawmill and encouraged more people to settle in the area. Within five years the settlers were well-established, and others soon followed. More land was reclaimed in the area referred to as *Beaubassin* (beautiful basin), and the animal herds increased, despite a few difficult years requiring huge amounts of work and effort.

Another attraction of Beaubassin was its location far from the meddling French officials at Port-Royal. New England merchants could slip quietly past Port-Royal toward Chignecto Bay, continue into the narrow basin, and trade with Acadians at the mouth of the Missaguash River. From there, a portage connected to the Baie-Verte, an important relay station in sea communications between Acadia and Canada and a strategic position commanding the isthmus of the Bay of Fundy.

Jacques Bourgeois and his group of settlers named their settlement Missaguash after the nearby river. The collection of settlements that formed in the area was also called Chignecto, after the narrow, 15-mile-wide isthmus that these settlements straddled. Around that time Michel de La Vallière de Beaubassin, son-in-law of Nicolas Denys, set up a fur-trading post on the isthmus. He also devoted some time to fishing, farming, and soldiering. In 1676, Governor Frontenac granted him seigneurial rights to a 100-square-league area, which became the *seigneurie* of Beaubassin. The grant to La Vallière specified that he leave any settlers there undisturbed and permit them to use the lands they occupied. The Bourgeois group was thus protected, but they were referred to as La Vallière's tenants.

A number of additional families came during the late 1670s and early 1680s. In 1686, Beaubassin was made a parish, and a church was built.[5] Settlement gradually spread up to Mill Creek, Peticodiac, Memramcook, and the Shepody Rivers. By 1715, Beaubassin was reported as home to 50 families (about 300 people), 32 acres of apple orchards, 800 hogs, and 1,000 head of cattle. The population increased to 2,800 by 1750, due in large part to influx of refugees from the southern regions of Nova Scotia in the aftermath of warfare.

Map of Acadia C. 1650 - 1700

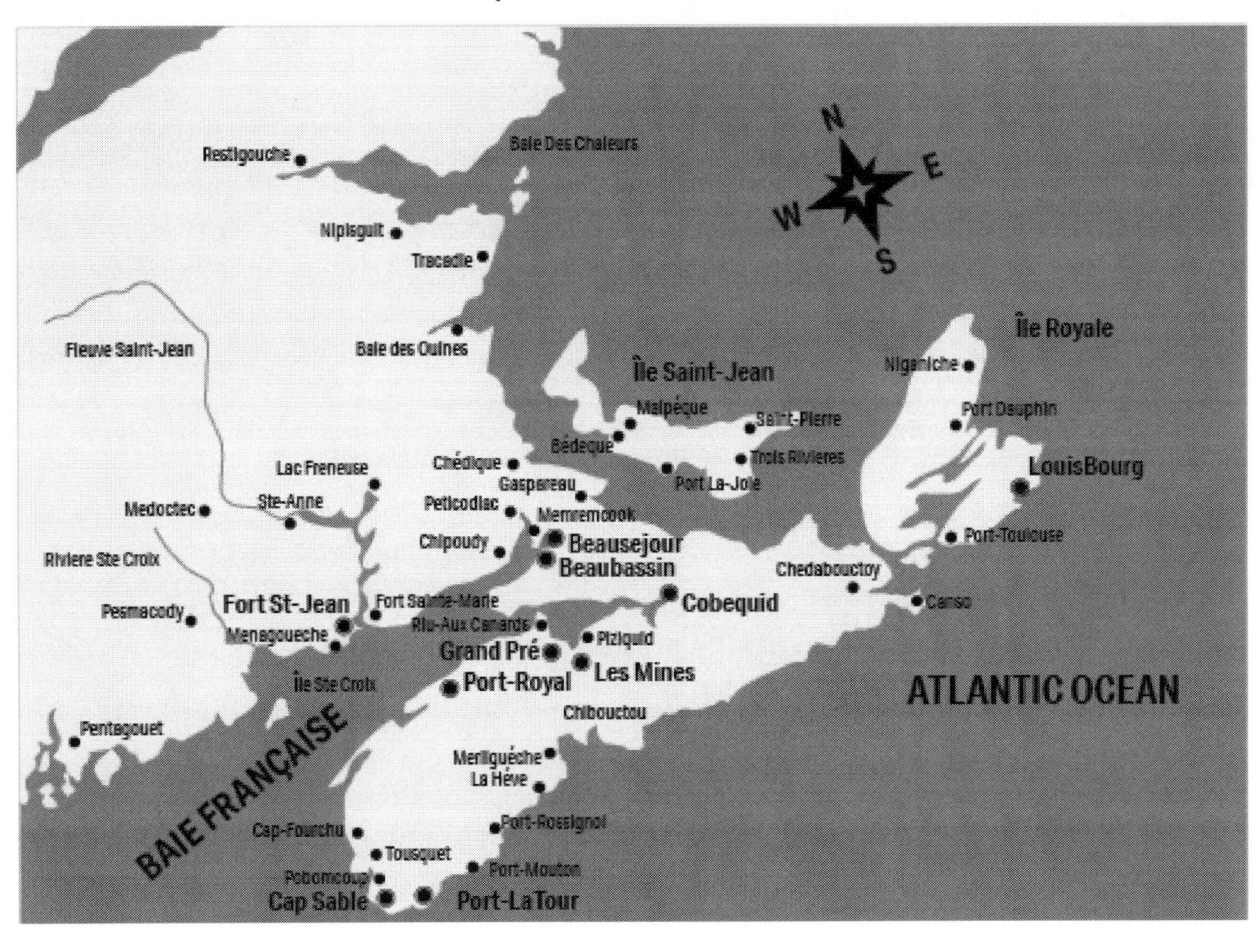

Jacques Bourgeois' third son, Guillaume, remained in Port-Royal attending his business endeavors. Guillaume and Marianne's daughter was born there in 1687, named Jeanne Anne Bourgeois. There is no record of other children, and it is probable that Marianne died in childbirth. Both Guillaume and Marianne were buried in Port-Royal; Guillaume in 1693 at age 38; Marianne's death date is questionable, but some sources record circa 1687. Jacques Bourgeois *dit* Jacob and his wife Jeanne Trahan had a large family of 10 children. He outlived his third son, returning to Port-Royal before 1699 and living there until his death in 1701.

Those Acadians who remained in the Port-Royal valley built more *aboiteaux* on both sides of the river above and below the fort, creating more agricultural land in the basin. Their settlements spread to the many smaller streams flowing from the uplands into the basin. As new settlers arrived, they moved to the new land and married into the nearby families. Even though they lived in plain view of French and British officials who ran the colony, Port-Royal valley Acadians went about their business undisturbed, much as their cousins did in the newer, more distant settlements of Beaubassin. Two church parishes were created to serve the Port-Royal area.

Port-Royal was the oldest settlement in Acadia and its administrative center until Halifax was founded by the British in 1749. The city's population was varied and included many transients, such as soldiers, merchants, administrators, and ecclesiastics. People living there were more aware of the general politics of the region, the influence of both French and English upon events, than Acadians living elsewhere. The permanent residents of the colonial capital built houses near the fort and engaged in legitimate commerce.[6] Probably Guillaume Bourgeois was among these residents, though we do not know what type of commerce he pursued.

Comparing the surnames of Acadians living at Port-Royal and at Chignecto, it appears that frequently there were members of an extended family living in both places. Or, as in the case of Jacques Bourgeois *dit* Jacob, they lived first at Port-Royal, then at Beaubassin, and then back to Port-Royal.

Jeanne Anne Bourgeois (1687-1766) – Jean LeBlanc (1684-1747)

Jeanne Anne Bourgeois. There is no indication that Guillaume Bourgeois remarried after his wife Marianne's death around 1687. It seems he remained in Port-Royal and raised his daughter Jeanne Anne there. The city was growing during the end of the 17th century. Governor Grandefontaine ordered a census taken in 1671, carried out by Récollet Father Laurent Molin, parish priest at Port-Royal. In this first Acadian census, 68 families and about 360 inhabitants were counted. They had 419 acres of cleared land for farming, about 500 cattle in pasture, more than 500 sheep, three dozen goats, and thirty pigs.[7] The census covered three generations of settlers, reporting that there were 15 sets of grandparents, including several having "… children of their own who were younger than one or more of their grandchildren." It was a youthful community, with nearly half of its residents under age 15. Women tended to marry and have their first child before age 18, some even younger. Most had a number of children, often bearing a child every two years. There were 3 families that had 11 children each.

To support such fertility, women could not be exhausted or underfed, attesting to a comfortable standard of living. In part, this fertility was due to genetic endowment and lack of disease, affecting both birth and survival rates. But the census data made clear that Acadia had experienced "… no major food shortages for over two decades nor any major epidemics of measles or chickenpox or smallpox."[8]

The town of Port-Royal extended 12.5 miles up the Rivière du Dauphin (now Annapolis River) and 5 miles on each side. Except in the town center, concentrated on a large outcropping that protruded into the river, family homes were scattered and built behind the marshes. Most farms had frontage onto the river, and the average size was 100-200 acres. Port-Royal became the capital of Acadia in 1700. It remained a trading town, a market for goods rather than a source of production. The main church was 12 miles from the fort, although there were small chapels for closer access.

Beginning in the 1670s, some of the city's population started moving, especially newly married couples. At first they settled in Beaubassin, but began to focus on the Mines (Minas) region a few years afterward. This area was a fertile basin 60 miles northeast of Port-Royal, halfway to the Beaubassin region. It was named for the copper deposits earlier explorers had found at Cap d'Or at the northern entrance to the basin. Champlain had noted these deposits, and some early settlers had mined the copper and other minerals. In 1680, prosperous Port-Royal settler Pierre Melanson, who married a daughter of Philippe Mius d'Entremont, sold his property and moved his large family to Grand Pré in the Mines region. This site lay between two small rivers flowing into the basin (Cornwallis and Gaspereau Rivers). Two years later Pierre Thériot started another settlement not far away. Others came to settle among the many streams flowing into the basin, quickly populating the area with their large extended families.

Although it was the last of the three main Acadian agricultural centers to develop, Mines soon became the leader in population and economy. It had fine marshlands, weak seigneurial control, and relative freedom from attention of French officials and New England raiders. The population in Grand Pré mushroomed from only 57 people in 1686 to more than 580 in 1707. Favorable characteristics of the region were noted: "There is no doubt that agriculture flourished in Minas beyond any experience at Port Royal or Beaubassin. It was the better balanced than the latter; not neglecting livestock, in which Beaubassin rather specialized, it developed the best and most extensive arable farming in Acadia."[9] Additionally, it offered easy access to the basin from the Bay of Fundy, which allowed the Acadians to pursue essential, though illegal, trade with New England merchants.

Another settlement began around 1685 a few miles southeast of Grand Pré along the upper stretches of the Pigiguit River, near the confluence with the St. Croix River. Two church parishes were established by 1722, the parish of Saint-Charles des Mines and the parish of Saint-Joseph de la Rivière aux Canards. These parishes attended to the religious needs of the growing communities, keeping records of marriages, baptisms, and burials. In addition, a Mi'kmaq mission was founded at Pigiguit. These Acadian families continued to have numerous children, contributing to rapid growth and making Grand Pré the principal settlement in Acadia.[10] This fecundity again testifies to good nutrition and lack of disease, for women cannot maintain repeated pregnancies close together unless well-nourished. Although childhood mortality was relatively high, they suffered less from common illnesses such as measles and smallpox that took a heavy toll in Europe.

Jean LeBlanc. Jeanne Anne Bourgeois was 16 years old and still living in Port-Royal when she married 20-year-old Jean LeBlanc in 1704. Jean was the son of André LeBlanc (1659-1743) and Jeanne Marie Dugas (1664-1734), both of Port-Royal. The LeBlanc family had been 2-3 generations in Acadia and was large; Jean had 11 siblings. Jeanne Marie Dugas' maternal grandmother was Marie Bourgeois (1597-?), daughter of Jacob Bourgeois (dates unknown), another family with numerous branches. Charles Bourgeois, the uncle of Jeanne Ann Bourgeois, married Anne Dugas in 1679 in Port-Royal; the families were probably interrelated.

By 1705, when their first son Jean LeBlanc *dit* Derico was born, they had moved to Grand Pré. At least one member of Jeanne Anne's family, her aunt Anne Bourgeois, also moved to Grand Pré with husband Rene LeBlanc and several children. Jean LeBlanc probably had other relatives in the Mines region. He was most likely a farmer, since this was the primary occupation of the Acadians who settled in Mines.

Jeanne Anne Bourgeois and Jean LeBlanc had a very large family; there are records of 11 children born over a period of 33 years. Their daughter Marie-Anne LeBlanc, through whom the Vial-Martin lineage descends, was the 10th child, born in 1732.

Life of Acadian Farming Families. In the three agricultural regions of Acadia, the farming families would have led similar lives during the late 17th and early 18th centuries. Each family had farmland of around 2-4 arpents width, a French unit for length and area (one linear arpent equals about 192 English feet; one arpent of area equals 0.85 acres). Typically farmers wanted their land to border a river, giving access to transportation and water. With 2-4 arpents width on the riverbank, their land stretched 40-60 arpents deep (7,800 to 11,520 feet). They planted wheat, potatoes, apples, pears, peas, turnips, cabbage, and other root vegetables. Farms also had cherries, wild mulberries, raspberries, and strawberries. Marshlands supplied rich salt-marsh hay for cattle, sheep, and pigs. These families had a long history of cooperation during generations as peasants in France, and their lineages were intermingled. Now they had developed new skills and a sense of independence, having learned to survive on their own in the new Acadian homeland.

Each farming community had flour and sawmills, essential for milling wheat into flour and cutting logs into boards for building. When new families arrived, their neighbors helped to build homes and barns. When wheat was harvested, the men worked together at the mill, bringing in wheat from fields and running the millstone, collecting and dividing flour into bags for individual homes. They aided each other building *aboiteaux* to reclaim salt marshes into fields and gardens. Each spring, they helped each other repair old dikes and build new ones. Over the winter, men and boys cut firewood, built or repaired homes, hunted, and trapped. Men made household furniture and family footwear; either wooden shoes as was common in France, or native moccasins. Such interdependence was essential to surviving and prospering and created a strong sense of community.

Farms at Grand Pré were exceptionally productive. The Acadians traded their excess products with the New Englanders who surreptitiously avoided Port-Royal and snuck up the rivers. These traders brought sugar, molasses, machinery, and other items not

Early Acadia 1635-1755   Claude T. Picard
Photo: ©Parks Canada/Claude Picard
By permission of Parks Canada and the Picard family.

available locally. Sweeteners were especially welcome, both for making tasty desserts and fermenting drinks.

Women tended home gardens, did household chores such as laundry and making clothes, and prepared and preserved food. They milked the cows and fed the chickens. Wool from sheep was carded, spun, and woven for clothes and blankets. Hemp and flax were also grown and their fibers woven into linen for clothes. Children worked hard, too. Boys helped in the fields, repaired dikes, and assisted with other tasks done by their fathers. Girls helped with household tasks as soon as they were able, the older girls providing care for new babies as they arrived.

Houses were made of rough-hewn lumber, squared logs that fit together at the corners forming a rectangle. Cracks between logs were filled with mud and straw to keep wind and weather out. Inside walls were lined with clay and whitewashed; roofs were made of thatch, birch bark, or cedar shingles. Homes were typically of good size for large families. The rectangular-shaped home had a lower floor with porches on one or two sides. The single large main room served as living, cooking, and dining areas with a hearth at one end. There was a sleeping area for husband and wife, cordoned off by drapes. At the foot of their bed was a crib or cot for the youngest child. The older children had bedrooms in the attic, accessed by stairs from the side porch outside.

The large fireplace provided both heat and cooking space. There was a slate or brick hearth with firewood stacked on one end. High inside the fireplace were hooks where meats were hung and slowly smoked, including pork, venison, salmon, ducks, rabbit, and other game. Racks or swinging arms held pots for making stews and soups. A frame for baking bread was built into the back. Most homes had a cold room dug in the basement for keeping food during the winter. Staples were stored in barrels, including potatoes, turnips, carrots, beets, onions, parsnips, and apples. Cabbage was sliced and combined with salt in earthenware containers for fermentation into *choucroute*. Other barrels were used for salted herring and pickled pigs' feet and shoulders, using vinegar made from apples.

Libations were made from locally available plants and berries, including wine from dandelions, gooseberries, and chokecherries. They made a drink called "fir water" by boiling branches in a kettle, straining the liquid and adding molasses, then pouring it into a barrel and adding yeast. It fermented for a few days, producing a type of beer that protected them against scurvy. Local grains were distilled into rough liquor, useful for relieving joint pain during cold winters. These libations livened up the frequent *fetes* when families gathered for fun and celebration. In summer months, the *fetes* were outside in a family's yard, where people gathered around wooden tables and benches. Musicians brought whistles, homemade fiddles or banjos, and *guimbard* or Jew's harps. The *guimbard* (Galician harp) consists of a flexible metal, wooden, or bamboo reed attached to a frame. The reed is placed in the performer's mouth and plucked with the finger to produce a note; each harp makes only one pitch, so several different sized instruments are used to make harmony.

The families feasted and partied late into the night, singing, dancing, and stomping feet. Sometimes there were sports among the men, such as running or wrestling. These *fetes* were opportunities for single men and women to watch each other, sorting out which might be a suitable match to begin their own families.

Young women often did not marry until they were 20 years old. The bride's father provided a dowry to help the young couple begin life together. Young women must know how to weave and cook before marrying; young men must have skills to make farm tools and implements, such as plows and wheels, before they could propose. It was usual for newly married couples to live for a few years with the husband's family, during which time a farm and barn was built for them. Older members of the community ruled over disputes and made decisions about what was best for the group or family. Women might become skilled with herbal remedies or as midwives, and attend their neighbors for illness and childbirth.

Acadian farming women typically dressed in wool stockings, long striped wool skirt, with white shirt under a black bodice with front laces, and a scarf over the shoulder tied in front. They wore simple white bonnets, wooden clog shoes, and aprons when working at home. Men wore wool socks or stockings, short pants, a shirt and vest, and felt hat with jacket in winter. They also wore wooden shoes except when out hunting or trapping, when moccasins were more suitable.

Traditions and rituals of the Catholic Church were very important to farming Acadians. They wanted to have services of priests available for significant life events, especially baptisms, marriages, and burials. Holy days and festivals in the church calendar shaped their lives, and they felt reassured to have confession and absolution readily available. Attending mass on Sundays and holy days, where they caught up on news, brought the community together. Priests and monks frequently provided leadership in farming communities, even becoming involved in fighting against the British. The Acadians at Grand Pré played an important role, supporting Father Le Loutre and his resistance fighters during the struggles leading to the expulsion. As the breadbasket of the region, Grand Pré had 11 mills and herds of several thousand animals and willingly responded to Le Loutre's call for basic food stuffs. Between 1749 and 1755 they sent supplies to embattled compatriots in Fort Beauséjour, Louisbourg, Île St. Jean, and Chignecto. During this time, men from Grand Pré provided labor to help build a church and dikes in Chignecto.

Grand Pré as 1755 Approaches. Life for the family of Jeanne Anne Bourgeois and Jean LeBlanc continued in this bucolic fashion for over 40 years. Most of these years were spent peacefully tending crops and animals, trapping and hunting, working on dikes and homes, and enjoying community gatherings. There had been a raid in 1704, around the time they moved to the area, by New England Ranger Benjamin Church.

He was delayed in approaching the village by the mudflats of the bay and river. Men and ships got stuck on these flats as the vast tides went out, giving the Mi'kmaq and Acadians time to get into position for defense. These long-time allies fiercely defended the village but were eventually overwhelmed by Church's forces, which burned the village and fields and destroyed some dikes. After Church left, the villagers rebuilt as quickly as possible. That following winter the village suffered a flour shortage, due to crop and stored grain destruction. Fortunately the winter was not severe enough to create significant hardship. The dikes were repaired by spring, and there was a successful harvest in 1706.

Though the direct effects of the raid were short-lived, the memory lasted in the community of Grand Pré. Even though they remained unmolested in the years that followed, they still worried about return of English raiders. They were cautious in dealing with British authorities into the 1740s, even after Acadia had become British Nova Scotia in 1713. When Britain assumed control, the Acadians were required to swear an oath of allegiance to the English king. By the Treaty of Utrecht the French colonists living in Acadia were allowed to leave within a year and take their movable goods. If they remained, they would enjoy free exercise of their religion, could occupy their lands, and have rights of British citizens after taking an oath of allegiance. In the agreement made during Queen Anne's rule, the Acadians pledged they would not take up arms against the English or the French, nor fight against any of Britain's subjects or allies. In essence, this was a position of neutrality, which in the end failed to satisfy either country.

Relations between Acadians and British became increasingly difficult over the ensuing years. While most Acadians tried to maintain neutrality and continue their lives, others became embroiled in resistance efforts. Their Mi'kmaq allies became hostile, joining forces with Canadians to institute raids against British and neutral Acadian sites. Rising tensions eventually led to the British policy to remove Acadians from Nova Scotia, an expulsion called *Le Grand Dérangement.* This complex and tragic process is described in the next chapter.

Families of Grand Pré were caught up in a second military struggle in 1747, called the Battle of Grand Pré, or King George's War. Grand Pré had been the staging ground for French and Mi'kmaq sieges on Annapolis Royal (former Port-Royal) in 1744-45, so English troops were sent there in late 1746, reinforced by more forces in January 1747. These troops were billeted in 24 homes in the village. In the battle that followed between combined forces of Canadians, Mi'kmaq, and Acadian resistance fighters against the British troops, numerous lives were lost. The battle was called a massacre, the bloodiest victory for the French in Acadia. Villagers reported they "saw buried by both parties one hundred and twenty men."[11] After the French forces left, the village remained in British hands. New Englanders returned in March 1747, took possession of a stone house there, and required the inhabitants to renew their promise of faithful obedience to the English government. They also sailed to Pisiguet and burned a Canadian ship. The area remained embroiled in conflict during the ensuing years.

It is likely that some neutral Acadian residents of Grand Pré and Pisiguet were also killed during the fighting. Jean LeBlanc died on June 10, 1747, probably in Grand Pré, although some sources mention Pisiguet. It is possible he was a casualty of the battle. Some genealogical sources list him as dying in Port-Royal or Falmouth, England. However, there is no logical reason why he would go to England in 1747, before the first wave of Acadian expulsion in 1755. And a later name for Pisiquid/Pisiguet is Falmouth, assigned by New Englanders who replaced Acadians there.

Jeanne Anne Bourgeois LeBlanc was now a widow with 11 children, two or three probably still at home. The records of these children's births and deaths make a powerful statement of the wide-ranging effects of *Le Grand Dérangement*, during which Acadians were forcefully expelled from their homeland and widely dispersed around the world. All of the LeBlanc children were born in Grand Pré (Mines) between 1705 and 1738. Three died in Liverpool, Lancashire, England in 1756. Two died in Sauzon, Belle Île, France (1772, 1779). One died in Calais, France (1759). Three died in Donaldsonville, Ascension Parish, Louisiana (1777, 1800, including Marie-Anne 1812). The place and dates of death of the remaining two are unknown.

Jeanne Anne also suffered the devastation of separation and expulsion from her homeland. She found her way to Louisiana, though probably not along with her children, who ended up in Ascension Parish. She is on record as dying July 18, 1766, in St. Gabriel, Iberville Parish, in Louisiana. Both parishes border the Mississippi River south of Baton Rouge, but there is some distance between the towns of St. Gabriel and Donaldsonville.

The three children who arrived in Ascension Parish were Claude, Desiré, and Marie-Anne. When her father died in 1747, Marie-Anne was 15 years old and living in Grand Pré. Over the next eight years, her entire world would be disrupted in the greatest tragedy to befall her people.

CHAPTER 6

The Acadia Expulsion: Le Grand Dérangement

Marie-Anne LeBlanc (1732-1812) – Joseph Bujol (1722-1806)

Marie-Anne LeBlanc was a fourth generation Acadian, descended from Jeanne de La Tour, daughter of Charles Amador de St. Étienne de La Tour by his Mi'kmaq wife, Marguerite Membertou. The La Tours were among the first families of Acadia. **Joseph Bujol** was a second generation Acadian on the paternal side; his father Joseph *père* was born in Pigiguit. His grandparents had emigrated from France to Acadia in the late 1600s. On the maternal side, he was fourth generation Acadian. His mother's Landry family traces to Port-Royal in the mid-1600s. Many Acadians were third or fourth generation by the 1700s. In a relatively short time, these French settlers had formed a distinct and resilient character.

Shaping the Resilient Acadian Character

One remarkable attribute of the Acadians is the endurance of their culture. Their unique blend of close-knit kinship and pioneer ingenuity persisted in the face of widespread dispersal and attempts at assimilation, done by the British in both Nova Scotia and Atlantic colonies. The Acadians had lived in Nova Scotia for slightly over a century when the British assumed control following the Treaty of Utrecht in 1713. The earliest Acadian families were in the third and fourth generations. Still, it was a short period of time to form such a unique and well-defined culture. According to a leading Acadian scholar: "The remarkable longevity of Acadian culture can be attributed to group cohesiveness and insularity."[1]

Key factors were geographic isolation, chronic neglect by the mother country, shared French peasant background, and demands of pioneering in a harsh yet abundant climate. As with other frontier settlements in North America, the Acadians were forced to acquire new skills in order to survive. They shared pioneer characteristics of individualism, adaptability, pragmatism, industriousness, egalitarianism, and closing ranks when facing a general threat. However, Acadians were different; they maintained extended kinship systems, distinctive language and speech patterns, and greater social equality.

The geography of the Canadian Maritimes effectively shielded Acadians from the outside world. Their settlements on Nova Scotia's peninsulas and islands were far removed from the heavily traveled sea-lanes to Quebec and Boston. Throughout the 17th and early 18th centuries, Acadia was an economic backwater, not easily accessible. Continued isolation magnified the impact of frontier conditions on the French settlers. It required that they become physically and economically self-sufficient, shaping a self-contained society. Communication with other colonies was tenuous; overland travel to the St. Lawrence Valley via the St. John River was difficult, requiring 12 days and a dozen major portages. Travel to New England settlements was even more inconvenient, due to lack of major arterial waterways. Even within the Nova Scotia peninsula, travel was arduous. The coastal lowlands were ringed by salt marshes, had exceptionally high tides, and the heavily wooded uplands were laced with many creeks, lakes, and bogs.

The Acadians were almost completely insulated against influences of cultural trends in neighboring colonial settlements and Europe. As a result, they developed a diversified economy and pioneer mentality adapted to the conditions of their new homeland. As farmers in France, they grew crops such as rye that could not prosper in Acadia. The first few years they lived mostly by trapping, hunting, and fishing, which they learned from friendly Mi'kmaqs. They adapted dikes (*aboiteaux*) and drainage systems to recapture fertile marshes above Port-Royal around 1630. They used new building techniques to construct homes and barns from local timber, learned which crops were suitable, and became the region's breadbasket. Some became cattle ranchers; nearly all had some livestock. Meeting the necessities for living, Acadians enjoyed their lifestyle in ways that perplexed French Governor Paul Mascarene, who wrote in 1720 that they live "... in a manner from hand to mouth, and provided they have a good field of Cabbages and bread enough for their families with what fodder is sufficient for their Cattle they seldome look for much further improvement."[2]

Large extended families were essential for their way of life. They needed communal labor pools to build *aboiteaux*, construct buildings, harvest and preserve food, and carry out hunting expeditions. For the former French peasants, communal labor was a long tradition. Their close-knit families were a unifying agent, most from the same regions in France. The early immigrants, arriving in 1632, were from the Loudon commune of central-western France. More Acadian settlers were from around Loudon than any other area; others came from the Provinces of Poitou, Aunis, Angoumois, and Saintonge. They shared subregional culture and language, agrarian background, and nonmaterialistic values. Their families had intermarried for generations, and this endogamy continued in Acadia. More French settlers, trapping and shipping engagés, soldiers, and officials added to the population and introduced fresh bloodlines. However, once married into an Acadian family, newcomers were quickly absorbed and assimilated.

The British occupation of Acadia from 1654 to 1670 encouraged stronger Acadian group identity. In the prior years, Acadians had become factionalized between followers of d'Aulnay and La Tour, but when facing a common foe, they closed ranks. Members of both groups intermarried and merged into a common society. When French rule was restored in 1670, Acadians chaffed at the bureaucracy. Nearly all prime arable lands at Port-Royal had been developed. Many young families sought opportunities at the newly founded upper Bay of Fundy settlements—Mines, Pisiquid, and Beaubassin. They persuaded relatives to relocate; the new settlements were often formed by adjoining clusters of 5-10 interrelated family units. Bachelors sought wives in neighboring settlements. Bonds through marriage led to an increasingly complex social network, creating a clan united by blood ties, common beliefs and lifestyles, and common goals.

Acadian families had many children; 4-5 children were usual but as many as 11-12 not uncommon. Women started having children in their early 20s and continued until their 40s. As noted before, the health and nutrition of both women and children supported their fertility and survival rates. Isolation shielded the Acadians from the ravages of war, famines, and epidemics that raged across Europe. They were not worn down to early deaths by hard work. Acadian lifestyle fostered longevity. Records of their population growth are revealing:

Acadian Population Growth 1654 – 1755[3]

Year	Total Population
1654 (all)	300-350
1671 (Port-Royal Census)	363
1686 (Port-Royal Census)	592
1701 (all)	1450
1714 (all)	2500
1737 (all)	7598
1755 (all)	12,000-18,000

Had this level of fecundity continued—a growth rate of 100% every 20-25 years—the Acadian population was projected to be around 7 million by 1975. In the early 1990s, there were an estimated 1.5 million Acadians scattered over two continents, reflecting long-term results of their expulsion.[4] The rapidly expanding population in Nova Scotia in the 1730s was troublesome to British officials, aptly expressed by visiting literary Parisian Dièrville: "… they are free to populate the World, which is, Moreover, that which they do best." He found "the swarming of Brats… a sight to behold."[5]

The Acadian community was significantly inbred. Especially after 1710, few women married outside the clan. Though some married lonely British soldiers, or found a new arrival from Quebec or France, most practiced endogamy. By mid-1700s, young women and men had to search long and hard to find spouses who were not second or third cousins. Nearly half of all marriages needed a priest's dispensation for cosanguinity. Not only was this insularity detrimental to their genetics, the Acadians also remained largely uneducated. Most could not—and would not—speak English; although some Acadian men learned English to trade with Boston merchants. There were no schools except in cities such as Port-Royal or Quebec and no tradition of educating children among most peasant farmers. What little news they got came from French priests or occasional voyages some Acadians made to Louisbourg, the main French stronghold on Isle Royal. Naturally, this news was slanted to the beliefs and goals of France. Acadians remained uninformed about changing British policies that would lead to their expulsion.

Two other defining characteristics of the Acadian character bear examining: their attachment to land and their legal contentiousness. These former French peasants had endured a difficult life in the mother country; where they were feudally bound to work land they could never call their own. Shortly before they came to Acadia, their lot was worsening due to rising agricultural levies imposed by their landlords and a declining standard of living. To the Acadians, land ownership was the key to their lifestyle, and they prized farmland above all. Long-standing oppression by French nobility made the peasants suspicious of any person in authority. They transferred this distrust to their provincial administrators in Acadia, whom they viewed with the same mix of fear and contempt.

Once in Acadia, the transplanted farmers were given land grants to farm and ranch on *seigneuries*, whose owners wanted the land developed. The *seigneurs*, mainly first families of Acadia, were often unfamiliar with the exact boundaries of their lands. Thus, they issued land grants with overlapping boundaries, leading to frequent disputes. Usually these disputes between Acadian families were settled peaceably by community consensus. But the Acadians were not loath to use civil courts, taking advantage of French and British colonial judiciaries. They viewed the colonial governments as convenient venues to serve their judicial and notarial needs, never as arbiters of their lives and properties. Civil suits were a form of amusement for Acadians, whose court costs were small. Apparently they enjoyed crafting legal arguments and found going to court a kind of social diversion.[6]

Court cases involving Acadian Resistance leader **Joseph Broussard *dit* Beausoleil** shed light on how these civil courts functioned. Four claims were brought against him before he was 24 years old. Beausoleil was a man who stirred controversy yet brought strong leadership. Two were land disputes, one a British charge of consorting with the Indians and concealing their activities, and the last was a paternity suit. Although Beausoleil denied fathering the child, the midwife's testimony that the mother named him during childbirth swayed the verdict. First imprisoned and then ordered to pay child support, the intervention of Beausoleil's mother and several relatives led to an acceptable solution, leaving the purported father free of obligations. The involvement of so many people in a civil suit demonstrated the Acadian's cohesion. The intervention of four women who crafted a solution shows their prestige in the community. Women played major roles in all aspects of Acadian affairs—social, political, and legal.

There was social variation among Acadians; not all were peasant farmers. Among the leading families were the colony's economic and political elite. Some of the earliest were descendants of **Charles de Saint-Étienne de La Tour**, Nicolas Denys, Charles d'Aulnay, and Philippe Mius d'Entremont (whose son Jacques married Anne de La Tour, Charles' daughter by Jeanne Motin). Another daughter by Jeanne Motin, Marie de La Tour, married Alexandre Le Borgne de Bélisle. Guillaume Trahan married Marguerite, daughter of **Jean LeBlanc** and **Jeanne Bourgeois.** The Richard family that arrived in the 1650s became quite large; some of their 12 children married into the Broussard and LeBlanc families. Their descendants settled at Port-Royal, Minas, and Chignecto.

Early settlers in the farming lands reclaimed by *aboiteaux* included **Jacques Bourgeois *dit* Jacob**, Port-Royal surgeon who led the settlement of Beaubassin. Pierre Martin and wife Catherine Vigneau arrived in 1636 and created the first Martin families in the colony (not related to the Martins who much later married the Vials). Pierre Comeau, Port-Royal cooper who arrived in 1632, had a large, influential family. Pierre's fourth son, Pierre *le jeune dit* The Sea Wolf, married Jeanne, daughter of **Jacques Bourgeois** and **Jeanne Trahan**, at Port-Royal. Of the 10 Comeau children, three daughters married into the Martin and Brun families.[7]

This gives an idea of how interrelated the Acadian families became. After Britain took over the colony in 1713, many of these elites moved to the French Maritimes and continued to serve imperial France. Others remained on their Acadian *seigneuries*, giving land grants to relatives or friends to develop. Branches of these families populated Pobomcoup near Cap-Sable, Mirliguèche and other Atlantic fishing settlements, and the Port-Royal basins (now Annapolis Royal). Many went to Mines Basin settlements, including Grand-Pré, Pigiguit, and Cobeguit. Others settled along peninsula regions, including Beaubassin, Rivière-des-Héberts, Menoudy, and Chignecto. Their descendants spread into territory claimed by both France and Britain, such as Tintamarre, Chepoudy, Petitcoudiac, and Memramcook. They reached Shediac and Miramichi on the Gulf of St. Lawrence; the middle regions of Rivière St.-Jean; Rivière Ste.-Croix, and the shores of Passamaquoddy Bay. Some went to the Maine coast at Machias and down to the mouth of the Kennebec River.

During 40 years of French colonial governance and benign neglect, the Acadian settlements created their own particular pattern of social relationships. These coalesced into a network of kinship, economic activity, political habits, and religious practices that evolved over succeeding generations into an enduring community identity.[8] Acadian culture moved into a "golden age" when the latest 12-year-long war ended. Called Queen Anne's War, or War of Spanish Succession, conflict ceased with signing of the Treaty of Utrecht in 1713. During the ensuing 30 years of relative peace, the Acadians thrived and consolidated their close-knit culture. After a quarter century of nearly continuous warfare, they welcomed the respite, even though now under the rule of their former enemies, the British.

Marie-Anne LeBlanc and Joseph Bujol in Grand Pré, Mines

Marie-Anne LeBlanc was about 18 years old when she married Joseph Bujol, age 29, about 1750 in Grand Pré, Mines, Acadia (now Nova Scotia). Marie-Anne was a native of Grand Pré; her parents Jeanne Anne Bourgeois and Jean LeBlanc moved there from Port-Royal. She was the 10th of 11 surviving children, 6 boys and 5 girls. She grew up in a farming community during a time of relative peace, called the Acadian "golden age." During childhood and adolescence, she learned domestic skills and was cared for by her numerous siblings. Surrounded by many relatives in the Grand Pré village, her young life must have been full of happiness and community activities. We can imagine a social gathering where she might first have noticed Joseph Bujol's attraction to her. After a successful harvest, families assembled for *fetes* to share abundant food and drink. Dishes included freshly baked bread, stews of vegetables and pork, beans and peas, tasty desserts of apples and plums cooked in maple syrup, and for adults alcoholic drinks such as fir branch beer and fruit ciders.

At a designated family farm, they gathered around wooden tables and chairs set out in the yard, using dishes and implements also made of wood, carved by men and boys. For entertainment there were contests among the young men, such as foot racing and wrestling. Eligible bachelors used this opportunity to show off their physical prowess, hoping to catch the eye of an attractive maiden. Perhaps they had already noticed a girl at church and exchanged shy glances, trying to read messages in dark, languid eyes. In the Acadian's patriarchal society, young men could not approach young women directly. They met and interacted at strictly chaperoned dances or feasts, where men asked the parents' permission to dance with their daughters and were careful to avoid spending too much time with any girl. Music for dancing was provided by fiddlers accompanied by wooden whistles and *guimbard* (Jew's harps), with revelers stomping and chapping to lively rhythms.

Joseph could have drawn Marie-Anne's attention in a wrestling match. Bare-chested to display well-developed muscles, his strategy and strength won the match and left her breathless. A quick exchange of glances between them spoke eloquently of their attraction, something that did not go unnoticed by mothers and aunts. Later, he asked and was given permission to dance with her, while the ladies gossiped about a blossoming romance, especially when he claimed the last dance of the evening. Several days later Joseph found opportunity to speak with Jean LeBlanc, Marie-Anne's father, requesting his approval for making visits at the family home. Everyone knew what this meant. Joseph was declaring his intention to seek a bride, should she accept him. Over the next few months, or sometimes years depending on circumstances, the suitor would visit his beloved's home, have dinner, win over parental approval, and woo his bride on the porch. Chaperones glanced out windows or doors to ensure propriety. Occasionally two or more suitors competed, until the young woman made up her mind and settled on her husband.

Joseph Bujol (Bujold, Bugeaud) was also born in Mines in a large family. He was the oldest of 10 children born to Joseph Bujol *père* of Grand Pré and Marie-Josephe Landry of Pisiquid. The Bujol and LeBlanc families would have known each other well, frequently taking part in common labor and community events. Perhaps Joseph *fils* waited so long to seek a bride because he was developing his own farm and getting established. In any event, he must have been a desirable match and good provider, as they began a family right away and had two children before 1755: Marguerite born in 1751 and Augustin born in 1753. Their next four children give testimony to the disruptions of the Acadian expulsion: Felicité was born in 1755 in Oxford, Maryland; Anne was born in 1759, and Marie-Magdeline was born in 1765, both also in Oxford, Maryland. Their last child, Joseph Paul, was born in 1769 and his baptism recorded at St. Francis of Assisi Church in Pointe Coupée, Louisiana.

The Acadians Persist as French Neutrals Under British Rule

The Acadians could never bring themselves to fully accept British rule over their beloved homelands. Despite the neglect from their mother country, they remained strongly identified as French. Their Catholic religion defined rhythms of the year through holy days and rituals and marked the milestones of their lives, though they never allowed priests to negate their independence. Most spoke only French; few were able to read it. Their immense attachment to family and farmland was characteristically Gallic. Through the initial years of British hegemony, they kept alive the belief that tides would turn again to favor France, as had happened so often before—changing 10 times between 1604 and 1710. Their hope was to remain on the periphery and avoid crossfire that future colonial clashes would certainly bring.

During the unstable years between 1710 and 1713 after the British took over Port-Royal, Acadians from Mines and Beaubassin conducted guerrilla warfare against the invaders. In 1712 these resistance fighters launched a siege of the provincial capital, but it was unsuccessful. Understandably, the British were wary of the Acadians and wanted to obtain an oath of allegiance to their ruler. Under the terms of Queen Anne's proclamation in the 1713 treaty, the Acadians were permitted to leave the colony within one year and take their movable property with them. Those who remained under British rule were guaranteed freedom of religion and full title to their lands and movable possessions. Many did choose to relocate, migrating from Port-Royal to Beaubassin and Shepody (Chepody), still considered French possessions. However, many Acadians preferred to remain on their now well-developed lands, but refused to take an unconditional oath of allegiance.

By 1717, the Acadians offered a compromise, seeing that British control was weak and expecting France to regain the colony soon. They agreed to pledge their loyalty to England under these conditions: freedom to exercise their Catholic faith; guaranteed neutrality in future Franco-English colonial wars; and recognition by the colonial government that they were a distinct community with property rights. Their stance on neutrality was agreeing they would not bear arms for England or for France; essentially they would not engage in warfare. A major factor underlying this stance was risk of retribution by local Mi'kmaq and other natives who were allied with French colonials, should the Acadians fight for England.

The new British provincial governor, Richard Philipps, was acutely aware that his garrison of 500 was greatly outnumbered by over 2,500 hostile Acadians. Although he was anxious to impose an oath of allegiance, he lacked military power to compel submission. In addition, his garrison was dependent upon Acadian farmers for food and supplies. Philipps avoided action, abruptly terminating negotiations by sailing back to England in 1723. His surrogate, Lieutenant Governor Lawrence Armstrong, delayed action during native uprisings over three years. Then in 1726 Armstrong demanded an unconditional oath of allegiance, leading to a minor wave of Acadian emigration to French-held areas of Cape Breton Island and Île St. Jean.

The preponderance of Acadians closed ranks and adamantly rejected the unconditional oath. They made a counterproposal restating their previous terms: neutrality, rights to property, and religious freedom. The resulting diplomatic impasse caused Philipps to return in late 1729. Over the next several months he negotiated with Acadian representatives, assuring them that the British government had approved their demand for neutrality. Based on Philipps' verbal assurances, the Acadians signed the unconditional oath of allegiance (though in their mind the condition of neutrality applied). Philipps returned to England carrying these signatures but told the Board of Trade governing the colony that the Acadians had abandoned their claims to neutrality. He felt his mission had been a complete success, although it proved untrue. This document became known as the "conventions of 1730" and "Queen Anne's agreements." The Acadians stuck by their understanding throughout all the subsequent confrontations resulting from the murky situation:

"Thus, through the so-called 'conventions of 1730,' the Nova Scotian governor managed simultaneously to please and deceive all parties to the escalating controversy over the unconditional oath of allegiance, thereby laying the groundwork for future Anglo-Acadian confrontations."[9]

Between 1730 and 1749, the British colonial government made only token efforts to control the Acadians, who adjusted cleverly to the new political realities. They used procrastination and litigation to delay or waylay demands they preferred not to fulfill. For instance, if they were asked to survey lands, build roads, quarter troops, or furnish firewood and provisions to the garrison, they found reasons why they could not at the present do these things, although they would eventually. Next they sent shrewd legal representatives to make prolonged arguments in courts, often leading to demands being dropped. The Acadians especially sidetracked surveys; they did not want the British to know the real conditions of their crops or herds. Under pretexts of poor harvests or unhealthy animals, they avoided provisioning Annapolis Royal (Port-Royal) while smuggling their agricultural surplus to Boston merchants and the French fortress of Louisbourg on Cape Breton Island.

Acadian intransigence irritated provincial administrators, who called the French Neutrals "ungovernable" and lamented their "insubordination," for they behaved "in most respects as independent of any Government" and "treated with so much contempt" the English authorities.[10] In addition, Governor Armstrong complained that "there is not an inhabitant that pays a farthing rent towards defraying of such necessary charges that attends all government."[11]

The Acadians did maintain neutrality when Annapolis Royal was attacked twice by French Canadians, and they refused to aid French and native raiders when they briefly captured the English garrison at Mines in 1747 (Battle of Grand Pré). Anne-Marie's father, Jean

LeBlanc, died that year, possibly related to the battle. The Acadians' situation was changing around this time, although they did not recognize it. Intercolonial tensions were escalating, European powers were taking more interest in their colonies, and the British were thinking about long-term solutions to the Acadian problem. It became increasingly difficult, and dangerous, to remain neutral.

Louisbourg was a glittering example of French potential during its short lifespan. By 1739, it was remarkable for commerce, sophistication, and military prowess with a population of over 2,000. Another 2,500 lived along the coast including Acadian farmers and fishermen. The state-of-the-art fort was well garrisoned and considered impregnable, the strongest French presence in the Maritimes. Officers and leading elite families led an opulent life, though supplies could be undependable. The fort commanded a key sea-lane for travel, communication, and commerce. Although New Englanders wanted to overtake Louisbourg, they thought it was impossible until several British prisoners, captured at nearby Canso, spent time inside. One of the captured officers, Lieutenant John Bradstreet, was himself half French and spoke the language. He was among the numerous progeny of Charles de La Tour and Jeanne Motin, born to their granddaughter Agathe who married a British lieutenant. He anglicized as fast as he could and followed his father in a military career. Bradstreet returned to Boston after his release, bringing information about the vulnerabilities of Fort Louisbourg.

Ironically, John Bradstreet's distant cousin was an officer in Louisbourg. François Du Pont Duvivier was the son of yet another granddaughter of Charles La Tour and Jeanne Motin. Initially his career was in commerce, and his family, the Du Ponts, became among the wealthiest merchants in North America. In Louisbourg, he enlisted when the colony was threatened in 1744. Duvivier led the successful attack on Canso during which Bradstreet was taken prisoner. Whether the two distant cousins, fighting on enemy sides, ever discovered their relationship is not known. Duvivier was chosen to head the invasion of Annapolis Royal, where he thought his La Tour heritage would win over Acadians. He postured himself as a liberator, freeing them from the British yoke. But he was unsuccessful in all regards—most Acadians held to their neutral stance. They refused to join his ranks, and the promised French warships to reinforce his siege never showed up.

British reinforcements did arrive, however, sent by Governor William Shirley of Massachusetts. The French decided to withdraw; Duvivier sailed to France seeking assistance. The British Colonial Governor attributed their victory to timely help from the governor of Massachusetts and the Acadians refusing to take up arms. He implicitly recognized the 1730 conventions by noting in a letter to the Acadians, "In consequence of your oath you owe every obedience and every assistance to the King your Sovereign; and you ought to take it as a great favour that he does not compel you to take up arms."[12]

Bradstreet's sojourn inside Louisbourg allowed him to gather intelligence about the design of the fortress, the food and supplies shortages, and discontent of the men defending it. This laid the groundwork for British forces to launch a successful attack, and the fort fell in June 1745.

The Gathering Storm. The backdrop in Europe for this conflict was King George's War (War of the Austrian Succession), fought among Britain, France, Prussia, Dutch Republic, Bavaria, and Spain over royal succession and land inheritance. It was a far-reaching war because many European countries and the American colonies were involved. It ended in 1748 with an uneasy truce and another reshuffling of rule in the North American colonies. Louisbourg, Isle Royal, and Île St. Jean were returned to France, while England retained its possession of Nova Scotia. Claims to other territory remained as tangled as before with hazy borders. Both England and France became more involved in colonial affairs. France used the years before the next war to reinforce Louisbourg, making stronger their claim to mainland Acadia. The British reconsidered their attitude toward the Acadians, altering their policy of neglect and amelioration.

European powers believed that control of Nova Scotia and the Chignecto Isthmus was essential to dominance of the North Atlantic region. The Acadians were in the crosshairs. The British began considering deportation of the Francophone population in the early 1700s, viewing them as a continuing risk whether or not they pledged allegiance. Nova Scotia Governor Mascarene favored forcible expulsion in 1720, but waffled in 1745 about such an extreme solution, worrying about who would replace the Acadians and hoping they would eventually make good subjects through assimilation. Members of the Annapolis Royal Council wanted them transported out of the Province and replaced by good Protestant subjects, faulting all Acadians for the few who joined the invasion of Annapolis Royal in 1744.

Boston Governor Shirley first favored expulsion, but expressed different views in a letter containing a message for the Acadians in 1746. He reassured them that King George had no intentions of transporting them elsewhere, as long as they remained neutral and stayed out of the way. The Annapolis Royal Council had Shirley's letter read all around the province (even though they favored deportation the year before). It was critical that the Acadians remain neutral, because military operations were escalating between France and England. The French were amassing forces on the Atlantic coast and Quebec, but their armada was destroyed in Atlantic storms. Father Le Loutre brought forces from Quebec to reinforce Louisbourg. The British expected a large army to arrive soon. They built a new capital city at Halifax and recruited settlers in 1748-49. Over the next two years, the population of Halifax grew to over 5,000.

Colonel Edward Cornwallis replaced Mascarene as governor of Nova Scotia. He was determined to bring order and obedience to this unruly colony. Part of Cornwallis' agenda was to assimilate the Acadians. He planned to build Protestant schools, encourage intermarriage, and give tax-free land grants to Acadians who cooperated. Acadians could continue to practice Catholicism and hold their current properties, but these were contingent on renewed oaths of allegiance. Cornwallis would tolerate no nonsense about not bearing arms; Acadians must take the oaths "without any Conditional Clauses understood or any reservation whatever."[13]

The Acadians were fearful of assimilation. A large part of their continuing struggle under British rule was aimed at preserving their unique culture. Converting to Protestantism meant eternal damnation for Catholics; it was inconceivable to them. The oaths situation, however, was nothing new. They had faced these demands a number of times before, always insisting on the conventions of 1730, and managed to prevail. They would continue this tact. The proclamation Cornwallis made in 1749 gave them three months. Acadian settlements sent representatives to Halifax demanding the old exemptions. This led to Cornwallis publishing another proclamation, saying the king was not willing to allow exemptions to any of his subjects possessing land and habitations in the province. He gave them a few more months to take unconditional oaths.

By report, over a thousand Acadians signed a letter to Cornwallis and the Council, again rejecting unconditional oaths. The letter reiterated the agreements made in 1730 with Governor Philipps, noting Governor Shirley's promises that they would be undisturbed as long as they remained neutral. They threw in the old argument that they risked "barbarous cruelty" from the natives if they sided with the English. Saying that they could not sign an unconditional oath, they pledged to adhere to the "old oath which was given at Mines... with an exemption for ourselves and for our heirs from taking up arms." Otherwise, they were resolved to leave the country.

Cornwallis' deadline passed and nothing happened. He complained to the Board of Trade, expressing his frustration and fears, and advising it was too risky to allow the

Acadians to depart and join ranks with French and Canadian enemies. Even though their loyalty was questionable, their numbers were significant, around 12,000. The Board of Trade told Cornwallis to allow them to remain, avoiding any forcible measures to remove them for the present. Despite British ships patrolling the coasts and forts built to prevent migration and commerce, a number of Acadian families managed to cross to Île St. Jean in the summer of 1750. About 800 Acadians emigrated, aided by missionaries and provided arms by French authorities at Louisbourg.

The military situation in Nova Scotia changed drastically around 1750. Acadian neutrality was useful when the British had lesser military presence and population in the colony. This changed after Halifax was established, with influx of British and German settlers. Local farming was undertaken by these settlers, reducing dependence upon Acadian agriculture.

The European adversaries both built forts at strategic points in the Chignecto Isthmus. The French created Fort Beauséjour; the English later situated Fort Lawrence just across the Missaguash River. A significant event happened in May of 1750, involving Father Le Loutre and his Mi'kmaq forces. Governor Cornwallis had sent Major Charles Lawrence up the Bay of Fundy, taking 400 British settlers to Beaubassin to counteract the Acadian presence. Lawrence encountered Le Loutre's band of Mi'kmaqs, who meant to prevent disembarkation of the settlers, and fighting ensued. Lawrence prevailed and brought the settlers ashore, which spurred Le Loutre and his Mi'kmaqs to set fire to the Acadian village. Le Loutre intended to force Acadians to join French forces by destroying their homes. Around 4,000 of these French neutrals crossed over to Fort Beauséjour some two miles away.

The destruction of Beaubassin village by formerly friendly Mi'kmaqs led by a French priest must have shocked the Acadians. Some were incited to join resistance fighters led by Charles de Champs de Boishébert; possibly Joseph *dit* Beausoleil Broussard was already among these forces. Conditions were difficult for the refugees in an environment with constant skirmishes and limited provisions. A letter written by one to friends in Quebec gives a glimpse of their tribulation: "... we were compelled to leave all our property and flee from under the domination of the English... If Acadia is not restored to France I hope to take my little family and bring it to Canada. I beg you to let me know the state of things in that country. I assure you that we are in poor condition, for we are like the Indians in the woods."[14]

Britain and France were officially at peace, holding negotiations about boundaries of their North American colonies. Guerilla attacks and skirmishes were frequent between

British forces and French resistance fighters with their native allies. It was a time of hardship and dilemma for the Acadians. The French wanted them to migrate and expand populations of Isle Royal and Île St. Jean, to create new settlements on the mainland (now New Brunswick), and to fight in the military. The British wanted them to stay and assimilate, turn into obedient citizens, and eventually become Protestants. After the destruction of Beaubassin, including homes, farms, dikes, and crops, Acadians of the Chignecto Isthmus had little choice except to go along with the French. Their population was overrunning the capacity of the two islands with undiked marshes and forested lands that were rocky and steep. Some moved west to Shepody Bay and the valleys of the Petitcodiac and Memramcook Rivers, but there was little cleared land and small chance of rebuilding their former life.

The Acadians of Annapolis Valley and the Mines settlements stayed home and hoped for the best. But they failed to perceive the gravity of escalating military forces or how their neutrality stance was setting the stage for disaster. British administrators began to view their presence as increasingly dangerous, taking their refusal of an unconditional oath as a demonstration of pro-French sympathies. Even as the British became more adamant about unconditional loyalty to King George II, the Acadians were more reluctant to make this pledge. For them, it was primarily an issue of preserving their way of life and culture—this unique blend of French and Indian folkways that was forged on the 17th-century Acadian frontier.[15]

Brief Reprieve at Mines and Annapolis Valley. Nova Scotia Governor Cornwallis returned to England in 1752. Although unsuccessful in getting the French neutrals to pledge an unconditional oath of allegiance, his firm stand about the oath was pivotal in shaping future British response to the Acadian problem. His legacy was grim determination to expel all who were resistant, even the entire Francophone population if necessary. But first came a brief reprieve.

Colonel Peregrine Hopson, former British commander at Louisbourg, was next to take over as governor. Hopson was a conciliatory person by nature and observed how ineffective the proclamations by Cornwallis had been. He wanted no more trouble about the Acadians taking an unconditional oath and advised the Board of Trade to delay pushing the issue. The Board as usual took the easier path of temporization, noting that although having the French neutrals take the oath was desirable, "… it would be highly imprudent to disgust them by forcing it upon them at an improper time, and when they are quiet and at peace."[16]

Marie-Anne LeBlanc and **Joseph Bujol** were among the Mines residents who probably breathed sighs of relief when Cornwallis left and Hopson took over. For the present, they could direct attention to their everyday lives, farming and raising their family. They already had one daughter, Marguerite, and Marie-Anne was pregnant with their son, Augustin, who was born in 1753. They heard good things about Governor Hopson that reassured them. He treated the natives fairly and respectfully and maintained friendly relations with French commanders for mutual exchange of deserters. He made efforts to conciliate the Acadians, believing their presence was necessary to the welfare of the province. Once when a British officer carried off some of their cattle, Hopson reprimanded him and paid for the cattle. He issued instructions to all officers to treat the Acadians as British subjects, taking nothing from them by force.

Like all her Acadian confrères, Marie-Anne loved the land and their way of life, following patterns determined by the changing seasons. As spring came after winter's frozen darkness, she welcomed new sprouts of grasses pushing through still frosty fields. She began planning her home garden. When the soil was warm enough to plant, her mother Jeanne Anne LeBlanc *née* Bourgeois walked the several miles between their homes to help, bringing along her youngest son, Jean Baptiste, who was 14 years old. Since her husband's death in 1747, Jeanne Anne spent as much time with her youngest daughter as possible, the older children having settled onto farms farther away. Donning their *garde soleils*—bonnets with flaps covering the back of the neck and sides of the face—the women spent happy hours in the bright spring sunshine, putting in seeds for cabbage, squash, beans, turnips, potatoes, and herbs.

The men and boys repaired *aboiteaux*, herded cattle and sheep to and from grazing fields, and tended to newly born calves and lambs. They sowed wheat and corn seeds, gathered shellfish along banks, and fished in rivers and bays. As weather warmed into summer, they sheared the large sheep for thick, luxurious wool from which women made a multitude of clothing items—from caps to socks, shawls to shirts, dresses to drawers. For summer wear they switched to cooler flax fabrics, but the wool kept away the winter's cold.

Summer was a favorite season for Marie-Anne, since it brought frequent social gatherings. Families from all around Grand Pré and Pisiquid met weekly at different homes; many *fetes* were planned, weddings and betrothals celebrated, and babies christened. Since priests visited the villages monthly or less, village elders assumed roles as lay ministers to perform these essential spiritual rituals until the church fathers could make them official. It was especially important to christen newborns, since infant mortality was about 50%. They believed even lay rituals could save from eternal damnation those infants who died.

As fall arrived, harvest began, and everyone was busy from dawn to dusk. Groups of workers, men and women, went from farm to farm to assist bringing in the crops. They walked several miles between farms in the coolness of daybreak, spent the day harvesting corn and wheat, and returned home in twilight. Sometimes they stayed at the farm and enjoyed dinner together on the lawn, prepared from fresh garden vegetables and recently butchered pork or chickens. Acadians rarely consumed cattle and sheep, since these animals were more important for milk and wool.

Women worked side by side with men during the height of harvest, pitching wheat onto wagons and picking ears of corn into shoulder bags. Always they protected their skin from the sun with their *garde soleils*. Those who were pregnant or had newborn infants stayed at home, harvesting the garden and preparing meals for workers. Marie-Anne was among these in fall of 1752, humming as she cooked a large meal assisted by her mother. Workers would eat well this evening.

Autumn sunset always thrilled Marie-Anne. She reveled in the golden-hued sky and the special vibrancy of colors as sunrays glinted at low angles over gently rolling hills, casting deepening shadows along banks of irrigation canals, fading into hues of pink-streaked clouds against the cerulean horizon. In the distance, low mountainsides turned magenta before darkening to indigo.

The land held magic, and abundance, and succor for Marie-Anne and her people. It was the home to which she, her parents, and her grandparents had been born. This was the only home they had known for four generations, now moving into the fifth. Theirs was a warm, supportive, close-knit society in which happiness seemed available for all. She could not even imagine leaving this land and their culture. She hoped to see her children and grandchildren continue to enjoy their beloved Acadia.

Winter was difficult, but the Acadians had learned how to thrive through the snow, chilling fogs, and bitter winds blowing across the Maritimes. Their homes and woolen clothes kept them warm; they had learned to use snowshoes and hunt game from the natives. They preserved food and kept cold cellars, salted and smoked meat and fish. With abundant forests nearby, they gathered wood for hearth fires that kept burning all through the winter. A treat was derived from tapping maple trees for their sweet sap. In the spring as sap was rising, they set pails to catch the amber liquid, later boiling down into the most delicious syrup.

Perhaps some threads of doubt, some whispers of fear, entered Marie-Anne's mind as she sat near the crackling fire, cording and knitting wool from their sheep. Word had reached the Mines settlements about the plight of their confrères at Beaubassin. She was deeply sorrowful over the suffering of families after their homes and farms were burned by Father Le Loutre and his Mi'kmaqs. It was hard for her to understand how this warrior priest could turn against his own people; even though she heard the men discuss the strategy. True, it forced many in Beaubassin to cross over to the French side, but was this best for them? She doubted it, having heard of their hardships on the French-held islands. It was rumored that some of these families wanted to return to former lands, including a group from Pisiquid who had migrated earlier.

In the depth of winter, her thoughts may have turned frequently to the issue of the oaths. Many community meetings had addressed this issue, given the adamant stance of Governor Cornwallis for an unconditional oath. As was true for as long as she could remember, the Acadians' unswerving adherence to the "conventions of 1730" had foiled British attempts to undermine their relatively autonomous status and to push them toward assimilation. Perhaps they could continue on this path and remain unmolested. Certainly the policies of Governor Hopson seemed to support their status as French Neutrals who had a special dispensation. She ardently prayed that this would remain so.

Administrative Shifts and a Turn of Fate. A tense incident in 1753 threatened to start another Indian war. Two British men plundered an Indian (Mi'kmaq or Abenaki) storehouse on Isle Dore, killed and scalped some natives, including women and children. The men were brought to court to answer for their deeds. When Hopson sent a schooner to protect the native shores, the Indians in retaliation seized it and massacred the entire crew, save one Frenchman who was ransomed. The prospect for a lasting peace with the natives vanished. Fear of native raids was less in Mines but still a possibility. Memory of the Grand Pré battle six years earlier was still fresh, and word of the razing of Beaubassin a recent nightmare.

A few months later the Acadian inhabitants of Grand Pré, Canso, and Pisiquid brought a petition to the Council at Halifax requesting that their priests be excused from taking an oath of allegiance. They were worried that the bishop of Quebec would not send priests if they were required to become British subjects. The Council deliberated, recalling the

Acadians were promised free exercise of their religion and concerned that no services by priests would provide a pretext for leaving the province. The petition was granted, on condition that priests would obtain a license from the governor.

Later that fall, another delegation of Acadians came before the Council at Halifax. These were former residents of Pisiquid who had migrated to French territory in Cape Breton because of the unconditional oath demanded by Cornwallis. Apparently living under French rule was not what they had hoped for, and they wanted to return to their old homes. They agreed to take only the conditional oath, believing they were in danger from the natives if they agreed to bear arms for the British. They also requested being allowed to move from the province when they desired, taking their effects with them, as provided in the 1730 conventions. The Council gave them permission to return and all the privileges conferred by this earlier treaty.

The situation for the Acadians seemed promising as 1753 drew to a close. No doubt the residents of Grand Pré and other settlements felt hopeful they would continue an era of relative peace. But fate had other outcomes in store. Despite Hopson's conciliations, there was growing Francophobia among English officers and colonial leadership. When Hopson was compelled to return to England due to failing eyesight, taking a leave of absence, he was succeeded by Major Charles Lawrence in 1754. Lawrence was a professional soldier who established fortifications on the Chignecto Isthmus and had frequent skirmishes with natives and French resistance. He was concerned about the growing French military presence in the Maritimes and the vulnerability of the British colony now under his charge. Though England and France were nominally at peace, Lawrence realized that each country was just waiting for a favorable opportunity to strike a decisive blow. The looming conflict was greater than control of Acadia; it portended who would have mastery of the North American continent.

Lawrence was determined to obtain an unqualified oath of allegiance from the Acadians, intending to brook no opposition. In his view, they were subversives whose continued presence jeopardized British security. In addition, he was concerned with the rapid increase in Acadian population; from about 350 people in 1654 to 12,000-18,000 in 1755. If left unchecked, he foresaw geometric increase each year with rising risk. The Acadian problem promised to be of long duration, while the escalating border war with French Canada demanded a quick resolution. Lawrence saw only two options: full integration of the Acadians as British subjects—or deportation.

Lawrence and New England Governor Shirley were in correspondence about deportation of Acadians as early as November 1754. Just a few months earlier, Shirley had informed the home government in England of intelligence from Halifax that Chignecto Acadians together with their Indian allies joined the French garrison at Beauséjour to break up British eastern settlements. Shirley received instructions to cooperate with Lawrence in attacking the French forts in Nova Scotia; the prelude to the Seven Years' War between France and England. Lawrence sent Colonel Robert Monckton against Forts Beauséjour and St. John in spring 1755; joined by troops from Shirley to bring the Nova Scotia regiments to full force. By early June, 2,000 troops arrived at Chignecto and faced off against French forces.

British troops quickly overtook outlying structures, and French forces retreated into Fort Beauséjour along with about 220 Acadians. The remaining Acadians, several thousand whose Beaubassin homes were burned by Le Loutre, threw away their arms. They preferred to surrender than be hanged. Fighting continued a few more days, but when the French learned they would not receive reinforcements from Louisbourg, plus the Acadians within the fort urged capitulation, the commander surrendered.

Colonel Monckton renamed Beauséjour as Fort Cumberland and proceeded to take the remaining French forts on Baie Verte and the St. John River. In these struggles, the majority of Acadians refused to assist the French commanders. Observing the complete success of British forces, the natives decided to stop fighting and gave assurances of their friendliness. This was a momentous development in the Acadian saga: "With the fall of Fort Beauséjour, the Acadians' fate was sealed."[17]

Lawrence ordered the Acadians to surrender all their guns in June 1755. He used the 300 Acadian conscripts captured at Fort Beauséjour—who had been forced to join the French and bear arms—as an excuse to revive the unconditional oath of allegiance. The governor chose to ignore the fact that the vast majority of Acadians had refused to fight. His opportunity to take action came quickly. On July 3, an Acadian delegation from Mines went to Halifax with a petition requesting they be allowed to use their canoes for fishing, which had been forbidden shortly before; they were accused of using canoes to bring provisions to the French at Beauséjour. They also asked to have their guns returned, since they needed guns for hunting and defense against Indians. The petition was couched in "language not as tactful as it might have been."[18] They argued that possessing a gun did not induce them to rebel, and neither did absence of a weapon make them more faithful. Loyalty, they said, was a matter of conscience. If they decided to remain loyal, they wanted to know the governor's intentions toward them.

The Acadians' petition, Lawrence declared, was impertinent. He ordered the delegation to remain in Halifax; they responded at once with an apology stating they intended no disrespect. Lawrence reprimanded them and proffered his leniency due to their ignorance of British protocols. Then he ordered them to accept, on behalf of their people, an unconditional oath of allegiance. The delegates reiterated their readiness to reaffirm their long-standing conditional oath. Lawrence told them the king would not now accept an oath with conditions. They were given until the next morning to consider this.

The next day the Acadian delegates declared they could not consent to taking the unconditional oath without consulting their people. The Halifax Council replied the oath was a personal act, and their refusal to take it demonstrated allegiance to the French king. They would no longer be treated as British subjects. Having once refused the oath, they would have no further opportunity and would be removed from the province as "Popish recusants." To drive the point home, Lawrence had the delegates put in prison. The Council issued an order for Nova Scotia's French Neutrals to swear unconditional allegiance—or face deportation.

Another Acadian delegation representing 200 residents of Annapolis Royal brought a memorial to the Halifax Council on July 25, stating that they would abide by the old oath but could not subscribe to the new one. The Council warned of the consequences of this decision, giving them a few days to reconsider. The final answer was polite but determined, restating the agreements of the past, and concluding: "... we will never prove so fickle as to take an oath which changes, ever so little, the conditions and the privileges obtained for us by our sovereign and our fathers in the past."[19] Inhabitants of Pisiquid brought a similar petition, and another memorial was presented by Mines inhabitants refusing to take the new oath. Deputies of these delegations were also imprisoned on Georges Island at Halifax.

On July 31, 1755, the colonial government at Halifax issued an order for the forcible removal of French Neutrals from all Bay of Fundy settlements.

Acting Governor Lawrence and the Council at Halifax actually did not have the power to make this decision. The Council could not enact laws; its action was limited to the authority vested in the governor by his royal commission. Lawrence did not have either commission or instructions; technically Hopson was still governor. Hopson's instructions were to report to the Board of Trade in case the French Neutrals refused the new oath, who would then determine His Majesty's further directions. By 1755, Hopson had informed the Board of Trade that the Acadians refused to take the new oath, and the matter rested in their hands. King George apparently did not yet know the situation. The actions about to be taken by Lawrence and the Halifax Council were being done without the knowledge or authority of the home government.

To fortify his legal position, Lawrence asked the chief justice, Jonathan Belcher, to prepare an opinion about deporting the French Neutrals. Belcher had arrived in Nova Scotia from New England nine months before and apparently did not examine the official correspondence or Council minutes for the years 1713-1755. Nonetheless, he wrote a document "... ill-founded in fact and contemptible in argument..." that the Acadians could not be permitted to remain as this would "... incur the displeasure of the crown and the parliament..." based on supposed instructions to earlier governors no longer in effect. In addition, he said that people "... are declared recusants if they refuse on a summons to take the oath... and can never after such refusal be permitted to take them."[20] Although the latter was true, King George had long ignored his own law. The earlier argument was baseless.

Le Grand Dérangement

Joseph Bujol would have closely followed events happening with the Grand Pré delegation, along with other men of the community. **Anne-Marie** and the women became concerned when news arrived about imprisonment of the deputies in Halifax. Word spread rapidly of the exact same fate befalling delegates from other Acadian settlements. Leaders of villages around the Bay of Fundy were incarcerated in Georges Island prison, a terrible place. In the late summer of 1755, groups of worried villagers discussed these unsettling developments as they congregated in ripening fields and orchards. They were fearful of further punitive actions by the British but still could not believe that deportation was a serious threat. After all, they had weathered years of British threats and posturing, and nothing much had changed.

In early August 1755, Anne-Marie was pregnant with her third child. Her son Augustin was 2 years old, and her daughter Marguerite was 4. Perhaps she worried more than most Acadians about the future, hearing from her Bourgeois relatives about the devastation in Beaubassin and having lost her father shortly after the Grand Pré battle. In her view, the British could not be trusted to keep their word, though repeatedly affirming the status of French Neutrals. Something she had heard kept festering in her mind: that the British coveted the rich Acadian farmlands and fields; that they intended to bring Protestant settlers to replace her people. Already this was happening in the Annapolis Royal basin, and Beaubassin was in the midst of a fiery and bloody transition. No doubt when the Isthmus of Chignecto lands were reclaimed, it would be by British settlers.

She did well to be wary of British intentions. Lawrence had been scheming with Shirley and engineer Charles Morris to design the Acadian deportation. They devised a "... diabolically clever scheme for assuring the Acadians' peaceable submission."[21] English commanders at the Bay of Fundy settlements would lure Acadian men and boys into their respective posts, where the unsuspecting villagers would be held captive until transport ships arrived, sent by England to carry them into exile. Village women and children naturally would remain close to home with their possessions and livestock, forced to take over responsibility while their men were detained. Keeping families close to home would expedite collecting them for the short march to the waiting ships. The plan was to bring the men and boys for boarding at the same time, attempting to keep families from the same village together. The final parts of the scheme were to confiscate Acadian property and livestock to reimburse the English government for the cost of removal, and to burn all Acadian homes and boats to prevent those who escaped deportation from returning.

On the whole, Lawrence's scheme worked very well. At Fort Cumberland (formerly Beauséjour), Colonel Monckton summoned Beaubassin men and boys to the post, ostensibly for an important decree by the governor regarding their lands. On August 11, around 400 local Acadians came; shocked to hear Monckton state that the Council had declared them rebels, that their lands and possessions were forfeited to the crown, and they with their families would be deported. In the meantime, they would be treated as prisoners and held inside the fort.

Captain Cobb was sent to Shepody, but warnings preceded him, and many Acadians fled into the woods. Search parties scoured the countryside, bringing in a few captives. Captain Lewis went to Cobequid and captured two vessels bound for Louisbourg, took several prisoners, and burned several villages in the area. Monckton sent several of his captains to search out escapees along the Memramcook and Petitcodiac Rivers, and along Baie Verte. They took prisoners and burned isolated homes or villages whenever possible.

On September 4, French Canadians and Acadian resistance struck back. A British landing party of about 60 was torching a village on the shore when they were attacked by around 100 natives and Acadians led by Charles de Champs de Boishébert, Canadian leader. Joseph *dit* Beausoleil Broussard was among the Acadian resistance fighters. Twenty-three British soldiers were killed and a number wounded; their forces retreated to Fort Cumberland with a few Acadian captives. However, over 200 buildings and large quantities of wheat and flax had been destroyed. Similar destruction took place all along Baie Verte.

British transport ships arrived in Chignecto Bay on August 31; the tedious work of moving Acadian families to the embarkation point took over one month. The most warlike men were confined inside Fort Lawrence, but most of these escaped following a bold scheme by Beausoleil, who was among them. Their wives had smuggled spoons, knives, and other tools in food and clothing which they brought to the captives. With these simple implements, the Acadians dug a tunnel under the fort's walls. Acadian tradition says the men went through the tunnel according to size, from smallest to largest. This way each man enlarged the passage as he squeezed through. The last man out was "Little René" Richard, largest of all prisoners. Under cover of a dark, stormy night in the predawn hours, 86 men eluded detection by guards and disappeared into the woods on October 1, 1755. Beausoleil was among them, along with several of his grown sons and nephews. His brother Alexandre and son Victor were not among the escapees. The British became so alarmed after the escape that they confined Alexandre, Victor, and 20 others on their gunboat in the harbor under tighter security.

British redcoats herded the remaining men and boys to the ships. Others forced distraught women and children in straggling lines to the shore. The exiles carried what they could of clothing and possessions, but they had to leave most of their belongings behind. On October 13, 1755, a fleet of 10 British ships took aboard 960 Acadians. The exiles who boarded ships at Chignecto were bound for English colonies in South Carolina and Georgia. After the vessels departed, soldiers destroyed every barn and house in the region, and drove several herds of cattle into Fort Cumberland.

The gunboat with Alexandre and resistance fighters escorted four shiploads of Acadian exiles to Charleston, South Carolina. The militant Acadians were sent to the farthest southern colony, where they were held in shackles on Sullivan's Island, labeled special prisoners. Despite constant surveillance, the wily Alexandre escaped along with four men, but not Victor. The group made their way back home on foot, getting help from natives along the western border of the British colonies. They rejoined Beausoleil and the resistance in Shepody. The remaining prisoners were sent to London.

At Annapolis Royal, Major John Handfield was less competent in rounding up Acadians. He was unable to lure the men into the fort, and when troops searched the river and valley they found Acadian farms deserted. Word of events in Beaubassin had given forewarning, and they all disappeared into the woods. After remaining in hiding over a month, the Acadians returned to their homes in early September and resumed their farming lives. Things remained quiet for another month, apparently because Handfield lacked enough troops. When a fresh detachment of British soldiers arrived, the removal was soon accomplished. On December 4, 1755, a total of 1,664 Annapolis Royal-area Acadians were rounded up and taken to transport ships. Men, women, and children were crowded onto the ships, which set sail on December 9, distributing them along the Atlantic seaboard colonies. Some were sent to England.

In the Pisiquid neighborhood, Captain Murray of Fort Edward began the removal process, capturing 183 men by deceiving them into gathering for pronouncements. He needed more time to collect the other residents and worried that his troops would shoot to kill on any pretense. By October 14, he had gathered 900 Acadians, but his transport ships had not yet arrived. Finally all four vessels were present, and he loaded around 1,000 people on October 23, 1755.

The Grand Pré Deportation. On August 19, 1755, Colonel John Winslow arrived at Grand Pré and set up headquarters in the village church. He had residents remove sacred items from the church, and created a compound enclosed by a picket fence. Village leaders were informed they must provide provisions for the troops, but the reasons for the occupation were not divulged. Fearing the Acadians would destroy crops if his purpose was known, Winslow stationed troops to protect the unharvested grain and corn. On August 30, three sloops from Boston came to anchor in the bay.

Mines Acadians were greatly concerned about what all this British activity meant. Since deportations in Chignecto and Annapolis Royal had not yet taken place, even though men and boys in these regions were being held in forts, information had not spread. On September 2, Winslow issued a proclamation that an important communication about new resolutions from His Majesty would be given on Friday, September 5. All men and boys were to appear in the church at Grand Pré that day at three o'clock; no excuse would be accepted for not attending, and they would forfeit their lands in they failed to come.

Although Winslow realized his position was not strong, and if the Acadians resisted they far outnumbered his soldiers, everything went smoothly. At the appointed day and time,

418 Acadian inhabitants walked pensively into the church. The modest structure was familiar to them from their childhood, associated with the most joyous and sorrowful events of their lives. But the sacred hall had been violated; British soldiers were at the door, and a table had been placed in the center, around which stood several more soldiers. Soon Colonel Winslow entered, attended by his officers. He stood before the Acadians who were seated on pews and chairs, and read the proclamation sent by Governor Lawrence, pronounced in the name of King George II.

In shocked silence and considerable disbelief, the men and boys of Grand Pré heard the words that doomed their people to exile, translated in French by their priest:

"By his orders (Governor Lawrence) you are convened to hear His Majesty's final resolution in respect to the French inhabitants of this his province of Nova Scotia, who for almost a half a century have had more indulgence granted them than any of his subjects in any part of his dominions. What use you have made of it, you yourselves best know.

"The duty I am now upon, though necessary, is very disagreeable... therefore without hesitation I shall deliver you His Majesty's orders and instructions, namely: That your lands and tenements, cattle of all kinds and live stock of all sorts are forfeited to the Crown with all your other effects, saving your money and household goods, and that you yourselves are to be removed from this his province... whole families shall go in the same vessel; so that this removal which I am sensible must give you a great deal of trouble may be made as easy as His Majesty's service will admit; and I hope that in whatever part of the world your lot may fall, you may be faithful subjects, and a peaceable and happy people."[22]

King George, however, knew nothing about this proclamation, and his quite opposite instructions were even then en route to Lawrence from England.

Winslow continued by informing the Acadian men and boys that they would remain in the compound under security of his troops. He issued orders that his soldiers were not to kill any cattle or rob orchards, as the lands and possessions were now the property of the king. Turning from the stricken faces of the Acadians, he left the church.

As the immensity of this decision sank into their minds, the Acadian men thought at once of their families. Joseph Bujol reflected bitterly on how his wife, Anne-Marie, had premonitions that this meeting would not end well. She wanted him to remain home, but the consequences were too dire. Now it appeared he would lose all his land and possessions anyway. Talking among themselves, the men realized they needed to let their families know the situation. A few elders were selected to speak with Colonial Winslow; after lengthy deliberations, he granted the request. Twenty men left the compound daily to communicate with their families and bring food and clothing back for the others. This continued until all families had been visited.

Of course, as soon as families had the first visit, word spread like wildfire in the community. By the time Joseph came home, Anne-Marie knew about the horrific edict. Through tears and embraces, they reviewed what must be done, finding some comfort in the promise that families would be kept together. Anne-Marie had already packed bundles for Joseph, one with his own clothes and personal items, another with food, blankets, and extra jackets and socks for others to use. Joseph hugged his two small children tightly and whispered to be brave, even though they did not understand.

The next several days were excruciating for Anne-Marie. While the Acadian men were impounded, British soldiers came to search homes for weapons. She tried to shield the children as brusque, red-coated men ransacked their home, raiding the orchard for ripe apples and pears, even though against orders. She packed and repacked bundles for herself and the children, trying to decide what to bring and what to leave, precious things never to be seen again. At night, unable to sleep, she worried about her unborn baby. Where would the little one come into the world? Would she lose the pregnancy from stress and hardship? Might she even die in childbirth, somewhere in a dank ship on the tossing oceans, without attending women who knew what to do? The birth was not expected for another 4-5 months, so she ardently hoped to be somewhere on land—but where?

No one knew where they were being sent. Everyone doubted the word of the British. Five days after the men were seized; good cause for doubt was given. On September 10, word rippled among the women in Acadian homes that some men were being hauled out of the church and taken somewhere by soldiers, apparently toward the coast. All the women who could ran from their homes to Grand Pré, soon the scene of total chaos. Hundreds of weeping women, many with their children present, were pushing against a line of British soldiers and New England militiamen attempting to hold them back. The able-bodied Acadian men were being herded toward ships waiting in the bay. The younger boys and elderly men were still being held inside the compound.

Anne-Marie took her daughter by the hand and carried her toddler son, going as fast as possible to her mother's home, which was closer to Grand Pré. By the time they arrived,

Jeanne Anne had news of what was happening. Apparently Colonel Winslow feared an uprising and was putting 50 stronger men aboard each of his four transport ships. A large contingent of British soldiers formed a line from the church door to the fence, and the men were counted off in groups of 50. When the men refused to obey unless their elder fathers could come with them, Winslow commanded the soldiers to fix bayonets and advance. Pushing and threatening with bayonets, the soldiers forced the men along through the line and out of the compound, continuing to guard them as they walked toward the ships. The road from church to ships was over a mile, by now lined with hundreds of women and children. Crying, calling, praying, some women on their knees begging to see their husbands, the scene was heartrending. A few might have sighted their slowly moving spouses, calling out helplessly or throwing bundles over heads of soldiers in hopes that it would find the right man.

Winslow observed, "They went off praying, singing, and crying, being met by the women and children all the way (which is a mile and a half), with great lamentations."[23]

Soldiers continued escorting groups until all who were considered dangerous had been removed. The transport ships had not received provisions, so the women and children came daily to the shore with food. They gave bundles to soldiers who distributed them on board. Winslow sent out search parties to find stragglers or escapees but caught only 30 old and infirm men. He decided to leave them ashore until the ships were ready to depart. Captain Lewis was sent to Cobequid but returned without a prisoner as the inhabitants had fled. He reported that his men had laid the habitations in ruins.

Winslow grew increasingly annoyed that the supply ship and other transports had not yet arrived. While he chafed and groaned, 24 young men imprisoned on the ships were able to escape. François Hébert was accused as the instigator, taken ashore, and forced to witness the burning of his house and barn. The inhabitants were warned that unless the escapees surrendered within two days, all their household furniture would be confiscated and their homes destroyed. If the escapees were captured they would receive no mercy. As a result, 22 young men returned to the ships. The other two were found by British soldiers and shot.

On October 8, 1755, once the other transports and supply ship arrived, the embarkation of Grand Pré Acadians began in earnest. Families had been notified to come on that day, bringing their bundles of personal effects. It was a scene of wild confusion and despair. Slowly moving lines of women, children, and elderly wended from villages to the shore.

Most were on foot, mothers carrying small children, youths assisting infirm and elders, all toting bundles. They were weary, tearful, and disheartened. Their greatest hope was to reunite with their fathers and husbands and sons already aboard the ships. In all, 80 families arrived at the shore.

The next day the men who were held onboard or detained in the church were brought to reunite with their families. However, bedlam resulted as hundreds of people desperately searched for family members. Amid cries of joy and shouts of desperation, the Acadian families did their best to find each other. Many were reunited, Joseph Bujold and Anne-Marie among these. Most likely Jeanne Anne LeBlanc and her youngest son Jean Baptiste were part of this reunion. Four days later, several ships were fully loaded with families and received sailing orders for Maryland, Pennsylvania, and Virginia.

Ships Take Acadians into Exile, 1755   Claude T. Picard
Photo: ©Parks Canada/Claude Picard
By permission of Parks Canada and the Picard family.

Joseph and **Anne-Marie Bujold**, and their two children Marguerite and Augustin, were deported from Grand Pré on October 13, 1755. Their ship was bound for Maryland.

Winslow kept loading transport ships; by November 1, over 1,500 Acadians from the Mines region had been deported. But there still remained over 600 residents to deport and not enough transports. Winslow also needed to search for stragglers and destroy all homes and barns to prevent reoccupation. After housing the Acadian remnants in Grand Pré for another six weeks, his transports finally arrived, and the last unhappy residents were put aboard, setting sail on December 20, 1755. Any remaining Acadians who escaped into the wilderness and evaded British soldiers either died during the harsh winter or wandered to the French-held islands or into New Brunswick and Canada. Despite deportation of most of their population, the Acadian resistance continued its struggle for another five years, based in remote camps in Chignecto Bay regions and New Brunswick.

By the end of 1755, over 6,000 Acadians had been forcibly expelled from their homeland. They were dispersed among English colonies along the Atlantic seaboard or sent to England. The objective was to keep them separated as a people, in hopes that they would abandon their religion and culture, gradually to assimilate into British Protestant society. Many consider this an early effort at ethnic cleansing and genocide of an "undesirable" minority population.

Governor Lawrence received a letter from the Board of Trade, possibly as early as August 13, 1755, conveying the king's wishes to him. In effect, the instructions said that the Acadians were not to be molested. Though the exact date the letter arrived is uncertain, it was surely before November 30, since Lawrence sent a reply on that day referencing the August 13th letter. If this letter had been received in time, possibly the scheme for deporting the Acadians would have been halted. Having already started, however, Lawrence seemed compelled to finish the nasty business.

History leaves many evil deeds unpunished. Lawrence might have faced serious consequences for assuming such authority without clear royal directions, but the Seven Years' War intervened. He had barely finished his deplorable eradication of Acadians when England and Prussia signed the treaty which formally inaugurated the Seven Years' War, known in America as the French and Indian War. England declared war on France in 1756, and the time of concessions was over. Now as the conflict heated up and any French-leaning group was clearly the enemy, Lawrence's actions could be regarded as a patriotic service. The Seven Years' War can be considered the first "world war," fought between 1756 and 1763, involving every European great power of the time. It spanned five continents, affecting Europe, the Americas, West Africa, India, and the Philippines.

Acadian Expulsion by Area 1755 – 1760[24]

Grand Pré	2182
Annapolis Royal	1664
Pisiquid	1100 (approximate)
Beaubassin	1100 (approximate
Total	6050 (approximate)

Distribution of Acadian Exiles in 1755[25]

Georgia	400
South Carolina	942
North Carolina	50
Virginia	1500
Maryland	913
Pennsylvania	454
New York	344
Connecticut	731
Massachusetts	735
Bound for North Carolina but escaped	232

Acadians Remaining in Nova Scotia and New Brunswick. Though the popular image of *Le Grand Dérangement* is that all Acadians were expelled, probably as many as 10,000 remained in their homeland. Many who evaded capture became fugitives, making their way to Île St. Jean (now Prince Edward Island). By 1758, between 3,400 and 5,000 Acadians were residing there. When Louisbourg fell to the British, two-thirds of them were deported to France, sent mostly to the Atlantic ports where they lived in poverty in slums, having little opportunity for work. Some were sent inland as "peasants" to farm estates of the nobility. But these now independent pioneers would not return to a feudal lifestyle. When Spain took over the French colony of Louisiana, these disgruntled Acadians arranged for transport there. The Spanish government was eager to settle Catholic French Acadians to bolster the small population in Louisiana and provide a buffer against English colonies to the east. At Spanish expense, 1,596 Acadians (70% of those still in France) sailed in 1785 to New Orleans in seven transport ships.

Many Acadians remaining on the islands migrated to Quebec or farther north to New Brunswick and Newfoundland, mainly St. Pierre and Miquelon. Settlements along the Petitcodiac and Miramichi Rivers, and near present-day Memramcook, increased dramatically in size. They endured hardship and continued skirmishes between British and Acadian resistance forces. When the Seven Years' War ended in 1763, Acadians in the Massachusetts colony arranged for their return to Canada. They took an oath of allegiance to Britain, and in 1766 about 720 from the Boston and Salem colonies left. They traveled either by ship to Quebec, or on foot to Nova Scotia where they found over 12,000 English settlers had occupied their farmlands. Unable to reconcile themselves to this situation, many continued to the Petitcodiac River valley of New Brunswick. Some returning New England exiles accepted lands offered by the British in the western extremes of Nova Scotia. Considered less desirable, the 40 acres per family were near Halifax at Chezzetcook and Prospect. Others settled along the Strait of Canso. By 1767, additional Acadian settlements formed at Baie St.-Marie, Tousquet, and Pobomcoup.

France tried to recoup some of its losses during the Seven Years' War by bolstering its colony in St. Domingue (now Haiti). Acadians in exile along the Atlantic seaboard were recruited with promises of land and sustenance until they became self-sufficient. However, the real purpose was to build a workforce for clearing dense jungle and constructing a large military facility. In 1764, 418 Acadians were transported there from the New England colonies. They grudgingly endured their new status as forced laborers, anticipating promised land grants. Instead, they labored in tropical climates with diseases to which they had no resistance; the death rate was appalling. More waves of immigrants facing the same fate arrived in 1765, where the despairing Acadians would "... prefer the galleys and the torture associated with that punishment rather than stay in this horrible place..." where administrators found "... some men bewildered, without shelter, dying under bushes..."[26]

Approximately 2,000 Acadians arrived in the Antilles by 1764. Others, deported from Annapolis Royal in 1756, eventually arrived in Martinique. Although they requested passage back to Quebec or Cape Breton Island, it appears most remained in the Antilles. Many Acadians in these tropical islands requested permission to leave, and some deserted, but few St. Domingue Acadians left the colony in the late 1670s for Louisiana. Some did board ships arriving from Halifax or the Atlantic seaboard, transporting Acadians who were en route to Louisiana, but who never settled in the islands. It appears that the few remaining Acadians in the Antilles gradually adapted to this radically different environment, integrating into the islands' economic system as plantation laborers, artisans, managers, or more rarely, plantation owners.[27]

In late 1758 and early 1759, a contingent of the Acadian resistance was compelled to surrender and sent to detention centers in Halifax. They remained there for the duration of the Seven Years' War, and in 1764 when the war ended, they arranged ships to emigrate. At first they considered St. Domingue, but upon hearing reports of the misery and death toll, decided to continue on to the Mississippi valley with the intention of forming settlements in Illinois. But they never made it that far, staying in Louisiana.

The dispersal of Acadians was widespread. The fate of some took them as far away as the Falkland Islands and French Guiana.

Sufficient Acadians remained in the New Brunswick settlements to form a core that sustained their culture. Their right to live in this area was formally sanctioned by the British in 1764. By the early 1800s, most of the 3,729 New Brunswick Acadians resided in this region. These early post-dispersal settlements provided the foundation for rebuilding Acadian society in Canada.

Beausoleil Broussard and the Acadian Resistance

Two centuries after the Acadian expulsion, the global upheaval of World War II gave descendants of Louisiana refugees a new perspective on their history. Fighting in France, they discovered that the French understood their colloquial language, which aided communication essential to the war effort. This spurred an Acadian Renaissance of reclaiming long-lost pride and overcoming low self-esteem, a result of ethnic persecution through humiliation and fragmentation. Their collective consciousness yearned for a grand hero, "... someone of their own cultural identification with the charismatic stature..." of such leaders as George Washington, Napoleon, El Cid, or Alexander the Great.[28] Eventually this cultural hero emerged as Joseph Broussard *dit* Beausoliel, who became known as leader of the Acadian Resistance and Freedom Fighter.

Beausoleil was born in 1702 at Port-Royal, son of François Broussard (Brossard) and Catherine Richard. The family, which grew to 11 children, had moved to Shepody (Chipoudie) to a settlement near the Petitcodiac River in 1678. Joseph was nicknamed *Beausoleil*, reportedly for the river near his home which had "beautiful sunlight" sparkling off its waters. Some say the stories of Beausoleil are a merging of both his and his brother Alexandre's actions. Joseph married Agnes Thibodeau in 1725 at Port-Royal, daughter of Michel Thibodeau and Agnes Dugas, one of the most influential Acadian families during that time. Alexandre married Marguerite Thibodeau, Agnes' sister, in 1724. When their parents returned to Port-Royal, the two brothers remained on land grants given to their wives at Shepody.

François Broussard was known early on by the British as a dissident. Shortly after they took possession of Nova Scotia in 1713, François was imprisoned along with four other Acadians from Port-Royal, as retribution for seizing a British soldier. Details are lost, but apparently Acadian men seized the soldier for some aggravating deed. The British were attempting to establish authority and make examples of the Acadian leaders. François was released after a short time but remained fiercely anti-British the rest of his life, an attitude that profoundly influenced his children, Beausoleil in particular.

For 30 years Beausoleil (Joseph) and his wife Agnes lived a mostly peaceful life on the Petitcodiac River, near present-day Moncton, New Brunswick. They had 11 children, farming land reclaimed from marshes using *aboiteaux* and raising cattle. Beausoleil traded with local Mi'kmaq settlements and developed close friendships with the natives. He learned to speak their language and methods of trapping and hunting, skills that enhanced his ability to provide for his family. British soldiers observed that: "They behave like the Indians, with whom they are on very intimate terms... There are two families on the upper (Petitcodiac), named *Beausoleil*, who, though they are not Indians, live as they do... These *Beausoleils* enriched themselves during the recent disorders, and boast that they did much damage to the English and took from them property of value and many cattle. They speak the language of the Indians and obtain from them ... (many) beaver skins..."[29]

Like his father, Beausoleil was identified by the British as a dissident while a young man. When he was 21 years old, he and companion Jacques Michel were warned by the Nova Scotia Council to stop associating with Indians and militant French missionaries.

A general proclamation forbidding Acadians to entertain Mi'kmaqs was issued in 1722. When the Battle of Mines took place in early 1747, Beausoleil assisted French colonial troops who were fighting the British. Because of these activities to provision the French, Governor Shirley declared Beausoleil and 11 other Acadian men "outlaws" and offered a reward of 50 pounds sterling each for their capture.

Beausoleil and his clan of rebel Broussards continued to terrorize the British using guerilla tactics they learned from the Mi'kmaq. In spring of 1754, 20 English settlers were brought to farmlands east of Dartmouth, given protection by 200 British regulars and rangers. Despite defensive buildings and a picketed perimeter, they were raided by natives led by Beausoleil. Four settlers and three soldiers were killed and scalped. Along with raids on land, Beausoleil led a fleet of privateers making raids on coastal shipping. These attacks earned him the epithet "An indefatigable foe of the British."

A number of Beausoleil's actions in 1755 were documented by French and British soldiers. During June 1755, he engaged in skirmishes against English troops and captured a British officer. A flag of truce raised at Fort Beauséjour informed the British camp of this capture, and Beausoleil was given safe conduct to negotiate return of the officer. He met with Colonel Monckton and proposed that he would act as mediator between the British and natives in exchange for amnesty. Monckton agreed contingent on later approval of Governor Lawrence.

Although Alexandre was considered an equal leader among the Acadian resistance, the British identified Joseph as leader. Beausoleil was known as an excellent marksman and inventive strategist. The harassment delivered by his forces was so effective that British troops at Fort Cumberland were afraid to leave its protective walls. By one report, "They lurked around the forts of the Isthmus, killing any soldiers who strayed beyond the safety of the posts and they were always ready to attack foraging parties. The guerilla bands moved swiftly from one place to another, keeping the British in a state of uncertainty as to when and where the next attack would occur."[30]

Peace did not come to the Isthmus of Chignecto with the Acadian expulsion. In February of 1756, Boishébert and his band, including Beausoleil, were reportedly at Shediac. When the British arrived, they found no one. But as they returned to Fort Cumberland, they were waylaid by the Resistance, and several soldiers were killed. Not much later, Resistance fighters burned two schooners at Baie Verte, killed seven British, and took one prisoner. British parties searching for Resistance fighters were afraid to light campfires lest they give away their position; many suffered frozen feet.

The commander at Halifax wrote, "These people are Spirited up in their obstinacy by one *Beausoleil* an Acadian, and two or three others who have already rendered themselves obnoxious to the English that they are conscious of the treatment they deserve at our hands..."[31]

In November of 1758, Commander George Scott was sent to "lay waste" to the Petitcodiac region. His men burned all Acadian villages, killed and scalped many, including women and children, in response to bounties offered by the government. During one guerilla encounter, Beausoleil was wounded in the foot. The wound was serious enough for him to take refuge on the French side of the Miramichi River to recuperate. The British repeatedly attempted to kill or capture Beausoleil but were not successful.

Fort Louisbourg, the last French stronghold in the Maritimes, was captured by the British in July 1758. This delivered a mortal blow to the campaigns of French colonials and Acadian Resistance. The fort was their source for acquiring arms and ammunition and supplies for subsistence. At some point in 1758, the Acadian insurgents realized that all hope for victory appeared lost. The harsh winter took a serious toll among British and Acadians alike. By March 1759, provisions were scarce, and many soldiers and captives died from exposure and starvation. As ice melted on the bays, a sloop which had been frozen in the basin all winter was able to break loose and sail to Boston for supplies. By April, flocks of fowl returned to nesting grounds on the marshes, providing a supply of fresh meat. Small numbers of Indians and Acadians gathered around the fort.

The British governor at Fort Louisbourg offered amnesty to the Acadian insurgents in October 1759. However, this was a ploy for capturing them, as revealed in a letter the governor wrote to Lawrence, and they were not fooled. The last French stronghold in Canada, Quebec, fell to the British; most Acadians realized that continued resistance was futile. On November 16, 1759, Beausoleil, Alexandre, Simon Martin, and Jean Basque, who were the elected delegates for 190 Acadians in the Petitcodiac and Memramcook regions, arrived at Fort Cumberland to give unconditional surrender and beg provisions for their starving comrades. Eight days later, delegates of 700 Acadians at Miramichi, Richibouctou, and Bouctouche arrived at the fort with the same submissions. Colonel Frye, Fort Cumberland commandant, accepted the surrender and agreed to provide support. Beausoleil left Alexandre as hostage and returned to assemble the rest of his followers. But he foresaw British intentions to deport everyone and left with a few remaining insurgents to join Boishébert's camp at Petit-Rochelle.

Time had run out for the Acadian and French colonial resistance. They finally surrendered to British forces in July 1760, at the mouth of the Restigouche River. By 1760, nearly all Acadian insurgents, an estimated 900 men, were imprisoned at Fort Cumberland. The able-bodied members were compelled to march to Halifax in early summer 1760, where they were held in open barracks. Those considered most dangerous, such as Beausoleil and other leaders, were imprisoned behind the palisades of Georges Island.

Beausoleil Broussard, his brothers, sons, nephews, and many other Acadian insurgents paid dearly for their years of resistance. Both Beausoleil and Alexandre lost their mother and most children. They lost their villages, homes, and abundant way of life. They lost their motherland, the only place they knew. Jean-Baptiste Broussard, Beausoleil's brother, refused to surrender, setting out on foot with his family in 1760 for Quebec. They struggled in the dead of winter across New Brunswick and into Quebec, facing extreme suffering and digging graves along the way for his wife, two children, and mother-in-law. Only Jean-Baptiste, one son, and one daughter survived the trek. Tragically, Quebec was in British hands when they arrived.

In 1763, Beausoleil was confined under highest level of security in Georges Island prison. Life was difficult for the prisoners; their warm clothing was taken away, and many became ill from malnutrition and exposure. Other Acadians living in barracks were put to work helping on farms they had formerly owned. The British settlers who had taken over the farms could not operate the complex *aboiteaux* system; the Acadian detainees had to rebuild dikes that had fallen into disrepair during the war. The government did allow the Acadians to earn wages for this work, enabling them to procure better rations and save money for future needs. After the Treaty of Paris ended the war, Beausoleil wrote a letter to the Halifax Council on August 18, 1763, requesting that the Acadians be allowed to depart from Nova Scotia to French-held land. There were approximately 1,019 Acadians wanting to leave, and the British made sure they would not settle too close by. They considered Beausoleil and his cadre continuing threats and did not want them as close as Quebec.

Led by Beausoleil, more than 600 Acadians used funds they had accumulated, plus what they earned by selling their possessions, to hire ships for emigration to other lands. Initially, they planned to sail to the French Antilles but heard frightening reports of maltreatment by French authorities and high death tolls from malnutrition and tropical diseases. Next they developed an ambitious scheme to join their cousins and friends in Quebec by sailing to New Orleans, then up the Mississippi River to Canada. Another option was to form a major Acadian settlement in Illinois. They left in two groups, the first in December 1764, and the next in spring of 1765.

These two groups included most of Beausoleil and Alexandre's families and cousins. Nearly all members of the groups were related, by either blood or association, to the Broussards and the Thibodeaus. Among the first group leaving in November 1764, were **Joseph Bourgeois, Jr.**, of Chignecto, age 29, with his wife Marie Girouard, age 27, and 2-year-old daughter Marie. Two younger, unmarried Bourgeois brothers accompanied them, Michel, age 24, and Pierre, age 20. In the next group leaving in 1765 was **Paul Bourgeois, Jr.**, also of Chignecto, brother of Joseph. These Bourgeois brothers were relatives of **Marie-Anne Bujol** *née* **LeBlanc**; her second cousins once removed. Marie-Anne's mother, Jeanne Anne LeBlanc *née* Bourgeois, was first cousin to the grandfather of Joseph and Paul, Claude Bourgeois, Sr.

After a brief stop at St. Domingue, where a few Acadians already there joined them, Beausoleil's group chartered another ship for the trip to the Mississippi valley, arriving at New Orleans on February 28, 1765. They were destitute, with little more than what they were wearing, plus some paper money from Nova Scotia that France was supposed to make good. However, France had failed to send supplies, and information about English fortifications and Indian hostility in the Illinois area discouraged plans to continue there. The French colonial government, though strapped for funds, did provide for these 58 Acadian families and welcomed Beausoleil as a hero. Finding this warm welcome, the group decided to stay in Louisiana. At first officials wanted to settle them near New Orleans, but frequent river floods and dense hardwood forest deterred the settlers. A few went to join other exiles who had settled upriver at St. James Parish. Most of the group, including Alexandre and Beausoleil, were authorized to migrate to meadowlands at Attakapas, near present-day St. Martinville in Southwest Louisiana.

Beausoleil, Alexandre, and their families settled in the meadows that came to be known as "French Prairie" and began ranching, with small side farms. By April 1765, 58-60 families of 231 people were in Attakapas and Opelousas Districts. Though they faced many difficulties, including problems with natives, the Acadians quickly prospered in their new homeland. By the 1780s, Broussard family land holdings extended from St. Martinville to Bayou Vermilion, and 235 cattle brands were registered in their name. Also in April 1765, the Spanish governor Charles Aubry issued a special commission naming Beausoleil as "Captain of the Militia and Commandant of the Acadians of the Attakapas."[32]

The two Broussard leaders, who conducted their families and confrères to a new home where they could thrive, did not have much time to enjoy their accomplishment. A severe epidemic of yellow fever spread through the Attakapas region in fall 1765. Many deaths occurred; it is uncertain when the brothers fell to the disease. Church records are not clear; it seems likely that Alexandre died on September 18, 1765, and that Joseph Beausoleil died on October 20, 1765. Recent investigations by Broussard descendants indicate that Beausoleil was buried at Fausse Pointe by Bayou Teche, and that Alexandre is probably buried in the Belle Place area south of Loreauville.[33]

The struggles and sacrifice of Beausoleil did have one lasting outcome: he led the way for an exodus of his people to Louisiana. His contingent was one of the earliest to settle in these new lands, setting an example and extending threads of hope. The path for preserving their beloved Acadian culture was forged by Beausoleil's strong determination, courage, and unwavering resolve.

Beausoleil Broussard
Joseph Broussard *dit* Beausoleil in Acadia   Oils on canvas,
original artwork by Herb Roe, 2009 Wikimedia Commons License
link: https://creativecommons.org/licenses/by-sa/4.0

CHAPTER 7

From Maryland to Louisiana

Marguerite Bujol (Bijeaud) (1751-1805) –
Juan Francisco Vicente Vives (1751-1822)

⚜

When Joseph Bujol and Anne-Marie LeBlanc were deported from Grand Pré on October 13, 1755, their daughter Marguerite was 4 years old and their son Augustin was 2. Anne-Marie was pregnant with their third child, worried that she might give birth during the months at sea. The Acadian exiles probably did not know that the ship was bound for Maryland. The months between late summer 1755, when they became aware that the British were up to something, and October when they were deported, were filled with confusion and anxiety. In the chaos of boarding Acadian families, with the men already on board scrambling to find their own, many families were separated. The Acadians were allowed to bring only clothing, a few portable household items, and food for the voyage. They stuffed as much as possible into bundles, but still were poorly provisioned.

The British were not forthcoming about where their captives were going or whether all ships departing Grand Pré were going to the same places. Added to the shattering loss of their homes and motherland was the fear that they might never see relatives and friends again. It is hard to imagine the state of mind, the despair, anger, and hopelessness that most Acadians must have felt. They were confined to below decks in large rooms without portholes, meant for storing merchandise. Several hundred exiles were packed into these dark, tight quarters, sometimes so densely that one recalled, "... we were so crowded on the transport vessels, that we had not room even for all our bodies to lay down at once."[1]

Most brought some type of bedding, even if only blankets or coats. They probably had no way to cook and ate whatever dried fruit or meat they brought. Soon food ran short and most went hungry, leading to malnutrition and disease. Hygiene was impossible; they had no way to wash themselves or their clothes and had to use chamber pots in a closely confined environment. Many became seasick and added vomiting to the excrement. The stench was horrendous.

Diseases spread, particularly fevers, typhus, and even smallpox, and quite a number of Acadians died during the sea voyage. This made the British sailors even more reluctant to have contact with them, so provisions were further reduced, and probably no exiles were allowed on deck. The first Acadian exiles arrived at Annapolis, Maryland, the provincial capital, around November 20-30, 1755. These 913 exiles had spent over a month aboard four seriously overcrowded ships and had consumed all of their provisions en route. Of this group, 493 were from Pisiquid and 420 from Grand Pré.

Little Marguerite Bujol looked around with her 4-year-old eyes and must have been totally disoriented by what she saw inside the transport ship hold. She was among her people, with her mother, father, and brother beside her, but their lives were radically changed. Much time was spent in darkness, in a huge wooden thing that heaved and bucked, groaned and creaked, as if it was going to break apart at any minute. Sailing the North Atlantic coast during winter months was guaranteed to offer frequent gales and storms. She heard scary sounds, wind howling and water crashing, if she could even identify these things. Probably she asked her mother Anne-Marie what caused the noise and sickening movements; she likely did not understand the answers, having no concept of a ship or an ocean.

Marguerite was hungry all the time—that is, when she was not nauseated and vomiting. Her brother cried lots and clung to their mother. But Anne-Marie had her own difficulties; she was nauseous and dizzy, suffering chills and fevers and diarrhea along with the other exiles. Through a fevered haze, she doubted that her unborn baby would survive the journey. Joseph tried his best to comfort his wife and children, to find scraps of food when they could eat, and especially to get water for them, even if fetid.

That the majority survived under these dreadful conditions is testimony to their good health and resilience. The Acadians were known for strong constitutions, along with stubbornness and unflagging loyalty to their religion and mother country. Beyond doubt they prayed frequently, both individually and collectively, during this ordeal. When someone died, the body was sewed into a blanket for disposal overboard. One of the elder men performed Catholic last rites; even if done by a layman they believed it was enough to save the soul from eternal damnation.

Annapolis was compelled to provide immediate support for these unexpected, and unwanted, guests. The Provincial Council would not allow the Acadians to disembark, and there was a furor over how to handle this burden. The *Maryland Gazette*, Annapolis' newspaper, reported: "While they have lain in this Port, the Town has been at considerable charge in supporting them, as they appear very needy, and quite exhausted in Provisions; and it cannot be expected that the charge or Burden of maintaining such a Multitude can be supported by the Inhabitants of Annapolis... it will be necessary soon to disperse them to different Parts of the Province."[2]

And dispersed they were. The Council adopted a resolution to partition the exiles among the Maryland counties; sending one ship to the Patuxent River, one to the Choptank River, and a third to the Wicomico River, where they would await orders from the governor. The fourth ship remained at Annapolis. The Acadians were understandably eager to leave their unhealthy, confined quarters, but the circumstances they were to face on land were equally challenging in other ways.

They had arrived at a particularly inopportune time in the Atlantic seaboard colonies. Maryland, along with all the others, was inflamed by anti-Catholic sentiment and rampant Francophobia. One might think that Maryland, established as a refuge for persecuted English Catholics, would be sympathetic. But the majority Protestant population hated the "papists" and went so far as to legally forbid Maryland Catholics from helping the exiles. Suspicion ran high against any French person, because England was now at war with France, and the colonies were threatened on their western borders by French troops and their Indian allies. Maryland residents saw the Acadians as French-speaking prisoners of war, detained in their colony which was vulnerable to French attack. They feared the Acadians would escape and join French troops. Recently the British had faced military reverses in the Appalachian Mountains, fueling the colonists' fears. Thus, the Acadians became a scapegoat for the fear, frustration, and vulnerability that was pervasive in Maryland at the time.

The Acadians actually did consider themselves prisoners of war. The Provincial government, however, saw them as British subjects who were merely immigrants. As such, they did not merit special assistance. The Acadians insisted they had been expelled from their homeland by force of arms, making them prisoners of war; therefore, they were wards of the state. One contemporary observer wrote to Maryland Governor Horatio Sharpe that the Acadians at Annapolis "... were treated as prisoners of war by Governor Lawrence (of Nova Scotia)... (so feel) duty bound to declare themselves prisoners, but also in that character to be entitled to better treatment than they have met with as faithful subjects."[3]

The Maryland government, however, rejected that claim and forced the exiles to fend for themselves. Failing to get public assistance, many faced dire circumstances if they were not fortunate enough to get help from private philanthropy. One group of Acadians was forced to huddle together without shelter or warmth in the countryside for several days. It was winter, and the ground was frozen and snow covered. Some Acadians were taken in by Protestants out of compassion, but because they needed so many basic services—food, clothing, shelter, medical care—this created a heavy financial burden. These Good Samaritans soon reached the limits of their philanthropy and had to abandon their wards. A few Acadian families did find long-term residence in private homes, usually in exchange for household or business services. Others were compelled to accept low-paying and degrading jobs, reluctantly offered by wary Protestants.

One example from Baltimore illustrates this experience well. In December 1755, a Baltimore resident named Andrew Stygar took in several Acadians, carting them from dock to his home and maintaining them for 11 days. After this, it became too expensive for Stygar, and he turned them out. Most of these Acadians gathered in an unfinished abandoned house and tried to make the best of it. Shunned by the local population, they drew upon their own abilities, finding work on small fishing vessels as sailors or as longshoremen. Many women took positions as domestics or cooks. After a few years, many Acadians moved into huts of mud and mortar that they built on lots along South Charles Street in Baltimore, the French District.

Economic opportunities differed according to which region of Maryland the Acadians occupied. Those exiled to tobacco plantations generally had to work as field hands alongside black enslaved people. Those debilitated by age, disease, or malnutrition were driven to beg for subsistence. At Oxford, a local tobacco farmer named Henry Callister, who had staunchly supported the Acadian dispersal, responded with humanitarian assistance. He drafted a petition for relief in December 1755, sent to King George III, because the poor wretches had been there three weeks "... and nothing has been done for them by the public... few have charity on them. I see no one interested for them but myself... There's a number of them now about me in tears, craving relief for their sick..."[4]

Callister also provided the Acadians with monetary assistance so they could buy badly needed clothing and provisions at a local store. He managed to find a place for almost all the families during the winter in Oxford private houses and sent over 60 exiles at personal expense to stay in homes in the Wye River area. But Callister's kindness did not go unopposed. Colonel Edward Lloyd, a prominent local planter, despised Catholicism and feared threats to security. Criticizing Callister, Lloyd believed the Acadians were so attached to the French king that they would incite the black enslaved people to revolt and join French forces.

Lloyd's sentiments reflected the prevailing Maryland attitude toward the Acadian exiles. Most Maryland Protestants stood aside and allowed the "papists" to die of exposure and malnutrition. The Maryland provincial government also closed its eyes to the Acadians' plight. Governor Sharpe asked the legislature to provide support as they judged proper and got little interest. He then coupled this plea with a bill to reduce the Acadians' freedom of movement with stringent penalties if they left the county. This was meant to prevent them from joining French forces. British troops were under orders to "destroy without hesitation" any Acadians seen in the western boundaries of the province.

The exiles, characterized as "insolent and obstinate," were required to provide for their subsistence using their own labor and industry. However, there were few employment opportunities, and the Acadians lacked marketable skills for the local economy. Any able-bodied Acadians found loitering around, wandering, or refusing to work would be incarcerated until they showed desire to work. If parents were incapable of supporting their children, no matter the reason, county magistrates were empowered to "bind out" their children to local farmers and artisans.

Keeping their families together, preserving their close-knit kinship culture, and maintaining their religious and cultural beliefs were primary values of the Acadians. Over the years, they saw their children gradually learning English and becoming more integrated into Protestant society. The vast majority of Acadians existed at the poverty level, with high rates of disease and mortality. Although a few humanitarians in Baltimore, Annapolis, and Oxford gave assistance to small numbers of families, most were destitute and "... cannot feed themselves, they cannot find Houses, Clothing, and other Comforts, in their Condition needful, without going from House to House Begging, whereby they are become a Nuisance."[5]

The Acadian population in Maryland shrunk from 913 in December 1755, to a low of 667 in 1763, when the Seven Years' War ended. As the Acadian leaders sensed that their group's cultural identity was being rapidly undermined, their hopes for repatriation waned as England appeared to be winning the war. The Treaty of Paris (1763) offered new possibilities. In the treaty negotiations, the French minister sought release of Acadians incarcerated in England, promising French King Louis XV's protection. Copies of this document were smuggled to the colonies, prompting an immediate response from Maryland Acadians. They expressed their fervent longing for "deliverance," and although the British government agreed to permit them to leave for any French possession within 18 months, they lacked means to travel.

Initially the Maryland Acadians wanted to return to Canada, but it was now under British control, and return to Nova Scotia was not an option. The Maryland legislature refused to finance their voyage, and British Canadian officials were opposed to Acadian repatriation. The Acadians knew about experiences of other Acadian groups who went to the French Antilles, where the climate was notoriously unhealthy and the plantation economy offered little opportunity for economic independence. Their best option appeared to be Louisiana; they had received letters from relatives in the Broussard group urging them to relocate to the lower Mississippi Valley.

By the mid-1760s, Maryland colonists were anxious to see the Acadians depart. They had been taxed to support destitute Acadians, burdened by begging, and worried about insurgency for years. A similar situation existed in Pennsylvania, where the Acadians suffered even more and the colonists wanted to be rid of them. The colonial governments of these two provinces agreed to facilitate departure of the problematic exiles, so assisted them to charter ships for Louisiana. Local governments gave subsidies to widows and those with large families. Additionally, the Acadians pooled their resources, selling anything of value to secure passage and escape a life of persecution and poverty.

Between 1766 and 1770, approximately 90 percent of Acadians in Maryland and Pennsylvania went in waves of emigration to New Orleans. At least 782 Acadians from these two British colonies boarded English merchantmen ships at Chesapeake Bay ports, bound for a new life in Louisiana.

Acadians in Other Atlantic Colonies. Similar experiences befell Acadians sent to other English seaboard colonies. Almost all exiles arrived in poor health, stricken by epidemics of typhus and smallpox. Their former robust health deteriorated due to overcrowding, poor diet, seasickness, and stress during the stormy ocean voyage. They arrived mostly unannounced at colonial seaports designated by Lt. Governor Charles Lawrence. The stunned colonial officials were reluctant hosts, wary of these destitute, sick, and decidedly hostile Acadians now in their charge. Officials lacked instructions from British authorities about how to handle the exiles and viewed them as a potential "fifth column" that might join French forces fighting along the western borders. For months, local newspapers had been filled with anti-French propaganda, due to fear roused by early skirmishes of the Seven Years' War.

Virginia flatly refused to accept the 1,500 Acadian exiles sent to this Southern colony. The ship was immediately dispatched to England at Virginia's expense, where the exiles remained in coastal detention centers for the duration of the Seven Years' War (1756-1763).

Georgia at first rejected and then ignored the 400 exiles dumped on its shores in December 1755. The government only recognized their existence when they petitioned for emergency assistance in January 1756. Those Acadians too ill to support themselves were given a week's supply of rice. Their relative independence permitted some Acadians to escape, sailing in March of 1756 for Nova Scotia. But their ships were not seaworthy, and they landed in Massachusetts Bay four months later, reduced to less than half of the 200 original voyagers. British authorities arrested and detained them. Few of the Acadians remaining in Georgia obtained work; most existed in poverty. When the Seven Years' War ended, they took advantage of the 18-month window for leaving British colonies and migrated to French St. Domingue. Few survived this disease-ridden climate where they were forced into work as laborers on sugar plantations.

South Carolina received 942 exiles between November 1755 and late January 1756. The Protestant population was distressed by these "bigoted Papists," whom they feared would incite local enslaved people to rebellion or join French-allied Indians. Initially sequestered along the beaches, many exiles attempted escape into the interior, but the government pursued them and recaptured most. A few managed to elude capture, but only two Acadians are known to have arrived at Fort Duquesne, the French stronghold in the Ohio Valley. The fate of the others is unknown.

Eager to be rid of these unruly captives, the colonial government funded two ancient vessels with poor provisions, in which a large number of Acadians set sail for Nova Scotia. Their leaky ships took water, and they landed twice on beaches in Virginia and Maryland. After repairing the ships, they finished the voyage to the St. John River in

Nova Scotia. Many male survivors joined Lt. Charles de Boishébert's small French force and waged guerilla warfare against the British. This courageous example inspired both hope for Acadians and repercussions by colonial officials. Acadian families were divided and forcibly distributed throughout coastal counties. Teenage boys were bound out as indentured farm laborers or apprenticed to artisans. Many had to be put in irons and carried from their families. This cruelty drove remaining Acadians in South Carolina to surreptitiously sail to St. Domingue or the Bay of Fundy.

Pennsylvania mirrored Maryland in its treatment of Acadian exiles. In November 1755, 454 Acadians were treated with hostility. They became scapegoats for the colony's raging Francophobia, fed by successful French and Indian raids on the western borders. The Acadians were quarantined for four months on Province Island and then dispersed throughout the easternmost provinces. Farmers were given 10 pounds' worth of agricultural implements, while those incapable of supporting themselves were placed on the dole for one year. After that, the Acadians were supposed to be self-sufficient. But most rural townships objected, while most Acadians refused to be separated from families. The exiles congregated in slums of Philadelphia, where they remained in poverty. Although they tried to support themselves making wooden shoes and cloth from rags, there was no market. Starving and desperate, many resorted to petty thievery. Attempting to solve the problem, the legislature passed a bill in 1757 requiring Acadian children to apprentice with Anglo-American artisans and be educated in the English language; the ill, aged, and infirm would receive government support. This drew adamant protest from the Acadians, who saw it as an effort to destroy their families and assimilate their children. They sought permission to leave but were ignored. Some outspoken leaders threatened to join French forces; they were arrested and shipped to England, though subsequently returned. In 1761, renewed efforts to bind out Acadian children led to a petition to King George, seeking redress of their grievances against the Pennsylvania government.

After describing previous agreements with British crown and officials, and the misery and tribulation of their stay in Philadelphia, the petition concluded: "We therefore hereby implore your gracious protection, and request you may be pleased to let the justice of our complaints be truly and impartially inquired into, and that Your Majesty would please to grant us such relief, as in your justice and clemency you think our case requires..."[6] Although nothing came of the petition at the time, it became a major document in the

20th-century British Royal Proclamation (2003), in which Queen Elizabeth II symbolically apologized for her country's treatment of the Acadians.

In 1763, Pennsylvania Acadians tried to migrate to France, but when this did not work, many went to St. Domingue and met the same fate as others before. The majority who remained near Philadelphia joined their confrères in Maryland in a massive migration to Louisiana.

New York reluctantly accepted three contingents of Acadians between 1755 and 1756; two were from Cape Sable and Annapolis Royal. The third group was from Georgia en route to Nova Scotia. The colonial legislature successfully dispersed the exiles in those counties farthest from French Canada: Long Island and Staten Island. Many Acadians were indentured to Anglo-Americans; a substantial number of these escaped but were captured and imprisoned. Subsequently, they endured captivity until the Seven Years' War ended. Most then left for St. Domingue and a sad fate. Twenty Acadians from this colony were more fortunate, making their way to Mobile and on to Louisiana in early 1764.

Connecticut enacted legislation to distribute Acadians among 50 designated towns, directing town leaders to keep nuclear families together. Public assistance was provided for indigent or handicapped, and strict control kept over movement of able-bodied men. In January 1756, 277 exiles arrived from Annapolis Royal, followed the next day by 173 from Mines Basin. Four months later, 260 arrived after being driven off course by a storm, originally destined for New York. Their movements were severely restricted, and they were very dissatisfied. Over 90% petitioned the French king in 1763 for transportation to France. When this did not materialize, some went to St. Domingue. In 1767, 230 Acadians pooled resources and chartered a merchantman vessel, sailing for Quebec or the St. John River in New Brunswick. A handful remained permanently in Connecticut.

Massachusetts conditions were generally no worse than other Atlantic seaboard colonies, though it is viewed as the darkest place of the Acadian Diaspora. Governor Shirley had conspired with Lawrence to deport the Acadians, and initially large numbers were sent to Massachusetts Bay, perhaps as many as 2,000. But most were destined for other colonies and stayed only long enough for their ships to be refitted. Massachusetts is listed as receiving 735 permanent exiles starting November 1755, primarily from Mines Basin. In 1756, these were joined by 90 Georgia escapees who were arrested and detained when they landed in Boston. Like the other colonial governments, Boston's primary concern was distributing and controlling the Acadians, not their welfare. Sent to country towns, Acadians were given farming and weaving implements and their children indentured, causing an outcry from their leaders. The policy was modified to prohibit dividing families except for dire circumstances. Acadian men had freedom of movement initially, and some left for Quebec or St. John River, or got work as sailors. Then, laws were passed confining them to town limits. After 1763, restrictions loosened, and 300 Acadians left for St. Domingue, while hundreds of others found their way to Quebec and the islands of St. Pierre and Miquelon near Newfoundland. In 1766, the remaining Acadians sought resettlement in Canada, which the weary Massachusetts government approved. Required to take an oath of allegiance to Britain, around 900 Acadians agreed and went to Quebec, either overland or by sea. A smaller group made a four-month trek through Maine, returning to their homeland in Nova Scotia. They found their farms occupied by over 12,000 former New Englanders. Most Acadians chose to move on and settle in the Petit Codiac River Valley, New Brunswick, which had not been occupied.

Nova Scotia, New Brunswick, and Maritimes. Acadians who had remained in their homelands, joined by returning exiles from New England, established numerous settlements in the northern and western extremes of Nova Scotia in 1763-1767: around Halifax, Strait of Canso, Baie St.-Marie, Baie des Chaleurs, Tousquet and Pobomcoup. Refugees returning from St. Pierre and Miquelon established settlements on Cape Breton Island, Chéticamp and Margaree areas. Hundreds of Acadians had escaped deportation by going to Île St.-Jean (Prince Edward Island), though after the fall of Louisbourg many were deported to France. Others went to join settlements near present-day Memramcook, Petit Codiac, and Miramichi along the northern New Brunswick coast. A small number of Acadians remained in the St. John River Valley, their presence formally authorized in 1767 after taking an unconditional oath of allegiance.

Enough Acadians remained in these areas to maintain the viability of the settlements, though beleaguered by war and displacement. In 1764, the British government sanctioned their presence. This group provided the foundation for rebuilding Acadian society in northern New Brunswick. They numbered nearly 4,000 by 1803.[7]

England and France. In 1763, it was recorded that 3,400 Acadians were in exile in France and 688 in England. Theirs were not happy experiences; kept in prisons in England until sent on to France, facing rejection and poverty in France. Various attempts were made in France to resettle Acadians from seaports to interior farmlands, but these independent pioneers would not retrofit into a feudal system. Many were eventually sent on to French colonies in **Cayenne, French Guiana** (1763-1765), and the **Falkland Islands** (1764-1765).

Thousands of Acadians remaining in France were increasingly disillusioned with failed resettlement attempts and government-sponsored colonization schemes. When first approached about migrating to Louisiana in 1783-1784, they were resistant. Louisiana had become a Spanish colony in 1763, and the French government refused to subsidize the voyage. The Spanish government, however, was eager to have French Catholic Acadians to bolster their small population in the large and militarily vulnerable colony. Through a series of negotiations involving Acadian cobbler Olivier Terrio (Theriot) and French soldier of fortune Henri Peyroux, an accord was reached between France and Spain. In late 1784, over 1,500 Acadians (70% of those still in France) volunteered to leave for Louisiana on ships paid for by the Spanish government. By May 1785, a total of 1,595 Acadians left France aboard seven ships and sailed to New Orleans.[8]

Ten Years in Maryland

Marguerite Bujol and her family lived for 10 years in Maryland. They had arrived in November 1755, on one of the four ships bringing Grand Pré Acadians to the colony. They left Maryland in early January 1766 when they boarded an English merchant schooner provided by the government, along with 40-50 other families. During that decade in the colony, the Bujols lived in Oxford, a town in Talbot County on the Tred Avon River. They were likely among the fortunate exiles taken in by kindly people and perhaps found ways to earn a living through their hosts.

Marie-Anne LeBlanc Bujol, Marguerite's mother, gave birth to her third child in 1755, named Félicité. The birth took place in late November or early December, shortly after the family arrived in Maryland. Since both mother and baby survived, they must have been sheltered and provided with the necessary care. Mothers who gave birth in makeshift housing, or outside in the wintry cold, and their babies would not fare so well. While residing in Oxford, the Bujols had two more children, Anne born circa 1757, and Marie-Magdeleine born in 1765. Their last child, Joseph Paul, was born after they arrived in Louisiana; his birth was registered in 1769 in Pointe Coupée, a community founded by early French colonists on the Mississippi River in the 1720s. Point Coupée had a Catholic Church, St. Francis of Assisi that served river Acadian settlements.

Life in Oxford was quite different than Grand Pré, although Marguerite probably had few memories for comparison. Her parents might have remarked how buildings were made of bricks or clapboards here, instead of logs. Homes sat flush with the ground and were crowded closely together with small yards. Instead of the one large communal room of Acadian homes, these homes had many rooms, each used for different activities—cooking, eating, sleeping, washing, and gathering took place in particular rooms. Many homes had multiple stories and upstairs bedrooms. In Acadian homes, attics were used for sleeping quarters of older children and for storage, but were not true upstairs rooms. Some of the finer Maryland homes had separate structures for cooking, storage, and washing.

The noise level within towns, even small ones like Oxford, would be jarring to the Acadians. In Grand Pré their homes were widely separated, situated on farmland with pastures. Their homes were a considerable distance apart; it took several minutes to go from one Acadian home to another, even if running. The quiet of dawn and dusk, the soothing sounds of breezes, creeks, cornstalks rustling, and farm animals would have been sorely missed. Added to the Maryland town's cacophony were the harsh cadences of the English language. It was comforting for the Acadians to converse in the fluid, soft sounds of French, and many never learned English. Marguerite and her siblings, however, most likely learned to speak English. They were exposed to it from their earliest years, when children learn languages easily. Perhaps the Bujol children were even sent to school; possible when Acadian families were living in supportive homes.

The two oldest children, Marguerite and Augustin, were 15 and 13 years old respectively when they left Maryland. They had mingled with Anglo-Protestant society throughout their growing up years, probably spoke English well, and might have been able to read and write. It is ironic that these Acadian children would be capable of reading and writing English but would not have the same competency with French. Their bilingual abilities were no doubt useful to the family; one can imagine them translating for their mother or father during market transactions or interactions with officials or visitors.

René LeBlanc was among the Acadian community leaders in Oxford; he may have been related to Marie-Anne. He negotiated with Maryland officials to secure permission for the Acadians to leave after the Seven Years' War ended. He was also in correspondence with Beausoleil Broussard about the Attakapas settlement and positive treatment received in Louisiana. He reassured his people that they would be accepted as equals in the Francophone community there. Louisiana was a French Catholic colony, even though changing hands from France to Spain around that time. They would be able to openly practice their faith and freely speak their language. They would no longer be humiliated simply for being Acadian. They could establish themselves as free people with land holdings, becoming self-sufficient once again.

Each family was advised to prepare for the voyage, which was set for January 1766. Hopes were high that families would be reunited with loved ones, now separated and at unknown locales due to *Le Grand Dérangement*. Many who had accumulated possessions over the decade decided to sell almost everything to help pay for passage and reduce baggage. Over several months, women and girls dried meat and fruit to sustain their families during the journey. They sewed and knitted incessantly, making quilts and blankets from fabric scraps, and clothing, socks, and sweaters from wool. They made bundles of household necessities such as soap, salt, candles, knives and spoons, coal for cooking, small bowls and pots, and personal care items. Precious things full of memories from their former life at Grand Pré, such as ribbons or pendants, were tucked safely away.

Around January 2, 1766, about 30 people set out from areas of Oxford, Town Creek, and Snow Hill and walked, carrying their bundles to the wharf on the Tred Avon River. They were joined by other Acadians who had settled in the regions of the Chesapeake Bay Coast in Worcester and Somerset counties. This group of about 40 families was pleasantly surprised to see friends and relations with whom they had lost touch. They waited a day or two in the port, as other families straggled in, carrying sacks and trunks filled with provisions. Families remained together as ferries took about 50 people at a time to the waiting ship. A merchant ship named *Elizabeth* had been chartered for this group departing from Maryland. The passengers stayed aboard the ship in Chesapeake Bay for several days awaiting favorable winds, finally sailing out into the Atlantic Ocean around January 8, 1766. The voyage to New Orleans, Louisiana, would take around three months.

Voyage to New Orleans

Conditions on the merchant ship *Elizabeth* were better than those on the Acadians' first sea voyage from their homeland. Their quarters below deck were still crowded, but they tried to give each other a little privacy. Each family set up a space with bedding and their possessions, but there was no way to hang curtains or form compartments in the long, open cargo space. As the ship set sail on the Atlantic Ocean, nearly everyone in the hold became seasick. The malodorous, dank hold contributed to illness, including fevers and diarrhea. They used chamber pots and emptied them through a deck opening, but they had no way to bathe or wash clothes effectively. Small pots holding coals were the best they could do for cooking; water and bouillon were urged on sick family members to keep them hydrated. When able to keep food down, they had salted meat and dried bread, along with dried fruit they brought aboard. During the voyage, several passengers died from illness and malnutrition. They were buried at sea, bodies sewn into blankets after lay-performed last rites, perhaps with a favorite trinket to accompany them into the depths.

Months of sailing on the open ocean without land in sight must have led to tedium. Children would invent games, as they do everywhere, playing hide and seek or searching for hidden objects such as mittens or scarves. They were allowed on deck when the weather was good and met members of the crew. Perhaps some unlikely friendships formed between Acadian children and young sailors. But storms were frequent in the wintry Atlantic, sending everyone below as the ship tossed and creaked in buffeting winds and crashing waves. The *Elizabeth* was forced to spend several days in Charles Town Harbor, South Carolina, waiting out a storm. Passengers below deck remained in dank darkness, wet and cold to their bones, struggling with seasickness and illness, listening to the pounding waves and creaking boards.

Their dream of warm, hospitable Louisiana, where their families could reunite and their culture be restored, kept them going. They believed they could take charge of their own futures and stop being pawns in the power struggles of England and France. When weather improved, the ship continued its voyage across deep blue seas, shimmering in bright sunshine. Warm days passed to be replaced by yet another chilling storm. Winds had their benefit, however, pushing the ship rapidly through the ocean and around the tip of Florida, where it entered the Gulf of Mexico. Although the water did not look different, the Acadians felt the warmth and softer tropical breezes as they approached Louisiana.

Fifteen-year-old Marguerite might have experienced sadness leaving the helpful family who hosted them in Maryland. She probably had friends among Maryland children, especially if she attended school. Maryland was really the only home she remembered, but the stories of Acadian suffering and hopes held for their new home in Louisiana would keep her anticipating the future. She was fortunate that none of her family members sickened and died on the voyage. Their life on a ship, spending three months sailing across vast oceans, offered many new experiences for her. Once in the Gulf of Mexico, she would have spotted porpoises leaping in the ship's wake and frigate birds soaring overhead. Exploring the ship with its masts, ropes, barrels, and sails would provide much of interest. She probably saw some spectacular sunsets, as changing shades of orange and yellow slowly faded into pink, deepening into purple. When she heard the cries of seagulls and saw them circling the masts, she knew land was not far away.

At last she sighted a dark, flat line on the horizon—Louisiana was in sight. As the ship approached shore, she could see grassy swampland, gray-green and lush, as they entered the Mississippi River Delta. Tall reeds rustled, gnarled tree limbs waved welcome, and numerous shore birds balanced on long stilt legs with pointed beaks, casting beady eyes in her direction. The ship anchored at an outpost called Balise for a few hours, then headed upriver following the curving waterway toward New Orleans. The *Elizabeth* arrived in New Orleans on April 6, 1766. Marguerite's family packed their belongings and rolled up their pallets, stuffed these into wooden trunks, and disembarked the ship on a warm spring day, April 7, 1766.

The Bujol family and other Acadians were hosted for several weeks in New Orleans in the homes of French and Spanish Creoles. In the early 1700s, a New Orleans Creole was defined as "A child born in the colony as opposed to France."[9] Common usage of "Creole" in the 18th century came to mean French-speaking groups of French or Spanish descent. They were Catholics and retained traditional cultural traits, many shared by the Acadians. It must have been immensely comforting to the exiles to be among people speaking their language and sharing their religion. New Orleans would appear to them a very large city, bustling with activity, full of strange but enticing scents and people of various colors and backgrounds. In their hosts' homes, they would first taste the exotic Creole cuisine that was a blend of French, Spanish, African, Caribbean, and Native American flavors.

The local government administrators provided material assistance to the Acadians. Each incoming family was given "… six hens, one rooster, one cow either with calf or pregnant, 160 to 240 superficial arpents of land, corn, gunpowder, bullets, and a musket."[10] The government of Louisiana was still in transition; the French administration continued to operate in New Orleans because the Spanish had not taken official possession of the colony in 1766.

The initial wave of exiles arriving from Maryland and Pennsylvania, including Marguerite Bujol's family, were greeted cordially by the Spanish government, headed by Antonio de Ulloa. He became much favored by the Acadians at first due to his generosity and flexibility. Acadians showed profound gratitude during his tour in April 1766, firing musket rounds in celebration and promising to follow Spanish King Carlos III as faithfully as they had Louis XV. They were given permission to write their fellow Acadians still in Atlantic seaboard colonies, inviting them to escape captivity by coming to Louisiana.

The roster of Acadian arrivals recorded:

"Joseph Bugeaud (Bujol, Bijeaud) of Pigiguit and Oxford, age 43, came with wife Anne LeBlanc, age unrecorded, and five children: Marguerite, age 15; Augustin, age 13; Félicité-Perpétué, age 11, Anne, age 7, and Marie-Magdeleine, age 1." In addition, Joseph's brother Étienne, age 42 and a widower, came with his four children ages 14 to 5.[11]

The Bujol family was sent by barge upriver to an area just above the German Coast, which soon came to be called the Acadian Coast. They settled in the Cabannocé region, which already had several Acadian families living there. In spring of 1764, four Acadian families with surnames Poirier, Richard, Cormier, and Landry, a total of 21 people, were the first documented group to reach Louisiana. The French colonial government gave them supplies and sent them to plantation owner Nicholas Verret, who assigned them farmland in his area on the Mississippi River west bank (now St. James Parish). This large plantation was named "*Cabanannocer*," a Native American term for a duck roosting place. The larger region was called "the Cabanannocer Coast." Over a few years, the strange indigenous word was corrupted by French speakers into Cabannocé.

Acadian Settlements in Louisiana

The group of Acadians arriving from Maryland in April 1766 was not the first to come to Louisiana. In February 1764, the four Acadian families described above arrived in New Orleans. They traveled a circuitous route after originally deported to South Carolina and Georgia in 1755, spending time in New York, then heading to St. Domingue. Learning that the island was not hospitable for Acadians, they changed course for Mobile in Eastern Louisiana territory. Although unexpected by the French government, they were eventually settled at a stretch of the Mississippi River called Cabannocé, a sharp bend along the west bank above the region called the German Coast. Other exiles soon joined them and were given narrow land grants bordering the river.

The next wave of exiles who embarked after ratification of the Treaty of Paris (February 1763) came from New York. This small group of 20 consisted of Acadians who were deported to New York in 1755, joined by their relatives released from detention camps at Fort Edward, Nova Scotia. They arrived in New Orleans in early April 1764, and were settled by the caretaker French administration near the boundary between present-day St. John and St. James Parishes. They were given land bordering the Mississippi River.[12]

In late February 1765, more Acadian refugees from detention camps at Halifax arrived in Louisiana. They had tried to relocate at St. Domingue in 1763-64, but found living and working conditions untenable. Many died from malnutrition and disease. This group was led by Beausoleil Broussard; an estimated 300 people eventually settled in the Attakapas District. About 80 late-arriving Halifax Acadians were placed by the French authorities in the Cabannocé area in May 1765. With several groups of Acadians in close proximity, it appeared their hope of reuniting families might be realized.

The remainder of Acadians detained in Halifax, about 300 people, chartered commercial vessels to St. Domingue but refused to stay there. Their plan was to join Beausoleil in Attakapas. Arriving in Balise in May 1765, they found that their plan proved futile. The caretaker French government lacked resources to transport the new arrivals to the prairie districts. After recovering several weeks in New Orleans, this group was placed in the nearest vacant lands above the city, at Cabannocé, where they joined the 20 earlier Acadian arrivals. In this group were Paul Bourgeois, Jr., and his brother Joseph Bourgeois, both born in Beaubassin and cousins to Marie-Anne LeBlanc (Bujol). The Bourgeois brothers both subsequently lived and died in St. James Parish in Cabannocé.

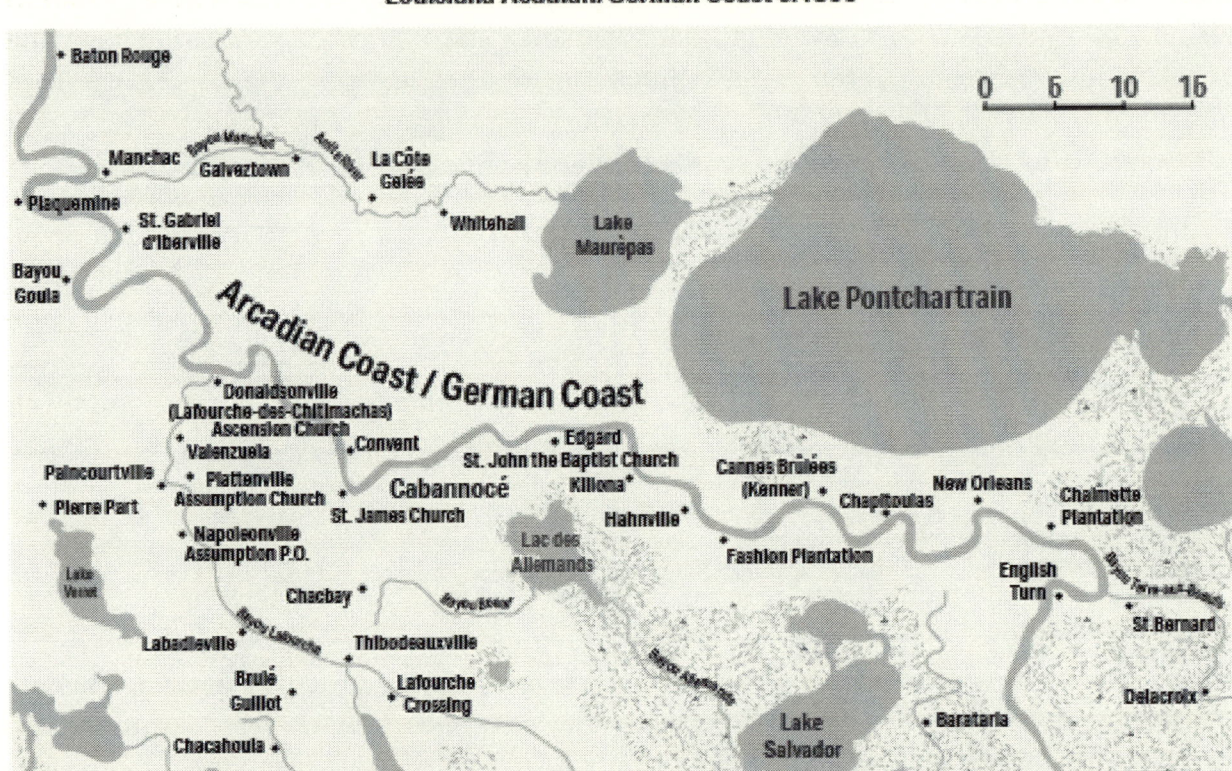

Acadian Coast/German Coast along Mississippi River c.1770-1800
Cabannocé Plantation was near St. James Church

Others of the Maryland and Pennsylvania groups were not as fortunate. As with other immigrants, they were offered land, seeds, livestock, and tools to establish their farms. But as they waited in New Orleans for their supplies and barges to carry them up the Mississippi River, Governor Ulloa changed tactics. He decided these Acadians should be strategically placed at vulnerable sites along the Mississippi River that marked the boundary between British and Spanish territory. Again, the Acadians were pawns in service of colonial powers. Over their protests, they were forcibly dispersed to areas that were isolated and often vulnerable to attack. Ulloa hoped that the Acadians' strong anti-British sentiments, combined with their highly regarded marksmanship, would provide an adequate defense in case hostilities broke out.

In July 1767, 210 Acadians were sent to Fort St. Gabriel, a considerable distance up the Mississippi River from Cabannocé. Another group of 149 was sent to San Luis de

Natchez, even further north, near present-day Vidalia. Other regions where Acadians located in 1766 included Côte Gelée, La Pointe, Fausse Pointe, La Manque near the Atchafalaya River, and Bayou Lafourche.

By 1768, the Acadians were the predominant cultural group in lower Louisiana outside of New Orleans. Hostility toward Governor Ulloa because of his dispersal policies led to their joining the French Creole rebellion of October 1768, when they marched on New Orleans, took up arms, and forced the Spanish governor to flee unceremoniously. Spanish control was restored in August 1769, and Ulloa's successor Alejandro O'Reilly was conciliatory toward the Acadians. He allowed the disgruntled San Luis de Natchez settlers to move to other settlements along the Mississippi River. This placated the Acadians, but Ulloa's dispersal policies may have discouraged further immigration, since very few new groups arrived between 1768 and 1785.

In 1770, a small band of 30 Acadians arrived at Natchitoches, Louisiana, after a harrowing journey that took 15 months. They boarded a British vessel at Port Tobacco, Maryland, in January 1769, bound for New Orleans. Delayed by fog in the Mississippi Delta, and then driven by easterly winds, the ship made land at Matagorda Bay, Texas. The passengers and crew were seized by Spanish authorities and arrested as smugglers. They spent time confined at hard labor in the Spanish Presidio de La Bahia, soon released to make their way as best they could. The group made a 420-mile overland trek to reach Louisiana at the Red River post, Natchitoches. The French commander tried to detain them to work there, but facing strong Acadian resistance, he relented and allowed the exiles to continue their journey to join their confrères. In April 1779, the group was given land grants on the west bank of the Mississippi River below Bayou Plaquemine, in present-day Iberville Parish.

A trickle of other exiles continued to make their way to the Acadian regions during this time. Although there are reports of long overland journeys from Nova Scotia, this is not documented. Only one Acadian group is known to have migrated to Louisiana from Canada. Nineteen Acadians sailed from St. Pierre Island to the Mississippi entrance, arriving in December 1788. They were allowed to join relatives living in the Cabannocé area in present-day Ascension Parish.

In 1785, the last large group of Acadian exiles came to Louisiana. These were 1,598 exiles sent to France but never successfully reintegrated. They were transported in five ships at Spain's expense, and like their predecessors, they sought family reunification.

Most of their relatives were situated along the Mississippi River, and they wanted to be settled nearby. Intendant Martin Navarro, who had worked under Ulloa in the late 1760s and witnessed the disastrous consequences of thwarting the Acadians' stubbornness, permitted the immigrants to choose their own homesites. The first contingent departed New Orleans in August 1785, finding new homes at Lafourche, Bayogoula, and Manchac. As additional ships arrived from France, the immigrants were given funds, supplies, housing, and medical attention at government expense. After short stays in New Orleans, these groups also selected their homesites. Many rejoined families in the Opelousas and Attakapas areas.

Finding available land was more difficult along the heavily populated lower Mississippi, and several families had to accept vacant sites in adjacent newly founded districts, including Lafourche, Chetimaches, Bayou des Ecores, Manchac, and Baton Rouge. Nearly 70% of these immigrants chose to settle in the Lafourche district, which was near existing Acadian settlements but not adjacent to thriving Anglo-American communities. Surrounded by virgin wilderness, lower Bayou Lafourche was sparsely populated. This helped insulate Acadian culture and protect against government interference. In this refuge, the long-suffering Acadians coming from exile in France were able to reconstruct their agrarian, non-materialistic, egalitarian, frontier society. They were determined to "... resurrect *vieille Acadie* on the banks of Louisiana's bayous."[13]

During the late 1770s and early 1780s, second-generation Louisiana Acadians began migrating to establish new homesteads. Acadian settlers tended to seek the isolation of prairies and bayous to preserve their culture, for family cohesiveness and economic independence, through land ownership. When they migrated, the family unit typically moved together. They consistently ventured no farther than the nearest prairie stream (*coulée*) or bayou ridge (*chènière*). Their homes were widely separated, though some communities created "villages" of temporary structures to accommodate new settlers until their homes were built. Movements to the southwestern prairies along the Vermilion River and Bayou Carencro, and into Calcasieu Parish, were also motivated by the desire to escape Creole colonists who were becoming increasingly hostile, and avoid meddling by European-born colonial administrators.

The settlement at Cabannocé formed the nucleus of a rapidly expanding settlement of Acadian immigrants. In this region of the Acadian Coast, population density increased dramatically. A total of 221 Acadians resided in present-day St. James and Ascension Parishes in 1766. By 1777, this soared to 786 people (226% increase). In nearby Iberville

Parish, the Acadian population grew 32%, rising from 220 to 291 people. The influx of Maryland exiles in 1766 caused most of these increases.[14]

Rapid population growth created pressure for intercolonial mobility. All the prime riverfront property was settled by 1786. Spanish Louisiana had inheritance laws that required all children to inherit equal portions of the parents' lands. This forced progressively smaller divisions of land tracts with each generation. The typical Acadian Coast land grant was 4-6 arpents river frontage by 40 arpents depth (1 linear arpent = 192 feet). The usual river parish family had 3-5 children to divide land among. Second-to-third generation Louisiana Acadians inherited long, very narrow strips of land, often less than 1.5 arpents wide by 40 arpents deep. Constant reduction of family landholdings made it difficult to continue farming effectively. Not infrequently, a family member bought property from relatives to continue farming. Those relatives then migrated to adjoining regions, frequently the Lafourche Valley, to begin a new home and farm. After 1795, many spread westward to Bayous Terrebonne, Blue, and Boeuf.

As the 18th century drew to a close, three increasingly different groups were forming: River Acadians living along the Mississippi, Bayou Acadians in the South Louisiana swamp regions, and Prairie Acadians in the vast open lands from Opelousas and Lafayette to Lake Charles in Calcasieu Parish. This region came to be called "The French Prairie."

River Acadians Adapt to Louisiana

When Joseph Bujol arrived at Cabannocé with his wife Marie-Anne LeBlanc and five children, he would have been given a land grant of 4 arpents river frontage by 40 arpents depth, on the west bank of the Mississippi River. Along with other immigrants, his work began with clearing the land, building a home, providing shelter for his animals, and starting crops. In the close-knit Acadian community, a large work force was available to help with these tasks. Those neighbors already settled provided a wealth of advice and assistance. The Bujol homestead was no doubt established before they had their last child in 1769. The Cabannocé census of 1769 listed Joseph Bujole (Bujol) as occupying lot number 74, with his wife and six children; the youngest boy, Joseph Paul, was age 3 months. His uncle Joseph Landry was also in the household which was next to brother Étienne's property. There was no local Catholic Church; the nearest was St. Francis of Assisi at Point Coupée. With few Catholic priests in the area, a visiting priest may have baptized Joseph Paul then later recorded it at the Point Coupée church.[15]

A year later, in August 1770, Marguerite Bujol was married in Cabannocé to Joseph Constant, a "publican" from d'Arbonne, France. Ten years and five children later, in 1780, Marguerite married her second husband, **Juan Francisco Vicente Vives**, one year after Joseph Constant's death. Her younger sister Marie-Magdeleine Bujol married Auguste Verret, son of former commandant Nicolas Verret, at Ascension Parish in February 1784. The two Bujol girls' husbands were among the French and Spanish Creole class, from socially prominent families.[16]

Juan Francisco Vicente Chevalier Vives

Joseph Constant, Marguerite Bujol's first husband, died in 1779; their last child was born only one year earlier. Probably two or three of their children died as infants; one surviving daughter married into the Zéringue family, and their son married a Landry. Very little time elapsed before Marguerite married her second husband, Juan Francisco Vicente Vives, in 1780. Born in Valencia, Spain, Vives was a prominent Spanish Creole, a physician and lieutenant captain who came to Louisiana in 1755, serving under Governor Bernardo Galvez. Don Juan Vives was knighted by the Spanish king for his military service, given the title chevalier, and awarded a 7,000-acre land grant along Bayou Lafourche in what was called Valenzuela, in Assumption Parish. His social status and wealth further enhanced the Bujol family's social standing, discussed more in the next section.

The Cabannocé Acadians wanted to recreate their former lifestyle from the Mines villages of Grand Pré and Pisiquid, where most had lived before expulsion from Nova Scotia. Mines was the breadbasket of Acadia, where they had cultivated oats, rye, and wheat along with many vegetables. The most fertile land in their Louisiana farms was called "riverbottom," near the waterfront and blanketed by dense thickets of hardwood timber. They often worked to exhaustion clearing the thickets in the hot, humid Louisiana climate. Work was difficult because they often lacked proper tools, or farm animals such as oxen. The Acadians were unfamiliar with the local, effective slash-and-burn technique to clear land. But persist they did, and by the 1770s, the average riverbottom farmer had cleared and cultivated around 2 arpents. They were required to protect their lands from annual inundations of the Mississippi River by building 5-6 foot levees.

Agriculture. The next challenge was growing crops in Louisiana's subtropical climate, vastly different than what they had known in Mines. Their new homeland had long growing seasons and high annual rainfall. The crops they had grown in Mines—wheat, barley, and oats—were unsuited for this climate, as they soon learned. They began cultivating maize (corn), a crop unknown in Acadia but suitable for the local climate, with seeds provided to them by the government. This substitute grain would serve as a staple in the Acadian diet for the next century.

In Mines, they had grown flax for summer clothing and used sheep wool for winter clothing. Flax would not grow in semitropical climates, and by 1770 the settlers had abandoned it in favor of clothes made from local cotton. Sheep were scarce in river settlements, and only a few could afford to buy them and rebuild large sheep herds. Woolen garments and stockings proved unbearably hot even in Louisiana winters. Soon they began growing cotton, which was more comfortable than wool, readily washable, and could be used as a year-round fabric. Cotton was easy to weave into cloth on looms that became common in Acadian homes. Cotton threads were woven into *cotonnade*, cotton broadcloth that quickly became known for its excellent quality.

Family gardens in Mines produced mainly field peas, turnips, and cabbage. The latter two could only be grown during Louisiana's short winter season and quickly declined in importance. Peas remained a staple, augmented by bean varieties such as red and butter beans. Acadian gardens also produced squash and pumpkins, and small quantities of rice and tobacco. Acadians were inveterate pipe smokers but previously had bought tobacco from their Mi'kmaq neighbors. In Louisiana, their relationship with local Native Americans was unfriendly, so they needed to grow their own tobacco. Rice was grown as a secondary crop, sown in lowlands subject to spring flooding. It provided them with another grain in years when corn failed, as happened in 1785. Lacking irrigation technology, Acadians could not depend upon rice, and it remained a marginal crop for many years. They called it "providence rice" since a successful crop depended upon nature providing enough rainfall, or river flooding.

By 1804, Acadians were growing small amounts of okra in river settlement farms. The vegetable's plump green pods had unique flavor and thickening qualities, which made okra an essential part of Creole cuisine, especially for gumbo. It probably arrived from West Africa, brought by enslaved people who were acquired by Acadians in the late 1790s. They continued their orchard tradition, but apple trees were replaced by figs, peaches, and apricots. By the 1780s, they were growing grape vines, including concord, white, and muscadine varieties.

Adapting to different growing requirements, rain, flooding, and insect pests required the Acadians to use new techniques. Flooding was alleviated by effective use of drainage ditches, but this required using plows to cut deep furrows between crop rows. In Acadia, they rarely used plows, since furrows were only 2-3 inches deep. Such shallow furrows led to root rot in the wet Louisiana climate. So, they quickly acquired oxen and learned to use plows to cut deep furrows and dig drainage ditches.

Livestock increased and diversified as the Acadians adapted to their new farms. Most had received two cows and seven chickens from the colonial government upon arrival. They soon acquired small numbers of hogs, which were a major source of protein in Acadia. Hogs and chickens proliferated quickly, and in 1772 the typical Acadian Coast household had 24 pigs and 22 chickens. They also had small numbers of cattle, but cattle ranching was not suited to the topography and dense population in the river and eastern bayou settlements.

River Acadians were able to augment their income by smuggling surplus grain, eggs, milk, and pork to the English east bank trading post at Manchac. This was a lucrative market where agricultural products fetched high prices. They traveled in pirogues by night, slipping past Spanish guards at Fort St. Gabriel. At Manchac, they acquired manufactured items, especially cast-iron tools and cauldrons, which were always in demand in their communities. Although they could sell their surplus crops in New Orleans, the Spanish regime kept prices artificially low in this market. Acadians continued their contraband markets until the American Revolution, when British holdings on the Mississippi River were captured by Spanish forces.

Housing. Non-materialistic values and frugality, characteristics of Acadians, carried over into their housing practices in Louisiana. At first, they tried to build houses the same way they had in Nova Scotia, because of familiarity and architectural simplicity. These *poteaux-en-terre* houses sat flush with the ground and had post-in-ground construction. Posts used in the walls were bound together with small branches, creating air pockets for insulation, and plastered on the interior walls with a mud-and-clay mixture that sealed the inside against blasts of arctic air. Weather boards were put on outside walls, and the roof thatched with reed, straw, and bark. Underneath the house was a small cellar for keeping food during the winter. Most Acadian houses had only one large room with a small attic for storage and sleeping quarters for boys, called *garconnière*. The chimney used for cooking and heat was built with the same materials, using extra coatings of mud plaster for insulation.

They quickly learned that this method of construction would not hold up in Louisiana's humid climate, propensity for floods, and frequent Gulf Coast storms. Putting posts into the ground led to rapid deterioration, the posts rotting in the high water table. Wood sitting in contact with the ground led to attack from termites; the insects rapidly destroyed dry wood. Houses flush with the ground were susceptible to flooding. The insulated walls and thick thatched roof prevented air flow and made inside rooms unbearably hot during sweltering summers. By the 1780s, their house design was modified to meet environmental conditions, evolving into the Louisiana Acadian house—a blend of Maritime Canadian, Norman, and West Indian architecture.

The simple lines of Norman country houses was brought by Acadians returning from exile in France, many trained as carpenters. West Indies influence is seen in use of piers to raise the floor off the ground. These piers were usually made from large cypress blocks, wood that is water and termite resistant. This elevation allowed air circulation for cooling and provided flood protection. Large doors and windows set in opposite walls allowed cross breezes for cooling the central living area; front and side galleries offered additional cooling. Cypress shingles replaced straw in roofing to permit heat to radiate upward from the attic at night. Massive cypress beams supported the floor, and the walls had lighter construction with diagonal bracing. Internal wall space was filled with *bousillage*, a mud-and-moss mixture that was less insulating. Above ground cellars were built as outbuildings.

Furnishings inside Acadian homes remained simple, in accord with their frugal lifestyle and non-materialism. Most homes had one or two rooms, attic, and at least one gallery. The great room had a table and a few chairs, beds had storage chests at the foot, usually made from readily available cypress wood. As they became more affluent, some bought imported cherry furniture and replaced chests with armoires. Earthenware dishes, tin cups and utensils were common; badly worn and dented after many years of use. Wealthier Acadians bought porcelain dishes and iron spoons and forks after the 1770s. For cooking, they used cast-iron cauldrons and frying pans, which were hung in the chimney hearth. Most meals were prepared by boiling in cauldrons over an open fire; frying pans used for quick-cooking food such as fish, eggs, and bacon, and also for baking cornbread.

Cuisine. Louisiana Acadian cuisine reflected traditional food preferences and styles of cooking but was adapted to local vegetables and proteins. Their traditional winter stew of turnips and cabbage morphed into maize-based soups with squash, peas, and beans. Later they began making gumbos, borrowing roux techniques and spices from the Creoles. Protein was primarily salt pork, which they boiled for hours to tenderize and remove saltiness. Long cooking times using the boiling cauldron was necessary for other proteins, such as game and old chickens, which were tough. They kept hens as long as eggs were still produced. The typical Acadian meal consisted of salt pork, corn bread, and seasonal vegetables and fruits. Their cuisine evolved over time, as they came to use seafood, shellfish, crayfish, sausage, and rice to make Creole-flavored jambalaya, etouffée, and gumbos.

Clothing. After the Acadians became adept at weaving cotton into cloth, production of fine cotonnade became the principal cottage industry. The fabric was often left in its natural tan state, or dyed indigo blue. Other colors, including red, black, and white were also used. Women wore ankle-length, striped cotonnade skirts, cotton corsets, and vests decorated with embroidery. Their *garde-soleil* bonnet was now made of cotton, covering shoulders and head, with rigid brims and side panels to hold it away from the neck, allowing air circulation. Their cotonnade stockings were of such fine quality that affluent Creoles sought them out.

Typical Acadian sabots, wooden shoes, proved unsuited to their new climate and topography. Both women and men wore moccasins during winter months but often went barefoot in the summer. Professionally crafted leather shoes with silver buckles were only worn by affluent farmers. Men wore soft felt hats during the winter, but switched to straw hats in spring and summer. They wore collarless, loose-fitting cotonnade shirts left natural or dyed white. Knee-length breeches were typically dyed indigo blue, their cotton stockings white or natural. In stormy weather or when doing tasks in the woodlands, they had leather leggings to wrap around calves, along with moccasins.

In typical frugal manner, Acadians wore clothing until it became tattered and threadbare. They were well aware of the time and labor required for the entire cloth-making process, so maximized the useful life of all clothing. It was usual for them to wear old clothes, even to church and social gatherings. This practice led European and Creole visitors to consider Acadians slovenly and poor, their clothes appearing as if they were "... thrown on with pitchforks."[17]

Social life. The Acadian extended family system retained its vitality, even though nuclear families were often separated during dispersal and resettlement. In Louisiana, they found themselves surrounded by numerous cousins who shared their values and language. Many families did reunite over the years from 1766 to the early 1800s. They preserved their culture of cooperation and group identity and continued Catholic religious traditions. Family ties pervaded all aspects of Acadian life; groups of related people worked, played, socialized, and worshipped together. Household tasks were usually differentiated according to sexes. Women and girls managed home gardens and barnyards, milked cows, cooked, preserved food, and made clothing. Men worked in the fields, cut timber and built structures, constructed levees and ditches. At harvest time, everyone went into the fields to pick cotton and corn. Older family members tended the young children and helped prepare meals.

The tradition of *fetes*, now called *bals de maison,* was continued; these weekly neighborhood dances were a most welcome diversion from hard work and a way to renew social bonds. These gatherings rotated among homes, everyone willingly traveling many miles to socialize and have fun. Initially, musicians were without their fiddles, unable to bring them or losing them during long years of exile. By late 1770s, most fiddlers had acquired new instruments, and the best of them attained regional fame. At the *bals*, even grandparents danced. Young men and women had opportunity to meet and exchange sly glances, dancing together under the scrutiny of matrons. Food and drink was shared, always featuring gumbo and corn bread.

Acadians provided assistance to each other during life's trials and tragedies, as well as sharing joys. Family and friends gathered at homes of those who were ill, stood vigil during dying, attended funerals, gave help and support to the bereaved. They celebrated life hallmarks with each other, including betrothal parties, weddings, and births. They shared the rituals of the church calendar, and gathered in small churches for major religious festivals. But as in Acadia, they retained an anticlerical attitude, resented church officials interfering in their lives, and wanted priests just to officiate for the sacraments—baptism, first communion, confirmation, marriage, last rites, and funerals. They found the Spanish priests more meddlesome than expected and resented their elitism and interference in secular affairs. This led to numerous bitter disputes between Acadians and their pastors, including some violent confrontations.

Acadian Metamorphosis. Although retaining most values of their culture, Louisiana Acadians did undergo a metamorphosis that was necessary in their new environment.

Their flexibility and adaptability allowed them to adopt new crops and farming methods quickly. Within 10 years, most immigrants attained a standard of living that compared well with their pre-dispersal status. By 1777, the typical Acadian resident of Ascension Parish owned 14.7 cattle, 11.59 hogs, 1.03 sheep, and 22.2 chickens.[18] The level of prosperity was fairly even, despite emergence of different agricultural patterns on a subregional basis. Their clothing and cuisine changed to reflect local influences and climate requirements. The uniformity of their culture reinforced group boundaries and differentiated Acadians from other local ethnic groups. Acadian society retained its inner strength but presented a new face to the world—a distinctly Louisiana quality that would come to be known as "Cajun."

However, change was ever on the horizon. As some Acadians became affluent, they aspired to membership in the Creole planter class. This required them to adopt different lifestyles and manners, which began separating them from the small farmer Acadians. Men congregated in local cabarets, many of which were Acadian owned, to gamble at billiards. They developed interest in horse racing, and horses became a status symbol to young, upwardly mobile Acadian men. Horses were a luxury until the 1790s, and having them for riding and pulling a sulky would impress neighbors. The La Pointe settlement in present-day St. Martin Parish first spawned the great Acadian pastime of horse racing. It spread to river and prairie parishes as more racetracks were built. Featured races were for pedigreed thouroughbreds owned by Anglo-Americans and Creole planters; but a great many races were for Acadian riding ponies and draft horses.

Jean Landry Chevalier Vives (1782–1809) — Marguerite Marie Bourgeois (1790–1815)

The Bujol family probably was among the earliest River Acadians to aspire toward the Creole class. Apparently Joseph Bujol became a prosperous farmer, building a large house and furnishing it with European imports, such as cherrywood furniture and porcelain dishes. He may have expanded his plantings into more lucrative crops such as sugarcane, especially after cotton production suffered "rot" caused by flooding and weevil attacks in the 1770s. Families joined by neighbors could harvest modest cotton crops, but growing sugarcane was labor intensive. It required more manpower than families and friends could provide. In the Ascension 1777 census Joseph Bujol had "6 arpents of land, 1 slave, 18 cattle, 2 horses, 0 sheep, 19 hogs, 1 arm" and his brother Étienne had "12 arpents next to brother Joseph, 4 slaves, 24 cattle, 3 horses, 3 sheep, 18 swine, 2 arms."[19]

Use of enslaved people was well-established in Southern Louisiana before the Acadians arrived, both as field hands and household workers. Between 1790 and 1810, a large majority of Acadians had acquired one to three. Initially, women were domestics serving as wet nurses; later, use of enslaved men in the fields became common. Owning enslaved people immediately increased a family's status.

Louisiana Acadians have been noted for equalitarian principles, which annoyed colonial administrators who found them lacking proper respect for authority and prone to insubordination. But their values seemed to extend mainly to their own ethnic group. Perhaps remnants of their mixed attitudes toward Native Americans, whom they viewed in Acadia both as economic partners and potential military rivals, made it easier to accept the slave economy. By 1850, most of the Bujol (Bujole) families in river parishes were slaveholders. Edmond Bujole (b.1818) of Ascension Parish was among the largest slaveholders; in 1850 he owned 36 and by 1860 this increased to 77 enslaved persons. This qualified him as a "great planter."[20] To be a large slaveholder and member of the planter aristocracy, one needed to own 20 to 50 enslaved persons. Acadian slaveholders aspired to the elevated social status of Creole planters, who lived in large, graceful mansions on extensive plantations. This required emulation of the materialistic lifestyle of Creole planters, building grand homes with fine furnishings, having horses and carriages, fieldworkers and domestic servants, high-fashion clothing, and entertaining lavishly.

Creoles and Acadians

Although Creoles considered themselves superior to the Acadians, there was one asset the Acadians had that drew them into relationships. Many single French and Spanish soldiers and administrators were living in Louisiana, and there was a dearth of eligible young women to marry. The Acadians had an excellent supply of marriageable daughters, many very comely. These marriages became common, frequently an Acadian bride marrying a Creole or Anglo-American of higher status. In 1770, Marguerite Bujol married French Creole Joseph Constant, a "publican" (common term for tax collectors or public contractors), placing him in the elite professional class. Marguerite's marriage must have been among the earliest such Acadian-Creole exogamous unions.

Marguerite Bujol and Joseph Constant lived in Lafourche-des-Chitimachas (present-day Donaldsonville) in Ascension Parish, near the point where Bayou Lafourche meets the Mississippi River. The French first colonized the area, previously occupied by Houma and Chitimacha native people. The settlers built the Ascension of Our Lord Catholic Church there in 1772. The newly married Constants were located not far from her parents' farm in Cabannocé, perhaps residing in the developing town where Joseph's work was based. Their first son, Paul Constant, was born in Lafourche-des-Chitimachas (Donaldsonville) in 1771, but may have died in infancy. The second son, Augustine Victor Constant, was born there in 1773, followed by a daughter, Anne Constant in 1774. The last two daughters, both named Magdeleine, born in 1775 and 1778, probably died young. Joseph Constant died at about age 35 and was buried at the Ascension of Our Lord Catholic Church on February 24, 1779.

Marguerite's second marriage increased her social standing even more. One can speculate about how she met Juan Francisco Vicente Vives and why he was drawn to marry a recent widow with at least three young children. Don Juan Vives had recently returned from a military expedition in 1779 against the British fort at Baton Rouge. The Spanish crown had awarded him a land grant of 9 arpents on the west bank of Bayou Lafourche where he built a large plantation-style home. The census of 1778 recorded that he possessed 10 enslaved persons, had 24 cattle, 15 horses, and 40 swine, and his farm had produced 200 quarts of corn. Born in 1751, he and Marguerite were the same age: 29 years old in 1780.

Perhaps recent military action, where he saw soldiers killed, made the young officer acutely aware of life's uncertainty. Having his own land and house possibly spurred him to desire a family with heirs. He was, clearly, well of an age to seek a bride. His land was located in Valenzuela, very close to Lafourche-des-Chitimachas. Undoubtedly he made frequent trips to the river town for business and to socialize. Given Marguerite Constant's status as a member of Creole society, they may have met at parties or dinners. Perhaps Marguerite was particularly beautiful; she certainly had demonstrated that she was fertile. However it came to pass, Don Juan Vives managed to court widow Marguerite Constant over a short time period, resulting in their marriage on February 8, 1780, in Ascension Church. It was just two weeks short of a year since Joseph had been buried at the same church.

The Bujol family became even more firmly situated in Creole society with the upwardly mobile marriage of yet another daughter. In 1784, Marguerite's younger sister Marie-Magdeleine Bujol married Auguste Verret of a socially prominent French Creole family. He later became Commandant of Assumption, and was the son of former commandant Nicolas Verret, who played a significant role in settling and supervising Acadians in the river parishes. It is interesting that Verret's son married an Acadian woman, since the commandant had several altercations with Acadian men during his administrative years. He experienced their insubordination firsthand and quarreled with Basile Préjean, an Acadian leader at Cabannocé. Such quarrels were verbal, legal, and at times physically violent. An example of Acadian and Creole tensions came in 1774, when Préjean burst into another commandant's office to launch an attack on a local Creole who was pressing charges against Préjean for a previous assault. The commandant was outraged and filed a complaint against Préjean, "... more as an example than for any other motive, in order to demonstrate to the Acadians that they must not strike anyone, least of all their betters."[21] The unruly Acadian was sentenced by the governor to three days' imprisonment.

Nicholas Verret was among the largest landholders along the Acadian Coast and a prominent leader with administrative positions in both the transitional French and subsequent Spanish colonial governments. When the first group of Acadian exiles arrived in Louisiana in 1764, the French administrators enlisted Verret to settle them on his land holdings along the Mississippi River in Cabannocé. His influence was woven into the Acadian experience over the next 20 years. He assisted groups arriving in 1766-1767 to find farms, reporting to Governor Ulloa in March 1768 that "... people who arrived as late as July have already cleared and opened up their land; are living in their own houses; are herding a little livestock; and no doubt will do some planting this year."[22]

Over the years, Verret encountered Acadian audacity and stubbornness, including handling a legal complaint filed by Father Valentin, curé of St. Jacques de Cabannocé church in 1771. The priest complained that four Acadian men smoked pipes in the presbytery and cursed his "Negro" cook in front of him. When he reprimanded them, they hurled curses at him. Father Valentin was unsuccessful in taking legal action against the "godless" Acadians, but such clashes served to increase Acadian-Creole polarization. By 1792, the colonial Creole aristocracy and the immigrant Acadians had been involved in two major conflicts: one a dispute over levee maintenance and the other about creating a new parish that would force increased financial support by parishioners, most of whom were Acadians.

Despite his checkered experience with Acadians, Nicholas Verret seemed to maintain a generally tolerant attitude. As increasingly prosperous Acadians began adopting Creole values and lifestyles, Verret would have mingled with them professionally and socially. Don Juan Vives would have been in his social circle, so it was natural that his wife's sister Marie-Magdeleine would meet Auguste Verret. One can imagine that the Bujol sisters were well-mannered and lovely, probably groomed for elite society, especially with their father aspiring to join the planter class. Their well-positioned marriages into Creole leading families served to advance their family's social status in the river communities.

Marguerite Bujol and **Juan Francisco Vicente Vives** had 7 children over the next 10 years. Probably all children were born at home; the Vives plantation house was five miles from Donaldsonville on Bayou Lafourche, in current-day Assumption Parish. However, most of their births were recorded at Ascension Church in the adjoining parish, because Assumption was not established until 1793. The first son, Antoine Maria Vives, was born circa 1780, probably near the year's end. Marguerite must have conceived immediately after her marriage in February 1780. A second son followed, born August 5, 1782. Named Jean Landry Chevalier Vives, the Vial-Martin lineage continued through him. Of interest, note the French spelling of his first name, Jean, instead of the Spanish Juan. Three daughters were born just one year apart; Anne Marguerite in 1784, Carmélite in 1785, and Marie Claire in 1786. Carmélite survived to adulthood; Ascension Church records contain her marriage in 1803 to Louis Landry. No later records of the other two girls were found, so they may have died young. Two boys followed: Juan Nicolas in 1788 (died 1789) and Paul (Pablo) "Hypolite" Augustin in 1790. Ascension Church records show that Paul "Hypolite" Augustin married Elise Eulalie Mollere in 1813.

The Vives children were born and grew up on their father's plantation in Valenzuela. Their large two-story house likely had a grand staircase rising from a curved driveway to the upper level. Having the main living quarters on the second floor took advantage of cooling breezes and expansive views. An elegant entryway would give access to the dining room, a sitting area, and several bedrooms. On the lower floor would be an office, library, rooms for domestics, and rooms for storage, food preparation, and kitchen. Some plantations had separate outbuildings for cooking and food storage.

In 1796, 41-year-old Juan Francisco Vicente Vives was promoted to First Captain in the Regiment of La Fourche. In the census of 1797, the Vives household consisted of seven family members and 20 enslaved persons. Most likely, Marguerite's children from her marriage with Joseph Constant were grown and had left the house. The oldest Vives child was 15, and the youngest was 1-2 years old. The family consisted of two parents and five children, further indicating childhood deaths for the other three. It is likely that the plantation was growing sugarcane by this time, in addition to corn. The number of enslaved people had doubled since 1788, putting Don Juan Vives among the larger planters.

The original home on Vives' plantation was destroyed by fire in 1830. The plantation remained in the Vives family until 1838, when part of the family land was sold by a son, probably Paul "Hypolite" Vives. Several tracts of sugarcane were bought by Charles (Carl) Anton Kock, a German immigrant, who created a successful import/export business and married Jean Heda Longer, daughter of a wealthy Creole family in New Orleans. He built a new plantation house on the Vives property in 1846, now called Belle Alliance Plantation. The couple started a life of sugarcane production. The plantation stayed in the Kock family until 1915.[23]

Belle Alliance is a two-story Greek Revival manor; it has 33 rooms with verandas on both levels. Six great square columns rise from the ground to the roof entablature, supporting the second-floor veranda. Cast-iron railings span the upper veranda from column to column, and turn toward the rear at the corners. House and columns are made of brick covered with stucco, painted white. The simple entablature has dentils on top, giving an ornate touch. A wide stairway with cast-iron railings rises to the second-story veranda. An oval driveway leads from the road to the front entry, huge oak trees shade the grounds, and massive gates with the Kock crest border the driveway entrance. Within the oval driveway are gardens with fountains, statuary, shrubs, roses, and seasonal flowers; the plantation is famous for its magnificent camellias.

A historical marker was placed on the land in 1965, commemorating the 1775 Spanish land grant to Don Juan Vives. This was part of ceremonies celebrating the second century of Acadian culture in Louisiana, attended by several direct descendents of Vives, with family names Breaud, Lear, and Fox, all of New Orleans.[24] Apparently, no Vials were in attendance. The plantation house was listed in the National Register of Historic Places in 1998. (See photo in Foreword)

Jean Landry Chevalier Vives married **Marguerite Marie Bourgeois** on May 8, 1808, at the Assumption Church in Plattenville. The bride was from nearby St. John the Baptist Parish, born July 12, 1790, daughter of Dominique Bourgeois, *fils*, and Marguerite LaGrange. The Bourgeois family lived in Edgard, one of the parish's first communities. This Bourgeois family was originally from France and not related to the Acadian Bourgeois who were Jean Vives' ancestors on his mother's side. Jean Baptiste Bourgeois (1695-1770), Marguerite Marie's great-grandfather, was born in Palisseau, Îll-de-France, in the Seine district of France. He came with his wife Marianne Chevalier to Mobile in 1718, continued on to New Orleans, and is listed as one of the two original Bourgeois to arrive in early colonial Louisiana. In the 1724 and 1731 censuses, he was listed as farming three arpents of land along the riverfront on the German Coast of the Mississippi. This land on the west bank later became part of St. Charles Parish near Edgard.

Jean Baptiste Bourgeois and Marianne Chevalier had six children. The fourth child was Dominique Bourgeois, *père,* born about 1730 in St. Charles Parish. Dominique married Reine Genevieve Duval (Uval) around 1751 in St. Charles Parish. Reine Genevieve was born in Oise, France in 1739. The German Coast census of 1766 listed Dominique, age 36, living with wife, age 23, one boy, age 6 months, and three girls. In all, they had eight children, the last born before 1777, when Dominique *père* died at age 47. Their sixth child, also named Dominique Bourgeois but identified as *fils*, was born around 1764 in St. Charles Parish. Dominique *fils* was married to Marguerite LaGrange on February 6, 1788, at St. John the Baptist Church in Edgard.

According to the colonial Spanish inheritance laws, each child received an equal part of the parents' land. Even with several children that died in childhood, the Bourgeois family was prodigious with its heirs. By the time Dominique *fils* inherited his land share, it would have become a thin, long segment with probably less than one arpent bordering the Mississippi River. Farming was the most common livelihood in the region. Edgard became a major site of the sugar industry. The majority of residents worked in sugar houses (mills), in the fields, or in other jobs that supported the industry. The huge Columbia Plantation, owned by the Caire and Graugnard families, leased land to many local families for growing their own sugarcane crops. Well into the next century, many family-owned sugar houses were still operating.

Dominique Bourgeois *fils* received a land grant of about 40 acres on Bayou Laforche in Ascension Parish. It was along the same road just 2 miles up the bayou from Jean Francisco Chevalier Vives' property.[25] Dominique and Marguerite had only two children, probably because Dominique died young, about age 26, sometime after 1790. His wife's date of death is not known. Their first daughter, Félicité Bourgeois, was born in 1788; the second daughter, Marguerite Marie, was born in 1790. Dominique had many siblings living in the area; perhaps the Bourgeois clan of aunts and uncles assisted the widow with her two small daughters. The LaGrange family also lived locally.

Nothing more is known about the first daughter, but Marguerite Marie entered the Vial-Martin lineage by marrying Jean Landry Chevalier Vives in 1808. The two were neighbors and knew each other from childhood. Jean lived only 2 miles from Marguerite Marie, and there were many social occasions that both attended. Both of their families were among the landholders, though the Bourgeois were smaller farmers in comparison to Jean Vives' well-to-do family. The Bourgeois would have enjoyed the status of French Creoles, especially as Marguerite Marie's great-grandfather was one of the first French immigrants to arrive in Louisiana. This would allow the young people to move in the same social circles. Their marriage took place on May 8, 1808, in Plattenville when the groom was 26 and the bride was 18. Perhaps they chose the Assumption Church in Plattenville, located alongside Bayou Lafourche, because it was a similar distance from the groom's home in Valenzeula and the bride's relatives in Edgard.

Jean Landry Chevalier Vives and Marguerite Marie Bourgeois had only two children, both daughters, who were baptized at Ascension Church, Donaldsonville. Marie Clementine Vives was born in1808, and married Hypolite Palloc on January 13, 1827, in Assumption Parish. The second daughter, Marie Malvina Vives, was born March 1, 1810. Her father Jean Vives, however, had died around November 3, 1809, and was buried at Ascension Church, Donaldsonville. His wife, Marguerite Marie, was pregnant with Marie Malvina when her husband died five months before their daughter's birth. She was only 19 years old at the time; Jean Vives was about 24 years old at his death. Perhaps an accident or seasonal epidemic claimed the life of the young aristocrat. He was survived by his younger brother, Paul Hypolite Vives, and an older sister, Carmélite. Apparently all other siblings had already passed away. Paul Hypolite was born around 1796 and was probably only 13 years old at the time.

Marguerite Marie Bourgeois Vives married again within 15 months of her husband's death. This pattern of rather quick remarriage of widows and widowers seems common in Creole-Acadian society of the time. Her second husband was François Mollere, and their union took place on February 22, 1811, at Ascension Church, Donaldsonville. Connections between the Vives and Mollere families must have been close, as Paul Hypolite Vives married Eulalie Mollere, sister of François, in 1813. It is possible that the merged families lived together at the Vives plantation. Marguerite Marie had one more child, a son, Juan Francisco Mollere, born in 1813. She lived only two more years and died at age 24 around February 15, 1815. Her burial was at Assumption Church, Plattenville.

The Vial-Martin family continued through her second daughter, Marie Malvina Vives, who married Martin Songy Reynaud in 1826. The Vives lineage passed down the distinct Spanish features seen later among the Vials, particularly the eyes and eyebrows.

CHAPTER 8

Statehood and Secession

Marie Malvina Vives (1810-1842) –
Martin Songy Reynaud (1801-1843)

By the time the 19th century was well underway, many River Acadians had moved solidly into the Creole class. The Louisiana descendents of *nouveau-noble* adventurer Charles Amador de St. Étienne de La Tour, early founder of Acadia, had either forgotten their Acadian roots or deliberately distanced themselves from their origins. Starting with Marguerite Bujol in 1780, exogamous marriages in the succeeding generations further obscured their Acadian heritage. Her upwardly mobile union with prominent Spanish Creole Juan Francisco Vicente Vives lifted the lineage into the plantation echelon, where it remained for at least two more generations. Their son, Jean Landry Chevalier Vives, married a French Creole, Marguerite Marie Bourgeois, whose parents were founding first-generation Louisiana Creoles, their lineage tracing back to Palaiseau, France. In the next generation, **Marie Malvina Vives** married **Martin Songy Reynaud**, a French Creole born in New Orleans. Martin's father, Jean Reynaud, was from Marseille, Bouches-du-Rhone, France. He came to Louisiana circa 1777, married into the prominent New Orleans Songy family, held important official positions, and acquired considerable wealth.

Martin's mother, Marie Charlotte Eleonore Songy, was married to Jean Reynaud at St. Louis Cathedral, New Orleans, in September 1784. Her father was François Valentin Joseph Songy, a native of New Orleans who held several government positions. He was appointed comptroller of Louisiana in 1762, worked at the Marine Bureau in 1765-66, and in the French colonial fiscal office in 1770. Her mother, Charlote Rillieux, whose family was from Lyon, Rhone, France, was also a New Orleans native. In their daughter's marriage agreement, this well-to-do family gave the future bride her rights in the succession of her father: "... one-third of which shall fall into the community the remaining two-thirds to be reserved for any children born of this marriage." The marriage agreement stipulated that the future groom make a marriage settlement of 4,000 livres on the future bride, the principal held intact for any children; another 1,000 livres went directly to the bride.[1]

Martin Songy Reynaud was the ninth child born of this union, although only five survived to adulthood. The Reynaud family was based in New Orleans, so all children were likely born there. Jean Reynaud, Martin's father, emigrated from Marseilles, France, to New Orleans in 1777-1778, and formed a partnership with Antoine Peytavin. They "... had large commercial dealings in the city of New Orleans, the interior of the province, and different parts of Europe and the West Indies, and were possessed of considerable property in the city and territory of Orleans, consisting of plantations, houses, negroes, and merchandise."[2]

The Reynaud-Peytavin properties included a lot and house on Royal Street and a plantation at Houmas, Ascension Parish. Their activities included overseeing a number of enslaved people sales, business agreements, and debt settlements. Jean Reynaud was noted to have given financial support to Spain's war against France, and he was a member of the Militia of New Orleans, gaining the rank of sublieutenant. After the United States acquired Louisiana, Jean became a naturalized citizen in 1806. His business ventures had extended into Ascension Parish by around 1800. Jean Reynaud disappeared under mysterious conditions when he was 49 years old. He was at the Houmas Plantation, owned by the Reynaud-Peytavin partnership, when he failed to return from some activity on January 13, 1807. There must have been widespread searches in the surrounding fields, but he was never seen again. As of 1813, Jean Reynaud was presumed to be dead, his death declared around the date of his disappearance.

Although Martin Songy Reynaud probably grew up in New Orleans, by 1822 he had relocated to the region of St. James Parish where he married his first wife, Marie Manette Françoise Malarcher, also from New Orleans. She died nine months later, probably in childbirth. Three years later, Martin married Marie Malvina Vives on January 26, 1826, at Ascension Church, Donaldsonville.

By this point in the lineage, Creole heritage outweighed Acadian. The last generation that was 100% Acadian included the children of Marie-Anne LeBlanc and Joseph Bujol, born between 1751 and 1769. The children of their daughter, Marguerite Bujol, and her husband Juan Francisco Vicente Vives, were 50% Acadian heritage. The children of their son, Jean Landry Chevalier Vives, and his wife Marguerite Marie Bourgeois, were 25% Acadian heritage. Their daughter, Marie Malvina Vives, and her husband Martin Songy Reynaud, further diluted the Acadian blood to 12.5% in their children. No new infusion of Acadian heritage through marriage had taken place in over 75 years. Culturally this upriver family had metamorphosed into Creole planters and plantation owners, along with some government functionaries and officials.

In 1839, the heirs of Jean Reynaud were challenging the Peytavin executors in the Court of Probates, Ascension Parish, over the distribution of their father's holdings in the partnership. Antoine Peytavin was also deceased by this time. The partnership properties had been sold in 1833, after the death of Madame Reynaud in 1828, and the executors had to take into consideration all the diverse assets, payment of debts, interest, management expenses, net proceeds of crops, and installment discounts. The Reynaud heirs objected to the Peytavin executors' accounting of assets, claiming that the amounts owed were:

"To Songy Reynaud in the sum of nine thousand and forty-three dollars. To Félicité D. Reynaud and the other heirs, a large sum not specified." The appeal case went to the Louisiana State Supreme Court, which returned a ruling in favor of the Reynauds, awarding the heirs the sums they claimed due.[3]

Martin Songy Reynaud was certainly a man of means when he relocated to Ascension Parish. He moved in leadership circles both economically and politically. In 1826, the local newspaper *Le Raconteur* wrote: "We are authorised to announce Songy REYNAUD, Esq., as a candidate to represent the Parish of Ascension in the next State Legislature."[4] Martin became wealthier due to the partnership settlement shortly after his marriage to Marie Malvina Vives. Of interest, two witnesses at this marriage were Peytavin brothers.

It is possible that Martin became involved in operations of the Vives sugarcane plantation, since the heirs through Jean Landry Chevalier Vives were daughters, Marie Malvina and her older sister Marie Clementine Vives, who married Hypolite Palloc. It appears that the surviving male heirs of the two other Vives brothers were not old enough to take charge at the time.

Marie Malvina Vives and Martin Songy Reynaud had seven children. Their first son, Jean Antoine, was born in 1826, almost certainly in the Donaldsonville area of Ascension Parish. He lived to the ripe age of 74 years. The next boy, Songy Reynaud (1827), lived only one year. Louis Songy (1829) lived to be 32 years. Felix Valery (1830) lived one year, and Felix David (1832) lived just two years. The next boy, Louis Felix (1834), had a life lasting 48 years. The seventh and last child was a girl, Louise Marie Malvina, born in Ascension Parish December 13, 1836. She lived to be 58 years old; through her the Vial-Martin lineage is descended.

Although Marie Malvina Vives Reynaud spent most of her life in Ascension Parish, and most likely all her children were born there, she was in New Orleans when she died. New Orleans was a large international city that stood out in comparison to other Southern cities and the rest of Louisiana. By 1860, it had a population of 168,000; the next largest city, Baton Rouge, had only 5,000 inhabitants. The elegant city offered excellent restaurants, opulent hotels, fancy balls, and renowned operas and theaters. There were less salient activities, too, such as gambling dens, horse racing, and houses of prostitution. Wealthier plantation owners maintained houses in New Orleans, where they brought their families to enjoy the opportunities and pleasures of the winter cultural season.

Of the four Vives-Reynaud children who survived to adulthood, two were married at Ascension Church in Donaldsonville and one at St. John the Baptist Church in the nearby parish with that name. Several grandchildren must have moved back to New Orleans, however, as their marriages are recorded there. The family ties to New Orleans remained strong, since they had numerous relatives there and owned a house in the city where they spent the winter cultural season.

Marie Malvina's death certificate reports she died "... in a house on Burgundy Street between Hospital and Barracks Streets in the first Municipality." The funeral was held at St. Louis Cathedral in Jackson Square, New Orleans. The funeral record says: "Died of yellow fever at 6:30 AM on Saturday, October 1, 1842, at her residence at 338 rue Bourgogne..."[5] She was buried at St. Louis Cemetery #2 in New Orleans. Only 32 years old, she must have been in New Orleans as the winter cultural season began, succumbing to an outbreak of the South Louisiana scourge, yellow fever. Martin Songy Reynaud lived only another year. His death is recorded on October 13, 1843, in Ascension Parish. He was just 41 years old, buried at Ascension Church in Donaldsonville.

Yellow Fever. Although a number of contagious diseases affected Louisiana, including cholera and smallpox, yellow fever caused the most intense and deadly epidemics. Transmitted by mosquitoes, the abundance of water in the region provided excellent breeding conditions. The cause of the disease was not understood until 1900, however. The first case was recorded in 1769, with an epidemic in 1796, when 638 people in New Orleans died out of a population of 8,756 (mortality rate 73 per 1000). There were yellow fever outbreaks for 67 summers in New Orleans between 1800 and 1900. While small numbers of people contracted the disease every year, the next major epidemics took place in 1811 and 1817, spreading from New Orleans to Baton Rouge, Saint Francisville, and Natchez.

All along the Mississippi River and into the bayou country, there were occasional cases of yellow fever. The worst epidemic was in 1853, when 1300 people died each week in August, resulting in 8,647 deaths in New Orleans; nearly 1 out of every 12 people. By this time, many Louisiana families had developed immunity from prior exposures. The hardest hit residents were Irish immigrants who lacked immunity; 1 out of every 5 died from the disease that summer. After this, there were three major epidemics until the final one in 1905.

Usual treatment was by bloodletting, blistering, purging, leeching, vomiting, and mercury. Believing yellow fever was caused by "miasma" in the air, cities would shoot cannons and burn barrels of tar during epidemics attempting to disrupt the bad air. Later theories held that yellow fever was transmitted by bacteria through contact with human waste, similar to cholera. In 1900 Dr. Walter Reed was sent by the U.S. military to Cuba to study the disease and verified that it was transmitted by the common mosquito. A Cuban physician, Dr. Charles Finlay, had developed this theory in 1881, but his findings were initially dismissed.

A viral infection, yellow fever begins with headaches and muscle aches, fever, vomiting, dizziness, and jaundice. This yellow tinge to the skin gave the disease its name. In later stages it causes internal hemorrhaging, delirium, and seizures. It was called "black vomit" due to bleeding from the stomach. Death may result 4-8 days after being infected due to hemorrhage, liver and kidney failure. People who recover become immune for life and cannot transmit the disease.

Once the cause was known, preventive measures included fumigation, closing all open water sources, screening cisterns, and even closing off holy water receptacles at entrances of Catholic churches.[6]

The Louisiana Purchase and Statehood

As the 19th century turned, big changes were hovering for the Louisiana territory. The young country that won independence from England just a quarter century earlier had its eye on this region. The newly minted United States wanted to acquire the area near New Orleans, mostly to secure passage of vessels down the Mississippi River to the port, from which they shipped goods to the Atlantic Coast and Europe. In 1800, this was still Spanish territory. The United States also aspired to possess the entire territory of Louisiana. There were many American settlers and merchants already in the region. This ill-defined territory offered wide-open access to the Western frontier, possibly to the Pacific Ocean, promising huge growth for the country.

Spain transferred Louisiana to France in 1801, and the U.S. tried to purchase New Orleans. Napoleon initially refused to sell; President Thomas Jefferson planned to send James Monroe to secure the deal. But, in April 1803, just as Monroe was to arrive in Paris, Napoleon offered to sell not only New Orleans but all of Louisiana. The deal was struck, and the United States purchased Louisiana for $15 million. President Jefferson selected William C. C. Claiborne, former governor of the Mississippi territory and highest-ranking civilian official in the region, to govern Lower Louisiana (south of the Arkansas River). On December 20, 1803, the transfer document was signed giving Lower Louisiana officially to the U.S. Three months later the U.S. took formal possession of the full territory of Louisiana, when France signed over the rights to Upper Louisiana.

The boundaries of this vast territory were vaguely defined, and the U.S. first had to explore and then settle it. President Jefferson commissioned Meriwether Lewis and William Clark to head the first transcontinental explorations, and in May 1804, they departed from St. Louis with 40 enlisted soldiers. Their journey up the Missouri River took them into uncharted lands, where they crossed the Great Divide, and followed the Columbia River to the Pacific Ocean. Their expedition took over two years, returning to St. Louis in September 1806.

South Louisiana was very different from other areas of America. Louisiana's population was more ethnically and racially diverse, and its political and social systems were deeply rooted in the French and Spanish colonial period. Claiborne's greatest challenge as governor was spanning the chasm that separated Anglo-American colonial political traditions from French and Spanish ones. His officials had to merge English common law, familiar to most Americans, with French and Spanish civil law procedures long used in Louisiana. Common law relied more on the judiciary for laws, whereas civil law used various agencies which weighed interests of groups instead of focusing on individual rights. The Civil Code of 1808 drew upon French and Spanish colonial law and the Napoleonic Code, but its drafters brought in Anglo-American and European views, leading to some unique aspects of Louisiana law.

From 1803 until 1812 when Louisiana became a state, it operated mostly under Spanish codes. Slowly, U.S. procedures replaced many from the colonial era, but Louisiana could not be molded into a state like all others. The Creoles united to resist imposition of Anglo-American political and cultural systems. In the resulting hybrid system, two unique structures were implemented: the parish system and the police jury system. In 1807, the territorial legislature replaced the 12 counties that were created shortly after the Louisiana Purchase and instituted 19 civil parishes. These were modeled on Catholic parishes that already existed. In Louisiana today, the parish, rather than the county, still constitutes the basic unit of local government.

In the parish system, the parish judge, justices of the peace, and a group of 12 citizens carried out administrative duties on a local level. This 12-person body was known as the Police Jury, modeled after the Spanish system of syndics; roughly equivalent to other states' county court systems.

One of the first tasks of the new U.S. administrators was to determine who had rightful claims to land ownership. They began assessments of ownership claims using evidence of grants given by the Spanish government when available. Other criteria were inhabiting and cultivating land for more than 10 consecutive years prior to the date when the U.S. acquired South Louisiana. One example found in papers recording the first settlers of the Louisiana Territory concerned Marguerite Rene Bourgeois, who "… claims a tract of land situate on the east side of the river Mississippi, in the county of Acadia, containing five arpents in front, and forty in depth, and bounded on the upper side by land of ETIENNE RENNE, and on the lower side by land of HENRY BERTHELOT. This is part of a tract of land of twelve arpents in front, for which there appears to have been a grant from the Spanish Government, and the land having been inhabited and cultivated for more than ten consecutive years prior to the 20th December, 1803. Confirmed."[7]

Claims were approved for Marie LeBlanc, Jean Pierre Richard, and Rose Bourgeois (widow of Richard) on the west bank of the Mississippi, and a number of Martins and Millets in parishes of Pointe Coupee, Iberville, and St. Mary. Dominique Bourgeois was not so fortunate; her claim was denied in 1805. She had purchased land from the Chetimachas tribe in Iberville, although she had no right to purchase land from Indians, as they could not sell land without authority and concurrence of the U.S. Government.[8]

By the 1810 census, over 76,000 people resided in the Territory of Orleans, about half black and half white. This area included most of what is now Louisiana. Since this number exceeded the minimum for statehood (60,000), the U.S. Congress authorized the calling of a state convention in 1811 to draw up a constitution. The convention had 43 delegates, half Anglo and half of French descent. They deliberated in a New Orleans coffeehouse, with prominent planter and politician Julien Poydras presiding. Louisiana's 1812 constitution provided for a two-house legislature, limited suffrage, and extensive executive powers that included the governor appointing all judges and local officials. The right to vote was limited to adult white males who paid taxes, disqualifying two-thirds of the adult white male population, all nonwhites, and women. There were age, property, and residency requirements for holding office.

On April 30, 1812, Louisiana was admitted as the 18th state in the Union, nine years after the Louisiana Purchase. In late June 1812, William Claiborne was elected as the first state governor.

Antebellum Plantations and Acadian *Petits Habitants*

Statehood and living under U.S. laws, even though adapted to reflect local political structures, brought about significant changes in the lives of Acadians and Creoles. Among the most notable changes were the freedom to sell land and move wherever they wanted, the expansion of technology and markets, and the infusion of Anglo-American population and money. Acadian society had already begun diversification in the late 1700s, when many sought improved social statuses, were slaveowners, and accepted materialism. Upwardly mobile Acadians aspiring to the planter class with its opulent lifestyle had to increase their wealth, which meant expanding both their real property holdings and their enslaved labor force.

Many Acadians rejected this trend toward materialism, however, seeking to perpetuate their traditional lifestyle. They aspired only to have a comfortable existence, to produce enough for their families, and have small agricultural surpluses which they sold to buy necessary household items that they could not make themselves. With increasing pressure from rising land values and taxes, many small farmers sold their land to expanding plantations along the Mississippi River. They retreated to the relative isolation of the lower Lafourche Basin and the prairies of Southwestern Louisiana. Others scattered among South Louisiana parishes and became involved in the sugarcane industry, which was increasingly lucrative. By the mid-1800s, there were 650 Acadian sugar growers in Iberville and 262 in West Baton Rouge parishes, and the numbers in Assumption and Lafourche parishes tripled. This was inevitably accompanied by growth in the number of enslaved people. By the Civil War, scores of Acadians were counted among planter aristocracy, each having acquired over 20 enslaved persons and $10,000 in real estate.

An antebellum Acadian upper-middle class developed; these were prosperous farmers but not included in the wealthy planter class. A large plurality of sugar growers along the Mississippi and bayous Lafourche and Teche were either farmers with small numbers of enslaved persons or planters of moderate means. They were not truly wealthy, however. For example, in Iberville parish, plantation owners held 80% of real property and 60% of personal property, while Acadian planters owned just 14% of real property and 11.7% of personal property.[9]

An ever-widening cultural gap separated the typical Acadian small farmer from the modest planter. Many Acadian planters had risen to the upper economic class and rapidly assumed the associated culture and its attendant social class. These *nouveau riche* Acadians quickly divested themselves of their traditional cultural practices and modeled themselves after the local Creole elite. In the early 19th century, their homes, furnishings, dress, and manners imitated the Creoles. They slavishly adopted Creole tastes for liquor and cuisine, frequented popular Gulf Coast watering holes, and began raising Kentucky thoroughbreds. When the newly arrived Anglo-Americans became the economic pacesetters, rich Acadians built elegant Greek Revival homes such as those introduced by the newcomers. Antebellum Acadian planters along the Mississippi River and both sides of the Atchafalaya with political aspirations began to identify themselves as Creoles. By this time the term "Acadian," or its 19th-century rendition "Cadien," was regarded as degrading.

In the late antebellum period, many Acadian planters diversified their business interests, following the lead of Anglo-Americans. They organized sugar-refining corporations, took active roles in developing banks, steam navigation companies, and railroads. To maintain their materialistic lifestyle, the planters demanded increasing output from their agricultural operations, which produced surplus disposable income. This income was used both for conspicuous consumption and to pay tuition; they wanted their sons to attend the finest schools in the Midwest, East Coast, and New England; and their daughters to be refined in the best regional Catholic finishing schools. These Acadian scions applied their schooling to manage their fathers' plantations or to the legal, medical, and education professions. They formed an Acadian bourgeoisie centered on local parish seats, becoming active in government.

Acadians from lower economic strata often became tradesmen by the mid-1800s. The 1860 census lists 17 categories of Acadian tradesmen in Lafourche Parish, such as carpenters, brick masons, and coopers. The planter class was the true economic force, however. In the river parishes, the census showed that nearly 16% of planter households owned 77% of real property and almost 72% of movable property. The same census reported that in Ascension Parish, the Creole, Anglo-American, and Acadian sugar planters possessed over 91% of all personal property, but the Acadian planters owned only 19% of this total and 28% of local real estate. Anglo-Americans were the economic leaders, since 19 households possessed 50.3% of local real estate and 62% of personal wealth.[10]

More tradition-bound Acadians were not deterred by this rapid accumulation of wealth by local elites, even while some Acadian confrères now identified as Creoles. They maintained the values and mores of their late colonial-era forebears, continuing to run small farms with assistance by sons and 2-3 enslaved persons. In the 1860s, although living in the shadow of the planter aristocracy, Acadian small farmers comprised 60% of Louisiana's Acadian population, most residing on sugar plantations east of the Atchafalaya River. Many owned 4-6 acres, enough to grow food for families and livestock, with a little surplus. There were others who owned no enslaved persons; they were called *petits habitants*, a smaller group of subsistence farmers. The sugar planters considered these Acadians nuisances who demoralized enslaved people by showing they could live comfortably without strenuous work, and who hired the enslaved for odd jobs, paying with luxuries the masters did not want them to have.

Wealthy planters attempted to buy out the nuisance Acadians, offering prices up to three times their properties' actual values. The *petits habitants* were not intimidated for the most part, remaining on their farms, except in river parishes. There, several pressures led to land sellouts, including police jury ordinances that mandated construction and maintenance of levees and public roads on waterfront land after the great flood of 1828. Some had gambling debt or large families that drained meager resources and were happy to accept planters' inflated offers. Several Acadian families who had long wanted to leave river lands to join relatives in Attakapas and Opelousas, but who were thwarted by restrictive Spanish settlement policies, could now sell and relocate. Other *petits habitants* were unhappy with changes taking place in their community, as the plantation system expanded and foreign customs took hold. They sold and moved to more isolated regions where traditional Acadian values still prevailed.

These displaced Acadians followed two patterns of migration: River parish residents sought new homes in the lower Lafourche Valley and St. Landry Parish. Those who were bought out in upper Lafourche Valley moved to north Terrebonne Parish and along Bayou Black, and the Pierre Part region of Assumption Parish. Many experienced lower standards of living after relocation, commonly working as day laborers and unable to afford land. Even those with land faced difficulties; their typically large families required more resources than their less fertile land offered. Many turned to hunting and fishing to augment protein in their diets. Subregional economic differences continued and widened among swamp, bayou, and river Acadians. While some families in these areas and the prairie regions of Lafayette, Vermillion, and Calcasieu became prosperous growing sugarcane or cotton, or accumulating large herds of cattle, most Acadians found their socioeconomic standing was falling.[11]

Significant cultural and economic differences emerged in Louisiana's Acadian community during the antebellum period. It was originally composed of an economically homogeneous group of subsistence farmers and ranchers but was transformed into rigid social stratification by changing economic conditions. The primary forces of change were the rise of sugarcane and cotton commercial agriculture, the attendant plantation system with accumulation of wealth and enslaved people ownership, and the aspiration of ambitious Acadians to join the planter class and identify as Creoles.

Francophobia. Ever since the Louisiana Purchase, when large numbers of Anglo-Americans flowed into the new territory to advance their fortunes, there was increasingly virulent Francophobia. As the Anglos became the dominant culture, their disdain became more public, especially through cultural and linguistic chauvinism. In the 1850s, this condescending statement appeared in a Baton Rouge newspaper regarding Acadians and their French language:

"[We possess] a sincere desire that their progress in the predominant language of the land, will enable us soon to communicate with them through the medium of that impressive tongue in which the constitution and laws of our country are written."[12]

It has been well-documented that when a cultural group loses its language, it becomes absorbed into the dominant society. In 1803, French speakers in Louisiana outnumbered English speakers by a 7-to-1 margin. By 1812, when the state was admitted into the union, that ratio had fallen to 3-to-1. Continued growth in Anglo-American immigration brought the state's free population to 70% English speakers by 1860. Newspapers and official communications began using English and eventually very few French language publications were available. Most of South Louisiana's 15 Acadian parishes did not experience this impact for many more years. In 1870, Acadians still outnumbered Anglos in 9 of these parishes. Anglo populations dominated portions of North Louisiana, Calcasieu, and Cameron parishes with their proximity to Texas and available cheap land. The Anglos heavily impacted river parishes.

The "nativist movement" of the 1850s added fuel to this flame, as large-scale European immigration brought thousands of Irish people fleeing the potato famine, Italians and Germans escaping European revolutions. There was a backlash against all things foreign, exemplified by the American party (the Know-Nothing party) that formed in the mid-1850s to oppose "the corruption of American institutions by the foreign-born."[13] This short-lived political party attracted numerous prosperous Acadians, mostly sugar planters who were previously Whigs, despite its anti-Catholic and anti-French language positions. The majority of Louisiana Catholics, including middle and lower class Acadians, voted the Democratic ticket; those of wealth supported the pro-business conservative Whig ticket. The Know-Nothings briefly scored political victories in St. Landry Parish, where they controlled the policy jury in 1854, in Whig strongholds in West Baton Rouge, St. James, and St. Martin parishes, and in Donaldsonville and Thibodaux in the Acadian sugar belt in 1855.

Upper class Acadians deserted their cultural heritage and migrated into the Anglo-American mainstream. This process was driven by vitriolic public denigration of their mother culture. The dominant culture's attitude toward Acadians followed a downward slope from "... condescension in the 1840s to disgust in the 1850s and 1860s..." reflecting a national perspective that was growing more hostile toward linguistic and cultural minorities. Acadian craftsmen and laboring classes were disinclined to make this cross-cultural migration and lacked the linguistic and educational skills to make the merger. "As sole heirs to their ethnic identity, they became an object of national and regional derision."[14]

Northerners visiting South Louisiana were struck by its natural beauty but found its French-speaking inhabitants repulsive. Southerners were viewed collectively as backward and morally debased, who had been left behind economically, technologically, and culturally by their more industrious and ambitious northern neighbors. Lower class Acadians embodied the worst of such attributes, seen as lazy, ignorant, and lacking in ambition while clinging to their tainted, archaic, and unjust social system. Even the swampy climate was blamed for their debasement. Famous lithographer A. R. Waud penned a report after visiting postwar Louisiana:

"These primitive people are the descendants of Canadian French settlers in Louisiana; and by dint of intermarriage they have succeeded in getting pretty well down in the social scale. Without energy, education, or ambition, they are good representatives of the white trash, behind the age in every thing... To live without effort is their apparent aim in life, and they are satisfied with very little... Their language is a mixture of French and English, quite puzzling to the uninitiated... so little are they thought of—that the niggers, when they want to express contempt for one of their own race, call him an Acadian nigger."[15]

(Note: This derogatory term is retained to give flavor of contemporary attitudes.)

Because these Acadians refused to assimilate, they were considered un-American. Due to their different culture and language, they were viewed as inherently inferior. Because they aspired just to a comfortable life, they were lazy and unambitious. Because they were Catholics, they were labeled pawns of the Pope and priest-dominated. They were considered dangerously inbred due to their strong extended family ties and close-knit neighborhoods. They were ignorant or stupid because they lacked formal education. They were backward because they did not embrace materialism and did not seek to acquire the latest consumer goods.

Albert Rhoads wrote for *Galaxy* magazine in 1873 that Americans wanted all foreign elements turned into the same mold, yet the Cajuns refused for generations, and this was most irritating. "He of Anglo-Saxon stock regards American civilization as the highest in the world, and insists that this Creole [Cajun] native shall square himself to it, but he persistently refuses—he prefers his own."[16] Apparently Rhoads did not appreciate the difference between Acadians/Cajuns and Creoles.

Northern biases were shared by Anglos living in the South, and these attitudes had taken shape by the early 1850s. Frederick Law Olmsted wrote these observations while traveling through the Acadian Coast of the Mississippi River: "At one corner of Mr. R's plantation, there was a hamlet of Acadians (descendants of the refugees of Acadia), about a dozen small houses or huts, built of wood or clay, in the old French peasant style. The residents owned small farms, on which they raised a little corn and rice; but Mr. R described them as lazy vagabonds, doing but little work, and spending much time in shooting, fishing and play. He wanted very much to buy all their land, and get them to move away."[17]

Emerge the Cajuns

Mutual antagonism between lower economic strata French speakers and Anglo-Americans pushed these groups ever farther apart. By the late 1800s they used these epithets for each other—*Américain*, implying swindler, and *Cajun*, signifying white trash. Contact between these groups was minimal, which helped preserve the Acadian's language and culture, but made it difficult for them to improve their condition since access to credit was linked to Anglo businessmen. The Cajuns came to be seen as a monolithic group without internal class, cultural, or religious distinctions, although this was untrue. Poor Creoles living in prairie and bayou regions became identified as Cajuns, primarily based on poverty and language. To these ranks were added large numbers of chronically poor and downwardly mobile Anglos and foreign French immigrants.

This sociocultural amalgam was created through multicultural marriages and held together by common bonds of poverty. The term Cajun was applied to this amalgam of several culturally and linguistically distinct groups that comprised the majority white population in several parishes—57% of all white households in the 15-parish Acadian area in the 1870 census. The highest proportions were in Terrebonne, Iberville, Lafourche, St. James, St. Mary, St. Martin, St. Landry, and West Baton Rouge. The lowest proportions were in Ascension, Calcasieu, and Vermillion. The middle range parishes were Cameron, Iberia, Lafayette, and Assumption.

Over the next 50 years, as these groups continued to coalesce, the foundation was set for the blended, Acadian-based culture that pervades South Louisiana in present times, called the Cajuns. Among the upper-middle and wealthy classes, however, prejudice against Cajuns persisted well into the mid-20th century. Cajuns were regarded as just a half-step above black people. They were seen as generally ignorant, not interested in bettering themselves, insular and clannish, and resistant to adopting mainstream "American" values.

A process of Americanization gradually took place after World War II, due to a number of events and resulting cultural and economic evolutions. These eventually led to an

"Acadian redemption" with rising ethnic pride and the near-adulation of Cajun cuisine, music, and culture that is now big tourist business in South Louisiana—a story that will be told later.

Louise Marie Malvina Reynaud (1836–1894) — Joseph Albert Bossier (1831–1868)

Louise Marie Malvina Reynaud was born on December 13, 1836, and baptized four months later at Ascension Church, Donaldsonville. She was the seventh and last child of Marie Malvina Vives and Martin Songy Reynaud. Only four of these children survived to adulthood. The family lived in or near the town of Donaldsonville, originally called Lafourche-des-Chitimachas. After the territory became part of the United States, many Anglo-Americans moved there. In 1806, landowner and planter William Donaldson commissioned a new town to be built at this site. It was renamed Donaldsonville after him.

Louise Marie Malvina Reynaud

Shortly before Louise Marie was born, Donaldsonville was designated as the Louisiana capital (1829-1831). This happened as the result of tensions between Anglo-Americans and French Creoles. Increasing numbers of Anglos wanted the state capital, then New Orleans, closer to their centers of population farther upriver and deemed the large port city "too noisy." The French Creoles wanted to keep the capital in its historically French location. Although Donaldsonville's moment in the sun as state capital was brief, it gained prestige for the growing town. The region was becoming wealthier, primarily due to the sugarcane industry. Sugar planters built fine mansions and public buildings in and around the town during the antebellum era. Donaldsonville's historic district is now considered one of the finest collections of buildings from the antebellum era of all Louisiana upriver towns.

The Reynaud family probably lived in one of those fine mansions in Donaldsonville. They were certainly well-to-do, given Martin Songy Reynaud's inheritance and business ventures. They owned a house in New Orleans and certainly spent part of the social season there. River steamboats were a major mode of transportation for trips up and down the Mississippi River. These elegantly adorned, two or three deck ships used steam engines to drive a huge paddlewheel at the back (bow). They were adeptly navigated along the river's strong currents and numerous twists. For the first class passengers there was fine dining, musical performances, dances, and promenades along the higher decks. The Reynaud family would have traveled first class and enjoyed these amenities.

Louise Marie Malvina endured many losses in her life of 58 years, which was average length for this time period. Both parents died when she was a child; she was undoubtedly raised by relatives. Thankfully, she had numerous aunts, uncles, and cousins that could provide care for the orphans. She lost her first child, Pierre Melville Bossier, when he was only a few months of age. Her three older brothers lived to adulthood.

Both of her parents, Marie Malvina Vives and Martin Songy Reynaud, died within a year of each other. Her mother died at age 32 of yellow fever in New Orleans (1842); her father's cause of death is unknown but he was only 41 years old and residing in Donaldsonville (1843). They left four children, none of them having reached adulthood. The oldest, Jean Antoine Reynaud, was 17 years old, followed by Louis Songy Reynaud age 14, Louis Felix Reynaud age 9, and Louise Marie Malvina Reynaud, age 7.

It is likely that the care of these children was spread among relatives, since there are records showing that Louis Songy Reynaud was living in Donaldsonville in 1861, while Louise Marie Malvina Reynaud was living downriver in Edgard, St. John the Baptist Parish, in 1860. Their father had two siblings still living when he died in 1843: Félicité Desiree, who married Isidore Valery Landry, and Charlotte Azelie, who married Louis Laroque Turgeau. There were Landry and Turgeau relatives who witnessed the parents' marriage and sponsored Louise Marie Malvina at baptism, along with Mrs. Albert Duffel. When she married into the Bossier family, her kinship network vastly expanded. There were numerous Bossiers in St. John the Baptist Parish, and she must have met many after she moved to live there.

Another shocking loss occurred for Louise Marie Malvina in 1861. Her older brother Louis Songy Reynaud was killed in a shootout with two other men in Donaldsonville. Louis Songy was living with his brother Jean and his wife and three children in the 1860 U.S. Census. His occupation was road inspector. When the Civil War broke out, he enlisted in the Confederate Army at Camp Moore, Louisiana, on June 7, 1861. Though he became a second lieutenant in Company F, 7th Louisiana infantry regiment, he resigned his commission and was back in Donaldsonville by that fall.

On November 20, 1861, the shooting incident was reported in local newspapers. Louis Songy was sitting on the bench at Crescent Park, near the Mississippi River, when two men accosted and fired at him. He fired back at the attackers; in all 14-15 pistol shots were fired, only five by Louis Songy, but he was hit by seven bullets. One assailant was hit in the arm, but the injury was mild. During the shooting, Louis Songy tried to escape to a nearby store, collapsed, and was taken to his brother's house. He died there a few hours later. The motive for the attack is not known. The attackers, David Pugh and Dr. James L. McCormick, were brothers-in-law; the Pugh family was very wealthy, owning 13 plantations and 1,500 enslaved people.[18]

Though there apparently was a trial, nothing came of it. In the 1870 U.S. Census, Dr. James McCormick still lived with his family in Donaldsonville, and David Pugh lived with his family in Lafourche Parish.

It is not clear where Louise Marie Malvina was living between the ages of 7 and 15 years, but most likely it was with relatives in St. John the Baptist Parish. In keeping with practices of upper class French Creoles, Louise Marie was sent to be educated in a Catholic academy school for girls. When she was 15 years old, Louise Marie was studying at the Nazareth Female Academy in Nelson County, Kentucky. The school was run by the Sisters of Charity of Nazareth, Kentucky, a Catholic religious order founded in 1812. They started the school in 1814, and enrollment steadily increased; soon they moved to the St. Thomas Farm site purchased by Mother Catherine Spalding, using a dowry provided by Ann O'Connor, a widow who joined the congregation. From humble beginnings at the farm, an educational ministry arose that would encompass 12 states and 4 foreign countries, to include several schools of nursing, many academies, and several colleges.[19]

The Nelson County, Kentucky, census of 1850 lists M. Reynaud, age 15, as a student, along with two Bossier girls ages 15 and 16, and one Duffel girl age 13, all of Louisiana. These girls were probably relatives, perhaps daughters in the family with whom she lived. It is not certain how long Louise Marie studied there, but she was back in Donaldsonville less than six years later when she married in 1856. In the 1860 census, she was living in St. John the Baptist Parish in Edgard, her husband's home.

From her pictures, it is evident that Louise Marie was a beautiful young woman and undoubtedly quite accomplished. She probably met her husband, Joseph Albert Bossier, in the French Creole social circles that were flourishing in the area. Perhaps the Bossier girls who attended the Nazareth Female Academy were his sisters or cousins. Family lore has it that Louise Marie was "an adopted child," though most likely this was not formal.

Certainly the Creole community was closely interconnected; Louise Marie and Joseph Bossier were second cousins and had to apply to the Catholic Church for a dispensation to marry due to third degree of cosanguinity.

The entangled bloodlines of French Creoles and Acadians made for numerous applications for such dispensations from the Church. Here is the pathway for Louise Marie Malvina Reynaud and Joseph Albert Bossier's cosanguinity:

- Louise Marie was the daughter of Martin Songy Reynaud, who was the son of Marie Charlotte Eleonore Songy, married to Jean Reynaud.

- Joseph Albert Bossier was the son of Félicité Desiree Songy, who married Pierre Maximilien Bossier. Félicité was the daughter of Martin Firmin Songy, who was the brother of Marie Charlotte Eleonore Songy, and uncle of Martin Songy Reynaud.

- Louise Marie and Joseph Albert shared common great-grandparents: François Valentin Joseph Songy and Charlotte Rillieux, making them second cousins.

Joseph Albert Bossier (Sr.) was born on September 14, 1831, and baptized five months later at St. John the Baptist Church in Edgard. He was the second child of Pierre Maximilien Bossier of Edgard and Félicité Desiree Songy of New Orleans. They had nine children of which three survived to adulthood. Joseph's parents were married in Edgard in 1818; Joseph was the last child born 13 years later. When Joseph was just a year old, his father died in 1832. His mother died in 1849 when Joseph was 18 years old; she had many Songy, Reynaud, and Bossier relatives so he had a wide family network.

The Bossiers were a military family originally from the Castelsagrat, Tarn-et-Garonne area of France. Joseph Albert's great-grandfather, Jean Pierre Bossier *dit* Lebrun, was born in Natchitoches in 1729. Jean Pierre's father, Jean Baptiste Bossier *dit* Lebrun, had relocated from Castelsagrat sometime around the 1730s. Jean Baptiste was married twice; both occurred in New Orleans. Apparently there were no children with the first

Joseph Albert Bossier Sr.

wife who died young; he married the second in 1728: Marianne Chagneau from Vérines, Charente-Maritime, France. He was residing in Natchitoches then, but went to New Orleans to marry, where a sergeant in the New Orleans troops was a witness. When he died in 1745 at age 69, he was residing in Natchitoches.

The town of Natchitoches was established in 1714 by French explorer Louis de St. Denis. It is the oldest permanent European settlement within the 1803 Louisiana Purchase territory. This French outpost on the Red River, near the border between French holdings and Spanish territories to the west (now Texas), had river access to Texas and New Orleans. Natchitoches was an important trading post with Mexico initially, and later a transfer point for cotton. Early settlers were French immigrants and French Creoles who acquired land grants that became cotton-producing plantations, such as the Magnolia and Oakland Plantations. This is known as the Cane River area.

Jean Baptiste Bossier *dit* Lebrun likely followed the pioneering steps of Louis de St. Denis when he came as a French immigrant soldier. His first son, Jean Pierre Bossier *dit* Lebrun (1729-1816), had moved to the German Coast along the Mississippi River before 1752. Jean Pierre was married to Marie Madeleine Manon Rommel (Rome) at St. Charles Borromeo Church in Destrehan on August 8, 1752. Her parents were from Rommel and Steiger families, early German settlers of that area. Their son, Jean Pierre Bossier (Bossie), was born in 1757, the fourth child; all born in St. John the Baptist Parish.

Jean Pierre Bossier (1757-1846) continued the military tradition of his family. He served as a second lieutenant in the Militia of the German Coast, Regiment of the Germans, from 1792 to 1797. This was probably not a full-time occupation, so he must have farmed in the parish. He married Marguerite Borne (1769-1846) at the parish church in Edgard on January 9, 1787. Her parents were Jacque Antoine Borne (1737-1809) and Anne Marie Heidel (Haydel) (1742-1810). Connections between the Bossier and Haydel families were close; two marriages between them took place in this generation. Jean Pierre's sister, Marguerite Bossier, married Jean Georges Haydel. When Jean Pierre died in 1846, one witness at burial was Jean Jacques Haydel, Jr. (1780-1863), son of the builder of Whitney Plantation, and a cousin by marriage.

Pierre Maximilien Bossier, son of Jean Pierre, was born on November 9, 1789, and baptized 2 months later at St. John the Baptist Church in Edgard. His was a large family; out of 12 siblings, all but three lived to adulthood. Before 1814, Maximilien had joined the 1st Division, Louisiana Militia, 5th Regiment of the German Coast. It appears that he might have fought in the War of 1812. He married in 1818, taking Félicité Desiree Songy as his wife at St. John the Baptist Church. In the census of 1830, Maximilien and his brother Justin were listed as heads of household; in their household were living 11 males and 10 females. They must have occupied a large home to accommodate 21 people; possibly a modest plantation in the Edgard area. Of the males, 6 were boys below age 10; 2 were teens; and 2 were adults between 21-40 years old. There were 6 girls below 10; 3 young women ages 21 to 30; and 1 mature woman between 31-40 years old.[20]

Maximilien was 41 years old at the time of the census, his brother Justin was 35, and both were married. The children were mostly those of Justin, since Maximilien and his wife Félicité Desiree were unfortunate with childbearing. Although Félicité Desiree had borne nine children, only her son Adam Bossier was alive in 1830, but he died in 1831. Later that year, however, they had Joseph Albert Bossier, who lived to age 37 and continued the family line with Louise Marie Malvina Reynaud.

The Bossier family of Edgard was evidently one of means. Joseph was able to attend college in 1846 at St. Louis University, in St. Louis, Missouri. He was 14 years old when he entered the university. His parent/guardian was listed in the student register as "Vve Marg. Bossie," and his name spelled "Joseph Bossie." It is possible that this guardian was Marguerite Borne, his paternal grandmother, although his mother was still alive then. He continued studies at the University of Louisiana, New Orleans, in the late 1840s. By 1850, he had graduated from Tulane University, New Orleans, with a law degree. The census of 1860 lists him as an attorney at law, with personal property valued at $5,000 and real property valued at $5,000. This consisted of substantial holdings at the time.[21]

Joseph Albert Bossier was a "product lawyer" living 40 miles above New Orleans. This type of lawyer specializes in legal issues involved with producing products, including government regulations, consumer protection, contracts, marketing, and commercial aspects. A subcategory of product lawyers deals with cases of people who are injured as a result of using or working with a product. Since Joseph lived and worked in St. John the Baptist Parish, a nexus of sugarcane production, undoubtedly many of his clients were involved in the industry. Given the litigious character of both French and Acadian people, Joseph was most likely well engaged and prosperous in his law practice. Lawyers, being familiar with economic details of their communities, could take advantage of financial opportunities. The close-knit nature of the profession allowed them to build wealth, connections, and political base. Their work time was usually flexible, so they could hold local political and public offices.

In 1853, Joseph married his first cousin, Clelia Bossier. They needed a Church dispensation for second degree of cosanguinity. There were no children and Clelia died in 1853, probably during the yellow fever epidemic in Edgard that year. His second marriage to Louise Marie Malvina Reynaud took place on June 2, 1856, in Ascension Church, Donaldsonville. Apparently Joseph had a propensity to marry his cousins; this time the bride was his second cousin. Joseph's sister Marcellite Marguerite Bossier was married to Valéry Justinien Laroque-Turgeau, first cousin to Marie Malvina. Their families undoubtedly had frequent interactions.

Joseph and Marie Malvina Bossier lived and raised their family in Edgard, not far downriver from Donaldsonville. Their first child, Pierre Melville Bossier, was born in 1857 but died that same year. The second son, Joseph Albert Bossier, Jr., was born in 1859 and lived to adulthood. Next was Louise Clothilde Malvina Bossier, born in 1860, who lived to 46 years old. Through her the Vial-Martin line descended. Oscar Louis Bossier, born in 1861, lived to a venerable 63 years old. The youngest daughter, Marie Maude Bossier, born in 1866, became one of the longest lived family members when she died at age 86 in 1952.

Joseph Albert Bossier, Sr., lived only until he was 37 years old. He died on December 2, 1868, at his home and was buried the next day at St. John the Baptist Church, Edgard. His obituary was printed on December 5, 1868, in the St. John News: "Joseph Bossier, one of our most eminent citizens and a distinguished lawyer, died last Wednesday at 7:00 AM in his 38th year. Mr. Bossier became a member of the bar in 1850 and since that time practiced his profession in our parish. His remains were deposited in the St. John the Baptist cemetery. He leaves a widow and four children."[22]

Louise Marie remarried on August 21, 1872, again at St. John the Baptist Church, Edgard. Her second husband was Pierre Nathaniel Ham, born about 1815 in Virginia. They had one child, a daughter Malvina Lillian Ham, born September 6, 1873. In the census of 1880, it was noted that Marie Louise "Keeps house." But in the 1890 census, she was listed as "Widow of Joseph Bossier." Pierre Nathaniel Ham must have died before this time, and she reverted to using her esteemed first husband's name. Louise Marie lived until 1894, when she died at age 58 years. Probably she is buried in one of the Bossier family crypts at St. John the Baptist Cemetery in Edgard.

The 1860 federal census of St. John the Baptist Parish reveals the concentration of economy in the sugarcane industry. Of the occupations listed for men, 62 residents were planters and 41 were overseers. The financial holdings of planters ranged from less than

$2,000 real estate and $8,000 personal estate to $200,000 real estate and $260,000 personal estate. Being a planter was by far the most prosperous occupation in the parish. The wealthiest planter was from Virginia. Overseers usually did not own land, and most had no personal estate listed; for those that did, the value was on average $1,000-1,500. There were four physicians in the parish with average holdings of $2,000 real estate and $5,000 personal estate. Of the three attorneys residing there, real estate was around $2,000 and personal estate up to $8,000. Teachers made considerably less. Of the 13 teachers listed, most had no real estate; only two had significant holdings between $2,000 and $4,000 combined real and personal estates.

At least half of parish residents in 1860 had no real estate and insignificant personal estate. Occupations for men were carpenter, cooper, mason, storekeeper, painter, tailor, shoemaker, blacksmith, printer, butcher, watchmaker, saddler, carriage maker, sawmill operator, trader, coffeehouse keeper, baker, druggist, priest, and sugar maker. The last category contained a single household, composed of people from Cuba, Poland, and Louisiana. They must have supplied small quantities of sugar to local households, while the planters were involved in commercial sugar making.[23]

The Bossier-Reynaud family lived through a tumultuous and conflicted era. As the sugarcane industry was expanding and creating extreme wealth for some, the widespread use of enslaved people was becoming more controversial and potentially dangerous. Economic disparity between classes had grown more pronounced; land ownership was concentrated among large plantation owners, while small farmers and traditional Acadians were falling into lower economic strata. Politics were heating up, and animosity between northern and southern states was growing. These divisions were propelling the fairly young United States toward its bloody and tragic Civil War.

Sugarcane Industry

The sugarcane industry shaped the lives of upriver families along the lower Mississippi River. By 1803, there were 75 sugar enterprises of varying sizes along both banks. The roots of plantation agriculture were established in the early 1730s, with Spanish land grants for cultivation of indigo and tobacco. Sugarcane plants were brought to New Orleans in 1742 by Jesuits from St. Domingue. Originating in New Guinea, sugarcane was brought by Columbus to the Caribbean from the Canary Islands. Though frost susceptible, cane survived in New Orleans' subtropical climate. The first sugar mill was built by Claude-Joseph Dubreuil of Esplanade Street in the late 1750s. Étienne de Bore is credited with starting economically successful sugarcane production in 1795, using improved cane varieties and his wife's fortune. He married the daughter of former Louisiana treasurer Jean-Baptiste Destrehan, and created a sugar manufacturing facility at his wife's property capable of making sugar granulate. This is now Audubon Park in New Orleans. With assistance of St. Domingue sugar maker Antoine Morin, de Bore's first crop produced 100 hogsheads (100,000 lbs.) of granulated sugar that sold for 12.5 cents per pound. Along with molasses selling for 50 cents per gallon, he netted a profit of $12,000, which was considerable at the time.[24]

The decline of other crops such as cotton and indigo set the stage for the spread of sugarcane cultivation. Plantations based on Spanish land grants already lined the lower Mississippi River and tributaries, situated upon better drained natural levees. The sugarcane region encompasses nearly 12,000 square miles in 20 parishes, where presently over 300,000 acres are used for cultivation. Strung like elongated rectangles on a string, these plantations form long, narrow strips following the undulating course of the rivers. By 1806, the northward expansion of sugar plantations reached around 35 miles north of New Orleans. Even the improved cane varieties were frost susceptible, so more cotton was planted than sugar in the north regions extending 15 miles above Baton Rouge to Point Coupee.

Although sugar was more profitable than cotton, it was a riskier crop and heavily labor dependent. Several factors combined to turn sugar production into a lucrative business. In the early 1800s, steam power was introduced for milling cane, making the milling process much more efficient than using animal power. Two new cane varieties came to Louisiana in 1825 which were more frost resistant.

An improved method for granulation was created in 1834 by **Norbert Rillieux (1806-1894)**, a free man of color born in New Orleans and educated in Paris. This triple-effect evaporator was widely adopted after 1844 and is still used today.[25]

Norbert Rillieux was a distant relative of the Vial-Martin families. His great-grandfather was François Rillieux, native of Lyon, France, who came to Mobile in the early 1770s and settled in New Orleans. Norbert's father, Vincent Rillieux Jr., was the nephew of Charlote Rillieux, daughter of François, and sister of Vincent Rillieux Sr. Charlote married Françoise Valentin Joseph Songy. They were the parents of Marie Charlotte Eleonore Songy, mother of Martin Songy Reynaud who married Marie Malvina Vives. François Rillieux was the great-grandfather of both Norbert and Martin, making them second cousins.

Vincent Rillieux Jr. (1778-?) was a prosperous engineer who invented a steam-operated cotton baler. Born in New Orleans, he "married" a free woman of color, Constance Vivant (1789-1868). Constance belonged to a respected free black family, among the large *gens de color libre* community of the city. This was probably not an official marriage, which was proscribed between the races by the *Code Noir*.[26] Their union was undoubtedly a *plaçage*, a recognized extralegal system in French and Spanish colonies. White men entered into civil unions with women of color, not legally recognized as wives, but given contracts that settled property on the woman and her children, often freeing them if enslaved. The women were called *placées*; some became wealthy and influential, including "voodoo queen" Marie Laveau. This system reached its zenith between 1769 and 1803.[27]

The seven children born of this union were considered Creoles, with access to education and privileges not available to most blacks. Relationships between such racially mixed families were complex; the *plaçage* system had particular rules, but men like Vincent bent laws of inheritance and propriety to advance their family.

After the Louisiana Purchase in 1803, Anglo-Americans poured into Louisiana, many joining the developing sugar industry. Although the War of 1812 temporarily slowed its development, the industry quickly rebounded and spread to plantations established west of the Mississippi, where the Anglos could acquire land. Between 1812 and 1850, Anglo planters bought rich, arable lands along the lower Bayou Teche, backlands of upper Bayou Lafourche, and public lands in Terrebonne Parish. Further westward expansion was hindered because the lands west of Bayou Teche were not included in the Louisiana Purchase.

By 1844, Louisiana had more than 700 sugar plantations in operation. Cotton prices fell precipitously in the 1840s, spurring more growth of sugarcane cultivation. As the antebellum period was nearing its end, there were over 1,000 sugar plantations in the state. The industry's incessant need for labor was solved by slavery, which had existed since the settlement of the area. There were 332,000 enslaved people in 1860, at least 45% of Louisiana's total population. Outside of New Orleans, they made up more than 60% of the population. Nine out of ten worked on rural plantations and farms. Concentrations of enslaved people were highest along the Mississippi River parishes, in some comprising over 90% of the population.[28]

The Civil War had catastrophic effects on the sugar industry. The number of sugar plantations decreased from 1,200 in 24 parishes in 1861, to only 175 plantations in 16 parishes in 1864. Before the war began, the sugar industry produced 264,000 "short tons" of sugar, which fell to only 5,971 produced in 1864. Currently there are 190 sugar plantations, although the sugar growing region covers the same area it did in 1844.[29]

Enslaved People. The economy and lifestyle of South Louisiana planters relied upon slavery. Although plantation owners and their families were just a small part of the agrarian population, they controlled much of the wealth and political power in antebellum Louisiana. Most were astute businessmen, buying and selling crops and enslaved people at the best prices. They reinvested profits into their plantations and bought luxury goods such as fine furniture, tableware, art, clothing, and jewelry. Many kept houses in New Orleans for the winter cultural season. Each plantation had a large mansion, set among moss-draped oaks on a high point in the property. Many had nearby outbuildings for cooking and storage.

Behind the great house were clusters of barns and sheds surrounding the sugarhouse, which had chimneys towering above cane fields. The sugarhouse was an agricultural factory in the field where cane juice was processed into granules and molasses. The enslaved people's quarters were nearby, essentially a village of nearly identical laborers' dwellings, small wood cabins usually housing two families. A central fireplace divided the rooms which contained minimal cooking and sleeping areas. The village was centered upon a single road in a linear pattern or grouped in a block pattern with a grid of streets. Larger plantations might have a church and company store.

Sugarcane fields were extensive, covering hundreds or thousands of acres without fences. These fields stretched in long, narrow rectangles from levee crests at riverbanks, into the back swamps that were down slope from the waterways. Long, straight ditches divided the fields for irrigation, giving the plantations a characteristic linear appearance. Sugarcane had a long growing and harvesting season, taking up most of the year. Planting, growing, cutting, and milling sugar was very hard work. Enslaved people worked the fields from sunrise to sundown; often they had to work around the clock during the grinding season. Many plantations imposed a minimum harvesting quota; those who failed to meet it were commonly whipped. Injuries and burns were frequent while cane juice was being boiled down to syrup.

Commonly, some male enslaved persons were trained as carpenters, blacksmiths, and other trades. Those trained and skilled in hunting were held in high regard, since their masters trusted them enough to carry arms. In addition to providing game for the plantation owners' family, these men supplied their own community with meat to supplement their mostly corn-based diet. Female enslaved persons worked primarily around or in the great house, preparing food and tending gardens. Others assumed responsibility for their community's children and meals. A subset of enslaved persons worked inside the planters' house, some living in first-floor rooms, to tend the master, mistress, and their children. Most plantations had overseers, usually white but occasionally black men. These were nearly universally dreaded and despised by enslaved people because of their cruelty.

The enslaved communities developed their own hierarchy, with those working in the house at the top and field workers at the bottom. Those living in the enslaved quarters often did not trust those who worked in the great house, fearing those closer to the master and mistress would be informers. African Americans throughout the antebellum South did not accept their enslavement and inhumane treatment and resisted regularly. On a day-to-day basis, this resistance took the form of slowing the work pace, breaking tools, stealing, faking illness, and even injuring animals. More violent resistance included poisoning overseers or planter families, aborting pregnancies, killing oneself or others, including their children, and running away. When caught doing something wrong, or if reported by those in the house, both enslaved men and women were whipped. Twenty lashes was light punishment; some were flogged nearly to death.

These beleaguered men and women were still able to create a sense of community, develop their own values, activities, and identity separate from white plantation society. They reinforced community ties by gathering together to eat, dance, sing, and tell stories. Few enslaved people were allowed to learn to read and write, and Louisiana legislation passed in 1830 made it a crime to teach them literacy. So, they used oral traditions to pass down history and stories, as their ancestors did in Africa. Among their community were religious leaders and midwives, held in high regard. It was difficult to maintain stable families, although some did accomplish this. Enslaved people were rarely allowed to marry formally in church services, though their masters might let them take on partners at other plantations. Such family ties were subject to the whims and fortunes of the plantation masters, who often sold unneeded family members, thus breaking up families. Most planters found it expedient to encourage family ties among their enslaved, since this would discourage adults from running away and would increase their enslaved holdings through more children.

When enslaved persons sought liberty, they headed for the swamps where they established maroon (runaway) communities. They raised and hunted food and raided nearby plantations for other supplies. Most runaways were captured after a short time, since rewards were offered for their capture and return. Runaways faced severe punishment and were usually sold on the slave market. Some plantation runaways with skills escaped to cities, such as New Orleans, where they merged into the free black community.

In 1811, the largest enslaved people revolt in United States history took place in Louisiana. Led by an enslaved man from St. Domingue named Charles Deslondes, a group of insurgents marched from upriver plantations down River Road to New Orleans. They burned plantations and crops, captured weapons and ammunition, and killed two whites. Planters organized vigilantes who were reinforced by U.S. Army troops from Baton Rouge and New Orleans. One company of free black militia joined the planter group. The two forces clashed outside New Orleans. Sixty-six enslaved people were killed; others were missing or captured and held for trial. Two whites were killed in the battle. Following the trial of captured insurgents, 21 were sentenced to death, shot, and decapitated. Their heads were placed on poles along River Road as a warning to other potentially rebellious enslaved people.

Life in the plantation house. Plantation great houses were of two basic types, Creole and Anglo, depending on the cultural identity of the planters. Creole plantation mansions had chimneys located on inside walls near the roofline center, likely a carryover from Acadian house styles. All the front rooms opened onto a gallery or porch, so there were multiple front doors. The interior floor plan was several rooms wide and from 1-3 rooms deep. It lacked a central hallway inside, with doors opening between rooms. Stairs were located on the exterior, never inside. Houses were 1.5-2 stories high with a hip roof. Living quarters were on the second story; the first floor used by servants and for cooking and storage. Additional rooms to the sides and rear were common. These features were inherently French traits. The French building style of *colombage* was popular in the 18th and early 19th centuries, using heavy cypress timbers pegged together and filled with brick or mud nogging (Spanish moss, shells, or lime to stiffen the mud), called *bousillage*. These houses had brick ground floors, green-shuttered French doors and windows, and exterior weatherboarding painted white.

Examples of Creole plantation mansions are **Home Place** (Keller) **Plantation** house built for the Fortier family (1801, St. Charles Parish); **St. Joseph Plantation** mansion built by C. B. Mericq about 1820 (St. James Parish); and **Whitney Plantation** built about 1800 by Jean Jacques Haydel (St. John the Baptist Parish). Whitney Plantation preserved many outbuildings and enslaved quarters and now is an extensive museum and monument to the lives and experiences of enslaved people.

Joseph Albert Bossier, Sr. was related by both blood and marriage to the Haydel (Heidel) family of Whitney Plantation:

- Ambroise Heidel (1702-1774) was his great-great grandfather through his grandmother, Marguerite Borne (1769-1846), daughter of Anne Marie Heidel (1742-1810). Ambroise was among the early German families who had land grants along the Mississippi River. This region was first called the German Coast; later the Acadian Coast was added.

- Anne Marie Heidel was the sister of Jean Jacques Heidel Sr. (1744-1826), who built Whitney Plantation. They were both children of Ambroise Heidel.

- Joseph's mother, Félicité Desiree Songy, was the granddaughter of Marie Borne, sister of Marguerite Borne. Thus, he had Heidel blood through both parents.

- His great-aunt Marguerite Bossier, sister of his grandfather Jean Pierre Bossier (Bossie), married Jean Georges Haydel (1753-1815).

- Jean Georges Haydel was the son of Jean Christophe Heidel (1731-1800), who was the brother of Jean Jacques Heidel Sr., who built Whitney Plantation. The younger generation changed the spelling to Haydel.

- The Heidel brother who built Whitney Plantation was the direct great-great-uncle of Joseph Bossier—and also his great-great-uncle-in-law! (Though he died before Joseph was born.)

Anglo plantation mansions were built in Upland South and Atlantic Tidewater styles. Their architects introduced Greek Revival and Georgian decorative styles. Anglo plantations were 1.5-2 stories high, with both floors used as living quarters. There was a central hall dividing the two rooms across the width, usually 1-2 rooms deep. Stairs were on the inside, and the chimneys placed at the ends, particularly at the outside ends of gables. Many had front-facing gables and galleries supported by columns, a portico, and pediments. Building materials were brick, plaster, and cypress wood. Walls were either entirely brick or wood, the same materials used on both floors.

Examples of Anglo plantation mansions are **Ashland-Belle Helene** built for Duncan Kenner in 1841 (Ascension Parish east bank); **Oaklawn Manor** built in 1847 by Alexander Porter (Bayou Teche); and **Madewood** built in 1840 by Thomas Pugh (Bayou Lafourche).

Secession and the Civil War

Political tensions were rising during the 1850s between northern and southern states in the U.S. Legislature. The main source of escalating differences among lawmakers was the issue of slavery. Those from northern states wanted slavery limited or banned; as a first step they sought to make slavery illegal in U.S. territories, particularly in the West. Initially, their proposals were to allow slavery already in southern states to remain, but to end any new importation of enslaved people. This they believed would eventually lead to phasing out the "peculiar institution." They believed that slavery was incompatible with republicanism, against the U.S. Constitution, and an inherently evil practice.

Southerners believed that eliminating slavery would destroy the South's economy and doom their society—slavery was an integral part of both. Although anti-slavery forces said their objective was containment and stopping expansion, slaveholding interests in the South declared this infringed on their Constitutional rights to state-based laws and economic practices. They had invested a large amount of capital in their enslaved people and were afraid of consequences if they were given freedom. The example of the horrors in St. Domingue was invoked, where a revolt of enslaved people killed nearly all the white people there—men, women, and children—even though many were sympathetic to abolition. Southerners mistrusted the containment strategy as a first step toward emancipation and found overwhelming the prospects of integrating millions of freed blacks into their communities.

With war clouds gathering in 1860, Louisiana's antebellum population was sharply divided along class lines. According to their divergent interests, the two major ideological groups were planters and large farmers, whose staple crop production depended on numerous enslaved workers; and small farmers and laborers who cared little about "Southern rights" and preferred to be left alone. Affluent Acadian as well as Creole and Anglo planters opposed any steps to ban slavery in the territories. Their delegate to the Democratic conventions in 1860 was former governor and current U.S. senator, Alexandre Mouton, a prominent Acadian. The tumultuous conventions produced a split with two presidential candidates resulting: Stephen A. Douglas and John Breckenridge. As talk of secession spread, two camps formed—those who wanted immediate secession and those who wanted southern states to coordinate an approach and negotiate a compromise over slavery, called "cooperationists." Planters along the Mississippi River and Lafourche Valley held on to the faint hope that cooperationists presented. They were worried about the disastrous impact a war would have on their business operations.

In the 1860 presidential election, Louisiana cast its electoral votes for John Breckinridge. However, he and the other Democratic candidate, Steven A. Douglas, could not command enough electoral votes, and the Republican Party won a plurality, making Abraham Lincoln winner of the election. Lincoln supported banning slavery in the U.S. territories but said, "I have no purpose, directly or indirectly to interfere with the institution of slavery in the United States where it exists. I believe I have no lawful right to do so, and I have no inclination to do so."[30]

Before Lincoln was inaugurated, however, seven slaveholding states with cotton-based economies declared secession and then formed the Confederacy. These states had the highest proportions of enslaved people, an average of 49%. Louisiana Governor Thomas Overton Moore called for a secession convention in the aftermath of Lincoln's election. When the convention met in Baton Rouge in January, 1861, public support for the cooperationist approach had dissolved, and the wave of secession swept over delegates, who voted 113 to 17 to dissolve "... the union between the State of Louisiana and other States."[31]

Louisiana became part of the Confederate States of America after it was formed on February 4, 1861. President Lincoln challenged the fledgling government's authority by sending reinforcements to Fort Sumter in Charleston Harbor in April 1861. The Confederate army bombarded the fort, setting off an armed struggle for independence. Soon the states of the Upper South joined the Confederacy, and a widespread call to arms went out. Louisiana rallied 12,000 volunteers by June 1, 1861, most sent to Virginia where fighting was taking place. As shown in muster rolls, participation in fighting units reflected cultural, class, and regional differences. Most poor, non-slaveholding Acadians had no affinity for the Confederate cause and sought to avoid conscription. In a letter to Confederate secretary of war, L. P. Walker, a recruiter lamented: "A goodly number of our citizens can neither speak nor understand the English language... Talk to them of our constitutional rights and the sires of the Revolution, they look upon you with astonishment."[32]

The prairie Acadians were particularly resistant to conscription and have a colorful history of deserting or going over to Union sides during the Civil War. The affluent river and bayou Acadians, many who had joined the planter class, had a real stake in the war's outcome. Often they entered military service as officers because of their high socioeconomic class, usually by raising regiments or through political appointments as aides-de-camp. The Donaldsonville Artillery Battery muster roll had 27% of men bearing

Acadian surnames, though just five Acadian families resided in the community. Leading Ascension Parish Acadian, J. O. Landry, entered service as lieutenant colonel of the 28th Louisiana, bringing with him "... five companies from his own parish, and as many blood relatives as the chief of a Scottish clan."[33]

Joseph Albert Bossier was 30 years old when Louisiana entered the Civil War in 1861. There is no clear evidence that he enrolled in the Confederate army or fought in the Civil War. Although two J. Bossier men from Louisiana are listed in the service records of Confederate soldiers, these are not likely to be Joseph Albert Bossier. One was in a Texas military unit (Waul's Legion—Infantry, Cavalry, Artillery) in 1863, and the other in the Second Cavalry, A-Br military unit from Louisiana in 1862.[34]

Louise Marie Malvina (Reynaud) Bossier was 25 years old when war descended upon her world. She had two young children under the age of 2 and was pregnant in 1861. Although her husband most likely did not leave to fight, many of her male relatives would have. It is difficult to imagine the fear and uncertainty that prevailed during the war years, the constant threat of loss, the grieving for those fallen in battle. As Union troops arrived in Louisiana and fighting swept across the fields and waterways, local residents faced shortages of food and materials, disrupted communications, and risk of their homes being raided. They came to fear both sides, since advancing or retreating armies behaved much the same, confiscating food and useful implements, stealing horses and slaughtering cattle, and at times burning fields and buildings to hinder opposing forces.

Union forces conducted several campaigns to gain and hold control of the Mississippi River, the major artery of transportation in Louisiana. Conflict came to Donaldsonville in 1862, the base for Confederate Captain Philippe Landry's guerillas, who had made repeated raids on Union shipping vessels going down the Mississippi. Federal gunboats bombarded Donaldsonville during the summer of 1862, led by Admiral David G. Farragut. The scene was described as:

> "The irate naval commander, Admiral Farragut, ordered the bombardment of Donaldsonville as soon as it could be evacuated. All of the citizens of Donaldsonville... left their homes and went to the bayou... a detachment of Yankees went to shore with fire torches in hand. The hotels, warehouses, dwellings, and some of the most valuable buildings of the town were destroyed. Plantations... were bombarded and set afire... A citizen's committee met and decided to ask

Governor Moore to keep the (Confederate) Rangers from firing on Federal boats. These attacks did no real good and brought only crude reprisals against the innocent and helped to keep the Negroes stirred up."[35]

A group of planters from Ascension and St. James parishes tempered their loyalty to the Southern cause with pragmatism. They observed that the Rangers were either unwilling or unable to protect Confederate property, and in fact were as bad as or worse than Federal troops; complaining that the Rangers entered their homes and pillaged everything they wanted. Although the planters decided that continued resistance was necessary, they wanted the local Confederate guerilla leaders to exercise greater discretion. Finding that their own discretion was the better part of valor, the planters took the oath of allegiance to the United States government, making a deal so they could retain their enslaved people and purchase provisions.

But they continued clandestinely to assist Confederate raiders from St. Martin Parish by operating an "underground railroad" that smuggled mostly Acadian conscripts, who deserted the Union forces or had been prisoners, as well as much needed supplies. This "railroad" used the network of waterways along the eastern and southern fringes of the Atchafalaya Basin, from Oscar Ayraud's Palo Alto Plantation near Donaldsonville, to Pierre Hébert's residence along Bayou Boeuf, to Pierre Daigle's farm near Brashear City. Daigle's residence was a vital link in this system, located at the confluence of Bayous Boeuf and Chemise. This system operated until the war ended, with peak use in the spring of 1865, and only died out when the fall of Richmond signaled the Confederacy's defeat.[36]

Union forces made Donaldsonville the base for their occupation of river parishes. They took over several plantations, using them to supply federal forces with food and materials and to produce cotton. In the fall of 1862, several skirmishes took place between Union and Confederate armies near Donaldsonville. One was called the "Battle of Kock's Plantation" and took place on the Palo Alto and St. Emma Plantation grounds. At the time, both plantations were owned by Charles A. Kock, together with nearby Belle Alliance Plantation. Kock was one of the largest sugar planters in the area, owning 124 enslaved people at St. Emma and 180 at Belle Alliance. The sugar houses of the plantations were used as quarters for Confederate troops. There was a field hospital outside Belle Alliance, and the first floor of the big house was used as an infirmary.

In the "Battle of Kock's Plantation" during the fall of 1862, Union forces were marching south from Donaldsonville to Thibodaux, heading across the St. Emma Plantation grounds. They met with Confederate forces, and during a series of engagements, 465 federal troops were killed. This battle was part of a campaign called "Taylor's Operations in West Louisiana" and was extremely important, as the Confederate victory left them in control over much of the interior in the Acadian region. Numerous Confederate generals and troops were present at nearby Palo Alto Plantation during the battle.[37]

To help secure Union possession of Donaldsonville, General Benjamin Butler built the star-shaped Union fortress called Fort Butler. The fort was made of earth and wood, 381 feet long on the Mississippi River side, with a deep moat on the land sides that was also protected by Bayou Lafourche. A high stockade surrounded the fort, made of an earth parapet. The fort could hold 600 men; many escaped enslaved people helped build it and stayed inside. In 1863, a small garrison remained in Fort Butler, made up of 180 Union soldiers, 1st Louisiana Volunteers, a few Louisiana Native Guard convalescents, and some fugitive runaways. In June 1863, Confederate forces attacked Fort Butler at night; more than 1,000 Texas Rangers led by General Tom Green. In the battle, free blacks and fugitive runaways helped Union forces mount a successful defense. This is one of the first occasions when blacks fought as soldiers for the Union, performing "daring deeds" and defending the fort "to the death."[38]

The cost of loyalty to the Southern cause was high for river parishes. The plantations suffered significant battlefield damage, the enslaved workforce was lost through emancipation, transportation and communication were seriously disrupted, loss of animals was substantial, many towns were partly burned, and an entire social system and economy was destroyed. The ravages of war had spread across all the Acadian regions of Louisiana.

By the end of the war, neglect and abandonment were rampant in sugarcane country. "Mansions stood empty and pillaged, with idle sugar-houses falling rapidly into ruin. Cane fields were littered with rottenness. Desolation brooded over the plantation country."[39] Creole and Anglo planters, as well as small farmers and ordinary citizens of towns, were in the same situation. As the war concluded, "… the crestfallen genteel Acadian planters of the river parishes and their plebian western cousins, the prairie ranchers, faced the same bleak future."[40]

War's Aftermath. Based on 1860 census figures, 8% of all white men aged 13 to 43 died in the Civil War, including 6% in the North and 18% in the South. It has been difficult to accurately account for war-related deaths, since records were spotty and often did not take into account soldiers who died later due to wounds, and civilian deaths resulting from disease and starvation. Recent estimates are that 350,000 Confederate and 411,000 Union military deaths occurred. War-related death rates among former enslaved people are hard to track, but losses were considerable, probably as many as hundreds of thousands. When they escaped or were set free, they went in massive numbers to areas under Union army control; but sufficient shelter, doctors, or food were often lacking. Escaping black people died from disease, starvation, or exposure. It is proposed that if black deaths are counted in the war's total, the rate would exceed 1 million.[41]

The Emancipation Proclamation and 13th Amendment set enslaved people free on December 6, 1865. The entire structure of plantation agriculture was forced to change, and there was a drastic contraction of business and economy. Federal blockades during the war had already reduced commerce and trade. Roads were completely neglected and became almost impassable; bridges were either destroyed by retreating armies or washed away for lack of maintenance. Steam navigation along rivers, which was the quickest and most reliable form of transportation in South Louisiana, virtually halted. Boats had been appropriated by both sides, and numerous sunken wrecks blocked ports and river confluences. These rusting hulks and floating debris collecting around them were not removed by government engineers until 1870-1871.

Much of the wealth that existed in the South was destroyed by the war. Investments in Confederate bonds were worthless, most banks and railroads were bankrupt, and income per person dropped to less than 40% of that in the North. Wealth amassed in enslaved people ended when the South's 3.5 million blacks were freed. Southern political influence in the U.S. federal government, formerly considerable, was greatly reduced for years. It did not return until the latter half of the 20th century.

Breakdown in communication and transportation, lack of adult white men, and flight of emancipated blacks seriously disrupted agricultural and business. Most farms, and even plantations, were reduced to subsistence gardening. The immediate concern was providing food for families to survive. By the war's end, most fields in Louisiana's Acadian parishes had been untended for 2-3 years; in the water-bottom regions, brush and saplings were rapidly reclaiming the fertile lands. Former Confederate soldiers who had returned home were wounded or disabled, unable to tend their lands or support themselves. Thousands of other rebels, deserters, opportunists, black camp followers, and former enslaved people returned to their South Louisiana haunts, adding to the strain on meager food resources. Food stocks in individual homes were nearly depleted, and grocery stores were unable to obtain provisions until late fall, 1865. The river parishes, along with bayou and prairie parishes, hovered on the brink of starvation.

Problems in resuming farming were compounded by lack of animals and equipment. Many cotton gins, sugar mills, and warehouses were destroyed during the war or were unserviceable due to years of neglect. Sugarcane growers had operated 1,291 mills in Louisiana on the eve of the Civil War; only 175 were in operation at the end of conflict. By 1870, this number had grown slightly to 300. Sugar production fell from a peak of 269,000 tons in 1861 to 42,500 tons in 1863, with another drastic reduction to just 5,400 tons in 1864. Few farmers could pay exorbitant prices being charged for animals and equipment, and most had difficulty obtaining credit due to land depreciation. Those who could get credit (usually at 10-15% interest) focused on producing staple crops that required the least labor and offered the greatest profit margins. Growing sugarcane was problematic due to high capital investment needs, lack of skilled laborers, shortage of seed cane, and a 2-3 year wait time to reach peak sugar production. Many planters and small farmers in the sugar region turned to other crops, especially cotton.

There was a prevailing view that the Southern planter elites somehow managed to hold on to their plantations and retain powerful positions. Recent studies dispute this view, reporting that although some Southern elites retained their economic status, the turmoil of the 1860s created huge economic mobility for opportunists. Unfortunately for most Acadians, economic mobility turned into a downward spiral. On the eve of secession, Acadians were the second most affluent group in rural South Louisiana, behind the Anglo-Americans. In the war's aftermath, the depression struck most severely at the extremes of the Acadian community's socioeconomic spectrum, reducing the very poor and formerly rich alike. Residents of the Acadian Coast were hardest hit; these parishes were most dependent on farm credit and enslaved labor. Many formerly successful Acadian farming ventures failed, the land offered for sale by desperate owners or their creditors, with few buyers in sight. When farms did sell, it was at severely depressed prices.

Between 1860 and 1870, Acadian real estate holdings decreased in value by over 52% on average. In Acadian Coast parishes, however, property values depreciated by over 77%, a devastating loss of equity built up over generations. Personal property holdings in 1850-1870 plummeted 86%, a remarkable loss of material wealth. The Acadian planter class virtually disappeared. Over 10 years between censuses, the number of formerly prosperous Acadian planters fell from 25 to only 1 in West Baton Rouge; 43 to 10 in Iberville; 17 to 4 in Ascension; and 18 to 3 in St. James parishes. Most had lost their farms and plantations. Acadian-owned real estate fell during that period by 70-90% in river parishes; about 49% in Lafourche Basin; and 19-82% in prairie parishes. There were just 136 large and medium-sized farms, and 56 small farms, owned by Acadians in river parishes in 1870. Wealth shifted from Creoles and Acadians to Anglos. This reflects the influx of Northerners and Easterners after the Civil War, taking advantage of the chaos and devastation in the South. Population and wealth percentages show the stark realities.[42]

- 1870 white population in river parishes—28.4% Creole, 30% Acadian, 23.2% Anglo.
- Ascension Parish wealth—Anglos were just 8% of the population, but owned 29% of wealth.
- Assumption Parish wealth—Anglos were just 7% of the population, but owned 57% of wealth.
- Iberville Parish wealth—Anglos were 11% of the population, and owned 58% of wealth.

The number of Creole planters was small in the 1870 census, ranging from 1 to 15 in most river parishes, including Ascension, Assumption, Iberville, St. James, and West Baton Rouge. The Acadian component was very small in St. John the Baptist Parish, however, which was predominately white Creole. With fewer large farms, it fared somewhat better.

River parish population (except St. John the Baptist) fell by 10,000 between 1860 and 1870—from 59,711 to 49,976.[43] This fall in population reflects the devastation the war wreaked upon agriculture and the economic depression that followed, as the entire plantation system that depended upon slavery collapsed.

In 1860, Louisiana's total population was 689,191—about equally divided between white and black, but most black people were enslaved (331,726). There were 18,647 "free colored" in the state; most lived in New Orleans and Cane River regions. In the census of 1870, taken five years after the Civil War ended, the 50-50 black-white division remained; there were 364,210 "free colored" people living in Louisiana. In the river parishes, the black-white ratio was closer to 2:1; almost twice as many blacks as whites, with a tiny number of Native Americans and Chinese.

Many small and subsistence farmers lost their land, migrating from river parishes to the parishes west of the Atchafalaya Basin. By 1870, day laborers made up the majority of the Acadian agricultural work force. Day laborers were regarded as having low status, at the same level as newly freed black people, beside whom they frequently worked. Acadian day laborers were drawn from the rapidly growing landless class and the beleaguered, dwindling small farmer class. To work for another man was considered the least desirable way to live by the traditionally self-sufficient Acadians. Most landless Acadians were actually share renters, a step above sharecroppers; they provided their own work stock, animal feed, fertilizer, and tools along with family labor. They had some choice over what crops to grow but had to give landlords over one-fourth to one-third of crop production and buy at the company store.

The Panic of 1873 virtually paralyzed the U.S. economy. Bank bonds had saturated the market, railroads were overbuilt; banks could not cover bad debt, many banks closed, and the securities market collapsed. The result was a long-standing, worldwide depression which did not recover until 1896. The financial crisis struck New Orleans hard, amplified by the flight of carpetbag investors who returned north with their remaining liquid assets. As many as 5,000 New Orleans families faced starvation due to chronic unemployment in 1874-75. Rural parishes also suffered, with malnutrition especially evident among laboring classes. Adding to this economic misery was the Mississippi River flooding in 1874 and 1876, destroying crops and reducing food and financial resources.

The Acadians After the Civil War

As the postbellum period progressed, Acadian culture divided into two basic groups: a small upper and upper-middle class that was co-opted by the dominant Anglo-American culture, and the impoverished, undereducated lower classes who still adhered to their cultural traditions. Due to intermarriage and downward economic mobility among many Anglos and recent immigrants, all those on the lower rungs of society merged with poor Acadians, becoming the Cajuns. Cajuns came to be widely regarded as poor and ignorant people.

After the Civil War, numerous unemployed and underemployed Acadian professionals, merchants, and craftsmen migrated to the towns and cities of South Louisiana, congregating in parish seats. Those Acadians living in larger cities were inevitably drawn into the American mainstream, source of employment and credit. They found it necessary to speak English well and began giving their children Anglo names. By 1870, Anglo first names were given to 56% of Acadian children in working class households. In parishes where Creoles predominated, such as St. John the Baptist, St. Charles, and Point Coupée, the small Acadian minority quickly blended into the lower socioeconomic strata of white Creole society and was able to preserve its French character better.

Upper class and professional Acadians strove to avoid the onerous social stigma assigned to their poor relations, now identified as Cajuns. Even the newly free blacks emulated their former masters and viewed their Cajun neighbors with derision. Poor Acadians were forced to abandon their traditional agricultural lifestyles and support themselves as cypress lumberjacks, fishermen, and trappers in the Atchafalaya Basin and coastal marshes. It is no coincidence that alcoholism and whisky consumption among Cajuns spiked, as they found themselves trapped in tenantry and poverty. This situation did not improve until the first two decades of the 20th century, with industrialization of the Texas Golden Triangle, the southeast portion where oil was struck in 1901; and the later growth of Louisiana's oil and gas industry.

Through forced cultural interchanges with black and poor white communities, the Acadians created the unique blend of music, cuisine, dance, and myth that is now identified with being Cajun. This metamorphosis was largely completed when the original prairie Creole settlement around Eunice, once distinct from nearby Acadian settlements, was officially designated as Evangeline Parish in 1910, drawing from Longfellow's famous (though inaccurate) story.[44]

Both Acadian and Creole antebellum gentry were profoundly affected by the aftermath of the Civil War. They lost not only their wealth and property but also were unable to attain prominent political positions for many years. At the dawn of the 20th century, a few Acadians and Creoles served in high offices, including chief justice of the Louisiana Supreme Court, United States senator and congressmen, police jurors, sheriffs, district attorneys, judges, and state lawmakers. The turbulence and violence that characterized the postbellum era led Francophiles to join in efforts to eradicate the local Republican Party. They formed vigilante groups to uphold local civic codes and values; combatting raids on farms and homes by vagrants and freedmen who were stealing livestock, confiscating property, and pillaging villages. There was little central government to enforce laws, and many desperate or opportunistic men roamed in the post-war chaos.

Many antebellum planters and large farmers who grew to manhood during or just after the Civil War could no longer find a niche in agriculture. These young men migrated to South Louisiana towns and villages, where they formed a professional class. Most had been classically educated in fine schools and applied their knowledge to careers as attorneys, dry goods merchants, sugar and cotton factors, clerks, bill collectors, and teachers. New Orleans was a magnet for professionals seeking to advance their careers. Since the language of business was now English, and the Anglo-Americans held most wealth and credit, these men moved quickly to assimilate into the mainstream. Acadian gentry made every effort to disassociate from their heritage and poor relations because of the associated social stigma.

In the early 20th century, the children of these acculturated Acadians and Creoles threw their energies into Americanizing their people. Public education was seen as the best way to bring illiterate French speakers into the mainstream. The Compulsory Education Act of 1916 and the compulsory English educational provisions of 1921 in the state constitution propelled this culture-leveling education. Most of the teachers who carried out the laws were Acadians or Creoles of the gentry class. They chastised students for speaking French and publically humiliated them. English was the language of the future, and all who aspired to status and success were bound to use it—even to the suppression of speaking French within families. The mother tongue and long-standing traditions were fading as the generations progressed.

The children of **Louise Marie Malvina Reynaud** and **Joseph Albert Bossier** were born into this time of immense cultural, social, and economic transitions. Four children grew to adulthood as the century turned, marrying into other local families or new arrivals in the upriver parishes. They faced a world vastly different than the one of their ancestors.

CHAPTER 9

A New Century in a Changing World
Louise Clothilde Malvina Bossier (1860-1907) – Louis Adolphe Vial (1842-1910)

⚜

The winds of war were swirling when **Louise Clothilde Malvina Bossier** was born on June 9, 1860. She had one surviving older brother, Joseph Albert Bossier Jr., born in 1859; the first brother born in 1857 died shortly after birth. Two siblings followed, Oscar Louis Bossier born 1861 and Marie Maude Bossier born 1866. Her father, **Joseph Albert Bossier Sr.,** was a successful and well-respected lawyer in the town of Edgard, St. John the Baptist Parish. There is no information about his participation in the Confederate militia during the Civil War (1861-1865), although his father and grandfather had belonged to earlier German Coast militias. He continued to practice law until his death at age 37 in 1868.

During Louise Clothilde's early childhood, her world was immersed in conflict that would permanently change society and economics in the upriver parishes. At first, the conflict seemed far away with most action in eastern border states. The river parishes mustered several militia groups, and many Confederate soldiers left for action on the distant front. Most plantation owners believed European dependence on their cotton and sugar would bring in allies, and southern armies would be invincible. Midway through 1862, New Orleans was taken by Union forces, and the situation turned sharply. With the Mississippi River under Union control, river communities were cut off from commerce and supplies and vulnerable to invasion.

Their optimism was dashed. "For the sugar planters, the gay, light days of faraway war were ended. No longer did they relax on their verandas, drinking mint juleps and discoursing on the ineffectiveness of naval blockade and the impending collapse of the Northern economy."[1] After New Orleans fell, federal troops attempted to occupy the parishes along the river up to Baton Rouge, but lacked manpower and were satisfied to control river traffic. There were a number of skirmishes and a few notable battles that took place in river parishes, but the most contested regions were along the western and northern stretches, including parishes along the Red River and Bayou Teche. There was a Confederate stronghold in Lafourche Parish, and federal troops attacked in that region, capturing the Boutte Station Depot and the Bayou des Allemands area in spring of 1862.

For three long, weary years the Civil War filled the river parishes with violence and destruction. When Union troops were advancing toward a town or plantation, many white people packed up a few necessities and fled toward the forests. Their enslaved people became resistant, refused to obey orders, and often left to join the federals. As forces from either side pushed across the landscape, they took what they needed from homes and plantations, trampled over crops, and appropriated animals for food or transportation. In this lawless environment, scavengers and opportunists were constant threats to life and property. Families who stayed at home could find their pantries emptied, their gardens and livestock raided, their bedding and clothes absconded, their tools and firearms taken.

The New Orleans *Daily Picayune* wrote in December 1862 of the precarious straits of people in the disputed territories. "They are between two fires; and, in many instances, can hardly escape either partial or complete destruction but by fleeing from their homes, and leaving them scenes of desolation—mournful momentoes of what the war has brought upon the people. The crops are left unharvested. The servants are demoralized and reduced to starvation and sickness. Property of all kinds goes to ruin. The members of the family seek a precarious living among distant friends."[2]

St. John the Baptist Parish lies between Ascension Parish upriver (north) and St. Charles Parish downriver (south). Civil War battles in Ascension Parish around Donaldsonville were described in the previous chapter. Although both the other parishes were little involved in direct combat, residents tried to give support to the Confederate cause. In St. Charles Parish, rebel supporters were gathering a herd of cattle on the west bank of the Mississippi to supply Confederate troops. Federal Colonel Thomas, who had occupied Boutte, got word of this and sent 200 soldiers to the St. Charles Courthouse where they camped overnight. At daybreak, the soldiers marched upriver toward the Bonnet Carré bend of the river. There they found 500 cattle that had arrived the night before from Texas. Colonel Thomas left some men to guard the cattle, and taking advice of local blacks, went further upriver to the bend where reportedly a considerable Confederate force was camped. After proceeding about eight miles above the Courthouse, he encountered a small rebel force. There was a short skirmish; a few rebel men and horses were captured, but most headed for the swamps. Thomas continued on about two miles but did not find more enemy forces. He turned back, collecting large numbers of horses, cattle, mules, and sheep from plantations on the way.

Colonel Thomas captured three white men and was joined by about 500 black people and other vagrants. He marched through the following night downriver to the Union camp at Algiers; his procession now three miles long comprised of the troops, black people and vagrants, almost 1000 head of cattle, and hundreds of sheep and mules.[3]

Plantations: Destruction and Desolation

Every plantation along the Mississippi River—and throughout Louisiana and other southern states—suffered during and after the Civil War. Although this might be considered justice for the suffering that plantation life visited on generations of enslaved people, everyone living on and around plantations faced dire consequences, whether white or black. The focus here is upon several plantations located in St. John the Baptist and St. Charles Parishes. Family members and ancestors of the Vial-Martin lineage had multiple connections with some of these plantations.

Fashion Plantation, St. Charles Parish, Hahnville. G.W. Fullerton was the first owner of Fashion Plantation, consisting of 1200 acres with a large plantation house built in raised West Indies design on brick piers, with a gallery and dormers. In 1851, it was bought by General Richard Taylor, one of the leading Confederate officers and son of U.S. President Zachary Taylor. Richard Taylor was born near Louisville, Kentucky, and his sister married future Confederate States President Jefferson Davis. Taylor was educated in Scotland, France, Harvard, and Yale. He accompanied his father, then a U.S. general, to fight in the Mexican War and learned military arts there. Richard used an inheritance when his father died to purchase Fashion Plantation. He had managed a previous plantation of his father's in Mississippi north of Natchez. A young man of 25 years when he took over Fashion Plantation, he increased the number of enslaved people from 64 to 150 and purchased adjoining properties to expand his holdings.

Richard Taylor held several important political positions, including state senator twice. He was a delegate from St. Charles Parish to Whig and Democratic Conventions. A strong proponent of secession, he was initially a cooperationist. In 1861, he became Colonel of the 9th Louisiana Regiment, serving under General Stonewall Jackson in Virginia, and then commanding Confederate troops in Western Louisiana in the summer of 1862. He had a number of victories at Donaldsonville, Des Allemands, and the Red River, and managed to capture Kenner from the Union army with plans to recapture New Orleans. But the Union victories at Port Hudson and Vicksburg squelched this plan, since they now controlled Mississippi River travel and could quickly move troops south to New Orleans.

Fashion Plantation had been left in the hands of an overseer, but federal troops overran the plantation in 1862. Taylor's family was living in grand style before the war, with an extensive library, works of art, and beautiful grounds. They had five children, although the two boys did not live to manhood. When Union forces overran the plantation, one soldier from Vermont wrote a letter describing Fashion as the most splendid plantation he had ever seen. He described how the plundering included "... hundreds of bottles of wine, eggs, preserved figs and peaches, turkeys, chickens and honey... all kinds of clothing, rings, watches, guns, pistols, swords, and some of General (Zachary) Taylor's old hats and coats, belt, swords ... every old relic he had is worn about the camp."[4] Livestock was driven off with the troops while families of women and children ran into the woods. The 175 enslaved people then working on the plantation were carted off to a federal camp in Algiers, except those too old to move. Some joined black Union troops, but many were forced to return to Fashion and continue working, now as wage laborers.

In September 1862, Union soldiers burned the plantation house to the ground. Richard Taylor, who became a Confederate general in 1861, was furious about the Union army's looting and destruction of his plantation. He vowed revenge by executing 10 Union soldiers for each further act of plantation looting. Although Union General Butler claimed he did not allow looting by his soldiers, it obviously did occur. Taylor never got over the loss of his home and possessions; his father's sword and other heirlooms were stolen and lost forever. Taylor was in Alabama when it became clear that the South had lost the war, and he surrendered on May 8, 1865. The U.S. government confiscated his land, since he was exempted from clemency through President Andrew Johnson's amnesty proclamation of 1865.

Taylor went to Washington to plead for release of ex-Confederate President Jefferson Davis but was not successful. With his plantation lands seized and sold, his enslaved people freed, his possessions lost, Richard Taylor was ruined financially. When his former enslaved people learned of his situation, they offered to loan him considerable amounts of money from their savings. He refused this generous gesture but promised them he would let them know if things got worse. After residing some time in New Orleans, Taylor went to Europe in 1873 as an agent for several business ventures. When his wife died in 1875, he returned to Virginia and became a writer. His primary work, *Destruction and Reconstruction,* included his reminiscences of the Civil War, published only one week before he died in New York City in 1879. Richard Taylor was buried in Metairie Cemetery in New Orleans.

Portions of the Fashion Plantation were bought in 1870 by **Jean Baptiste Martin Sr.**, whose lineage eventually merged with that of **Louise Clothilde Malvina Bossier**. Martin was then living in St. Charles Parish and purchased the land from two unmarried sisters of the local Labranche family. The property was part of the succession of Martin's own grandparents, Jean Louis Labranche and Aimee Trepagnier. Probably the Labranche family bought portions of Fashion Plantation from the U.S. government after the property was confiscated in 1865. J.B. Martin Sr. acquired two-sixteenth part of the property described in records of the St. Charles Parish Clerk of Court:

"A sugar plantation situated in the Parish of St. Charles, on the right bank of the Mississippi River, about twenty-seven miles above the City of New Orleans, measuring twenty-five arpents (21.15 acres) front on said River and having a depth of eighty arpents (25.38 acres), between lines opening about the thirteen degree, bounded on its line by the plantation of Richard Taylor and on its lower line by a tract of land now belonging to Mr. Bernard Soulie, but formerly forming part of the present plantation. Together with the buildings, improvements, laborers' cabins, sugar-house with purgery, mills to steam engines, stables, granaries, farming utensils, mules, oxen, carts, etc. thereon and all other appurtenances thereto attaching including crops on said plantation and the Roy Villeré concession in the rear thereof..."[5]

Martin paid the Labranche sisters, his cousins, $10,000 in United States currency in cash. The transaction was recorded on February 15, 1870, by T. T. Baudouin, Recorder for the St. Charles Parish Clerk of Court. The U.S. government sold the remainder of Taylor's Fashion Plantation lands in 1883 for $17,250.

In 1888, **Louis Adolphe Vial** bought land at Fashion Plantation from Damien Haydel, who also had bought Home Place Plantation. L.A. Vial built a home there when he moved from the Killona area where his parents lived, and started his large family with **Louise**

Clothilde Malvina Bossier. Their oldest son, **Leon Charles Vial I**, later acquired the adjoining tract of land that was part of Fashion Plantation and built his family home there. This house is still in the Vial family and descendants are living there.

The lands that were once an expansive plantation were subdivided over the years. Today the once-grand Fashion Plantation is simply commemorated by a historical marker beside River Road in Hahnville. The marker stands on the river side, just across the road from property still owned by the Vial family. It says: "Fashion Plantation: Home of General Richard Taylor, son of Zachary Taylor, Louisiana Statesman and member of 1861 Secession Convention. Commanded Louisiana District, 1862-64; defeated Banks at Battle of Mansfield, 1864. Federals plundered home in 1862."

Home Place Plantation, St. Charles Parish, Hahnville. Near central Hahnville is the Home Place Plantation. Today it is the only large plantation house left in St. Charles Parish, standing on the west bank of the Mississippi River in forlorn dignity. It is also known as the Keller Homestead, after the last family to live in the house. In 1970, it was designated as a National Historical Landmark and a historical marker plaque set at the entrance. Located about a half-mile south of the Hahnville post office, the two-story house is set back from River Road (LA 18). It has a hip roof with three dormer windows facing the front, and second-story gallery porch on all four sides. The lower floor is built of bricks made on the plantation and covered with stucco, as are the pillars supporting the gallery. The second-story walls, floors, ceilings, and gallery are constructed of cypress. In the traditional Creole building style, walls were chinked with Spanish moss and clay.

The house originally had three chimneys and two front stairways that weathered over the years. The upstairs was two rooms deep and four rooms across, in local style. Downstairs rooms were for storage and servants' quarters, with a separate kitchen. There was a plantation bell tower on one side and a cistern on the other, plus several outbuildings and barns. Many have admired the craftsmanship that went into Home Place, considered a fine example of large French Colonial raised cottages. The outer stairway with oak handrails and crafted iron vertical rails was of superior quality. Some rooms had imported Italian marble, and the dining room flooring was marble. Along the lower story walls were gun portals for defense.

Although reports disagree, in the prevalent view the house was built for Pierre Gaillard in 1791. Probably the builder was a mulatto named Charles Pacquet, who also built Destrehan Plantation house on the east bank of the river. The home passed through several hands, acquired by Louis Edmond Fortier between 1806 and 1812. Fortier served as captain during the War of 1812, and his pride was his stable of fine thoroughbred horses kept at the plantation.[6]

Fortier married Felicite Labranche; she acquired the plantation through a First Judicial District of Louisiana Court judgment against her husband in 1843; details of the marital discord are unclear. By the Fortier family's report, Louis died at Home Place in 1849; after his death Felicite lived in their New Orleans home. The property passed through her son and several other families; by the Civil War it was reputed to have the rarest shrubs in the state, fine garden and fruit trees, and 25 large pecan trees.

The ravages of the Civil War disrupted Home Place Plantation's productivity, and it went to a sheriff's sale in 1868, passing through two owners until purchased in 1885 by Damien Haydel. Originally from Edgard, Damien and his wife Delphine Hart produced small sugar and rice crops on the land. His son-in-law Pierre Anatole Keller, also from Edgard, moved into Home Place to become overseer because none of Haydel's sons wanted the position. Pierre Keller had married Elvire Haydel, Damien's daughter, and had managed another plantation as well as selling several lots in Hahnville which became known as Keller Acres.

Pierre Anatole Keller bought Home Place from his father-in-law Damien in 1889, in conjunction with Ulysse Haydel. Damien and his wife continued to live there until their deaths. Keller ran the plantation, continued with sugarcane production, and increased the rice crop. In 1893, the property was divided between Keller and Ulysse Haydel. Keller kept the house and upper portion, while Ulysse got the lower portion and called it Caneland Plantation. The lower portion passed back to the Kellers in 1896.

Over the years, weather and changing needs brought renovations to Home Place. Bathrooms were built upstairs and the kitchen outbuilding moved closer. Cane fields suffered damage in the hard freeze of 1911 and flooding from the Hymelia Crevasse in 1912, when the levee broke upriver. Storms in 1915 and Hurricane Betsy in 1965 caused structural damage and knocked down the bell tower. During this time the sugar mill and machinery and the blacksmith shop were dismantled and sold. The levee was raised as the river moved farther away, and River Road was eventually widened and paved.

Most of the Kellers living in Edgard moved into Home Place, and five children were born to Pierre and Elvire Keller there. When Pierre died in 1932, the house passed into his estate; his youngest son, Richard L Keller, was residing there into the 1970s. The house is still owned by the Keller family but is currently unoccupied and in need of repairs and maintenance.

In addition to being nearby neighbors, the Vial-Martin families are related by marriage to the Kellers. **Leon Charles Vial I** (1878-1939) was the son of **Louis Adolphe Vial** and **Louise Clothilde Malvina Bossier**. His second wife was **Marguerite Marie Keller** (1886-1967), daughter of Pierre Anatole Keller and Elvire Haydel.

Home Place Plantation House Hahnville, LA 2019

Destrehan Plantation, St. Charles Parish, Destrehan. On the east bank of the Mississippi River about 18 miles above New Orleans sits one of the oldest plantations in the South. The plantation house, once situated on natural high ground, overlooked the river. The system of levees built over ensuing years have since blocked this view. The plantation house was built by free mulatto Charles Pacquet in 1787 for Robin Antoine de Logny, appointed commandant of the Second German Coast by Governor O'Reilly. Two years after construction was completed in 1790, de Logny died, and his son-in-law, Jean Noel d'Estrehan, purchased the plantation. An old Louisiana family, the d'Estrehans had arrived with Bienville, founder of New Orleans. The name was changed to Destrehan, and the present town named after the family.

Jean Noel Destrehan was educated in France and married Marie Celeste Robin de Logny, sister of Robin Antoine. He was a successful indigo and sugarcane planter; a prominent politician who served as Speaker of the House in the territorial legislature and helped draft the first state constitution. He ran for state governor but lost, was elected U.S. Senator from Louisiana but declined due to business affairs. The Destrehans were gracious hosts and entertained Governor Walter C. Claiborne, as well as the pirate Jean Lafitte. Jean Noel and his wife, who lived until 1823-1824, had 14 children.

Destrehan Plantation passed down through several generations, arriving in 1848 in the hands of Eleanora Zelia Destrehan. She was courted by 50-year-old Scotsman Stephen Henderson, known throughout Louisiana for his business acumen. Although the Destrehans were well-to-do, Henderson's fortune far outstripped theirs; he was a multimillionaire. Legend has it that the couple made a prenuptial agreement in 1816—whoever died last would retain the estate. Since Zelia was just 16 years old, half the Scotsman's age, it seemed a safe bet for the Destrehans. After a short, happy marriage, young Zelia died in 1830 while traveling to New York. Stephen acquired the plantation, purchasing it from the estate. He built a magnificent tomb for her in the Red Church Cemetery where he joined her in 1838.

In the provisions of Stephen's will, a town was to be built named Destrehan, and all his enslaved people were to be set free with a choice: either a $500 ship passage to Liberia or an acre of land, cabin, mule, cow, and supplies to start out as a free man. He also wanted to build a factory on the land for making shoes and clothing for the black people, under direction of Scottish workmen, "To give employment to the poor and inculcate in them habits of industry, sobriety, and thrift."[7] However, his nephews from Scotland contested the will with litigation stretching over years, even through the Civil War. Most of the will was nullified, and the enslaved people were not freed.

In 1839, Pierre Adolphe Rost purchased the plantation from the Henderson estate. He married Louise Adele Destrehan, sister of Zelia. Rost was from France and had served under Napoleon. After Waterloo, he settled first in Mississippi and became a lawyer, held political offices, and moved to New Orleans where he married Louise. Now in the elite Creole society, he was involved in politics and served as Louisiana Supreme Court justice from 1845-1853. He and Louise remodeled the house in Greek Revival style in the 1840s. The house was formerly built in the raised West Indies or Creole style, two stories with interior chimneys and many outbuildings. The Rosts replaced wood columns of the façade with plastered brick and enclosed the rear gallery to create an entrance foyer. The winding staircases were removed from the rear gallery and installed in the center hall. The exterior stucco was scored to resemble stone.

During the Civil War, Rost was sent as a diplomatic representative of the Confederacy to Spain. He remained there with his family through most of the war. When the war ended in 1865, the plantation was seized by the Freedmen's Bureau, which established the Rost Home Colony to provide freedmen with medical and educational aid. They could also work for wages or for a portion of the harvested crops. This was the most successful and profitable Colony among those created in Louisiana after the war. When Pierre Rost returned from Europe, he received a pardon from President Andrew Johnson and demanded his property back. This was granted, but the Colony continued for another year, paying Rost rent. The last colonist left in December 1866.

Pierre Rost died in 1868, and his wife Louise continued living there until she died in 1877. Ownership passed to their son Emile Rost, a Harvard lawyer who acted as his father's secretary in Europe. He took over managing Destrehan Plantation in 1869 but was in frail health and did not enjoy the climate, often traveling to more hospitable settings. Emile served as St. Charles Parish policy juror and school director, was involved in local politics, and became judge of the 21st Judicial District. Emile never married, living at the plantation until 1910, when he sold it to the Destrehan Planting and Manufacturing Company, a syndicate of planters. This ended family ownership of Destrehan Plantation after 123 years.

In 1914, the Mexican Petroleum Company (predecessor of American Oil Company) bought the plantation house and 1,050 acres. The company built an oil refinery, tore down ancillary buildings, and created employee housing. The mansion became a clubhouse and office complex. In 1959, the oil refinery was demolished and the property abandoned. Over the next 12 years, the venerable plantation house went through decay and vandalism. With no protection, the house was robbed of Spanish-style ceramic tiles, glass windowpanes, Italian marble mantels, and cypress paneling. The local sheriff prevented theft of the original 1840s iron entrance gates and a 1,400 lb. marble bathtub, rumored to be a gift from Napoleon Bonaparte.

Because the house once hosted Jean Lafitte, local children and thrill-seekers snuck in to search for Lafitte's ghost or treasure. Tales related that the ghost appears on dark and stormy nights, points a bony finger at a spot on the floor or walls, and vanishes. Gaping holes were left where treasure-seekers tried to find Lafitte's cache.

The River Road Historical Society was organized in 1968 to save and restore the house. In 1971, American Oil donated the house and four acres to them and donated more money and land in 1990. The Historical Society raised funds to restore the house and grounds to their former beauty, recently recreating the authentic plantation community around the manor house. Now Destrehan Plantation offers guided tours which interpret lives of former residents, both free and enslaved.

St. John the Baptist Parish Plantations. Several plantation houses in St. John the Baptist Parish survived the Civil War.

Evergreen Plantation is on the west side of the Mississippi River near Wallace, along River Road (LA 18). The grand house was constructed in 1790 and renovated in Greek Revival style in 1832. The main crop was sugarcane, cultivated by enslaved labor until emancipation, then by wage laborers. It continued operating until around 1930, when the owners abandoned the house during the Depression. Under directions of the bank that owned it, the plantation continued producing sugarcane and is still a working sugar plantation today. In the 1940s, the house was extensively restored. The plantation had 37 outbuildings, most antebellum, making it among the most complete plantation complexes in the South. There are 22 enslaved people's quarters arranged in pairs in rows along an alley of oak trees. A picturesque building with graceful flying staircases, Evergreen has been the set for many movies. It was designated as a National Historic Landmark in 1992 and is included on the Louisiana African American Heritage Trail.

San Francisco Plantation is a historic plantation house located in Garyville. Built in 1849-1850 for Edmond Marmillion, it is an architecturally distinctive style in the South, called Steamboat Gothic. Situated on eight acres, it is now surrounded by oil tanks. The 1½-story structure is set on a full-height basement with a brick floor. Brick piers rise to support the main structure, which has an ornate sheltered porch on three sides. Fluted columns with Corinthian design and overhanging decorative cornices gives the house a "steamboat" appearance, topped by a dormered hip roof. The name is thought to come from a comment by Edmond's oldest son, who declared about the huge debt he faced when he took over the estate, that he was *sans fruscins* or "without a penny in my pocket." The house was called St. Frusquin at first, which was changed into "San Francisco" around 1879 by the next owner. It was restored to 1850s appearance and designated a National Historic Landmark in 1974.

Whitney Plantation is located near Wallace on River Road. It was acquired in 1752 by German immigrants **Ambroise Haydel** and his wife, where they cultivated indigo and later sugarcane in the early 1800s. Jean Jacques Haydel Sr., youngest son of Ambroise, was granted the land claim in 1803, passing it to his sons Marcellin and Jean Jacques Jr. Marcellin's widow, Marie Azélie Haydel, took the plantation over and developed it into a huge agricultural endeavor, producing over 400,000 pounds of sugar in a single season. She enhanced the interior with murals and frescos by Dominici Canova, which still adorn the main house. The Haydel descendants owned the plantation until 1867. After the Civil War, the plantation was sold to Bradish Johnson of New York. He named the property after his grandson, Harry Whitney. It passed through several owners until purchased in 1990 by the Formosa Chemicals and Fiber Corporation, which sold it in 1999 to the Cummings family of New Orleans.

The main house is raised-style French Creole, built in 1803. Numerous outbuildings have been preserved, including a *pigeonnier* (pigeon coop), plantation store, and barn. The Cummings family turned the plantation buildings and grounds into the Whitney Plantation Historic District, a museum devoted to slavery, in 2014. Enslaved people's quarters were moved from other plantations, along with other buildings typical of working sugar plantations. The grounds have exhibits and art, including life-size sculptures of enslaved children. Oral histories of many last survivors of slavery were collected and published, now held by the U.S. Library of Congress. There are archeological sites being explored. The plantation was listed on the National Register of Historic Places in 1992, and it is part of the Louisiana African American Heritage Trail.

The relationships by blood and marriage between the **Vial-Martin** and the **Haydel** families were described in the prior chapter.

Reconstruction and Civil War Aftermath

The Federal occupation lasted longer in Louisiana than any other Southern state, from 1865 to 1877. Initially the U.S. government used New Orleans as a testing ground for Reconstruction policies, but there were few lasting transformations. Black people were now legally free, and for a short time black men could vote and hold office. Freedom from servitude and the right to vote had only symbolic value, however, if people could not earn enough to provide their families with basic necessities. This did not improve their potential when their children could attend only substandard, underfunded schools. In the war's aftermath, most Louisiana blacks and many whites could not afford to purchase a plot of land. They resorted to tenant farming, sharecropping, and debt peonage that kept them in continual dependency.

Louisiana was hit hard with economic depression as well as social chaos. The state lost one-third of her assessed wealth between 1860 and 1865. Population decreased during 1860-1870, especially in the lower river parishes that were so dependent on the sugarcane industry. More than half of the livestock was gone. There was no capital for plantation owners and businessmen to continue their activities. From a high of 1,291 sugarcane plantations in operation in 1850, this dropped to around 200 producing even a token crop by 1865.[8]

When enslaved people were freed, there was a huge loss of capital investment without any compensation to former owners. In sugarcane regions, 139,000 previously enslaved people were emancipated, most with no means of earning a living. Out of the destruction of war and chaos of reconstruction, many racial problems crystallized that would plague generations of Southerners, both black and white.

While some white citizens of Louisiana championed emancipation and urged cooperation with Union authorities, others strongly resisted and sought vindication for the loss of lives and properties. Early on the U.S. Congress created the Freedmen's Bureau—Bureau of Refugees, Freedmen, and Abandoned Lands—which began in 1865 to solve problems associated with ending slavery. Bureau agents tried to resolve labor disputes, protect freed blacks from violence, keep former enslaved people on plantations where they could work, and distribute food, clothing, and fuel. The Destrehan Plantation was used as an educational and medical facility for freedmen. Although many individuals were helped, there was no lasting impact of this work.

Louisiana had the first black newspaper in the South, initially called *L'Union* in 1863 and later the *New Orleans Tribune,* but the paper had a short life, only six years. There were a number of contested elections and restrictions on freedmen's rights through the Louisiana Black Code of 1865. U.S. Congress passed the Civil Rights Act of 1866, which granted all citizens to enjoy equally without regard to race the rights to protect person and property, make contracts, and bring lawsuits. Though this federal legislation prevailed over state laws, and the Republican Party in control became more radical, there was continued resistance among whites. This led to several riots between 1866 and 1877 in which a number of people were killed. The state adopted a new constitution in 1868, with a bill of rights that extended voting to black males, established a free integrated public school system, and gave blacks access to public accommodations.

The new constitution did little to end racial discrimination. Blacks could rarely afford court battles or have means to take advantage of transportation and entertainment. Early black leaders were generally free before the Civil War, financially secure, and literate; many owned property and previously had their own enslaved workers. Several black men held government offices, including U.S. congressman, lieutenant and acting governor, state treasurer, mayor, and member of the police jury. Some terrorist organizations formed during Reconstruction, primarily to intimidate Republican voters and officeholders of both races, including the Knights of the White Camellia and the White League. White members of these groups killed three state legislators during this era. Tensions between Radical Republicans and Democratic white supremacists peaked after the disputed gubernatorial election of 1876, in which both parties' candidates claimed victory. There were two separate governments for a time, but Democratic candidate Francis T. Nicholls sent 3,000 men to intimidate the State Supreme Court, charged with deciding who won. The court justices stepped down, and Nicholls appointed new judges who confirmed his election.

The national presidential election was also contested that year, with the parties disagreeing whether the Democratic or Republican candidate had won. A compromise was worked out in 1877—if the disputed votes were given to Republican Rutherford B. Hayes, in exchange he would permit Southern Democrats to assume control of local governments in the three states still occupied by the Federal military: Florida, South Carolina, and Louisiana. The agreement was struck, Federal troops left, and the Nicholls faction took over Louisiana government. In 1879, a mostly Democratic convention drew up a new constitution that returned the state to "home rule," putting white supremacists in control of most state, parish, and municipal institutions.[9]

Daily life continues, even in the wake of war and destruction. Residents of the small towns along the Mississippi River banks suffered less than those living in rural lands or on plantations. Transportation and commerce were re-established after the rivers were cleared of warships and debris. One major impetus for recovery was the arrival of the Texas & Pacific Railroad in 1871, with tracks following the west bank of the Mississippi River from New Orleans to Donaldsonville. The railroad had stops at most sizeable towns and provided both passenger and freight services.

Louise Clothilde Malvina Bossier was 11 years old in 1871. Her father died in 1868, and her mother remarried Pierre Nathaniel Ham in 1872. The census of 1870 listed Louise and her mother as living in Ward 1, St. John the Baptist Parish.[10] They were most likely living in their home in Edgard where her father had practiced as a lawyer. He was reasonably prosperous and died at the height of his career, probably leaving his widow an inheritance to maintain the family. Edgard was a small town, although it became parish seat in 1848. It had two newspapers in 1860 that were still operating into the next century.

Reserve Plantation near Edgard was able to return to sugar production more rapidly than most. Beginning as a small rice farm in 1764, the main house and plantation grew through a succession of owners to become a large, profitable operation until onset of the Civil War. Of interest, the plantation was owned by two free families of color, including François Rillieux and Jean Baptiste Fleming. During the war, the owner was a widow who ran into financial problems and sold it to Leon Godchaux, a French immigrant who became a wealthy clothing store owner. After acquiring Reserve Plantation in 1869, Godchaux applied his financial acumen and started centralizing sugar processing. He and his sons consolidated nearby plantations, used modern production techniques, and applied good management to make the plantation again profitable. This sugar operation provided many jobs to local communities.

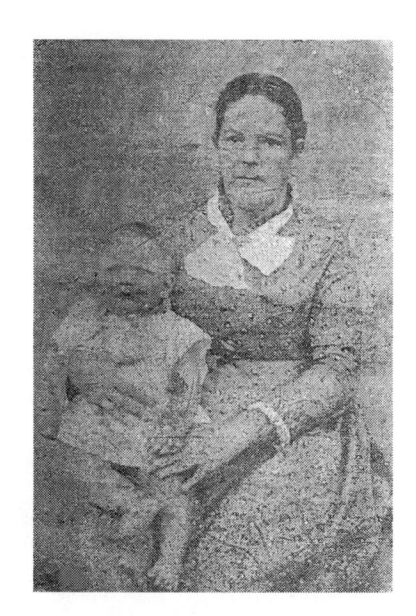

Louise Clothilde Malvina Bossier

Private schools that taught in the French language were started in Edgard around 1869. The first high schools at Edgard and Reserve were built in 1909. Children from area towns went to school by horse-drawn busses or commuter trains. We can imagine that Louise Clothilde went to school during this time since her father and mother were both well educated. She would also have taken the train with her mother and aunts to go shopping in Donaldsonville. The Texas & Pacific Railroad made its last stop in this larger town, around 30 miles upriver from Edgard. Donaldsonville was returning as a center for commerce after damages suffered during the war, due to its location at the junction of the Mississippi River and Bayou Lafourche. Now the railroad became another asset to the city's economy.

A favorite shopping destination was J. Lemann & Son Department Store, whose motto was "fair dealing, courteous treatment, and money refunded if goods are not satisfactory."[11] Jacob Lemann started his store in 1836 after selling goods from a horse-drawn cart. A large stone and stucco building, the Lemann store was once the oldest family-operated department store in Louisiana. Shoppers could find anything from clothes, dry goods, and groceries to agriculture supplies and implements; buggies, carriages, and saddlery to hardware and paints. Various products were located in separate subdivisions, and manufactured goods from all over the world were offered. Once, Lemann's even had a mail-order business.

It would have been an all-day excursion, but women, children, and men looked forward to these outings. Bringing basket lunches, they boarded the earliest train at the nearby stop; this was often simply a wooden platform next to the rails. It took several hours to reach Donaldsonville, as the train made many stops. Once there, they got off at the impressive new train station, with its three-dormer building and long platform with covered walkway. The town also offered a 5 & 10 cent store, women's clothing and hats, rice mill, hotel, and the Opera Cafe.

In 1873, the town renamed its main street Railroad Avenue. A ticket from Donaldsonville to Gretna, at the outskirts of New Orleans, was $1.85. Shoppers might walk from the train station to the stores, or take a buggy if the streets were flooded. Standing water in streets was common from spring flooding, when the Mississippi River topped the levees. Streets could stay under water for months at a time, until the levees were raised later on.

In 1872, a railroad bridge was built across Bayou Lafourche. The *Donaldsonville Chief* newspaper remarked, "The pile driver is at work at the site of the railroad bridge... We hope it may be steadily continued, and our railroad extended somewhere or other, we are not very particular where."[12] Eventually the rails did continue to Baton Rouge and headed west to Texas. If travelers wanted to proceed down Bayou Lafourche, they boarded mule-drawn barges towed from a path along the levee. The bayou was dammed in 1904 to prevent flooding, but the results also altered agriculture, reduced silt deposition to refurbish marshes, and affected transportation to the Gulf of Mexico. A pumping station was built in the 1950s to resupply water to the bayou, which never returned to its former conditions.

Much of Louise Clothilde's social life was centered around church activities. Near Edgard, the oldest chapel in the region, *La Paroisse de St. Jean des Allemands*, was built in 1723 in Karlstein, on the west bank of the Mississippi River near present-day Taft. It was constructed of handmade cypress lumber. When it fell into disrepair, the church was relocated to what is now Destrehan, across the river from Edgard. In 1740, this church and parish became known as St. Charles Borromeo. The original cypress log structure burned down in 1806; when rebuilt it was painted red. The "Little Red Church" on the east bank of the Mississippi River became a landmark for riverboats going to New Orleans, signaling that their destination was not far away. In 1921, the "Little Red Church" burned down, and the present church was built on the property.[13]

After the church and parish relocated to Destrehan, the people of the west bank had no church from 1740 to 1771. West bank residents had to take boats across the river to attend services. The Edgard community built a wooden church in 1772, which was named St John the Baptist Church. It served until 1821, when it was destroyed by a flood caused by the Poché Crevasse. A second church was built in the same place in 1822, constructed of handmade bricks with a high center steeple. Fire destroyed this church in 1918, and the congregation raised $90,000 in one day to build a beautiful, twin-spire, red brick church in 1920 that still stands today. St. John the Baptist Church Cemetery in Edgard contains graves of many Vial-Martin family ancestors, especially Bossiers and Vials.

There is a curious tale associated with this church, called "The Curse of St. John the Baptist Parish." In the late 1800s, conflicts developed between Father Alexander Juillé, pastor, and the church wardens who thought he had too much power. Another story says he accused a young couple of kissing in the church, and the girl's parents were outraged because he was destroying her reputation. Whatever the reason, Father Juillé was arrested and put in jail. When told he could leave, he refused and said he would stay in jail until the people who put him there spoke with him. Many days passed and some feared he would never leave. To ease tensions, the Catholic Church transferred him to Lafayette, and the local church was closed for over three years. When Father Juillé did leave jail, legend says he climbed to the top of the levee and pronounced a 100-year curse on the parish. Supposedly this curse led to the murders of a priest, his housekeeper, and a nun in the rectory in 1975 and the church burning down in 1918.[14] But other accounts say Father Juillé forgave his accusers and left in good graces.

Catholic churches were pivotal in each important life transition, from christening at birth to marriages to funeral services at death. It is likely that Louise Clothilde and Louis Adolphe Vial met at a church or social function, as they lived close to each other in the Lucy community, three miles east of Edgard where the Mississippi River made a large curve. The Bossier family had numerous relatives in the river parishes, attended church regularly, went to local fairs and soirées, and visited socially. Louis Adolphe Vial was a relative newcomer to the region. Their courtship and marriage took place between 1870 and 1876. By the censuses of 1880 and 1890, Louise Clothilde was living in St. Charles Parish. She moved there following her marriage to Louis Adolphe, which took place at St. John the Baptist Church, Edgard, on August 8, 1876.

Louis Adolphe Vial was born on December 23, 1842, in New Orleans. His baptism took place just over three years later, an unusually long time, at St. Louis Cathedral in the Vieux Carré. The Vial family was from Lyon in the Rhone region of France. Louis' father, **Charles François Leon Vial**, was the son of a rich ship owner, Claude Vial, a merchant of Lyon. Claude Vial's wife was Magdeleine Françoise Josephine "Fanny" Daram (d'Aram family from Versailles and Toulouse). Claude and Fanny had at least three more children after Charles François Leon; all their children were born between 1813 and 1818. One daughter, **Adelaide Augustine Herminie Vial**, was a student of Franz Liszt. The famous Hungarian composer and virtuoso pianist was employed teaching wealthy female students at a school in Paris in the 1830s. Liszt acted as a witness to the marriage of Charles François Leon Vial and **Marie Magdeleine "Lise" Richard** in 1833 in Paris.

Louis Adolphe Vial

Franz Liszt was apparently a friend of the Vial family, and his school was located near their home. A month after he witnessed the marriage, he wrote a letter to his lover, Marie d'Agoult, telling her to forward her letters to him through Madame Vial, saying "I am completely certain of her." Herminie was a favorite student of Liszt, and he dedicated his work *Grande Fantaisie di Bravura sur la Clochette de Paganini* (1834) to "Mademoiselle Herminie Vial." Liszt and Herminie performed a dual piano concert at the Hotel de Ville in Paris on April 9, 1835. This concert is famous because the composer fainted at the conclusion. Other letters by Liszt state that he dined at the home of "mère Vial" only once (1836); and referred to a charitable project for children for which Madame Vial had requested his patronage (1841). These references are most likely to Fanny Daram, by then widow of Claude Vial.[15]

Charles François Leon Vial married Marie Magdeleine "Lise" Richard in 1833 in Paris, which was her family's home. The Vial family was from Lyon, Rhone, France. They moved to Paris, probably because Fanny Daram inherited property that had belonged to her father, Marie-Joseph Daram, before the French Revolution. Although his possessions were confiscated when he left Paris, some property was returned to owners after the Restoration of Louis XVIII. If so, this would explain the family's move to Paris and apparent wealth. Little is known of the lives of Charles François Leon Vial and Marie Magdeleine "Lise" Richard until their marriage, although there were notable people in the family trees.

Marie Magdeleine "Lise" Richard was the daughter of Baron Joseph-Étienne Richard, a lawyer and public prosecutor of the commune of La Flèche, who became a well-known politician involved in the French revolution. He served as a deputy for Sarthe to the Legislative Assembly in 1791-92 and voted for the death of King Louis XVI at the ruler's trial. After holding several positions in Public Safety and the War Ministry, he served under Napoleon I as préfet of Haute-Garonne and Charente-Inférieure during the First Empire. Napoleon I awarded him the Legion of Honour in 1804 then granted him the titles of chevalier de l'Empire (1809) and baron de l'Empire (1810). Under the Bourbon Restoration and King Louis XVIII, Joseph-Étienne was dismissed but soon recalled and appointed préfet of Calvados in 1815, retiring quietly to Saintes in Charente-Maritime when a law was passed in 1816 proscribing regicides. No action was taken against him for his vote to kill the former king; apparently he was exempted from this law and even given a pension of 6,000 francs.[16]

Shortly after their marriage, the couple went to Mexico City and established a business there. It is not clear why they relocated to Mexico. There is a hint that the families may have disapproved of the marriage; neither surviving parent on either side appears to have been present for the ceremony. According to family lore, "Lise" Richard was of noble birth while Charles Françoise Leon Vial was not, and her family objected to the marriage.[17] If the Richard family was noble, it seems of recent vintage. The couple may have left to advance their financial situation. Lyon had a substantial silk industry with considerable trade in Mexico City, and there was a large French community.

France was a major trade partner with Mexico at that time. However, during the early years of the new Mexican republic, competing factions struggled to control the government, resulting in widespread civil disorder. Private property was looted, and foreigners had no way to obtain compensation from the Mexican government. French merchants complained to their home country, which demanded repayment of damages. The initial complainant was a French pastry chef, giving the conflict its name "The Pastry War." When Mexico made no payment, France blockaded ports along the Gulf, and fighting seemed imminent.

On November 27, 1838, French forces attacked Veracruz and briefly occupied it. Due to escalating hostilities, French nationals living in Mexico were ordered to leave their homes within three days and the country within two weeks. Fearing for their lives and property, many French people left Mexico during 1838-1839, including Charles F. Leon Vial and his family.

Their first son, Emile Fernand François Xavier Vial, was born on January 12, 1835, in Mexico City. The next two children were also born in Mexico City: Gustave Charles Marc Lino Vial in 1837, and Jeanne Marie Catherine Vial in 1838.[18] The Vials departed shortly afterward and arrived in New Orleans on February 11, 1839. The passenger list of the Bark General Foy, sailing from San Sacrificios, Mexico, includes "Vial & wife & three children."[19]

According to the 1840 census, the family had settled in the Third Ward, First Municipality of New Orleans.[20] From 1842 to 1844, they resided at 130 Old Levee Street, and Charles F. Leon Vial operated a grocery store, Leon Vial & Co., grocers.[21] Their next son, Louis Adolphe Vial, was born in New Orleans in 1842, while the family resided at Old Levee Street. His sponsors at baptism were Adolphe and Marie Louise Vuez, who operated a fancy dry goods and millinery shop on Bourbon Street in New Orleans. Two more daughters were also born at the Old Levee Street home, Stephanie Clementine Vial in 1846, and Herminie Françoise Romualdine Vial in 1848. Stephanie was baptized at St. Louis Cathedral in New Orleans in July 1847, but the family moved soon after, and the last daughter Herminie was baptized at St. John the Baptist Church in Edgard on February 7, 1849.

The national recession of 1838-1843 caused financial difficulties for Charles Leon's grocery business. He had to turn his store over to creditors, although he did not file bankruptcy. Around this time, his wife Lise Richard Vial filed in 1845 to separate her property from that of her husband. This was granted in the St. Charles Parish court; they must have been planning to move away from New Orleans. The move must have occurred in 1847-1848. This legal procedure no doubt preserved some of their assets in Lise's name.

The census of 1850 lists the Vial family living in St. John the Baptist Parish, where the family head was listed as a grocer.[22] Their home was on the west bank just above the St. Charles Parish line, probably in Lucy. Members of the family listed in the census were Leon Vial, Grocer age 36; Lise Richard age 36; Emile Vial age 15; Charles Vial age 13; Marie Vial age 11; Adolphe Vial age 7; Fanny Vial age 4; and Herminie Vial age 2. In 1859, Lise bought some land in St. Charles Parish just downriver from Killona, consisting of a store standing on ½ arpent of river fronting.

Killona is located about halfway between Edgard and Hahnville, just downriver of the parish boundary line. It was the site of several large sugar plantations in the mid-1800s. The original name was Karlstein, referring to a collection of German colonial villages founded under the leadership of Karl Friedrich d'Arensbourg in 1721. The region extended from Taft to Lucy. The Killona, Mary, and Waterford Plantations continued operating after the Civil War, until most of the properties were acquired by Louisiana Power & Light in 1963, and then the Waterford nuclear plants in the 1970s.

River Parishes Map Contemporary

An article appeared in *L'Avant Coureur*, a local newspaper, on February 5, 1859, describing an accident suffered by Charles F. Leon Vial: "Mr. Charles Vial of St. John the Baptist was the victim these last days of an accident which fortunately will not have grave results. He worked on the river bank removing some driftwood with the aid of a worn 'tour' (crane) when the cable broke and the pole of the 'tour' struck Mr. Vial in the middle of the chest. Dr. Chabaud was immediately called to bleed the patient, whose condition today does not inspire any anxiety."[23]

The three oldest children married during the 1850s, all at St. John the Baptist Church in Edgard. Jeanne Marie was married on January 20, 1855, to Louis Chevalier D'Arensbourg, and the oldest son Emile Fernand married Marie Celima D'Arensbourg on August 25, 1855. Gustave Charles Lino Vial married Clotilde Malvina Songy on August 8, 1859. All the Vial children except one were married in the Edgard church, including Louis Adolphe Vial, wed to Louise Clothilde Malvina Bossier on August 8, 1876. The 1860 census shows only three children remaining in the household, ages 12 to 17, with Charles F. Leon Vial's occupation as storekeeper. His personal property was valued at $1,000, and it was noted that his daughter Herminie had attended school within the last year.[24]

During the Civil War, Union forces made two excursions upriver to St. Charles Parish after New Orleans fell, in August and September 1862. It is not clear if members of this Vial family served during the Civil War. There was an "A. Vial" who was a private in a New Orleans artillery company for the Confederate Army, but this is unlikely to have been Louis Adolphe Vial. His brother, Emile Fernand Vial, was captured and taken to New Orleans, even though he was not in the Confederate Army. He died there of typhoid fever. On the second raid, the Union forces landed right at the Vial store in St. Charles Parish, which had frontage on the river, and they looted the store. Twenty years later, Lise Richard Vial filed a claim for this looting and was actually awarded about $2,000 for the property taken. Hers was one of the rare claims for damages done during the Civil War to be successful.[25]

It appears that Charles F. Leon and Lise were operating the store near Killona in the 1860s, although they were still listed in the 1860 census as living in St. John the Baptist Parish. They probably moved shortly after the census was taken. Their two youngest daughters, Stephanie and Herminie, were married on the same day, February 7, 1867. Double weddings were common among siblings, but the sisters' weddings apparently did not take place in the same church. Stéphanie married Jean-Charles (Jules) Médoux; their marriage was reported in 1868 in *L'Avant Coureur*, a St. Charles Parish newspaper, provided by the parish priest of St. Charles Borromeo Church in a recap of sacraments done in 1867. Herminie married François Mathéo Songy; their marriage was recorded in St. John the Baptist Church. Stéphanie died 20 months later, probably from complications of childbirth.

Records are lacking to explain this odd occurrence. St. Charles Borromeo Church rectory burned down with the parish registers in 1877. Civil records of marriage licenses at St. Charles Parish courthouse start with 1878. No family members signed Stéphanie's church funeral record in October 1868; there is no civil death certificate. This suggests estrangement from her family; possibly her parents did not approve of her marriage to Jean-Charles. The cause of this apparent rift remains a family mystery.

At the 1870 census, Charles F. Leon Vial and family were listed as residents of St. Charles Parish. They were living in the First Ward, Boutte Station. He was 54 years old and working as a storekeeper; his wife Lise was age 51 and keeping house. Living in the household was Celima D'Arensbourg Vial, age 28, widow of Emile Fernand Vial, and her four children ages 13 to 6. All the children were listed as attending school. Real estate value was shown as $1,000, and personal property was $1,500. In February 1872, Charles F. Leon Vial sold his St. John the Baptist property consisting of "one dwelling house, one kitchen, one building formerly used as a store." This store and cooperage was located on the batture at Bonnet Carré.[26]

Charles François Leon Vial died on August 9, 1873, and was buried the next day at St. John the Baptist Church in Edgard. His obituary appeared in *Le Meschacébé*, in French:

"Saturday last, 9 August, at 9 AM, died at the age of 60 years, M. Charles Leon Vial d'Areng (his mother's maiden name, Daram) de Saffon (his maternal grandmother's maiden name). Gout had confined him to a sickbed for more than two months, and his death was foreseen. The life of this excellent man, whom many friends will mourn, shows once more how much history is stranger than fiction." The newspaper article then relates the story of his sojourn in Mexico and move to New Orleans, noting he "practiced honorably the commercial profession" in St. John the Baptist and St. Charles Parishes.[27]

His wife Marie Magdeleine Lise Richard lived another 22 years in St. Charles Parish and died at 89 years of age. She was buried in the Edgard cemetery the next day beside her husband. Their son, Louis Adolphe Vial, was appointed to administer the estate, but it was so burdened with debt that the property had to be sold by the sheriff to raise money to repay these. Four generations later, their direct descendent Wayne Charles Vial would write: "Although Leon and Lise's monetary legacy amounted to little, they left a heritage of integrity and resiliency, as well as many descendants who were to play an active role in the future of St. Charles and St. John the Baptist Parishes."[28]

Louis Adolphe Vial, though born in New Orleans in December 1842, moved with his family to St. John the Baptist Parish as a youth. He was listed in the 1850 census taken there when he was 7 ½ years old. His father had established another mercantile business in Lucy, and later in Boutte. Louis Adolphe grew up in Lucy and was still living there in the 1860 census when he was 17-18 years old. By the 1870 census, he was no longer living with his parents, who had relocated to St. Charles Parish.

Louis Adolphe was the third son and did not continue in his father's grocery enterprises. Instead, he acquired land in 1862 that was part of Fashion Plantation and became a farmer.[29] Around this time he moved from Killona, where his parents lived. He married Louise Clothilde Malvina Bossier in 1876 when he was 34 years old. In the years between, he must have been developing his sugarcane business and building a house on the property. By the late 1870s, Louis Adolphe and his wife Louise Clothilde were considered "well-known sugar planters."[30]

In 1888, Louis Adolphe Vial bought another part of Fashion Plantation from Damien Haydel, located on the west bank of the Mississippi River, 27 miles above New Orleans. This property had 4 arpents (3.384 acres) river frontage and was bounded on the downriver side by land of Mrs. J.B. Martin Sr. (Celeste Triche). This property was later divided among the Vial children.[31]

Later the Haydel and Vial families became related by marriage. Louis Adolphe's oldest son, Leon Charles Vial I (1876-1939), took the granddaughter of Damien Haydel as his second wife in 1916. Damien Haydel (1825-1899) was the father of Josephine Marie Elvire Haydel (1853-1914) who married Pierre Anatole Keller (1854-1931). They were parents of Marguerite Marie Keller (1866-1967) who became the second wife of Leon Charles Vial I. Louis Adolphe died in 1910 and did not live long enough to see this subsequent relationship take place with the Haydel family.

Louis Adolphe and Louise Clothilde Vial had 13 children born in St. Charles Parish; only two died in infancy. By 1876 when they married, they were living in St. Charles Parish. The 1880 census recorded the Vial family at this residence along with two boarders from the Borne family. The 1900 and 1910 censuses identified their residence as Ward 2, St. Charles Parish, and Louis' occupation as farmer.[32]

Their first child, Joseph Adolphe Vial, was born in 1877 but only lived for three years. He was followed quickly by Leon Charles Vial I in 1878 and Leonide Mary Vial in 1879. These two Vial children are the direct ancestors of the Vial-Martin family featured in this book. The next children were Martha Alice Vial (1881), Melchior Claudius Vial (1882), Richard John Vial (1883), Antonia Felide Vial (1885), Louise Malvina Vial (1886), Hortaire Joseph Vial (1887), Melville Louis Vial (1889), Emile Denis Vial (1891-1893, died age 2 years), Eric Oscar Vial (1892), and Ella Zulma Vial (1895).

It is obvious that most of Louise Clothilde Vial's adult life was consumed with having babies. She was pregnant most of the 18 years between the birth of her first child and the birth of her last one. The fact that she and all but two of her children survived is a testimony to strong constitutions. One can imagine that Louise had domestic servants to assist with housekeeping and caring for this immense brood and a large house. As a sugar planter who acquired large holdings after the war, Louis Adolphe no doubt did well financially once the economy recovered.

In 1892, St. Charles Parish was described as one of the best in the state. "The alluvial lands along either side of the Mississippi furnish the almost entire cultivable lands of the parish. These lands are of the very richest and yield immense crops of cane and rice, in which they are chiefly cultivated. There are in the parish a number of the finest sugar plantations of the state. A great majority of the agriculturists of the parish own small tracts of land, which they cultivate largely in rice. Of late, however, sugar-cane culture on a small scale has become quite popular."[33]

The parish had other assets, including heavily wooded swamps with cypress and other timbers, while the southern portion was mainly sea marsh and marsh prairie. There were now four railroads, two on each side of the river that connected with New Orleans and went both north and west. Initially the seat of government was simply the St. Charles Parish Courthouse. In 1870, a Republican, Judge Othello Jerome Flagg, acquired land near the courthouse. He had it surveyed and subdivided in 1872 for a town he named Flaggville. But shortly after Flaggville was created, it was merged with a nearby town, Hahnville, located just north of Home Place Plantation. In 1872, this town was laid out by ex-governor Michael Hahn on the site of his sugar plantation.

Hahnville became the parish seat. Its population at the time was 340, most being black people. The town had two stores, a newspaper, and three business houses in the surrounding country. The *St. Charles Herald* newspaper was established in 1873 by Hahn, who conducted it until his death in 1885. It was the official means of reporting government actions, taken over by J.C. Triche & Co. and called itself "... independent in politics, and devoted to local interests."[34] Although he lived in the South before the Civil War, Hahn was a Northern sympathizer who was appointed military governor by President Lincoln. Hahn also served as congressman, director of St. Charles Parish Schools, state registrar of voters, police juror, and district judge. While Hahn was alive, the newspaper "... always reacted strongly to him and his party. The paper remained a strong Republican organ."[35]

Michael Hahn remains notable in Louisiana history because he served during a brief period when the state had two governors. Toward the end of the Civil War, the state was in chaos as the Union army pushed toward occupation. From February 1864 to March 1865, Hahn was the federally appointed governor of Louisiana, while Henry Watkins Allen was governor of the Confederate part of the state. Hahn was elected to the United States Senate in 1865, but due to national political compromises around the presidential election, he was prevented from being seated in the congressional Reconstruction agreements.

St. Charles Parish was predominantly Republican after Reconstruction, and several early parish officials were black men. Accusations were made that many were not qualified for office, some being illiterate, penniless, and used as political tools. All the local sheriffs during this time were Republicans. In 1876, there was a push to unseat the "Radical Republicans" by the Democratic-Conservative Party. However, the election that year was won by Republicans, including putting **J.B. Martin Sr.** in as clerk of court (1877-1896) and George Essex as sheriff. On the losing ticket was E.D. Sellers running for sheriff. By 1883, defections and scandals affected the Radical Republican Party, and the Democrats prevailed, with B.S. Labranche as sheriff and Joseph L. Martin as deputy sheriff; he was the brother of J.B. Martin Sr. Theodule T. Baudouin became assessor and later moved into the sheriff position when Sheriff Labranche died.

The next sheriff, Lewis Ory, was the first Republican to hold the office long term, from 1884 to 1903. Ory was killed in the line of duty and replaced by deputy sheriff Anthony Madere, serving 1903-1912. Years later, a secret illegal agreement between them came to light giving insight into political trading that took place during the time. Both men signed a document in 1899 to support each other in the 1900 election since there were a number of candidates. Madere agreed to support Ory for sheriff and tax collector and influence his friends to vote favorably. Ory agreed that after his expected election in 1900 for four years, he would appoint Madere his chief deputy and jailor, and they would divide the proceeds of those offices equally.[36]

The Madere, Vial, and Martin families had numerous interconnections through marriage and kinship over the years spanning the late 1800s into the mid-20th century.

Politics were volatile as the new century approached with people switching sides, and party distinctions began to blur. In Louisiana, the typical governing body of most parishes is called the Police Jury. It is the legislative and executive government of the parish and is elected by the voters. Its members are called jurors, and together they elect a president as their chairman. (Initially St. Charles and St. John the Baptist Parishes had Policy Juries; later they changed to a home rule charter.) Appointments to and by the Police

Jury led to many disputes, with seatings and un-seatings and at times two men claiming right to an office. Issues were appealed to the Louisiana Supreme Court with protests and countercharges. By 1900, the parish was transitioning to Democratic Party dominance, which lasted through most of the century. Instead of two parties, there was bifactionalism with competing factions within the same party. It was into this volatile environment that members of the Vial and Martin families ventured and attained leadership positions. But the families were placed at odds with each other in political competitions.

Louise Clothilde Malvina Bossier Vial died at age 46 on April 15, 1907, while hospitalized in Hotel Dieu, a highly regarded hospital in New Orleans. She was only in the hospital for one day when she died from "pleura-pneumonia."[37] Since there was limited medical care available in rural upriver parishes, she was probably taken to Hotel Dieu because she was critically ill. It is likely that her husband, Louis Adolphe, accompanied her and was there when she died. Her body was transported back to Edgard for burial at St. John the Baptist Church on April 16, 1907. Her youngest child, Ella Zulma Vial, born in 1895, would have been 12 years old, and her youngest son Eric Oscar Vial, born in 1892, would be 15 years old.

The Vial home in Ward 2, St. Charles Parish, often was a multifamily household. This was not unusual among the Creole families along the Mississippi River, particularly those who had large homes. In the 1910 census, Louis Adolphe was living with his two youngest children and the family of his son, Richard John Vial. Richard was the fifth living child and had married Marie Josepha Hymel in October 1907, six months after his mother Louise Clothilde had died. Richard and Marie Josepha Vial had two young children by 1910. One can assume that Marie Josepha assumed the role of "woman of the house" after the death of Louise Clothilde.

Louis Adolphe Vial died at age 67 on April 28, 1910. The census must have been done in the earlier months of that year. He was ill the last several months of his life, although the illness is not specified, and he would have been cared for at home. His obituary was published in the *New Orleans Daily Picayune*:

"Hahnville, La., April 28. – After a lingering illness of five months, Mr. Louis Adolphe Vial, aged 68 years, died today. He was a successful farmer, following the rice and cane culture. He married Miss Louise C. Bossier, daughter of a well-known lawyer. From this issue were born, and are now living, eleven children: Leon C. Vial, parish assessor; Mrs. P.D. (J.B.) Martin, Mrs. O.P. Schexnayder, R.J. Vial, Mrs. Dr. A.J. Melancon, Mrs. P.D. Lorio, Messrs. M.C., H.J. and E.C. Vial, Miss Ella Vial and Mr. Melville Vial. He is survived by one brother, C.L. Vial of St. John Parish, and one sister, Mrs. Chevalier Darensbourgh, also of St. John, besides other relatives. The ceremonies will be held at Our Lady of the Rosary Church, of this parish, and interment will follow at St. John's Church on Friday at 3 p.m."[38]

He was buried in St. John the Baptist Parish Church Cemetery, Edgard, alongside his wife Louise Clothilde who had been buried there three years earlier.

Children living at time of Louis Adolphe Vial's death (1910):

Leon C. Vial I	age 32	m. Celeste Irma Martin 1902
Leonide Mary Vial Martin	age 31	m. Jean Baptiste Martin 1903
Martha Alice Vial Schexnayder	age 29	m. Olide Paul Schexnayder 1905
Melchior Claudius Vial	age 28	m. Nina Agnes Melanson 1900
Richard John Vial	age 27	m. Marie Josepha Hymel 1907
Antonia Felide Vial Melanson	age 25	m. Ashbel Denniss Melanson 1906
Louise Malvina Vial Lorio	age 24	m. Pierre Desire Lorio 1908
Hortaire Joseph Vial	age 23	m. Alice Clare Fielder 1920
Melville Louis Vial	age 21	not married
Eric Oscar Vial	age 18	m. Blanche Elizabeth Scherer 1914
Ella Zulma Vial Baudouin	age 15	m. Elmer Lucius Baudouin 1927

Surviving siblings at time of L.A. Vial's death:

Gustave Charles Marc Lino Vial (C. L. Vial)	age 73	m. Clotilde Malvina Songy 1859
Jeanne Marie Catherine Vial D'Arensbourg (Mrs. Chevalier Darensbourgh)	age 72	m. Louis Chevalier D'Arensbourg 1855

CHAPTER 10

Vial and Martin Families in St. Charles Parish

Leonide Mary Vial (1879-1964) –
Jean Baptiste Martin, Jr. (1881-1955)

⚜

At the dawn of the 20th century, St. Charles Parish was largely rural and agricultural. The large sugar plantations had been dismantled after the Civil War, leaving the sugarcane industry in collapse. A great deal of property exchanged hands during the post-war years of 1865 to 1900, as an influx of Northerners, Easterners, and recent immigrants from France and Europe had money to purchase land. Many plantation owners in financial arrears began parceling their property and selling smaller pieces, which became modest farms or homesites. Landholders during this time doubled in number, although the average size of their holdings was cut in half. Various crops were grown, though the region gradually returned to sugarcane as new technology reduced labor demands.[1]

St. Charles and other Mississippi River parishes were created in 1807 from what was called the *Côte des Allemands* (German Coast). The area began 25 miles above New Orleans and extended along both sides of the river for 40 miles toward Baton Rouge. First settled by Germans from the Rhine region led by Karl Friedrich D'Arensbourg, the collective name Karlstein was given to the colonial river villages around 1724, extending from present-day Taft to Lucy (now part of Edgard), including contemporary Killona. Several large land grants became plantations, including Mary Plantation, Killona

Plantation, and Waterford Plantation. Killona opened a post office in 1887, which was closed in the 1980s.

The St. Charles Courthouse was established in 1804, and a community grew up around it using that name. The first post office opened in 1843; it closed in 1880 when the Hahnville post office opened. In 1872 civil engineer Thomas Sharpe laid out a village around the courthouse and named it Flaggville, after district judge Othelle J. Flagg. Around the same time, Michael J. Hahn, an attorney who held numerous public offices including congressman and Louisiana governor, laid out the streets of Hahnville on his sugar plantation just upriver from Flaggville. Hahnville and Flaggville were separated by the Home Place Plantation; in time the entire area became commonly called Hahnville.[2]

The 295 square miles of land in St. Charles Parish is largely rich, fertile alluvial soil deposited by the Mississippi River over many ages. The river divides the parish roughly in half into the east bank and west bank. Although the Mississippi River generally flows north to south, in St. Charles Parish it runs west to east. Facing north, the land to the right of the river is the east bank, in which the towns of Norco and Destrehan are located. On the west bank, the left side of the river is Hahnville, Taft, Killona, Luling, and Ama. The parish is bounded on the northeast by Lake Pontchartrain, a brackish-water lake about 40 miles long and 20 miles wide. On the southwest is Lake Des Allemands, a large body of sweet water.

Originally lands in this region were flat and sloped from 14 feet above natural sea level along the banks of the river, to about 1 foot above sea level at the shore of Lake Pontchartrain. The last 4-5 miles east of the river were swamplands giving way to marsh nearer the lake. Only 3-4 miles of land closest to the riverbanks were suitable for cultivation. Land to the west also descended into marshes and swamps as it stretched farther from the river. Flooding was a perennial problem; serious attempts at levee building began around 1743. These levees were only about 5 feet high, not enough to protect from floods which occurred almost yearly. Each landowner was responsible for building and maintaining levees along his property, so the quality was unreliable. In 1928 a controlled outlet for flooding was created, named the Bonnet Carré Spillway, located just north of Norco. It saved the region from the greatest recorded flood in 1937. Since then, better levee height and maintenance by Federal Corps of Engineers, plus the spillway, have protected St. Charles Parish from disastrous flooding.

The Mississippi River played a central role in the area throughout its history. It was the major route for travel from upriver parishes to New Orleans, for commerce and shipping from northerly cities and the Port of New Orleans, and as a source of fishing and wildlife. Through the years, it has been the waterway to prosperity and the gate to the world. Although the river also brought yellow fever and malaria, immigrants and opportunists, and at times devastating floods, it spurred the region's development from wilderness colony, to plantations, farms, and growing towns, to its present status as an industrial center.

Due to the importance of river access, property in the river parishes was divided from the beginning into long segments, all with frontage on the riverbanks. The properties extended back to border markers such as railroads, swamps, or lakes. Maps of early land grants and properties along the Mississippi River look like a snake with thin rectangular strips fanning outward on each side. As these large properties were divided due to family inheritance, and again as plantations broke up after the Civil War, the strips of land became thinner.

Although the Mississippi River was the main artery of transportation, roads were built along both banks of the levee from New Orleans to Baton Rouge in the 1800s. River Road was a narrow dirt trail for many years. Travel was uncomfortable on the dusty, muddy, winding, potholed road. It was easier to take a riverboat going from one town to the next along the river. Small ferries took people and horse-drawn buggies across the river from bank to bank or the destination landing. In 1900 normal river height nearly reached the tops of the low levees. Every village had a landing with riverboats and ferries. Large paddlewheel steamboats would only stop at bigger towns, although the showboats came to small villages. This created excitement and was a significant source of entertainment, and local children brought items to sell.

River Road on both sides still exists today. Now it is paved, but still narrow and winding. These were the only roads between Baton Rouge and New Orleans until Airline Highway was completed in 1935. As auto travel increased, the state built a ferry large enough to hold 15 cars based in Luling in 1948. Workers needed to get across the river to jobs in the developing petrochemical businesses around Norco.

Railroads came to the river parishes in 1871 with a line running from New Orleans to Donaldsonville. Between 1900 and 1930 people often traveled to and from New Orleans by train, and towns along the route had depots. Stores and merchants in river towns still got their wares delivered from boats traveling upriver from New Orleans.

In the early 1900s industry moved into the parish with the first sawmill opening in Taft in 1907. The abundance of cypress and oak trees provided a good supply of lumber. In 1908 the Louisiana Cypress Company began harvesting local cypress trees, built the Cousins Canal, and moved more than 100,000 board feet through it by 1912. The Colonial Dairy Farm, one of the largest in the state, was also located in Taft.

In 1902 the discovery of oil in Jennings, 150 miles west of St. Charles Parish, would indelibly shape the character of the river parishes. Oil companies saw them as ideal locations for refineries because of their access to the Mississippi River and ample portage for huge oil tankers. In 1914, Destrehan Plantation was sold to the Mexican Petroleum Company. It was the first River Road plantation to shift from an agricultural to an industrial economic base. Through several buyouts and mergers, the American Oil Company acquired the property and deeded the plantation house to the River Road Historical Society for preservation. In 1916 the New Orleans Refining Company acquired land in the small east bank town of Sellers, then an agricultural site. Known by the acronym NORCO, it bought 366 acres of sugarcane fields from the Good Hope Plantation to establish a marine petroleum supply terminal. By 1920 the company built a refinery there with significant impact on the parish landscape. Paved roads were built for trucks to service the refinery. Workers streamed into the area seeking jobs; housing and services quickly followed. Soon the town of Sellers adopted Norco as its name.

Shell Oil Company acquired the Norco refinery in 1929 and expanded it, adding a large chemical plant. Many other industries and oil companies soon followed, bringing huge storage tanks, oil barrels, railroad tanker cars, and noisy trucks. From oil refineries protruded coiling tubes, tall chimneys spouting black smoke, conveyor belts, and towering pipes lighting the sky with perpetual flames casting an eerie glow all night. Hissing noises and mechanical clamor filled the atmosphere as petroleum and chemical industries eventually lined the river. Oil was discovered in St. Charles Parish in 1938-1942. In the following years many petrochemical companies located nearby, including Monsanto, Lion Oil Co., Shell Chemical, Union Carbide, and others.

The Waterford Nuclear Generating Station was constructed in 1974 on 3,000 acres in Killona. It began operating in 1985 and has an annual output of 8,402 GWh electricity to serve the region. The 50-mile contamination exposure risk zone includes all of St. Charles Parish and New Orleans, which is 33 miles from the plant. It was temporarily shut down in 2005 due to Hurricane Katrina and in 2011 during a river flood.

Leonide Mary Vial was born on August 19, 1879, in the Vial family home built by her father, Louis Adolphe Vial. He had acquired property on the Fashion Plantation grounds in the early 1870s and built the house, probably before he married Louise Clothilde Malvina Bossier in 1876. The house must have been sizeable since they had 13 children, all born before the turn of the 20th century. The first son born in 1877 only lived for three years, followed quickly by Leon Charles Vial I in July 1878, and Leonide Mary a year later. The children were spaced one to two years apart and kept coming in regular succession, until the last daughter was born in 1895. One other boy died in infancy, living two years.

Leonide Mary Vial

Although no pictures exist of this first Vial house, one can imagine it had two stories and was constructed in typical Creole style common in river parishes. In the early 1900s kitchen stoves were wood or kerosene burning, and electricity was nonexistent. Lighting was by kerosene lamps or candles; heat from wood or coal-burning fireplaces or cold oil heaters. Rainwater was collected in cisterns, using gutters to funnel runoff from the roof. Wooden buckets were used to carry water from cistern spigots for household use. Another outbuilding was used for laundry, with large metal tubs and washboards for scrubbing clothes, which were then hung with wooden clothespins on lines to dry outside. The ground level of some houses had rooms for laundry or cooking purposes, perhaps bedrooms for servants or storage. Ground-floor rooms were often flooded, however, either from heavy rains or levee breakages. Wealthier families often had an icebox, supplied by regular visits from the ice man who used huge tongs to haul blocks of ice from his wagon. This was the best way to keep perishable foods from spoiling. Underground cellars were impractical since they would always fill with groundwater. Sometimes watermelons were placed in streams or gullies to cool them down before eating.

The second story contained bedrooms and possibly sitting rooms which would be confiscated by the growing family for sleeping. In families as large as the Vials, children shared rooms, sometimes sleeping in the same bed. For boys there were bunk beds, often in an attic (*garçonnière.*) Free-standing dressers or armoires held clothes and bed linens. There were no inside bathroom facilities until many years later, so every bedroom had slop pots for night use, to be carried downstairs and emptied each day. An outhouse or two were located in the yard, not far from the house. Washbowls and pitchers were kept on dressers for morning cleanup, needing daily emptying and replenishment. One room was dedicated to bathing, containing a metal bathtub and shelves for towels and bathing supplies. This room might be on the second floor, if the family had household servants. If the family hauled their own bathwater, however, the bathing room was most likely on the first or the ground floor. Grander homes often had second-story balconies, allowing the family to enjoy breezes and pleasant sitting areas just outside the bedrooms.

Home Life. In rural upriver parishes, families grew their own vegetables and fruit trees and kept livestock including chickens, pigs, cows, and occasionally goats. Horses and mules were necessary for pulling the carriage and working the fields. Barns for the animals and chicken coops were not far from the house. Vegetable gardens were also close by, and the herb garden flanked the back stairs to the house. Family gardens usually provided potatoes, squash, tomatoes, beans, corn, melons, celery, carrots, peppers, and onions. It was essential to grow the "holy trinity" of vegetables for making Creole and Cajun dishes: onions, bell peppers, and celery. Tomatoes and garlic also have key roles in this cuisine, as well as okra, eggplant, and cabbage. Essential herbs and spices included parsley, oregano, thyme, and filé (dried, ground sassafras leaves).

Abundant waterways and marshes provided crabs, shrimp, crayfish, frogs, turtles, and waterfowl. Most families kept shrimp boxes along banks of the river, which the children would check daily, bringing home the small, sweet river shrimp. Many types of fish were caught; large river catfish, called "channel cats," were especially favored for frying. Families butchered their hogs, beef, and chickens as needed for meals. When a pig was butchered, nearly all parts were used. There would be pork roasts and pork chops, bacon, fat rendered until the chunks formed crisp cracklings, and less-choice meat ground for sausage. Most famous was andouille sausage, smoked and aged with a unique blend of seasonings. They made hogshead cheese and pickled pigs' feet and ears in a big crock with salt and vinegar. Pickling was one way to put up food, both meat and vegetables, to keep for months.

Although the Vials had servants, girls were expected to become good cooks and started learning early. Leonide and her sisters were taught to make gumbos, red beans and rice, stuffed crabs, fried chicken and fish, Creole specialties such as etouffée and au gratin dishes, jambalaya, bouillabaisse, smothered cabbage or okra, and numerous others.

Baked delicacies were made for social occasions, and crisp-crusted French bread baked for everyday consumption. Not every chore required for a self-sustaining household could be done by servants, so no doubt Leonide and her siblings had assigned daily duties. These might be collecting eggs from the henhouse, feeding chickens and pigs, weeding gardens, picking ripe vegetables and fruit, assisting with meal preparation. The boys contributed by fishing, hunting small game, and preparing meats.

Since a new baby sister or brother appeared every year or two, Leonide as the eldest daughter would have assumed childcare responsibilities early. Along with her sister, Martha Alice, who was two years younger, she probably watched over the next several siblings: Melchior, Richard, Antonia, Louise, Hortaire, Melville, and Eric. When the last daughter Ella was born in 1895, Leonide was 16 years old and approaching marriageable age. The children no doubt had black nannies as was common during that time, but with such a huge brood, additional watchful eyes were always needed.

Girls learned to sew clothes and do needlework, essential skills since virtually all family clothing was made at home. There were mercantile stores in the region, including the Vial family store in Killona and the Caire's Landing general store in Edgard. The Caire store was the biggest in the area, and people came from up, down, and across the river to shop there. What was not available in the store could be ordered through the Sears catalog; every imaginable type of merchandise from food to household goods to farm equipment. Occasionally the family would take an excursion to New Orleans, made easier by the railroad. In the "Big Easy" were opportunities to shop nearly undreamt of, including ready-made dresses beckoning from the windows of Krauss or Maison Blanche stores.

Medical doctors were few in rural areas but provided essential services for residents. They seldom saw patients in offices and primarily made house calls. It was common for doctors to make regular rounds in their area. People who needed a doctor visit would tie flags on their mailboxes to catch his attention. If need was urgent, someone would be sent by horseback to summon the doctor to the house. A typical rural doctor of the early1900s was described this way by the New Orleans *Times-Picayune*:

"Lionel Waguespack, who graduated from Tulane Medical School in 1900, had a flourishing practice. He'd deliver babies, dispense medicine, pull teeth, treat typhoid and fight off yellow fever. He kept a stable of three or four horses so he'd always have a fresh one in case of an emergency. And every day he'd make his rounds... Waguespack put in long hours and sometimes he'd have to spend the night at a patient's house. He could always sleep in the buggy, though, the horse could find his way home alone. Four times a year, he would attend meetings with other country doctors in the area. Medical advances were coming along rapidly, and they'd try to help each other keep up."[3]

Midwives often attended women in childbirth, especially when no difficulties were expected. Doctors were scarce and needed for more serious problems. Given the restrictive morals of the Victorian period, most likely girls of good families were not involved in assisting family births directly. They probably served by "running and fetching" things the midwife needed, such as warm water and clean linens. Of course, they were delighted once the baby came and vied to be first to hold the swaddled newborn. Girls growing up on a farm inevitably were exposed to facts of reproduction, however, given all the animals surrounding them.

Education. Rural 19th-century Creole planters educated their children by hiring tutors to teach in the home. When the boys were old enough, they were sent to colleges in New Orleans or other southern and eastern cities. Schooling for girls usually ended when they reached adolescence, if it continued that long. Some families, however, sent daughters to finishing schools or academies for women. Leonide Vial's grandmother, Louise Marie Malvina Reynaud (wife of Joseph Bossier), went to a Catholic school in Kentucky, the Nazareth Female Academy, for four years in the mid-1850s. It is unlikely that Leonide's mother, Louise Clothilde Malvina Bossier, had education beyond childhood, as she married Louis Adolphe Vial when she was 16. Alice Dugas, a resident of Donaldsonville, was dubbed "the town's *enfant terrible,* a one-woman intellectual elite with a sharp tongue and a sharp mind to match."[4] Born around the turn of the century, Alice Dugas earned bachelor's, master's, and doctoral degrees and traveled around the world, living on several continents while working as a librarian.

St. Charles Parish had two public schools in 1850 funded by taxation with Jean M. Dieudonne as superintendent. There were three public and some private schools in the 1860s, but little is known of them. The new state constitution created by the Reconstruction Convention of 1868 prohibited separate schools for blacks and whites, and a system of school districts with school boards and superintendents was established. The white population of South Louisiana was not ready for integration and railed about the absence of white schools. The *St. Charles Mirror* reported: "The white people of Hahnville, having given up all hope of ever obtaining a school for their children from the Radical School Board, have employed a competent teacher and opened a private school."[5]

The earliest board minutes of 1879 record T.T. Baudouin as superintendent of St. Charles Parish public school system. School sessions began in February and lasted four to six months. Schools were located in homes, churches, and halls, with few buildings belonging to the school system. Superintendent Baudouin visited all schools during each session. Although during Reconstruction there had been black members of the school board, by this time all were white, and there were separate schools for the races. In 1891 there were 17 public schools and four private schools. One teacher operated a private school located just above Hahnville; advertising that he was a professor of French, English, Spanish, math, and all branches pertaining to a thorough education. Both Hahnville and Fashion had public schools for whites by 1895. In 1896 the parish had 10 schools for whites and 7 for blacks.

Although the Vial home was near the Fashion School, it is unlikely that the older children went there. They probably attended a private school or were tutored at home. A report by the School Board circa 1904 contains a photograph and list of its students; Ella Vial was then attending Fashion School. She would have been about 8 years old. Around 1915 a young Flaggville native related that "Fashion School was one room, with grades one to six… Fashion adjoined Superintendent Johnny Martin's yard (J.B. Martin Jr.). Just a fence separated the school from his house. I went to school with Dick (Richard) and Marie Vial, Helen Martin and Leon Vial Jr. I sat behind Leon at Fashion School. We attended Fashion for six years."[6]

As the early 20th century unfolded, various members of the Vial-Martin families began playing key roles in education, governance, and politics in St. Charles Parish. They were among the earliest teachers and distinguished themselves as principals and school superintendents. Several played prominent roles in government as public officials. Their stories are told later in the chapter.

Farming and Agriculture. The main crops in the parish were rice and sugarcane. Rice farming required less labor force and could be managed by families and friends. Low mounds were created surrounding what were once cane fields, and these were flooded to grow rice. Rice, however, was not as lucrative a crop as sugarcane, which continued as a major product of the river parishes. After Reconstruction, large plantations could not afford to hire workers needed to for sugarcane production, which was labor intensive. Many plantations were divided and sold, creating smaller scale sugar operations. A sharecropping system was devised, in which large landowners rented land out, taking a percentage of the crop's proceeds. Due to the poverty of most blacks and working-class whites, sharecroppers usually incurred heavy debts from the landowners to get crops into production, and more for harvesting. The sharecropping system became, essentially, an indentured-servitude system.

Producing sugarcane was an intense, season-driven endeavor. In January, seed cane saved from the previous season was planted in furrows dug by mules pulling plows until the appearance of gasoline-powered tractors. Seed cane laid in furrows was covered by hand in the early 1900s. When the young cane shoots appeared, the rows were weeded and tended through spring and summer using hoe crews. By July, the cane stood 5-6 feet high; weeding continued to keep drainage flowing between rows, which emptied into the swamp. Harvesting usually began in October but was heavily influenced by weather. The longer the cane grew, the sweeter its sugar content, but an early frost could ruin the crop. Harvesting cane was still done by hand at this time by cutting crews. Using a big cane knife, crews stripped leaves with two sweeping vertical blows, cut the stalk at the ground, and chopped off the top. Mule carts came by and cane stalks were tossed in for transport to the sugarhouse. Years later this process became mechanized.

Most large scale sugar operations had their own sugar house; smaller ones sent cane to nearby houses for processing. The house had a mill to grind cane, pulled by mules, though some used low-pressure steam. Juice was squeezed from the cane between great iron rollers, and impurities strained from the raw juice. Originally the juice passed through a series of open kettles on hot fires until it crystallized. By the mid-1850s most large operations used machinery that improved quality and efficiency. Vacuum pans created steam condensing, boiling cane juice at lower temperature thus reducing molasses byproduct, creating a superior grade of sugar. Bone-black filters were introduced which strained out remaining impurities and bleached the product. Crystallized sugar was placed in barrels (hogsheads) and taken to docks for shipment to sugar wholesalers and retailers.[7]

Although these mechanizations improved the process, it was still hard labor over long hours. A large sugar farm required around-the-clock crews during the height of sugar house operations to quickly harvest cane if weather was inclement. To be readily available, the laborers—mostly black—lived in houses on the property called "the quarters." Big sugarcane farms could have 4-5 rows of 10 houses each, the small wood shacks not much different from slave times. Children lived there with parents, often helping by working in the cane fields and sugar houses. There were distinct social divisions between whites, blacks, and Creoles of color. The Creoles and better-off blacks prided themselves on having their own house and not residing in "the quarters."

Irene Oubre LeGaux from Donaldsonville described her family's situation around 1900: "We never lived in the quarters… My daddy would never bring us in the quarters. He was a proud man… We always lived in a good house in the front… We didn't much come from slavery because… his grandfather was a pure German. At the time of slavery, he bought his children's right so they was free. He bought their freedom. They never was slaves."[8]

Leonide Vial's parents were described as "well-known sugar planters," so their operation must have been quite substantial. The Vials probably used sharecropping and had a cluster of laborer rowhouses, "the quarters." They likely had a sugar house on-site and ran the entire production process there, sending many barrels of crystallized sugar to the local river landing for shipment to New Orleans. The Vial children would have been familiar with the seasonal rhythms of sugarcane production. They might sneak into the sugar house to grab snacks of fresh-cut cane to chew or be sent there to collect jars of molasses syrup, which was a staple, poured over pancakes or grits or crusts of bread. It was frequently used to sweeten cakes and baked goods.

Vial Influences in St. Charles Parish. It's not clear how long the Vials continued their sugarcane operations. In 1897 Leonide Vial's older brother, **Leon C. Vial Sr. (I)**, was "taken out of the sugar fields" at age 17 and went to work for the parish clerk of court as a copyist. Jean Baptiste (J.B.) Martin Sr. held the clerk of court position but died in office later that year. He was posthumously to become Leonide's father-in-law in just a few years. J.C. Triche Sr. was appointed by the governor to fill the unexpired clerk of court term. In 1899 when Leon came of age, he was made chief deputy clerk of court.

Between 1900 and 1910, Leon built a large house on a portion of Fashion Plantation that his father, Louis Adolphe Vial, had acquired in 1888 and divided among his children. This property had four arpents frontage (768 ft.) on the Mississippi River. It was bounded on the north side by property belonging to Mrs. J.B. Martin Sr.

Leon Charles Vial Sr. (I)
By permission of Henry E. Yoes, III

(Celeste Triche, sister of J.C. Triche Sr.). The next three generations of Vials lived in this two-story house, and the latest are still there today.

In 1904, Leon was elected to the State House of Representatives, also keeping his position in the clerk's office. In 1908 he was elected parish assessor and held that position until 1916. Becoming active in national politics, he served as delegate to three national conventions, acting as secretary to the Louisiana delegation in 1924. In 1916 he was elected sheriff of St. Charles Parish and held that position for 22 years, until his death in 1939. Despite some controversies over the years, he remained in office and was a popular public official. He was accused of overcharging the parish for feeding prisoners in 1924, which he attributed to political opponents and called it "an absolute malicious falsehood." He faced an impeachment for failing to report poll tax receipts and permit inspection of public records in 1932. Sheriff Vial said he was not aware he had to report poll tax payments to the clerk of court and assessor, in addition to the election committee. Since he remained in office, the impeachment failed.[9]

While holding political offices, Leon continued farming sugarcane and truck crops, also raising cattle for a number of years. As his duties became heavier, he found it necessary to give up farming and the cattle business. He promoted parish interests in many ways, such as keeping taxes low to attract business interests, pioneering the area's first gravel highways and then hard-surfaced roads, organizing the drainage district to assist farmers, building sidewalks in town, and improving school and government buildings including jails. Late in life he saw great possibilities for prosperity through developing oil fields in the region.

His Memoriam in *Louisiana Today* aptly declared: "A testimony to the popularity of the late Sheriff Vial might be taken from the fact that he had been elected to public office on ten different occasions and was never defeated in an election."[10]

The Triche, Martin, and Vial families became interconnected through several marriages. Members of these families held numerous political and public offices, shaped and modernized the educational system, and found themselves at odds more than once. Leon C. Vial Sr. (I) initiated what is called the "Vial Era" in St. Charles Parish leadership. After he died, he was succeeded in office by his widowed second wife, Marie Keller Vial, who finished her husband's term. His oldest son was soon to follow.

In 1944, **Leon C. Vial Jr. (II)** (1904-1976), the oldest son of Leon C. Vial I by the first wife Celeste Irma Martin (1876-1913), was elected sheriff and served five successive terms spanning 20 years. While his father was alive he had stayed out of politics. He was serving as a Catholic lay brother with the Order of the Sacred Heart, but family ties called him away from this vocation. As the heir apparent of the well-known Vial family, Leon Jr. easily displaced incumbent Sheriff Ralph A. Dubroca. The hotly contested elections in 1940 and 1944 created what is called the "Vial-Martin Feud," described later. His only serious challenger during these years was Edward A. Dufresne Sr., who ran against him twice, in 1948 and 1952.

"Big Eddie" Dufresne yearned for a political career and was the most persistent critic of Vial leadership during the 1940s, producing the "Second Vial Feud." Dufresne lived on neighboring Esperanza Plantation, just downriver from the Vial property. But he failed to oust the firmly entrenched Sheriff Vial and never attained public office. Eventually Dufresne gave up the quest and focused instead on his plantation and horses.

In 1964, Sheriff Vial lost the election, ending the "Vial Era." For over 50 years, the Vials provided public service, including Leon C. Vial I's brother, Richard J. Vial Sr., school board member for over 40 years, primarily as president. He established his son, Richard J. Vial Jr., as superintendent of schools in 1945. The next generations of Vials included an assistant district attorney/parish attorney, parish coroner, and judges.

The transition of power involving the school board and school superintendent in the early 1940s provoked conflict between the Vial and Martin families. Emotional stress was enhanced by deep intertwining of the families, including a "double marriage" that occurred in 1902-1903. Leon C. Vial I married Celeste Irma Martin on January 28, 1902, at Our Lady of the Most Holy Rosary Church in Taft, St. Charles Parish. Celeste Irma Martin was the older sister of Jean Baptiste (J.B.) Martin Jr. Leonide Mary Vial married Jean Baptiste (J.B.) Martin Jr. on October 7, 1903, at the same church. J.B. Martin Jr. was the youngest brother of Celeste Irma Martin. These Vial-Martin couples were double in-laws, and their children double first cousins.

Jean Baptiste (J.B.) Martin, Jr. Other prominent figures in St. Charles public office came from the Martin family. J.B. Martin Sr. (1847-1897) was clerk of court from 1877 to 1897, a term of 20 years. When

J.B. Martin Jr. (II)

he died in office, he was succeeded by J.C. Triche Sr., who was to become his son's uncle. J.B. Martin Jr. was a teacher and long-time superintendent of schools, serving from 1913 to 1944, a period of 31 years. Other Martins were teachers and principals in nearby parishes.

The Martin family descended through a lineage from Collobriéres, Var, a region in Southeastern France between Nice and Marseille. The paternal line, going back to 1670, married women from the Martine, Caroune, Bernard, and Ginouves families, also of the Var region. The great-great-grandfather of J.B. Martin Jr., Joseph Auguste Therese Martin (1766-1839), left France and settled in New Orleans. He became a "socially prominent physician" and acquired a house in the French Quarter around 1831, where he practiced medicine and resided until his death. In New Orleans he met and married Marie Elizabeth Jacques Guibert (Guivert), born in 1781 in Port-au-Prince, Saint-Domingue. Their wedding took place in 1809 at St. Mary's Church, New Orleans. The Guibert family was from Bazenville, Calvados, in the Normandy region of Northwestern France. The maternal line was from the Ossone de Vierre family from Paris, who had also relocated to Port-au-Prince. Joseph Auguste and Marie Elizabeth had six children, all born in New Orleans between 1810 and 1822.

Joseph Honoré Edouard Martin (1818-1864) was their fifth child and only son. He was sent to France to be educated, commonly done by French families. First he graduated as a civil engineer, and afterward as a medical doctor in 1843. The second Dr. Martin was a leading surgeon in New Orleans for many years; his practice located in the house he inherited from his father. There was a dispute with a tenant, a Martin relative, but Joseph Honoré acquired ownership through a sheriff's sale in 1847. He saw patients and dispensed medications at this house in the French Quarter. In those days medicines were dispensed at an apothecary's store where many were made on-site. Although beyond the age for military service, he enlisted with the Confederacy in 1861, became surgeon of his regiment, and served until his death in 1864.

Dr. Martin's house located at 709-711 Royal Street was described in the sale document: "A two-story house with attic and forming two distinct tenements. The first story consists of a store, brick store, cabinet, yard, kitchen and servant's rooms, fixtures for the waterworks, etc., and separate corridor. The second story of five rooms, cabinet and pantry, and in the attic of three rooms and a cabinet, a three-story brick building in the yard and consisting of a kitchen, ironing room, stable and six servants' rooms, fixture for the waterworks, etc., with a separate corridor."[11]

Joseph Honoré Edouard Martin married Aimée Colette Labranche (1826-c.1877) in New Orleans in 1846. He was 28 years old, somewhat late to marry, but there is no evidence he was married before. The Labranche family was descended from German immigrants who settled on Louisiana's German Coast in the early 1700s. She was probably born in New Orleans where her father had a home. Her family was related to the Trepagnier, Haydel, and Sarpy families of New Orleans and the river parishes. Joseph Honoré sold the Royal Street house in 1849; he and Aimée Colette were still residing in New Orleans in the 1850 and 1860 U.S. census reports. They had five children, all born in New Orleans between 1847 and 1854. The first child was **Jean Baptiste (J.B.) Martin Sr.**, born in 1847; he became the first of three in his lineage to bear that name. His siblings were Marie Anthimia (1849), Louise Marguerite (1851 lived one year), Joseph Euphemere Labranche (1853), and Marie Henriette (1854).

J.B. Martin Sr. attended schools in Louisiana and New York. In 1867, right after the Civil War ended, he became a clerk in a New Orleans store. After a few years in that position, he left New Orleans and went upriver in order to run Labranche Plantation, which his family had owned and operated before the Civil War, producing sugarcane. His mother, Aimée Colette, was the daughter of Jean Baptiste Labranche (1777-1837), whose family established the original Labranche Plantation in 1765. Jean Baptiste Labranche resided in New Orleans in the early 19th century and owned plantations on the German Coast. This family descended from Johan Zweig, an early settler of the German Coast listed in the 1724 U.S. census. The Zweig name was changed to a French translation: Zweig means "twig" in German, so in French this became Labranche, "the branch." Such name changes were common as French became the dominant language in the region.

The Labranche Plantation lands spanned the Mississippi River. The large home in St. Rose was by many accounts one of the grandest on the German Coast until it was destroyed during the Civil War.[12] All that remains of the original buildings is the "Dependency House," originally the *garçonnière* (young men's quarters). The Lentini family of Kenner purchased and restored it in 1983. The Dependency House is listed on the National Registry of Historic Places.

J.B. Martin Sr. managed the Labranche Plantation sugarcane operations until 1871. In the 1870 U.S. census, he is listed as residing there with Michel Labranche; his occupation stated as planter. This must have been a challenging job because the area was going through difficult post-war recovery. The life of a sugar planter during an economic depression probably held little appeal for the well-educated, multilingual, metropolitan-raised young man. He was no doubt relieved when the plantation was sold in 1871.

Most of the plantation on the west bank was sold to Charles Lafitte, a New Orleans businessman, who named it Esperanza. He is probably not related to infamous pirate Jean Lafitte, who grew up on Louisiana bayous and often docked along the Mississippi River. It continued producing sugarcane as one of the oldest continuously operating plantation sites in St. Charles Parish. Esperanza was acquired by Edward A. Dufresne ("Big Eddie") in 1937; he built the modern showplace plantation house in Luling in 1957.[13]

Seeking a career elsewhere, J.B. Martin Sr. applied for the assistant position in the St. Charles Parish clerk of court office. Upon being accepted, he left plantation work and never returned. In 1874 he became deputy clerk of court. In this position he met several influential men, including J.C. Triche Sr., who was editor of the *St. Charles Herald* and soon became his brother-in-law; T.J. "Colonel Mulberry" Sellers, who owned two plantations and was an early school board member; the "Colonel's" son, T.B. Sellers, who was made school superintendent; Theodule T. Baudouin, who held several positions including assessor, sheriff, and school superintendent; and two Labranche sheriffs, who were his relatives. These prominent river parish families shared social as well as political and business connections. On social occasions, J.B. Martin Sr. would have met J.C. Triche's sister, Celeste Triche.

J.B. Martin Sr. and Celeste Triche were married in 1875. Celeste was the daughter of André Triche III (1826-?) and Marie Irma Millet (1830-1910), born in 1852 in Reserve, St. John the Baptist Parish. On her mother's side the lineage went back to Germany in the 1600s with surnames of Rommel, Steiger, Altofer, and Schneider. The Rommel name was shortened to Rome in the 1700s after immigration to Louisiana. The Triche lineage was French but married Germans in the 1700s and 1800s.

There were several children in Celeste's family; she was the fourth with three older siblings and several younger. Her brother J.C. Triche Sr. was born 10 years later in 1862. The Triche family managed the *St. Charles Herald* newspaper for many years, from 1888 to 1954; it passed through the hands of his sisters Polymnia (Polly) and Beatrice, and his sons J.C. (Clem) Jr. and Lucien Taft. For a short time Triche's nephew, J.B. Martin Jr., ran the paper for the family out of a small office in front of his home in Hahnville.[14]

During the first several years of their marriage, J.B. Martin Sr. and his wife Celeste Triche probably lived in Reserve. Their first child, Celeste Irma, was born in Reserve in 1876. Two sons followed but neither survived; Edouard Andree (May-October 1878) and Joseph Victor (1879-1883). J.B. Martin Jr. was born in 1881, followed by Anna Colette

(1883-1959), Paul Antoine (1885-1887), Dana A. (1888-1942), Josephine Rene (1890-1922), Marie Andre Emilie "Keet" (1892-1981), and Charles Antoine (1895-1901).

Reserve was then a small town on the east bank of the Mississippi River, across from Edgard on the west bank. J.B. Sr. worked as clerk of court at St. Charles Parish, with public offices located in Hahnville. The distance between Edgard and Hahnville along River Road was about 20 miles, but transportation was slow and the road conditions poor. In addition, he needed to take a ferry across the river from Reserve to Edgard. The commute would have taken him several hours.

In January 1883, the heirs of Colonel Richard Taylor, son of U.S. President Zachary Taylor, sold Fashion Plantation. In March 1883, a portion of the plantation was recorded as sold to Celeste Triche Martin, wife of J.B. Sr. At the time her brother, J.C. Triche, and her husband were public office holders. Probably Celeste bought the property through an agent in her name because of these political connections. By the end of 1883, J.B. and Celeste recorded the construction of a home on the property. They also provided a small lot for the Fashion School, though public records during that time are lacking. The Fashion School is listed in public records in April 1895 but had opened earlier. One condition of this donation was that the school be used for education of whites only.[15]

The Martin family relocated to the home on Fashion Plantation in late 1883. Their property was next to the Vial family property. This part of Fashion on the west bank of the river had been subdivided in 1882 into Lots 16, 17, and 18. Lot 15 to the south belonged to the Vials. Lot 19 to the north belonged to Homer J. Smith and, later, the Bisso Realty Company and Richard Vial. The original property owned by the Martins consisted of 162.66 acres, a long narrow rectangle extending west from the Mississippi River to a wooded, swampy area and the railroad tracks. River Road cut through the east side of the property along the levee. Included was the batture, a buffer zone of trees and sandbars between the levee and river that often was filled with water. Several canals and drainage ditches crossed the property.

Toward the center of the property J.B. and Celeste situated a large two-story house built in typical French Creole style. The house was set well back from the road with a long driveway leading to outbuildings such as barn, garage, and storage shed. A porch bounded by railings ran the width of the front, and plain square columns supported the roof. A stairway led to the porch center and elevated first floor. Projecting behind was an extension containing the kitchen, bathrooms, pantry, and storage rooms. Two chimneys rose from the roof to vent fireplaces. Later a three-window dormer was added to brighten the upstairs bedrooms.

The four younger children were born in this house. It remained in the family and became the home of the youngest daughter, Marie Andre Emilie "Keet," and her husband,

252   Upriver Families Acadian Roots and Creole Heritage

Laurent J. Labry. When J.B. Martin Jr. grew up and married, he bought another house on the adjoining land around 1903. After his parents' deaths, the Fashion property was subdivided in 1929 into five lots, one for each of the siblings. The 1929 survey document by H.E. Landry describes this division:

Lot A	J.B. Martin	35.59 acres
Lot B	Dana A. Martin	29.86 acres
Lot C	Marie Martin	29.87 acres (wife of L.J. Labry)
Lot D	Anna Martin	29.91 acres (widow of L.A. Charbonnet)
Lot E	Heirs of Irma Martin Vial	37.43 acres

J.B. Martin Sr. – Celeste Triche Home in Hahnville, LA, c.1890
By permission of Henry E. Yoes, III

Only two years after the birth of his last child, J.B. Martin Sr. died unexpectedly at age 50. He was still working as clerk of court when he died in 1897, having served for 20 years. His brother-in-law, J.C. Triche Sr., was appointed to finish his term. The oldest son, J.B. Martin Jr., was 16 years old, and the second son, Dana Martin, just 9 years old. It must have been difficult for Celeste, having to manage a household and property with six young children. She did have a large extended family, however, and would have received plenty of assistance. Celeste lived to see the dawn of a new century and the success of her oldest son as an educator and superintendent of schools. Her youngest daughter, Marie "Keet," was also a noted teacher and principal in the developing public school system. Celeste Triche Martin died in 1924 at age 72 and was buried beside her husband in St. Charles Parish, Our Lady of the Most Holy Rosary Church Cemetery in Taft.

J.B. Martin Jr. was born on August 13, 1881, in Reserve and grew up in Hahnville at his parents' home on land that once was part of Fashion Plantation. His early education was in parish elementary schools, but there were no parish high schools, so he attended the Boys' High School in New Orleans. He went to college at Louisiana State University and A&M College in Baton Rouge. Entering as a freshman in 1898, he would have been 17 years old. He graduated in 1902 when he was 21. The university was instituted 40 years earlier, located in the former U.S. garrison at Baton Rouge. Students were called cadets, retaining a military atmosphere and dress. LSU Yearbook *Gumbo* boasted the campus was "one of the most beautiful and healthful spots in the South" and provided "cadets' quarters lighted with electricity and supplied with purest artesian water." Tuition was free; expenses for sessions of nine months for board, lodging, washing, fuel, and electric lights was $108. Other expenses included incidental fee $5, surgeon's fee and medicines $7, furniture rent $5, textbooks about $10, and uniforms $15 per suit of cap, blouse, and trousers.

To qualify for admission to the freshman class, applicants had to know arithmetic, algebra through quadratics, and two books of plane geometry. Also necessary was "corresponding advancement in other subjects." Courses of study included mathematics, languages and literatures, engineering, agriculture and botany, civics, civil engineering, law, history, military science, physics, psychology, geodetic and railroad surveying, commercial geography, zoology, and others. Education was not a separate field in those times. If you had a college degree, it was taken for granted that you knew how to teach.

Although what J.B. Martin studied is not known, his interest in learning and education is apparent from his long career in the field. The college yearbook *Gumbo* described the various kinds of college men that made up the student body at LSU: the politician, the sport, the digger, the ladies' man, and the athlete. Humorous portraits described each type, and one can glean that "the digger" would fit best for J.B.

"The digger is never looked for, for he can always be found, when not in the classroom and laboratory, poring over his textbook. His dress though neat is modest and the demerit book gives a good account of him. In some cases you will find him 'Digger' and 'ladies' man' combined, but all things are sacrificed when necessary to that for which he entered the University... you will see his light timidly appear and burn till late... He is a good companion when he has time for a stroll, and at any athletic contest you will find him as enthusiastic as anyone else."[16]

J.B. was among class officers as the Historian for the Second Term Junior Class. Maybe he concentrated on history in his studies. He graduated as one of 44 young men in 1902. As the *Gumbo* noted, "Some men were born for great things, some were born for small, but the good Lord only knows why some were born at all." J.B. was certainly among the first, because "The digger we must have. He needs no eulogy, for he is the backbone of the University."

On October 4, 1902, J.B. was appointed as a teacher in the St. Charles Parish public school system. School board records note a new "graded school" would be established if finances justify, and "Prof. J.B. Martin be appointed at $45 per month." However, he needed to guarantee not less than 20 pupils, or the school would be closed. The earliest schools combined students of all ages in one classroom; these were "un-graded" schools. "Graded schools" emerged in the late 1800s with four loosely defined grades that grew into eight grades. Finishing the eighth grade meant the end of education for most students.

Some years earlier, in 1897, J.B.'s mother, Celeste Triche, had donated a lot on her Fashion property for a school in Hahnville. The donation stipulated that her son would be the teacher, and it would a graded school with classes not lower than the sixth grade. J.B. obviously attained the board's enrollment stipulations of 20 students, as he continued teaching there for 10 years. He was being paid $5 per month more than any other parish teachers. According to his sister Marie "Keet," he not only taught, but "he built all the desks and chairs."

The same year that J.B. was appointed teacher he also started to operate the *St. Charles Herald* for his uncle, J.C. Triche Sr. The newspaper was printed in a small building in front of his house, with the assistance of other Martin family members. J.B. was an editor of the newspaper, although never officially listed. To keep the public informed about school board activities, the board authorized payment of $150 to J.B. for improving the "quality of the St. Charles Herald" in 1903. At the next meeting, the wording was changed for this "donation," and it was identified as money appropriated for publishing the written records of the school board. J.B.'s publishing and editing work continued until 1913.[17]

On October 7, 1903, J.B. Martin Jr. and Leonide Mary Vial were married in St. Charles Parish. They knew each other from childhood, since their families lived on adjacent properties and interacted frequently. The year before, Leonide's brother, Leon Charles Vial I, had married J.B.'s sister, Celeste Irma Martin. Leonide was a beautiful young woman and accomplished pianist. She was spending her time as most well-off Creole belles did, socializing with friends, doing fine needlework, reading and playing music, attending church functions, and occasionally making a shopping trip to New Orleans. Fifty years later she said of these times, "I wasn't working or anything—just having a good time. The work started after we were married."[18]

Around that time J.B. bought a large six-bedroom, two-story house that had been built circa 1850, part of his father's Fashion Plantation property acquired from a New Orleans agent. The Creole-style home sat on stone pillars and had screened porches in front, side, and back entrance leading to a large kitchen and pantry. On the first floor were a kitchen, formal dining room, living room, entrance and office room, and two bedrooms. The only bathroom was adjoining the rear bedroom. Cisterns collected rainwater that supplied kitchen and bathroom, and the house had electricity by the early 1900s. A long driveway led from River Road, passing along the right side of the house and making a circle behind. The outbuildings included laundry and servants' rooms, garage, barn, and chicken house. Fruit and nut trees and a vegetable garden also supplied food.

The second story had bedrooms for the children. Dormers gave outside views to two bedrooms used for the girls, on east and west sides of a long central room that had bunk beds for the boys. There was no upstairs plumbing so water was hauled up for wash basins and slop pots used at night. Two fireplaces provided heat, one shared between the downstairs bedrooms and one in the living room. Cold oil or kerosene space heaters were used upstairs.

The Martin's first child, Helen, was born in 1905. The next two followed quickly; J.B. III (Jr., Johnny, Manny) in 1906 and Minerva Louise (Min) in 1908. The last three were all boys: Louis A. (Bébé, Major) in 1910, Frederick Charles (Fred) in 1913, and

Roy H. (Peter) in 1915. With a school superintendent father, all the children were well-educated and went to college. All four boys and one daughter attended LSU. The older siblings were bilingual and spoke French fluently. However, English became the predominant language in the river parishes, and the younger boys did not learn French. Minerva went to graduate school, earning a PhD in English and teaching at the University of Maryland. She lived in Europe for years and taught at the university extension in Munich.

J.B.'s older sister, Anna Colette, was the first Martin to enter the school system. She taught in Luling in 1900, resigning after five years when she married L.A. Charbonnet, and moved to New Orleans. The youngest sister, **Marie Andre Emilie "Keet,"** was also a teacher. She is regarded as a school pioneer in St. Charles Parish, starting to teach when she was 17 and teaching at Taft, St. Rose, Fashion, Paradis, Luling, and on the east bank of the river. Her brothers and sisters called her "Mox," and later generations called her "Tante Keet," though no one can remember why. Born in the late 1800s, she initially spoke only French and had to learn English in school. She was first taught by her brother J.B., who was 12 years older, and had to call him "Mr. Martin," saying he was strict but good.

Marie Keet taught school after finishing the 10th grade and later went to the Teachers' College in Natchitoches. There she completed high school while doing college studies. In 1914 she was transferred to teach in Paradis just west of Hahnville, where a Chicago firm planned development. It built a bank, courthouse, and structure they called a high school, but it was not official. There was a moss gin, sawmill, park, hotel, and even streetlights. But the business soon failed in the small rural community, and after teaching a year, Marie Keet was sent to Montz on the river's east bank. It was a long commute, so she stayed in Montz for the week. To get there she needed to go to Killona, sometimes by train, and walk to the riverbank to catch a ferry across. It was easier to take a ferry upriver from Hahnville to Montz. When she arrived, someone would take her in a horse and buggy to the school. Usually schools were one room and ungraded, so she divided time between age groups, having older children tend the little ones until she was ready for them.[19]

Her long career in education spanned 44 years, a good part spent as both teacher and principal of Luling and Hahnville schools. When she retired in 1954 at age 62 and was asked if she had any regrets, she said, "Yes, I wish I was still teaching." She was considered ahead of her time by developing music programs in public schools, organizing a band at Hahnville School, and giving private lessons after hours.[20]

Politics and Education

As the Martins were making their imprint on education in St. Charles Parish, the educational and political systems were changing. The interplay between public institutions, political influence, and the flow of money created a volatile environment. In rural parishes with limited economies, the influx of resources brought by public education had major impacts. Vying for power within these systems became inevitable. Some background will put this into perspective.

The Louisiana Constitution of 1868 provided for public schools in parishes "without distinction of race, color, or previous conditions" funded by proceeds of poll taxes and local fundraising. The State Board of Education was created to oversee public schools; in 1871 parish school board directors were appointed for two-year terms. In St. Charles Parish, the first school board included both black and white directors. The 1879 Constitution gave these boards power to appoint parish superintendents, who were ex-officio secretaries of the board. School board directors were appointed for a four-year term, and had power to make contracts, including written contracts with teachers. The St. Charles Parish Public School System was established in 1879, placed under the jurisdiction of the Police Jury.

The first superintendent was Theodule Telesphore (T.T.) Baudouin, serving from 1878 to 1888. Initially there were 10 schools throughout the parish, located in churches, private homes, and other buildings with 393 black students (1,595 eligible) and 113 white students (356 eligible) in 1882. Most white children were still educated at home by tutors. Transportation was provided for students living over two miles from schools. The General School Act of 1888 decreed that Police Juries must assess a minimum of 1.5 mills on property to fund public schools. (The millage rate in property tax: 1 mill = $1 in property tax levied per $1,000 of assessed value.) In 1896 the parish had 17 public schools; 10 were attended by white students and 7 by black students. A new state Constitution passed that year provided free but separate public schools for white and black children.[21]

Subsequent parish school superintendents had short terms until the appointment of Thomas B. Sellers, who served from 1896 to 1913. His father, Thomas J. "Colonel Mulberry" Sellers, had served briefly as a school board director and was credited with manipulating the superintendent appointment for his son. The elder Sellers was somewhat legendary, owning eight plantations and fighting several duels, but living to die a natural death. He was friends with Mark Twain; both were steamboat pilots on the Mississippi

River in pre-civil war times. He inspired a character in a play whose famous saying was "There's millions in it." "Colonel Mulberry" Sellers was known as both a clear-headed businessman and riverboat speculator who lost fortunes gambling. He was reputed to have harvested timber from school board properties for personal gain, but investigating committees found no violations.

School board directors held considerable power. They made rules and set policies for schools, students, teachers, and numerous other school employees. They administered the budget and controlled expenditures. And they selected and appointed the school superintendent, who managed the details of the parish educational system. By 1898, the superintendent office was a desirable position with salary up to $1,200 per month.

Thomas B. Sellers, who held the superintendent position at the turn of the century, was the target of an ouster movement by the Baudouin family. T.T. Baudouin was a prior superintendent and long-time school board member, president much of that time. His son, James Baudouin, was on the board in 1900 and tried to reinstate his father as superintendent but lost the vote. Sellers retained the office and was serving when J.B. Martin Jr. and family began to influence school affairs around 1902.

Initially Sellers approved of J.B. as an educator with excellent credentials. J.B. was teaching at Fashion School when an incident occurred, probably a disagreement with Sellers over some education-related decision. School board records indicate a resolution was passed on August 7, 1911, declaring "whereas J.B. Martin has proved himself guilty of insubordination, (we) dispose with his services."[22]

"Insubordination" generally implies that someone was disobedient to a superior, or became defiant, or refused to carry out assigned duties. J.B. Martin kept a "diary" of school board activities, but his entry does not give details of the incident. He was listed as a faculty member at Fashion School in 1912, so must have been reinstated.

Sellers tendered his resignation as superintendent in April 1911 and had picked a successor, J.W. Plauche. Both Plauche and Martin were nominated as the new superintendent, with Plauche winning by a 3-2 vote. But Plauche had trouble posting his bond (required for public office). Some intrigue took place; both Sellers and Plauche were missing from subsequent school board meetings, along with the minute books. No mention was made of Plauche in the next several school board minutes, but Sellers continued to act as secretary (a job assigned to the Superintendent) through June and July 1911.

Plauche apparently was unable to qualify for superintendent because of a lawsuit filed by Richard J. Vial Sr., brother-in-law of J.B. Martin. The lawsuit alleged that Plauche was not qualified for the office since he was not a resident of St. Charles Parish. This derailed Plauche's attempt. After that, Sellers withdrew his resignation and continued as superintendent until early 1912. By then, new state laws provided for the election, instead of appointment, of school board members, and the configuration of the board changed. In this time of transition, J.B. undoubtedly continued cultivating his relatives and allies. Forces were now in place to move ahead with his appointment as superintendent.

On January 4, 1912, a new board took office and appointed J.B. Martin Jr. as the first full-time school superintendent of St. Charles Parish. Sellers signed minutes as the outgoing superintendent, and J.B. finished his term at Fashion School in March. On July 5, 1912, after resolving a dispute over his bond, J.B. took his seat as superintendent. He served in this position for 31 years until he retired in 1944.

School Superintendent J.B. Martin Jr. In his long tenure, J.B. accomplished numerous objectives to expand and improve the parish public school system. Under his leadership, the Destrehan and Hahnville High Schools were established. Among his accomplishments were expanding the school year to the nine-month term, starting bus transportation, developing a school lunch program, adding physical education programs, and including courses in business and music. He directed an elementary school building program in the 1930s, considered one of the best in the state. He was considered the brains of the parish during this time, and the *Times Picayune* called him "the Father of St. Charles Parish Schools."[23]

The *Times Picayune* article in 1938 featured J.B.'s Silver Jubilee luncheon, continuing with praise: "… many of the great advances made in education in St. Charles Parish can be attributed to the determination and conscientious work of its first professional superintendent… J.B. Martin Middle School in Paradis is named in his honor." In addition to the ambitious school building program, he was a leader in the health movement well before it was taken over by the state. He was one of the first superintendents to introduce a school band, and was a pioneer in the audiovisual field, bringing to the classroom the "last word in the line of teaching… the motion picture machine." The success of the South Central Athletic association can be largely attributed to him, including the philosophy of participation rather than competition.

Dr. F.H. Miller of LSU concluded the Silver Jubilee Fete for Superintendent Martin by complimenting him on his achievements and faithful service, saying, "We respect your ability; we admire your courage, and we love Johnny Martin."

Louisiana State Superintendent of Schools T.H. Harris once said of J.B., "Superintendent Martin is held on a high pedestal in the educational circles of the state and the St. Charles Parish School System leads in educational development." Dr. J.M. Foote, statistician for the Louisiana State Department of Education, gave a vignette of J.B. while recognizing his work building new schools. Dr. Foote recalled standing on the levee in 1915 and taking a picture of J.B. in a Model-A Ford, with the characteristic cigar in his mouth. A copy of this photograph is kept in the State Department files alongside a picture showing one of the old schools. "What a contrast," declared Dr. Foote, "to this wonderful structure of brick, mortar and iron we are seated in on this happy occasion." He further said the St. Charles parish schools were in the front ranks in the field of education in Louisiana.[24]

J.B. was honored in 1950 at a dinner given in Thibodaux by 14 school superintendents from South Louisiana parishes. He was one among three retired superintendents; the others were from LaFourche and Assumption parishes, serving 35 and 41 years respectively. These three former superintendents were noted as leaders in the advancement of public school education in their parishes. Each honoree was presented with a floral offering, and after the dinner party they were guests of the Thomson Machinery Company.[25]

Not everyone lauded J.B. so highly, revealing a different side. One long-time educator described him as "a dictator, a little czar." J.B. was quite a short man, yet forceful and strong-willed. The critic added, though, that he "was a loved man, an honest man that you could trust. He wasn't a man who said one thing and meant something else, and he was a man who didn't say one thing to your face and something else behind your back. No matter how big the guy was he was talking to, he spoke his mind."[26]

J.B. was also a member of the board of directors of the Luling-Hahnville Bank for 25 years. He was a multifaceted person, a musician himself who played the trumpet. Perhaps his most sensational accolade is that one of his early pupils was famous jazz musician "Papa" Celestin.

Oscar Phillip Celestin (1884-1954) was born in Napoleonville, LA, to a black Creole family, son of a sugarcane cutter. In his youth he worked on rural plantations, as a cook for the Texas & Pacific Railroad, saved up money, and bought used musical instruments. He played guitar and trombone before deciding on cornet as his main instrument. As a youth, he took music lessons from J.B., also studying with Claiborne Williams who traveled down Bayou Lafourche from Donaldsonville. He played with the Algiers Brass Band by the early 1900s and with various small-town bands before moving to New Orleans in 1904 at age 20. He formed the Tuxedo Band which became highly popular and frequently hired for society functions, both black and white. He often played on Bourbon Street in the French Quarter, made regular radio broadcasts, television appearances, and recordings. In 1953 he gave a command performance for President Eisenhower at the White House. His last recording singing was on the album "Marie LaVeau" in 1954. The song by the same title became a voodoo cult classic. Near the end of his life he was honored as one of the greats of New Orleans music, and the Jazz Foundation of New Orleans placed a bust of him at the Delgado Museum. When he died, 4000 people marched in his funeral parade.[27]

Tangled Roots and Conflicting Ambitions. The leading families of St. Charles Parish were closely connected and shared tangled roots. They frequently intermarried, and after a few generations, it seemed virtually everyone important was second or third cousins. In particular, the Vial, Martin, Triche, Labranche, Songy, Keller, Madere, and Dubroca families were interconnected by blood or marriage—and often by both.

After 1900, only a few Republicans held office in St. Charles Parish. There were factions within the Democratic Party, however, and a system of bifactionalism developed in which the primaries became the real contest. Whichever candidate won the Democratic primary had in essence won the election. The Democratic election commissioners operated the primary and reported the returns to the chairman of the election committee. Trouble began with the January 1908 election for sheriff. Thomas B. Sellers was running against the incumbent Sheriff Anthony Madere in the primary.

When the election committee met to tabulate results three days after the primary, Sellers protested that the election was improper. He said polling booths were not in accord with the law because they were open and accessible through windows by which voters could be watched from outside. Non-official people were allowed within the barriers around the voting places, which were maintained by incumbent Sheriff Madere. In addition, a poll watcher for Madere had intimidated 15 voters by going into the booth with them, claiming he was helping them vote. Supposedly these voters wanted to vote for Sellers. Another 10 of Sellers' supporters were denied the right to vote. In some voting wards there were illegal actions by clerks, votes were counted in private, and non-eligible persons counted votes.

The Democratic election committee upheld Sellers' protest and declared him winner of the nomination. But the contested election was far from over. Two other offices were also challenged: clerk of court between incumbent J.C. Triche and S.H. Labiche, and tax assessor between incumbent Leon C. Vial Sr. and Charles Elfer. The same reasons were given as in the challenge to Sellers. The election committee ordered new elections in both cases.

Madere, Triche, and Vial filed suit immediately, stating that the committee's decisions were illegal and fraudulent. Noting who was on the election committee sheds light on possible motives for overturning the primary results. There were "interested parties" who wanted certain outcomes: Thomas J. Sellers was the father of sheriff candidate Thomas B. Sellers; Sheriff Madere, assessor candidate Charles Elfer, and another Elfer were members of the election committee. The trial judge found in favor of the incumbents. But all decisions were appealed to the Louisiana Supreme Court, which concluded that "the election was fairly conducted," and that the Democratic election committee had produced no defense of its actions.[28]

Anthony Madere continued as sheriff for another four years. One of his sons bought property from J.B. Martin Jr. and built a house on the section between River Road and the levee. The Madere family operated a garage in Hahnville; they were related to the Vials through marriages with Keller daughters, and thus the Martins were in-laws. Leon C. Vial Sr. continued as assessor until 1916 when he was elected sheriff, holding that office for 24 years. J.C. Triche Sr. only continued one more year in the clerk of court office, which he had held for 12 years. He was replaced by Ralph A. Dubroca.

The "Vial Era" began with Leon C. Vial Sr. taking office as sheriff in 1916. The power structure remained stable for another decade until the election of January 1928. By that time bifactionalism had produced two fully organized factions battling each other: the "New Regulars" versus the "Old Regulars." The Old Regulars included Sheriff Vial, Assessor Ralph Dubroca, and Clerk of Court Irby Baudouin. J.B. Martin Jr. could be considered among this group, as long-term superintendent of schools and brother-in-law to Vial.

The New Regulars regarded themselves as the reform faction. They began a hard-hitting campaign early on and utilized the new house-to-house method of contacting voters.

Their message was mostly to elect different and non-corruptible officials. Although the established incumbents did not feel threatened at first, their attitude changed when they saw how effective their opponents' campaigning was. They launched an aggressive campaign calling on all resources, including gathering in old favors. Campaigning grew to a fevered pitch. The *St. Charles Herald*, owned by the pro-Old Regulars Triche family, publically lashed out at the New Regulars for the "falsification and vituperation" to which they resorted. Further criticism accused them of bringing the public schools into the fight, even though this had nothing to do with the offices being contested.

The Old Regulars won a landslide victory with every one of their candidates being elected. The powers that be continued in key parish offices for another four years.

In the election of 1932, Sheriff Vial was challenged by Adolph Levesque, a shopkeeper from Des Allemands. Levesque was a supporter of Huey "The Kingfish" Long, legendary Louisiana governor from 1928 to 1932. Long was a member of the United States Senate from 1932 until his assassination in 1935. Sheriff Vial and Governor Long had recently had a falling out, so the governor supported his opponent. Vial won the election but was accused of voter fraud by failure to comply with laws requiring reports on poll tax receipts and refusing to allow an inspection of poll tax records in his office. Levesque and supporters petitioned the state Attorney General to investigate, claiming Vial was "guilty of nonfeasance, malfeasance and misfeasance" in these violations of election laws. A special representative was sent to investigate, but he reported conflicting data on both issues. Vial ignored the first charge and pleaded ignorance on the second.[29] Governor Long offered to oust Vial in favor of Levesque, but the challenger declined, saying he wanted to be elected rather than appointed.

Other charges floated around in newspapers, but despite the flurry nothing happened. Leon C. Vial Sr. remained sheriff. Friction continued in the parish, but the incumbent candidates once again swept to victory in 1936. An American Oil Company worker ran against Vial, but the sheriff was re-elected by the largest majority ever. Three years later, however, Sheriff Vial died while in office and his second wife, Marie Keller Vial, completed his term. She ran for the office in the 1940 election, losing to Ralph A. Dubroca, who had been serving as tax assessor. When Clerk of Court Irby Baudouin threw his support behind Dubroca, this probably sealed the election.

It is likely that the growing division within the Vial faction was an underlying factor in this loss. Below the surface internecine struggles expanded after 1940. These were to flare in particular between the Vial and Martin families, previously firm allies in political ambitions but soon to be rendered into hostile factions.

The Vial-Martin Feud

The interplay of parish educational and political systems underlay the Vial-Martin family split. To grasp the situation, it's necessary to understand parish economic structures and the patronage system in the mid-1900s. Parish school boards were responsible for overseeing huge and complex enterprises. In Louisiana, they were often the largest employer in the parish, managing the expenditure of millions of state and local taxpayer dollars. They employed thousands of teachers, transportation drivers, and support staff for buildings and grounds. They made contracts with architects and engineers for new schools or renovations, water supplies and plumbing, electric supplies and equipment, safety programs, paving roads and parking lots, and other infrastructure. They made provisions for special events such as sports and fairs. Busses and boats used for transportation were commissioned and purchased. Books, desks, and equipment were purchased. Fiscal agents such as banks and law firms were contracted. A newspaper was selected to print official minutes and notices. And the board made resolutions for levying authorized taxes, called special tax elections for bond issues, as well as renewal of tax millage on property to support schools.

School boards had considerable leeway to establish policies relative to school curricula, students, teachers, and other employees. They had an obligation to inform the public about progress and needs, financial status, and accounting for receipts and expenditures. The public school system was, in essence, big business.

The patronage system seems inevitable where there is money to be spread around. Patronage is the practice by elected officials of filling government positions with people of their choosing, and of offering contracts to selected firms. State and local governments have used extensive patronage systems for years. It is also long-standing on the federal level. Usually politicians award their supporters, encouraging future support. At its best, patronage brings in loyal people who are qualified for their positions. At its worst, it is used to pay back political debts, garner future funds, and aid cronies in making profits off the government. History shows that patronage systems extending far down the organizational chain are susceptible to inefficiency and corruption. In Louisiana, as in much of the South, the "good ol' boys" used the patronage system to augment and maintain their positions of power.

St. Charles Parish in the mid-1900s was no different. One native said he grew up "related to 90 percent of Hahnville," and he knew everyone by name when he was a teenager. He was related to the Maderes and Triches. His grandfather Keller had a country store where people came to sit on the porch, play cards, and talk. Politics was a favorite topic, and everyone voted. Political controversy was on everyone's lips and family political affiliations were all-important. "If you gave a Madere a job, that took care of the Maderes," he said.[30]

Political office holders and school board directors and superintendents used their considerable hiring, purchasing, and contracting authority as a huge patronage system. A lot of money and desirable positions were involved. Two of J.B. Martin's sisters (Anna Colette, Marie "Keet") and two daughters (Helen, Minerva) were teachers; one son (Frederick) was parish supervisor. Leon C. Vial Sr. had several relatives who were teachers, and his wife and son succeeded him as sheriff. Richard Vial Sr.'s son was a teacher and music director, brought in as superintendent after J.B. resigned. Among teachers, school staff, and contractors were members of the Songy, Keller, Baudouin, Sellers, Madere, and Dufrene families.

School Board Directors vs. School Superintendent. Directors had full financial and governing authority to set academic goals, adopt policies, and approve the budget. They were elected by the public, and they hired the school superintendent. As the chief executive officer, the superintendent was charged with administration of the school system in accord with policies adopted by the school board. Superintendents had primary responsibility for personnel and recommended teachers and other staff to the school board for hiring. They acted as secretary and treasurer of the board. Details of school operations and implementing educational policy were in the superintendent's hands.

School boards were supposed to remain focused on the big picture and not micromanage day-to-day operations and personnel matters. But this has remained a major issue over the years. Boards or individual directors were not supposed to interfere; although the superintendent was bound by decisions made by the entire school board, he was never bound by what any individual board member said. This was such a problem that legislation was passed in 2020 making interference in personnel matters by individual school board members illegal.[31]

Richard J. Vial Sr. became an influential school board member after he was elected in 1920. He was an ally in 1911 of J.B. Martin—his brother-in-law—and the brother of Sheriff Vial. In 1931, Richard was elected president of the school board and served mostly in that position until he resigned in 1960. During the 1920s-1930s the St. Charles Parish school system was expanding rapidly, and there was some discord between Superintendent Martin and the school board. At one point the board revoked what it called the "excess powers" given to the superintendent, restricting him to powers allowed by the State Constitution. Reading between the lines, it is likely that J.B. was taking actions on employment or expenditures that the board believed were their right. In 1929, a special meeting was called to review the work of the superintendent; this was the strongest threat to J.B.'s leadership. However, J.B. had enough supporters on the board, and no action was taken on the review.[32]

Of interest, in that year the *Good Hope News* printed an article, "Hahnville School Has Splendid Record." The article praised the high school for beautiful grounds, excellent equipment, and specialized teachers; adding that it was run along the most progressive lines advised by advanced psychologists and teachers. Specifically noted was the cooperative approach to sports and contests that avoided the bitterness of rivalry.[33]

The Great Depression had significant impact on the school system, leading to pay cuts, discontinuing the parish health nurse, issuing script instead of money, and attempting to sell certificates of indebtedness. Many teachers resigned rather than accept pay cuts, and volunteers filled classrooms. School sessions were limited. There were fundraisers, donations, and some staff offered free services, such as transfer operators (bus/boat drivers). The school term was shortened. By the mid-1930s the Depression was improving; bands were started and athletics expanded.

Some new figures entered the school system and played important roles in the fomenting campaign to oust Supervisor Martin. School Board President Richard Vial's son, Richard J. Vial Jr., was hired to teach, soon becoming assistant principal and then music director at Hahnville High School. A favorite of Supervisor Martin's, Eual J. Landry, became principal of the high school. Aubin A. Songy became assistant principal. James N. Poche, principal at Destrehan High School, was writing a book about character education and citizenship. He was made classroom supervisor, a new position, and replaced by Aubin A. Songy as principal. Poche presented reports to the school board in 1934-1935 on teacher development that received accolades.

Over the next few years, several glowing reports were issued about St. Charles Parish schools. The Hahnville High School band under Richard Vial Jr. won state band contests, and Eual Landry's introduction of "moving pictures" in education received commendation throughout the state. Education for "colored students" progressed with addition of a high school. Despite earlier praise for Poche, in 1937 Superintendent Martin reported that the classroom supervisor position had not given the results anticipated. On his recommendation, the board discontinued the position.

The school board and the superintendent seemed to be working well together. In January 1938, a letter from the state superintendent of schools praised Superintendent Martin for introducing moving pictures, in particular a film that "tells the story of educational development in one of the parishes much more forcefully than could possibly be done in any number of speeches or books."[34]

On May 3, 1938, the board unanimously reappointed J.B. Martin as superintendent for the next 4 years, commended him on his first 25 years in the position, and expressed the desire that he serve another 25 years.

Just a month later, controversy about levying the millage tax on property owners to support the school system fueled the Vial-Martin Feud. Among the largest taxpayers were the oil industries, particularly the Pan American Petroleum Company. Negotiating the rate of industry taxation had traditionally been handled in committee, out of public view. Agreements would be reached among the school board committee, oil company representatives, and the most powerful political figure in the parish—Sheriff Vial. In the June 1938 special school tax election, however, this precedent was broken.

The meeting took place in the parish courtroom with a large crowd present. The school board had called a special election for a 7 mills tax, and the Pan American Petroleum Company representative asked that be reduced to 5.25 mills. He told the audience that the reduced millage would receive 100% support by industry. Superintendent Martin supported the need for the tax but took no stance on reduced millage. He inquired if the oil company representative had spoken with the sheriff about the reduced millage. He was told yes and that the sheriff was in complete support.

The school board voted 3-2 to rescind the prior tax vote for 7 mills. Board President Vial and one other member voted no; the other three members voted yes. Superintendent Martin went on record as supporting the change the oil industry wanted. A member of the audience, James Percival Vial (son of Sheriff Vial and nephew of School Board President Vial) spoke up, telling the superintendent that if he wished to know how his father stood on the school tax, he should visit him at home. Perhaps James Percival meant the issue was best discussed there or that Sheriff Vial's health often kept him home (he died seven months later).

A struggle for political leadership was already underway within the Vial faction. Disagreements were evident between J.B. and Richard Vial and between Richard and Sheriff Vial. In openly opposing the tax millage reduction sought by the oil industry, Richard had broken precedent of settling differences quietly in committee. He was also taking an opposing stance to the political leader, Sheriff Vial, whose health was ailing.

To make matters worse, in the next school board meeting in July, Board President Vial offered a resolution seconded by his ally to hold aside "certain discussions" from school board business, and that these be "obliterated from the records of the minute books." These records were to be declared null and void, except a portion dealing with loans. The motion passed unanimously. On the next motion by the same two, the tax vote was "recalled, rescinded and set aside."[35]

Motions were also passed to abide by a letter from the state superintendent of education (about limiting financial powers of the superintendent) and suspend all financial obligations by the board. A finance committee was created to take over the authority previously granted to the secretary of the board (Supervisor Martin) to purchase, contract, and obligate the school board. Then, the tax was proposed at the millage set by Sheriff Vial and the oil industry (5.25 mills). The votes on these motions were unanimous.

Something had shifted with the three members who previously supported J.B. The impact of these actions was to significantly restrict his authority as school superintendent. J.B. had lost his majority, a good deal of his power, and his job was in jeopardy. But he was not done fighting.

J.B. was instructed to alter the minutes of the June school board meeting to reflect the changes made in the July meeting. He was then told to remove any record of the original June meeting from the books. He did so in his inimitable "insubordinate" way. The previous year's minutes book was full after the June meeting. He simply started a new minutes book with the June meeting as amended. But he kept his copy of the original minutes book retaining a record of the board's unusual actions, probably stashed away where it could not be found easily.

As the election of 1940 approached, J.B. faced significant odds. His brother-in-law and constant ally, Sheriff Vial, had died. Vial's first wife, J.B.'s sister, was also dead, and Vial's second wife was acting sheriff while planning to run for office herself. This left the critical position of parish political leader uncertain, with jockeying for political leadership. J.B. had no desire to assume that role but did work behind the scenes to influence the outcome of the elections. Irby T. Baudouin Sr. was clerk of court and considered an ally of J.B. and the "old" Vial faction. Baudouin supported Tax Assessor Ralph Dubroca as candidate for sheriff, while he sought the tax assessor position for himself.

Richard Vial Sr. wanted to retain control of the school board, contain the powers of the superintendent, and promote candidates for the "new" Vial faction. His sister-in-law Marie Keller Vial was running for election to her deceased husband's post as sheriff. Richard "carried the Vial banner. The resulting election was bitter, interesting, and made a crucial impact on schools. The impact did not come immediately."[36]

The Bitter Election of 1940. There was widespread speculation about how the political void left by Sheriff Leon Vial's death would be filled. Hundreds gathered on the spacious lawn at Fashion, Sheriff Vial's "plantation home," to attend his funeral on Feb. 7, 1939. Schools were closed for a day, and a page set aside in the school board minutes book as a memorial for this "friend and counselor to thousands."[37]

Political skirmishing was immediately underway: "Who will succeed Sheriff Vial is problematical... No doubt the good Sheriff wanted the job to remain in his family as he had held the position since 1916. But... his death was so sudden that he may not have had time to build the foundations for this move... We don't know."[38] Sheriff Vial, who suffered from a bad back for years, had died of a heart attack while enjoying a meal at his son's house.

Details of the political maneuvering by the two Vial factions—Richard Vial Sr. group vs. the "old" Vial-Martin alliance—are mostly legends. Martin family lore tells that on the eve of the election, certain Martins, children of J.B.—Helen, Louis (Major), or Minerva—guarded the ballot boxes with shotguns (one version says Major had a submachine gun). Their reason was to prevent the opposition Vials from "stuffing the ballot boxes." This opposition Vial faction retorted that the Martins had already stuffed the boxes. Feelings were running high, and animosity became so great that some members of the Martin and Vial families did not talk to each other for many years afterward.

Leon C. Vial Jr. (II) had stayed out of politics during his father's life, but he joined forces with his uncle Richard Vial Sr. to support his stepmother's candidacy against Dubroca for sheriff in 1940. This spurred him into the political arena, and at the urging of family members he ran for sheriff in the next election of 1944. Vial won his first political office, ousting Dubroca by a slim margin. This election shifted power back to the "new" Vial faction; an expression of the forces that led to ending J.B. Martin's long career as school superintendent.

The Martin allies won in 1940. Ralph A. Dubroca served as sheriff from 1940 to 1944, and Irby T. Baudouin Sr. was tax assessor from 1940 to 1960. Power also shifted within the school board after this election. "On March 6, 1940, Martin took control of the School Board away from Richard J. Vial, Sr. T.C. Dufrene, by a vote of 4-1, became president. Vial cast the lone dissenting vote. Martin once had a 3-2 majority of members, now had four. Flavin Keller became vice president… It is almost certain that Martin's political allies, including Irby Baudouin, Sr., engineered the change."[39]

Stability in the school board power structure was not long-lived, however. A member resigned to join the parish Policy Jury; the Louisiana governor was charged with appointing replacements to unfinished terms. In 1940, Sam Jones became governor as Huey Long went to the U.S. Senate. The Vial family had traditionally been aligned with Huey Long. Governor Jones appointed Stanley F. Keller to the vacant position, which did not cause immediate controversy. Another resignation from the school board was replaced by Vial ally Landry Dufrene, but still J.B. maintained his majority. Flavin Keller, school board president, died in December 1942, setting off a period of frantic political activity.

Governor Jones appointed Percy Alleman to fill Flavin Keller's position. Alleman was allied with the Vial faction and the Huey Long regime, knowledgeable about the school system and laws. A "delegation" had rushed to the state capitol in Baton Rouge to secure Alleman's appointment, which could swing control back to the Vials. At that time, Richard Vial was again president of the board and Landry Dufrene was a Vial ally, so adding Alleman would return the majority to Vial.

J.B. had been outflanked by his opponents. But his supporters soon invaded the capitol and somehow obtained a second appointment by Governor Jones, getting him to rescind his former appointment and give the vacant position to H.A. Dufresne. The St. Charles Parish clerk of court duly recorded these events. Both Alleman and Dufresne presented their commissions to the school board, which voted to accept Dufresne. Richard Vial voted "blank" while all the other members approved. Thus, J.B. retained a majority of school board members, at least for a while.

Percy Alleman appealed to the district court and was initially ruled against. Dufresne became vice president of the school board, serving for one and one-half years while Alleman's further appeals went through state courts. At the appellate court level, it was ruled that Alleman was the rightful school board appointee, because he had the earlier commission (dated December 28, 1942) while Dufresne's commission was dated later (January 4, 1943). But Dufresne refused to step aside, and Alleman had to file a proceeding "for intrusion into office." While this was in progress, the District Attorney rendered a "second opinion" that Dufresne's appointment was not legal. In April 1944, Dufresne resigned at a special meeting.

During the interval between the seating of Dufresne and his replacement by Alleman, neither Richard Vial nor Landry Dufrene attended any board meetings. But they did attend the April 7, 1944, meeting when Percy Alleman took his seat. Vial was confirmed as president and formed an executive committee composed of himself, Landry Dufrene, and Alleman. They gave all "Martin appointees" notices of dismissal. The balance of power had shifted back to the Vial faction, and J.B. knew he was on the way out. He signed the school board minutes as secretary for the last time.[40]

Although J.B. remained as superintendent through the end of May, he did not sign any meeting minutes that month. On June 6, 1944, he submitted this simple resignation letter on a sheet of school board stationary:

> "To the President and Members of the St. Charles Parish School Board.
>
> Hahnville, La.
>
> Gentlemen:
>
> Kindly accept this my resignation as Superintendent of St. Charles Parish Public Schools.
>
> Thanking you for your many past Courtesies.
>
> I am with the very best of wishes
>
> Yours Truly,
> *J.B. Martin* (signature)"

The reason given by the school board executive committee for forcing J.B. Martin to resign as superintendent was "because of his political activity." A member of the Martin family said his reason for resigning was that the school board had become "too political." They were rejecting his professional recommendations in favor of "political appointments." An educator who served under J.B.—and who was not a relative—believed that Martin was frustrated with the school board for making patronage appointments over his recommendations of qualified candidates. He did not want to deal with school personnel who could make political end-runs around him when they disagreed with his decisions as superintendent.[41]

After J.B. Martin's ouster, the school board was solidly under President Vial's control and already had chosen his son, Richard J. Vial Jr., as the next superintendent. But the junior Vial was a soldier in World War II at that time. He was sent a letter and accepted the position, being appointed in 1944 after J.B.'s resignation. Critics questioned his qualifications, pointing out that he held only a bachelor's degree and had never served as a principal. The board requested his early release from the Army, and he assumed the superintendent position in October 1945.

Aubin A. Songy, principal of Destrehan High School and school supervisor, was asked to be acting superintendent until Vial Jr. returned from the war. Songy had worked in the school system under J.B. for more than a decade and reportedly suffered emotional stress in the role he played after the resignation of Martin. He became board secretary and signed the final minutes in the Martin years, serving as acting superintendent from 1944 to 1945. When Richard J. Vial Jr. assumed the position, Songy continued as a school supervisor. The two men worked closely together, and each had a particular role: Vial concentrated on the political aspects of the superintendent's position, and Songy focused on the academic aspects of the school system.

The Aftermath of Vial and Martin Eras

Richard J. Vial Jr. (1908-1973) was a successful school superintendent. The former band director was popular in the parish, and the Vials were regarded as among the best-educated people in the community. Even though family conflicts caused J.B.'s resignation, he had a mentoring relationship with his nephew, "Dick" Vial. It appears that J.B. wanted his nephew to succeed him, just not in the way it happened. The transition was easier because of Dick Vial's distance during the ouster; he was half a world away fighting in the Philippines. His sister, Marie Vial Dufrene, described their close relationship: "If Dick had a problem as Superintendent, he would not hesitate going to Uncle Johnny to ask his advice."[42]

A curious communication process took place in the estranged families. Leonide Vial Martin would bring coffee and ask her nephew Dick about his father, her younger brother, the main force in ending her husband's superintendent role. J.B. would inquire about Dick's mother, his sister-in-law. Minerva, J.B.'s daughter, recalls friendly talks between her father and her cousin, Dick, saying "Our families were always close." Minerva and Dick were in the first graduating class from Hahnville High School. The family rift was probably hardest for Leonide, who could not see her siblings, but she fully supported her husband. In later years her nephew, Leon C. Vial III (Sunny), acted as her attorney.

Richard "Dick" Vial ushered the parish school system smoothly through racial integration during the 1960s. The black supervisor of schools, Raymond Smith, believed integration went well because "people accepted the leadership in the school system. We did not have one day of rioting or unpleasantness."[43] Several major building programs included two new high schools in the 1970s. Vial held this office until his death in 1973, six months before his scheduled retirement. As Vial's retirement approached, the school board wanted the selection of his successor to be free of politics. They asked professors from Tulane and Nicholls University to review the 38 applications and recommend the best candidate. Using these evaluations, the board selected Dr. Bruce Meeks, who became assistant superintendent in 1971. Upon Vial's death, he assumed the superintendent position.

School board elections in 1962 and parish elections in 1963 signaled decline in Vial control, with victories of several opposition candidates. A runoff election was necessary for sheriff in 1963 between Leon C. Vial Jr. and John St. Amant. The results were close, but St. Amant won. Opposition candidate Edward "Little Eddie" Dufresne Jr. won clerk of court, while sometimes Vial ally Julius Sellers Sr. won tax assessor. As elected officials took office in 1964, the Vial reign ended.

Subsequent generations of the Vial-Martin family continued to play important roles in the affairs of St. Charles Parish. They served as parish administrators, lawyers, judges, educators, assessors, and in public charitable organizations. With many Vials in public service in the late 20th century, they rightly proclaimed, "We're back!"

As Leon C. Vial III (Sunny) said in a 2001 interview with *L'Observateur*, "Politics has been good to us, but I didn't see the glory of it." He described the "political feud" that erupted within the Vial-Martin families, saying "I saw the misery daddy went through. I never got that interested in politics." As soon as that feud died down, the Vial-Dufresne feud flared over the sheriff position election in 1948. "Big Eddie" Dufresne, long-time critic of Vial, ran unsuccessfully for sheriff. Vial was too popular; people would "come to him with whatever problems they had," Sunny said of his father.

Sunny stayed out of politics, practicing law and serving briefly as parish attorney. His brother Dr. Jerry Vial served as parish coroner. "Little Eddie" Dufresne advanced his political career, moving from clerk of court to judge on the Court of Appeals. The Vial-Dufresne feud ended with the marriage of Dr. Vial's son, David, and Debra Dufresne, daughter of "Little Eddie." Sunny's cousin, Mary Ann Vial Lemmon (daughter of James Percival Vial), became the first woman appointed as a federal judge in the parish.

The article concluded, "Nonetheless, St. Charles Parish would be unrecognizable without the Vial family."[44]

The Vial-Martin feud slowly resolved as later generations reconnected in the early 2000s, discovering cousins they never knew before.

J.B. Martin Jr. spent 11 years in quiet retirement with his wife Leonide at their home in Hahnville. All four of their sons served in armed forces during World War II, some seeing action in the Pacific theater. Fortunately, none were injured, and all returned home safely. By the time J.B. retired in 1944 and the war ended in 1945, the only child still living in Hahnville was Louis (BéBé, called Major after his military service). He worked with the state conservation commission in Hahnville.

At the golden wedding anniversary of J.B. and Leonide Vial Martin in 1953, the dispersed Martin children were described as: "The children are Mrs. Roscoe Cole of Alexandria, Va.; Dr. Minerva Martin of Washington, D.C. who is with the English department of the University of Maryland; Dr. J.B. Martin Jr. (III) a Lake Charles (dermatologist);… Fred C. Martin, comptroller of the Southern Construction Company in Lake Charles; and Roy H. Martin of Houma, who is with the Texas Oil Company's production department."

Three of the Martin children were married, about which J.B. said, "That's 50 percent, a fairly good average. We also have five grandchildren from 3 to 13 years old." Reminiscing about St. Charles Parish, he continued, "I've seen this area change from an agricultural to an industrial parish. This used to be a big sugarcane and rice producing place; now there are nearly 200 oil and gas wells on both sides of the river. We still have quite a bit of cattle pasturing here, but that's husbandry—not agriculture. The farmers just can't compete with industrial salaries. About 40-50 years ago the population was around 8,000; chances are now it's 17 or 18 thousand, and still growing."

Asked how they spent their time, Leonide replied she mostly worked around their home and that flowers were her big interest. She still liked to play piano but was limited by arthritis in her hands. J.B. said his wife got a yen to visit New Orleans about once a month, so they would go "just to see if it's still there."[45]

All their children had come to New Orleans earlier that month for the big golden wedding anniversary celebration. The Martins planned to celebrate the actual date of their anniversary (October 7) with family living in Lake Charles.

J.B. Martin Jr. is still remembered as the "Father of St. Charles Parish Schools," and his silver jubilee as superintendent was celebrated on April 30, 1938, with the day dedicated to him. He died of a heart attack on January 15, 1955, at his home in Hahnville. He is buried at Our Lady of the Most Holy Rosary Cemetery in Taft. He was 73 years old.

Leonide Mary Vial Martin lived another nine years in their family home in Hahnville. She tended her flowers and enjoyed grandchildren. Her handwritten will (March 27, 1959) contains a plea to her children: "I leave for all of you to decide what to do with property and home. Just do not be too hasty to dispose of home—it is home for all of you." She died on October 7, 1964, in Hahnville and is buried at Our Lady of the Most Holy Rosary Cemetery in Taft. She was 85 years old.

The children agreed to give lifetime rights to the old house and yard to Louis. Within a few years the old house was torn down and a small, modern one built. Louis lived there until his death in 1976; the remaining children decided to sell the property.

Leonide Mary Vial Martin
c.1930

Leonide Vial was the link to an unrealized richness of family history. She passed on the distant Acadian roots and entangled tendrils of Creole heritage to her descendants.

EPILOGUE

Acadian to Cajun

⚜

When our grandparents and great-grandparents were growing up in St. Charles and St. John the Baptist Parishes, they had little concern with Cajun and Creole distinctions. The word "Acadian" was not in their lexicon. They knew, however, they were from good families that were leaders in their society and connected to everyone of importance. If asked, they would certainly say they were not Cajuns, a group widely regarded as lower class, backwards, and unambitious who were content with simple, though sensuous, lives. The Cajuns living all around them were workers and laborers, just a step above the black classes.

After my father, Fred Martin, returned from World War II, our family moved from New Orleans to Lafayette. I was 6 years old and went to the Southwestern Louisiana Institute (now University of Louisiana, Lafayette) teachers' training elementary school. We lived in Arbolada, a neighborhood adjacent to the college campus. I have fond memories of playing on campus fields and adventuring at Cypress Lake, the arcades, and gardens. Lafayette is in the heart of Acadiana, the 22-parish region designated by the state in 1971 as "Cajun Country." It never occurred to me that I was in the very bastion of Cajun culture—despite most of my friends having classic Cajun surnames such as Theriot, Thibodeaux, Hebert, Plauche, LeBlanc, Broussard, Landry, and Breaux.

Their families were just like mine. They lived in my neighborhood, dressed and talked the same, and had the same things. Although their families descended from Acadian émigrés, they did not identify as Cajuns. Using that term was tantamount to an insult; they wanted to be known simply as Americans. Cajuns lived in shacks out in the bayous, fished and trapped, spoke heavily accented English, were poorly educated, and were lazy and fun-loving. That stereotype was prevalent in the 1950s-1960s; their parties with dancing to fiddle and accordion music—*fais-do-do*—things of legend.

Among my life's ironies was how I strongly opposed our family move to Lake Charles when I was 12. To me, moving to that city, just 75 miles straight west, was going to live among the lowly Cajuns. I refused to attend school with them, badgering my parents to send me to an elite boarding school in Mississippi catering to better families. This isolated, strict Catholic girls' boarding school was a shocking ordeal; I didn't last an entire year before pleading to come home. But that's another story, where I learned some hard lessons.

As the Cajuns renewed themselves, so did our family's view of them. We now regard their culture with admiration and appreciate their many gifts. Although the thread connecting us is gossamer, we are honored to share Acadian roots.

How did the Cajuns come to be so reviled in South Louisiana society? The answers lie in the forces buffeting their culture in the aftermath of the Civil War and subsequent depression. The very nature of Acadian culture set the stage for the transition—and also their resilience and rebound into an almost mythically exotic people.

A Marginalized Culture

The thousands of Acadian exiles from Nova Scotia shared a common culture. They had resilient bonds of language, kinship, religion, and social customs. During their first 150 years in Louisiana, they retained this culture with adaptations to the new environment, including changes in cuisine, agricultural practices, clothing, and building materials. Preferences for a simple lifestyle, disdain of materialism, intermarriage, and family-centered society persisted through the first half of the 20th century. French was the predominant language of most households, and often the only language spoken. Catholicism remained strong, although practiced in their unique and often irreverent way, with emphasis on life-transition rituals. Already lines had blurred between some Acadians and white Creoles. Forces that shaped distinct Cajun identity intensified after the turn of the 20th century.

The Civil War and depression that followed profoundly altered Acadian ethnic patterns. Planters and large farmers lost their property; Acadian real estate ownership fell up to

90% in the river parishes.[1] Acadians working in agriculture became tenants, sharecroppers, or day laborers. Many migrated to cities for jobs; others retreated into bayou and swamp regions to work as trappers, fishermen, or lumberjacks. They were stuck in poverty and lacked educational opportunities. Cultural stereotypes of the backwards, hedonistic, isolationist Cajuns became prevalent. The better off, better educated, professional Acadians eschewed their poor confrères and avoided associating with those onerous Cajuns.

A significant proportion of other ethnic groups such as French, Spanish, and German also suffered impoverishment. They were lowered to the social stratum of the Cajuns, resulting in intermarriage and blending into the larger Francophone group. This blending of ethnicities, including some Native Americans, created the culture now considered Cajun. It was also influenced by Afro-Caribbean enslaved people who shared a French-Catholic heritage, especially in cuisine and music—products of this melting pot.

Most Cajuns remained culturally isolated from mainstream America until World War II. Radio made its way into South Louisiana by the 1930s, with many stations broadcasting news in Cajun French and featuring Cajun music. But less than half of Cajun homes had radios. By 1940, only 17% of rural dwellings had electric lighting, and 22% had indoor plumbing. They were so immersed in poverty that most did not even notice the Great Depression.[2]

The Americanization of the Cajuns

It took a worldwide crisis of unprecedented scale to propel the Cajuns into mainstream American society. World War II impacted their lives as nothing before, creating a sense of unification with the country and desire to be part of Anglo-American culture. Alarmed and incensed by the global threat to freedom, Cajuns were spurred to join the war effort and participated by the thousands. Young men left South Louisiana for the first time, encountered solely English-speaking Americans, and quickly learned to speak the language. They went to strange new places, were exposed to diverse values, and gained different perspectives. They faced culture shock and ethnic slurs, but many excelled as soldiers and some became invaluable translators.

Cajun civilians joined with other Americans to support the war effort as volunteers, participating in numerous activities bringing them in contact with mainstream culture. Others left Acadiana to take jobs in Texas or New Orleans. They watched wartime newsreels and movies, listened to radio, and read books and magazines, all in English. United to fight "foreign" enemies, their identity as Americans was powerfully reinforced. Nearly 25,000 Cajuns served in the military, including those who volunteered and who were drafted.[3] The wartime imperative was to blend in, speak English, and let go of ethnic alliances: to be American.

There was an influx of outsiders into South Louisiana to work in oil refineries and industries. This caused friction but also exposed Cajuns to other points of view. Children were influenced through participating in wartime drives, popular media, and by classroom emphasis on Americanism. Teachers promoted the American way of life as superior, to be emulated by all, and gave students basic citizenship training. Churches and youth groups joined the effort to produce mainstream children, encouraging Cajuns to put aside their ethnicity, speak English, and take part in war-support activities. Increasing numbers of Cajuns were learning to read in the 1940s, and the state supported literacy with rural bookmobiles and library services.

When the war ended, Cajuns celebrated victory along with other Americans around the country. People shouted, horns blared, bells rang, and citizens held parades. Cajun GIs returned home after experiences in countries from Europe to Asia, but they were not the same boys who had left Acadiana. Those who remained at home had also changed during these four transformative years. A series of trends was set into motion that would continue the group's assimilation into mainstream society.

Many war veterans completed schooling with the GI Bill of Rights or used it to buy homes and start businesses. Economic conditions improved, and good jobs were available in the booming oil industry. Rising out of poverty, Cajuns put aside their traditional antimaterialism and embraced rampant consumerism along with most Americans. Television sets were the most popular item, bringing expanded contact with an English-speaking world beyond the Cajun homeland. No longer isolated from countrywide and worldwide events, Cajuns were embroiled in the upheavals of the civil rights movement, anti-communism, and tensions of the Cold War and atomic age.

Change was all around, but it was not always smooth. Cajun children growing up in the postwar period were caught between two worlds: one familiar, rural, French-speaking; the other mysterious, urban, English-speaking. This new world was more enticing than the outmoded one of their forebears, so most Cajun youth emulated mainstream peers. A Cajun from Ville Platte recalled about his friends during the 1950s: "They read comics about Archie and Jughead… in dress and liking for hamburgers were very much like…

all-American teenagers."[4] Many were discontent with their surroundings, wanted more opportunities, complained about "old people" in a break with traditional reverence for elders. They were willing to move to cities for jobs and liked fast food, clothes, cars, and rock 'n' roll music.

Language and Culture. Speaking French became a casualty of Americanization. Use of Cajun French as a first language declined significantly around World War II. For Cajuns born at the dawn of the 20th century, 83% used French primarily; that plummeted dramatically to 21% of those born around 1960.[5] As Cajun parents assimilated after the war, they chose not to teach French to their children and spoke English at home. The French language became a mystery to postwar Cajun children. It was a peculiar code their parents used for communicating in confidence.

Although a large part of this decline can be attributed to postwar Americanization, the process was in place much earlier. An anti-foreign surge followed World War I, leading to school policies for enforcing use of English. In 1916, the Louisiana Board of Education banned French from classrooms, codified in the State Constitution in 1921. Official education policy did not mention punishment, but many teachers used such methods as paddling, writing lines in English on blackboards, public shaming, whipping, or walking around the flagpole holding bricks. Punishment for speaking French was variable, and most children continued using it at home. Some did not attend school and escaped this humiliation, but many were traumatized well into adulthood.

By the 1975 generation, only 8% of Cajuns spoke French as a primary language; for about the same it was a secondary language. Journalists reported that the unique bilingual character of South Louisiana would soon die out. They found Cajun children nearly indistinguishable from Anglo-Americans and unaware of their ethnic heritage, with Louisiana college students so similar that they might have been from New York, Kansas, or Oregon universities.[6] By the 1980 generation, only 3% spoke primarily French. This is an astounding 95% drop from the World War II era.[7]

According to sociologists studying language patterns, the critical mass for linguistic survival is 20% of a people.[8] It appears that Cajun French may disappear as an everyday means of communication in South Louisiana. Some believe that a culture cannot continue without using its traditional language. Efforts were undertaken to preserve the language beginning with the 1968 creation of CODOFIL (Council for the Development of French in Louisiana), a state agency charged to "… accomplish the development, utilization, and preservation of the French language as found in the State of Louisiana for the cultural, economic, and tourist benefit of the State."[9] CODOFIL imported French-speaking teachers from Quebec, Belgium, and France, and started programs in elementary schools. Throughout its controversial history, the organization promoted Cajun ethnic pride, battled slurs and stereotypes, tried unsuccessfully to eliminate using "coonass" (slang for Cajun), and managed to teach French to thousands of children. Despite its efforts, French continued to disappear at alarming rates.

A Cajun grassroots pride and empowerment movement had already started, running parallel and at times contrary to CODOFIL's top-down, elitist, organized agenda. This movement was centered around Cajun music and food, which began to gain national attention in the mid-1960s. Tourism mushroomed as prosperity allowed Americans to travel and enjoy luxuries, and they flocked to exotic South Louisiana to indulge in energizing music and piquant cuisine. Finding new value in cultural traditions, Cajuns modified them to accommodate modern tastes and took full advantage of tourism.

Exploitation and Authenticity. Cajun was no longer a derogatory term. It became a cultural icon replete with ethnic pride and profitability. Demand for Cajun music and cuisine spread nationally and internationally, with restaurants featuring Cajun dishes and clubs promoting Cajun bands. Louisiana sported Cajun and Acadian festivals, created Evangeline State Park and Acadian Village, and provided tours of alligator-infested bayous and tongue-blistering McIlhenny Tabasco tastings. Tourists could attend a "genuine" Cajun *fais-do-do*, crawfish boil, boudin sausage tasting, and dine at innumerable restaurants featuring Cajun and Creole cuisine. Even New Orleans got into the Cajun act, promoted as the heart of Cajun country (which is actually Lafayette) with a plethora of ethnic restaurants and dishes. In truth, only a very small number of New Orleans residents are Cajuns.

Two of the most famous "Cajun" dishes were 20th-century inventions. Crawfish étouffée was originally known as crawfish courtbouillon. This rich stew of seasoned onion, bell pepper, celery, and crawfish tails is served over rice. It had Creole flavor origins and was a standard dish among Cajuns for years. In the late 1940s, the owner of a Lafayette restaurant was preparing a batch for herself. A well-to-do customer was watching, and asked in French what she was making. She replied, also in French, that she was smothering some crawfish— *étouffée* being French for "smothered." Later the customer returned with friends and ordered "crawfish étouffée," coining the name by which the dish became known.

Blackened redfish has become another icon of Cajun cuisine, but it has shallow roots. Redfish, or red snapper, is a popular Gulf of Mexico staple originally prepared in bouillabaisse or courtbouillon. In the 1970s, rising Cajun chef Paul Prudhomme opened K-Paul's Louisiana Kitchen in New Orleans, where he popularized the dish. He learned cooking techniques in his large family, using fresh ingredients because they had no electricity. Unable to afford a commercial grill in his restaurant, he cooked well-seasoned redfish fillet on a superheated iron skillet, creating the culinary phenomenon. It was so popular by the mid-1980s that the redfish population fell dramatically, leading to a government ban on commercial redfishing.[10] Prudhomme published many cookbooks and became a "culinary god," taking his restaurant on the road to San Francisco and New York City.

While Cajun food was widely adored, it was also mangled, imitated, hyped, marketed, and misinterpreted. This exploitation included Cajun pizza, chicken, pasta, and all kinds of fast foods. Perhaps the worst is Popeye's, a chain capitalizing on the Cajun theme and serving nothing that remotely resembles authentic cuisine. Louisiana's Department of Agriculture fought back by creating a "Certified Cajun Product" logo and threatening non-Louisiana companies with false advertising lawsuits. But keeping cuisine authentic is a losing battle. Even prestigious New Orleans restaurants now serve such nouveau Cajun dishes such as shrimp and grits.

As a native South Louisianan, I can attest that we ate shrimp with rice and grits with eggs and bacon.

The double-edged sword of tourism brought money but also disrupted already declining folk practices in South Louisiana. Tourists invaded obscure Cajun nightclubs, interrupting the weekly ritual of Saturday night dancing and bourré card games. There were so many at Mardi Gras festivities that locals vacated the scene, leaving tourists wondering why no Cajuns were dancing. Some Cajuns accommodated tourists by providing what they wanted to see, staging cultural events and putting on shows for money but abandoning them as soon as the tourists left. The entertainment industry also took advantage of the Cajun craze, producing films and television programs in the 1980s-1990s stereotyping Cajuns as ignorant, violent, and oversexed swamp dwellers. Cajun music festivals drew large crowds as traditional styles morphed into Zydeco and Cajun rock.

Cajun pride and empowerment also found expression through legal and political activism. In the landmark 1980 lawsuit *Roach v. Dresser Industrial Valve and Instrument Division*, employee Calvin Roach challenged the company for ethnic slurs in accusing Cajuns of stealing and calling them "cheap crooked coonasses." The defense argued that the Equal Opportunity Act of 1964 did not protect Cajuns because they were not a bona fide ethnic minority, since Acadia had never been an independent nation. But the court ruled in favor of Roach, declaring that Cajuns were indeed a minority and protected by the ban on national origin discrimination.[11]

Modern Adaptations and Symbolic Ethnicity. Like other minorities, Cajuns entered the 21st century transformed yet able to retain their core identity. With their knack for perseverance, they took advantage of the information age to create a digital presence. Many internet websites, online discussion groups, and webzines are dedicated to preserving their history and culture. Entering the search term "Cajun" currently results in over 46 million hits; this virtual community has been called "Cyberacadiana."[12] Universities created centers for Louisiana studies, and published books and journals focused on local culture. Interest in Cajuns continues through both academic and popular sources.

Cajuns have adapted to the modern world by pursuing high-tech careers: everything from rocket science to molecular genetics. DNA research by one at Tulane University discovered a common Cajun genotype, providing evidence that Cajuns are truly a distinct ethnic group. Genealogical websites abound, assisting Acadian descendants to trace their roots and learn about their lineages. Cajuns can be found in nearly every occupation—chef, musician, painter, politician, activist, baseball and football player, actor, businessman, physician, and international entrepreneur.

Though Cajuns have found ways to flourish in the contemporary global community, they have also paid a price. Many folk traditions have been lost or changed beyond recognition. French as an everyday language is moribund, even as ethnic pride is soaring. Their music and cuisine have been appropriated and altered, even while gaining in popularity. They have blended beyond recognition into modern society, yet vast resources have been devoted to their history and culture. Action Cadienne, an ethnic preservation group, declared that Cajun French was the source of their identity and its demise would inevitably destroy the entire culture.[13]

However, sociologists argue that ethnic groups who have mostly assimilated can retain much of their cultural heritage through "symbolic ethnicity." Many minorities are replacing their actual cultures with symbolic cultures, which permit them to feel ethnic by taking part in traditional holidays and festivals, eating traditional food, and listening to traditional music. They may dedicate certain days to wearing traditional clothing and having parades. Thus, they feel connected to their culture without the effort of practicing folkways on a daily basis. With symbolic ethnicity, minorities can experience their culture as a leisure-time pursuit rather than a customary way of life.[14]

South Louisiana Cajuns already participate in symbolic ethnicity. Street signs in French accompany English signs in Acadiana cities, even though most Cajuns cannot read them. Folk and music festivals are frequent, providing events for immersion in Cajun culture. Consuming ethnic cuisine is a common practice, whether in restaurants or through prepared foods readily available in supermarkets. Mardi Gras is a big expression of symbolic ethnicity, offering costumes, dancing, drinking, and eating along Cajun and Creole themes.

The authenticity of such activities can certainly be questioned. Symbolic ethnicity allows Cajuns who might spurn folk practices to "… 'feel' Cajun, to express their 'Cajunness' when convenient, without disrupting their everyday lives."[15] Such practices do, however, keep people connected to their traditions. It might prevent total Americanization of the Cajuns into the foreseeable future. For a people so capable of retaining cultural roots through hundreds of years, overcoming expulsion and upheaval and establishing new foundations, this path to cultural expression may preserve traditions for future generations.

Acadian Redemption

Four hundred years after the first French settlers came to the land called Acadia, the human rights violation of their forced expulsion and resultant diasporas was rectified. In the century and a half between their arrival in 1604 and expulsion in 1755, a unique Acadian identity was formed. Under authority of the British king, soldiers confiscated their lands and possessions, herded them onto ships with only what they could carry, and sent them off to faraway places. Often, families were separated, some never to reunite. They were not welcomed in British colonies and were used as labor on French feudal farms or Saint-Domingue sugar plantations. Some 12,000 Acadians were deported. Many died of disease and hardship. Over the next 15 years, about 4000 Acadian refugees came to South Louisiana, re-established their culture, and gradually became the Cajuns.

Some Acadians fought against this expulsion. They are called the Acadian Resistance, Freedom Fighters who became cultural heroes. The best-known leader of the resistance in Nova Scotia, who later settled in Attakapas, near present-day Opelousas, is Joseph *dit* Beausoliel Broussard. A colorful and charismatic man with a checkered history, Beausoleil led a band of guerilla fighters that challenged British forces for five years. Poorly armed, they were no match for His Majesty's Army and eventually were captured and jailed. After their release, Broussard led a group of Acadians to Louisiana's bayou country and served as a symbol for "New Acadia."

Beausoliel Broussard left an impressive legacy that has spread widely. He is featured in the main exhibit of the Acadian Museum of Erath, LA. His face appears on T-shirts sold to support the museum, and he is the subject of many poems, stories, and songs. The town of Broussard was named after him, and his descendants formed a foundation to save French language and history. His memorial is near the town. A play was commissioned about him for the celebration of the 250th anniversary of the Acadian deportation, hosted by the Acadian Cultural Center in Lafayette. Acadian museums and culture centers in Nova Scotia and New Brunswick have books and memorabilia featuring him.

One of his descendants undertook a 15-year campaign to obtain an apology from Queen Elizabeth II of England for the Acadians' expulsion. Warren Perrin, a lawyer and law professor at Loyola Law School, married another descendant of Beausoliel, and they had three children. In 1988, his youngest son asked him what the Acadians had done wrong to be expelled, and that struck a nerve. Perrin began intensive historical and legal research, becoming increasingly incensed about human rights assaults tantamount to ethnic cleansing. He viewed the British actions in 1755 as a violation of English and international law, and a violent and cruel case of genocide and scattering of an oppressed minority. The Acadians were exiled as criminals when they had not broken any laws, were British subjects, professed neutrality, and had pledged allegiance to the Crown with previously agreed stipulations.

Perrin further contended that the British stripped the Acadians of their rights in order to confiscate their lands and property, and the Crown had a moral obligation to acknowledge that a wrong had occurred. He believed repercussions continued into the present, both economic and psychological, from this tragedy of the Acadian people. Since their expulsion as criminals had never been revoked, contemporary Acadian descendants were technically banned from Canada. A retraction and apology was needed to set matters right.

In 1990, Perrin wrote a petition seeking redress, in which Beausoleil was named to symbolically represent the Acadians. He sent it to British Prime Minister Margaret Thatcher and the Queen of England. Six issues were set forth: restoration of French neutral status to Acadians, an inquiry into the deportation, a declaration annulling the Order of Deportation (officially ending Acadian exile), acknowledgement that tragedies occurred, acknowledgement that the action taken was contrary to international and English law, and erection of a memorial for the end of the exile. The petition was not filed in a court of law and sought no compensation.[16]

The petition received widespread support among Acadians, after initial reticence in Canada. Louisianans enthusiastically endorsed it, even non-Cajuns. Interest was spurred by the first two *Congrès Mondiaux Acadiens*, the Acadian World Congresses held in 1994 in Canada and 1999 in Louisiana. Initially the British government contended that it was too late to raise these issues, but after substantial media coverage, examples of other government restitutions, and support by international organizations, Perrin received a satisfactory response to his petition.

On December 9, 2003, Queen Elizabeth symbolically apologized to the Acadians. The Royal Proclamation on Deportation, signed by the governor of Canada, repudiated the wrongs committed during the Acadian deportation in the name of the British Crown. It designated July 28 of each year as "A Day of Commemoration of the Great Upheaval," beginning in 2005. In selecting the date that the first wave of Acadians was expelled, the Proclamation acknowledged the suffering and tragic consequences of this historic action. It noted the Acadians have made a remarkable contribution to Canadian society for almost 400 years and expressed hope of turning the page on this dark chapter of their history.[17]

Although this did not produce the monument that Perrin originally requested in his petition, it did bring the Acadian experience to international attention. It was an impetus for the Canadian government to officially recognize National Acadian Day in 2004, celebrated since 1881. Millions of people are reached by these Acadian celebrations. Perrin's patient and non-confrontational approach has been praised as an example of how victimized people can obtain redemption without violence. In Perrin's words, "By repudiating the wrongs committed during the exile, the Crown has sent a clear message that such actions are wrong. Arguably, in a time of peace, there has never been a tragedy with more unnecessary human suffering than the Acadian exile… *Beausoleil* and the Acadian people have been redeemed."[18]

National Acadian Day, Bouctouche, Nova Scotia (2013)
Kathi Bonnabel and Lennie Martin proudly wore their Bourgeois family nametags.

Descendants of J.B. Martin Jr. and Leonide Mary Vial Martin
First Generation

Roy (Peter), Frederick (Fred), Louis (Major), J.B. (Junior) III, Helen, Minerva
J.B. Martin Jr. (II), Leonide Mary Vial Martin
Hahnville, LA c.1950

Second-Fourth Generations

Back Row: Cary Martin, Doug Martin, Frederick Charles Martin Jr., Lara Anderson,
Middle Row: Katherine Bonnabel, Dorothy (DeeDee) Heathman, Helen Celeste Martin,
Leonide (Lennie) Martin, Corinne Martin
Front Row: Tyler Heathman, Valerie Heathman
New Orleans, LA 2012

Appendix

#1 Martin-Vial Family Tree: LaTour-D'Aprendestique-Bouregois-LeBlanc-Dugas

- **Marie-Anne LeBlanc (1732-1812)**
  - **Jean LeBlanc (1684-1747)**
    - **André LeBlanc (1659-1743)**
      - Daniel LeBlanc (1626-1686)
        - René LeBlanc (1595-?)
        - Unknown
      - Françoise Gaudet (1623-1698)
        - Jean Gaudet (1575-1672)
        - Marie D'Aussy (1580-1628)
    - **Jeanne Marie Dugas (1664-1734)**
      - Abraham Dugast (c1616-1698)
        - Abraham Dugas (1590-?)
        - Marguerite Carsonac (1590-?)
      - Marie-Marguerite Louise Doucet (c1625-1700)
        - Germain Doucet dit Laverdure (1595-?)
        - Marie Bourgeois (1597-?)
  - **Jeanne Anne Bourgeois (1687-1766)**
    - **Guillaume Bourgeois (1655-1693)**
      - Jacque Bourgeois dit Jacob (c1619-1701)
        - Nicolas Grandjehan (1570-1620)
        - Marguerite Bourgeois (1585-1620)
      - Jeanne Trahan (1631-1701)
        - Guillaume Trahan (c1601-c1680)
        - Françoise Corbineau (?-c1660)
    - **Marianne d'Aprendestique (1662-1687)**
      - Martin d'Aprendestique dit Martignon (1616-1689)
        - Janis d'Aprendestiguy (?-?)
        - Unknown
      - Jeanne de La Tour (1626-1696)
        - Charles Amador de St. étienne de La Tour (1593-1666)
        - Marguerite Membertou (c1606-c1684)

#2 Vial-Martin Family Tree: LeBlanc-Bujol-Bourgeois-Vives

Appendix 293

- Marie Malvina Vives (1810-1842)
  - Jean Landry Chevalier Vives (1782-1809)
    - Juan Francisco Vicente Chevalier Vives (1751-1805)
      - Joseph Causin Juan Thomas Vives (1719-?)
        - Jaume Vives (1682-?)
        - Josefa Maria Lacomba (1690-?)
      - Francisca Maria Xaviera Planells (1720-?)
        - Augustin Planells (1692-?)
        - Clara Maria Cortes (1694-?)
    - Marguerite Bujol (1751-1805)
      - Joseph Bujol (1722-1806)
        - Joseph Bujol (c1699-1758)
        - Marie Josephe Landry (?-?)
      - Marie-Anne LeBlanc (1732-1812)
        - Jean LeBlanc (1684-1747)
        - Jeanne Anne Bourgeois (1687-1766)
  - Marguerite Marie Bourgeois (1790-1815)
    - Dominique Bourgeois *fils* (c1764-1777)
      - Dominique Bourgeois *père* (1730-?)
        - Jean Baptiste Bourgeois (c1695-1770)
        - Marianne Chevalier (c1700-?)
      - Reine Genevieve Uval/Huval/Duval (1739-1797)
        - Henri III Uvalle (c1700-?)
        - Marie Jeanne Uvalle (c1700-?)
    - Marguerite LaGrange (c1770-?)
      - Jean Baptiste LaGrange (1728-1795)
        - Unknown
        - Unknown
      - Marie Louise Fontenot (1741-1820)
        - Jean Louis Fontineau *dit* Colin (1686-1755)
        - Louise Angelique Henry (1700-c1777)

#3 Vial-Martin Family Tree: Vives-Songy-Reynaud-Bossier

Louise Clothilde Malvina Bossier (1860-1907)

- Joseph Albert Bossier Sr. (1831-1868)
  - Maximilien Bossier (1789-1832)
    - Jean Pierre Bossie (1757-1846)
      - Jean Pierre Bossier *dit* Lebrun (1729-1816)
      - Marie Madeleine Manon Rome (c1734-?)
    - Marguerite Borne (1769-1846)
      - Jacques Antoine Borne (1737-1809)
      - Anne Marie Heidel (c1742-1810)
  - Felicite Desiree Songy (1805-1849)
    - Martin Firmin Songy (1773-c1824)
      - François Valentin Joseph Songy (1736-1776)
      - Charlotte Rillieux (c1746-1789)
    - Euphrosine Folse (1781-1860)
      - Antoine Folse (c1756-c1822)
      - Marie Borne (?-1798)
- Louise Marie Malvina Reynaud (1836-1894)
  - Martin Songy Reynaud (1801-1843)
    - Jean Reynaud (1757-1807)
      - Pierre Reynaud (1701-1770)
      - Marie Marguerite de Becaris (1721-?)
    - Marie Charlotte Eleonore Songy (1767-1828)
      - François Valentin Joseph Songy (1736-1776)
      - Charlotte Rillieux (c1746-1789)
  - Marie Malvina Vives (1810-1842)
    - Jean Landry Chevalier Vives (1782-1809)
      - Juan Francisco Chevalier Vives (1751-1822)
      - Marguerite Bujol (1751-1805)
    - Marguerite Marie Bourgeois (1790-1815)
      - Dominique Bourgeois *fils* (1771-?)
      - Marguerite LaGrange (c1770-?)

#4 Vial-Martin Family Tree: Vial-Richard-Bossier-Reynaud

- Leonide Mary Vial (1879-1964)
  - Louis Adolphe Vial (1642-1910)
    - Charles Francois Leon Vial (1813-1873)
      - Claude Vial (1782-1832)
        - Jean-Charles Vial (1754-1829)
        - Catherine Satin (1758-1802)
      - Magdeleine-Francoise Josephine Daraïn (1787-1854)
        - Marie-Joseph Daraïn (1747-1805)
        - Marie-Francoise de Saffon ca.1764-1838)
    - Marie Magdeleine Richard (1806-1895)
      - Joseph Etienne Richard (1761-1834)
        - Fabien Richard (1718-1772)
        - Francise Jeanne Simon Dujpont (1733-1803)
      - Marie Louise Dupille (?)
        - Yves Florentin Dupille (?)
        - Marie Elizabeth Liard (?)
  - Louise Clothilde Malvina Bossier (1860-1907)
    - Joseph Bossier (1831-1868)
      - Maximilien Bossier (1789-1832)
        - Jean Pierre Bossier (ca.1757-1846)
        - Marguerite Borne (ca.1769-1846)
      - Felicite Desiree Songy (1805-1849)
        - Martin Firmin Songy (1773-ca.1824)
        - Euphrosine Folse (1781-1860)
    - Louise Marie Malvina Reynaud (1836-c1894)
      - Martin Soncy Reynaud (1801-ca.1843)
        - Jean Reynaud (1757-ca.1807)
        - Marie Charlotte Eleonore Songy (1767-1828)
      - Marie Malvina Vives (1810-1842)
        - Jean Landry Chevalier Vives (1782-ca.1809)
        - Marguerite Marie Bourgeois (1790-ca.1815)

Appendix 295

#5 Vial-Martin Family Tree: Martin-Guibert-LaBranche-Triche-Millet

- J.B. Martin Jr. (1881-1955)
  - J.B. Martin Sr. (1847-1897)
    - Joseph Honoré Edouard Martin (1818-1864)
      - Joseph Auguste Therese Martin (1766-1839)
        - Joseph Bernard Martin (1726-1790)
        - Anne Magdeleine Ginouves (?-?)
      - Marie Elisabeth Jacques Guibert (1781-1845)
        - Pierre Gabriel Guibert (?-1809)
        - Jeanne Magdelaine Ossone deVierre (~1760-1790)
    - Aimée Colette Labranche (1826-1877)
      - Jean Baptiste Labranche (1777-1837)
        - Michael Labranche (1738-1767)
        - Louise Fortier (1755-1828)
      - Aimée Trepagnier (1785-?)
        - Jean Trepagnier (1747-1811)
        - Marie Labranche (1751-?)
  - Celeste Triche (1852-1924)
    - Andre Triche III (c.1826-1890)
      - Andre Triche II (1795-?)
        - Andre Baltazar Triche I (1754-1829)
        - Marie Delphine Lasseigne (1763-1813)
      - Celeste Clement (?-?)
        - Jacques "Santiago" Clement (1776-1851)
        - Therese Helfer (1774-1852)
    - Marie Irma Millet (1830-c.1910)
      - Pierre Millet (1804-1853)
        - Jean Millet (1770-1805)
        - Felicite Hautin (1770-1847)
      - Benjamin Poche (1792-1837)

Acknowledgements

Putting this book together has truly been a family effort. The core acknowledgement goes to Minerva Martin (Aunt Min) who inspired our ancestor quest. Immense thanks are due to Wayne Vial, our cousin whose extensive genealogy website provided a treasure of family trees and historic documents. Wayne also served as a beta reader, as did cousins Leon (Sunny) Vial III, Jara and Jeffrey Roux, and Lennie's husband David Gortner. Their assistance with fact-checking, information, and finding errors in the text were invaluable. Family members who reviewed portions of the text and offered helpful suggestions include Nanette Vial, Mary Ann Vial Lemmon, and Tim Vial.

Great appreciation goes to friends and family members who contributed photos which give context and intimacy to people and places. The St. Charles Parish Virtual Museum developed by members of the St. Charles Museum and Historical Association was a rich source of background information. Photos and books of Louisiana publisher and historian Henry E. Yoes III were of immense value. We owe them all beaucoup thanks.

Many thanks to Dorothy (DeeDee) Healthman, editors, and illustrators at Made For Success Publishing who did a great job of getting the multiple components of this book into final form.

And at the root, we honor and appreciate the Acadians—who became the Cajuns—for the rich and diverse history and culture they have passed down to our family.

About Authors

Leonide Martin, native of New Orleans, is an award winning author, editor, and California State University Professor Emeritus. Interest in describing the genealogical and historical background of her South Louisiana family grew out of the Acadian ancestor quest undertaken with her daughter Katherine Bonnabel in 2013. Nearly a decade of research revealed the 14-generation lineage back to Acadia, mostly through maternal lines. This process reconnected many cousins in a shared exploration of roots and heritage, bringing us closer together as a family.

Katherine Bonnabel was born in Southwest Louisiana and spent her early childhood in Metairie and Hahnville. Her deep connection to her family, the land, and the culture of these places fueled her passion to explore the rich heritage of the Acadian people. *Upriver Families* was inspired by a life- changing genealogical journey to Nova Scotia and New Brunswick with her mother Leonide Martin, where they discovered the places that their Acadian ancestors called home.

Corinne Martin was born in Houma and grew up near family in the upriver parishes. After 40-plus years living away from the state, during which she practiced as a clinical herbalist, interfaith minister, and a university professor publishing three books, she was drawn back to her Louisiana roots following the death of a beloved aunt. There was a sudden visceral longing to return. Responding to the tugging mysteries and bonds of family, she joined two newly re-found cousins, now co-authors, in the adventure of tracing family roots. Deeply anchored in South Louisiana now, as family twines all around, she couldn't be happier.

References

Chapter 4

1. Samuel de Champlain. *Voyages of Samuel de Champlain*, 1604-1618. Ed. W.L. Grant, Charles Scribner's Sons, New York, pp.36-37.
2. M.A. MacDonald. *Fortune & La Tour: The Civil War in Acadia*. Methuen Publications, Ontario, Canada, 1983, pp. 5-6.
3. Steven A. Cormier. "Acadians in Gray. Book One – French Acadia." Acadian/Cajun History and Genealogy Website, 2001-2019. www.acadiansingray.com
4. Cormier, "Acadians in Gray. Book One – French Acadia."
5. Cormier, "Acadians in Gray. Book One – French Acadia."
6. Cormier, "Acadians in Gray. Book One – French Acadia."
7. Dictionary of Canadian Biography. "Membertou." http://www.biographi.ca/en/bio/membertou
8. MacDonald, *Fortune & La Tour,* p.13.
9. Father Clarence d'Entremont. "A Father Assails His Son In Combat." Charles I de Saint-Etienne de La Tour. http://acadie1755.tripod.com/lrr01/lrr01_003.htm
10. Father Clarence d'Entremont. "A Father Assails His Son In Combat."
11. Father Clarence d'Entremont. "First Nun in North America Was Born At Our Doorstep." Antoinette de La Tour. http://acadie1755.tripod.com/lrr01/lrr01_003.htm
12. MacDonald, *Fortune & La Tour,* p.49.
13. MacDonald, *Fortune & La Tour,* p. 69.

14. MacDonald, *Fortune & La Tour,* p. 100.
15. MacDonald, *Fortune & La Tour,* p.148.
16. MacDonald, *Fortune & La Tour,* pp.170-171.
17. Cormier, "Acadians in Gray. Book One – French Acadia," Chapter 1 note 34.
18. MacDonald, *Fortune & La Tour,* p.178.
19. MacDonald, *Fortune & La Tour,* p.198. (Includes surnames: Amirault (Amero, Amiro), Aucoin, Belleisle, Bourgeois, Comeau, Couillard, d'Entremont, D'Eon, Dugas, Dupont du Chambon, Duvivier, Landry, LeBlanc, Leborgne, Melanson, Mius, Petitpas, Poirier, Richard, Robichaud, Theriault, Thibodeau, Viens, and a host of others.)
20. Jeanne (De Latour) Saint-Etienne de La Tour. WikiTree, https://www.wikitree.com/wiki/De-Latour.
21. Dictionary of Canadian Biography. "Apprendestiguy (Daprandesteguy, Arpentigy), Martin D', Sieur de Martignon." http://biography.ca/en/bio/aprendestiguy_martin_d

Chapter 5

1. Steven A. Cormier. "Acadians in Gray. Book One – French Acadia." Acadian/Cajun History and Genealogy Website, 2001-2019. www.acadiansingray.com
2. Jacques-Jacob Bourgeois Family Tree. www.geni.com
3. Stephen A. White. *Dictionnaire Généalogue Des Familles Acadiennes, Centre D'Études Acadiennes,* University of Moncton, Canada. Vol. 1 A-G.
4. Cormier, "Acadians in Gray. Book One – French Acadia." Ch. 1 ref.89.
5. Cormier, "Acadians in Gray. Book One – French Acadia." Ch. 1 ref.91. Family names of settlers coming in late 1670s and early 1680s include: Chiasson dit Lavallée, Larché, Cormier, Caissie, Belliveau, Bernard, Boucher, Bourg, Brun, Carret, Clémençeau, Daigre, Doiron, Doucet, Dugas, Forest, Gaudet, Gravois, Guénard, Hébert, Hugon, Labauve, Lambert, Landry, Lanoue, Livois, Martin, Melanson, Morin *dit* Boucher, Mouton, Olivier, Orillon, Pothier, Quimine, Richard, and Thériot.
6. Cormier, "Acadians in Gray. Book One – French Acadia." Ch. 1 ref.98. Among those engaged in commerce were the Boudreau and de Goutin families; Alexandre Le Borgne de Bélisle and his descendants held the *seigneurie* at Port-Royal for several decades. Among the other families living there were: Allain, Babineau, Bastarache,

Belliveau, Blanchard, Bonnevie, Bourg, Bourgeois, Breau, Broussard, Brun, Comeau, Doucet, Dugas, Duon, Dupuis, Forest, Gaudet, Gauthier, Gautrot, Girouard, Gousman, Granger, Guédry, Guilbeau, Hébert, Henry, Jeanson, Landry, Lanoue, Lavergne, LeBlanc, Léger, Levron, Martin, Martin *dit* Barnabé, Melanson, Michel, Moyse, Orillon, Part, Pellerin, Préjean, Prince, Richard, Robichaud, Roy, Savary, Savoie, and Thériot.

7. Cormier, "Acadians in Gray. "Book One – French Acadia." Ch 1 – First census 1671.
8. Cormier, "Acadians in Gray. "Book One – French Acadia." Ch 1 – First census 1671.
9. Cormier, "Acadians in Gray. "Book One – French Acadia." Ch 1, ref.93.
10. Cormier, "Acadians in Gray. "Book One – French Acadia." Ch 1, ref.94. Settlers surnames in these regions were Arsement, Babin, Barillot, Benoit, Boudrot, Boutin, Brasseur, Breau, Broussard, Bugeaud, Chauvet *dit* La Gerne, Comeau, Corporon, Daigre, Doiron, Forest, Gaudet, Gautrot, Girouard, Guédry, Hébert, Landry, LeBlanc, Lejeune, Martin, Michel, Mire, **Pitre**, Prince, Richard, Rivet, Roy, Savary, Thibodeau, Trahan, and Vincent.
11. Wikipedia. "Battle of Grand Pré." https://en.wikipedia.org/wiki/Battle_of_Grand_Pré.

Chapter 6

1. Carl A. Brasseaux. *The Founding of New Acadia: The Beginnings of Acadian Life in Louisiana, 1765-1803*. Louisiana State University Press, 1987, p.1.
2. Brasseaux, *The Founding of New Acadia*, p.1.
3. Carl A. Brasseaux. *Scattered to the Wind: Dispersal and Wanderings of the Acadians, 1755-1809*. University of Southwestern Louisiana, Center for Louisiana Studies, Lafayette, 1991. Tables I and II, pp.2, 4.
4. Brasseaux, *Scattered to the Wind*, p.1.
5. Charles D. Mahaffie Jr. A *Land of Discord Always: Acadia From Its Beginnings to the Expulsion of Its People, 1604-1755*. Nimbus Publishing, Halifax, Nova Scotia, 2003, p.119.
6. Warren A. Perrin. *Acadian Redemption: From Beausoleil Broussard to the Queen's Royal Proclamation*. Andrepoint Publishing, LLC, Opelousas, 2005, p.9.
7. Steven A. Cormier. Acadians in Gray. Book Ten: "The Louisiana Acadian 'Begats.' Website http://www.acadiansingray.com/

8. Naomi Griffiths. *The Acadians: Creation of a People*. McGraw-Hill Ryerson, Toronto, 1973.
9. Brasseaux, *The Founding of New Acadia*, p.15.
10. Brasseaux, *The Founding of New Acadia*, p.16.
11. Mahaffie, *Land of Discord Always*, p.186.
12. Mahaffie, *Land of Discord Always,* p.204.
13. Mahaffie, *Land of Discord Always,* p.230.
14. Arthur G. Doughty. *The Acadian Exiles*. Toronto, 1920. Letter from A. Doucet to Mde. Langedo of Quebec, August 5, 1750.
15. Brasseaux, *The Founding of New Acadia,* p.20.
16. Mahaffie, *Land of Discord Always,* p.240.
17. Brasseaux, *The Founding of New Acadia,* p.23.
18. Arthur G. Doughty. *The Acadian Exiles: a Chronicle of the Land of Evangeline*. Chronicles of Canada, Eds. George M. Wrong and H.H. Langton, Toronto, 1916, p.45.
19. Doughty, *Acadian Exiles,* p.43.
20. Doughty, *Acadian Exiles,* p.46.
21. Brasseaux, *The Founding of New Acadia,* p.24.
22. Doughty, *Acadian Exiles,* p.54. Winslow's Journal part ii, p.94.
23. Doughty, *Acadian Exiles,* p.55. Winslow's Journal, Part ii, p.109.
24. Andrew Hill Clark. *Acadia: The Geography of Early Nova Scotia to 1760*. Madison, 1968.
25. Brasseaux, *Scattered to the Wind,* p.8.
26. Brasseaux, *Scattered to the Wind,* p 44.
27. Brasseaux, *Scattered to the Wind,* p.46.
28. Perrin. *Acadian Redemption*, p.vii.
29. Perrin, *Acadian Redemption*, p.6-7.
30. Perrin, *Acadian Redemption*, p.23.
31. Perrin, *Acadian Redemption*, p.27-28.
32. Perrin, *Acadian Redemption*, p.44.
33. Perrin, *Acadian Redemption*, pp. 46-47.

Chapter 7

1. Carl A. Brasseaux. *Scattered to the Wind: Dispersal and Wanderings of the Acadians, 1755-1809*. University of Southwestern Louisiana, Center for Louisiana Studies, Lafayette, 1991, p.9.

2. Carl A. Brasseaux. *The Founding of New Acadia: The Beginnings of Acadian Life in Louisiana, 1765-1803*. Louisiana State University Press, 1987, p. 38.

3. Brasseuax, *The Founding of New Acadia*, p. 38.

4. Brasseaux, *The Founding of New Acadia*, p. 40.

5. Brasseaux, *The Founding of New Acadia*, p. 43.

6. Warren A. Perrin. *Acadian Redemption: From Beausoleil Broussard to the Queen's Royal Proclamation*. Andrepoint Publishing, LLC, Opelousas, 2005, p. 141.

7. Brasseaux, *Scattered to the Wind*, p. 34.

8. Brasseaux, *Scattered to the Wind*, p. 38.

9. The Indigenous Louisiana French Creole People. Website: www.frenchcreoles.com

10. Brasseaux, *The Founding of New Acadia*, pp.79-80.

11. Steven A. Cormier. Acadians in Gray. Book Eight. Website: http://www.acadiansingray.com/

12. Brasseaux, *Scattered to the Wind*, p. 62.

13. Brasseaux, *The Founding of New Acadia*, p. 110.

14. Brasseaux, *The Founding of New Acadia*, pp.106-107.

15. Jay M. Schexnaydre. Personal communication. February 2022. President, German-Acadian Coast Historical & GenealogicalSociety, LaPlace, Louisiana.

16. Cormier, Acadians in Gray. Book Eight. Website: http://www.acadiansingray.com/

17. Brasseaux, *The Founding of New Acadia*, p.139.

18. Brasseaux, *The Founding of New Acadia*, p. 121.

19. Steven A. Cormier. Acadians in Gray. Appendices: Acadians Who Found Refuge in Louisiana, February 1764—Early 1800s. Bijeaux/Bujole, Joseph, Ascension census 1777. Website http://www.acadiansingray.com/ ©2007-21.

20. Cormier, Acadians in Gray. Appendices: Acadians Who Found Refuge in Louisiana, February 1764—Early 1800s. Bijeaux/Bujole. Conclusion. Website http://www.acadiansingray.com/ ©2007-21.

21. Brasseaux, *The Founding of New Acadia*, p. 173.

22. Brasseaux, *The Founding of New Acadia*, p. 84.

23. Belle Alliance Plantation Circa 1846 in Louisiana. Website: http://oldhouseaddicts.com/index.php/2017/11/20/belle-alliance-plantation-circa-1846-louisiana/

24. Claire Puneky. "Vives' 1775 Land Marker Dedicated in Assumption. Descendants of Officer, N.O. Group Attend." *Times Picayune,* New Orleans, 1965.

25. Jay M. Schexnaydre. Personal communication. February 2022. President, German-Acadian Coast Historical & GenealogicalSociety, LaPlace, Louisiana.

Chapter 8

1. Archives of the Archdiocese of New Orleans, LA. 70116-2596, 1988, Vol. 2, 1751-1771 – 239, SLC B5/176.

2. Biographical and Historical Memoirs of Louisiana. www.ancestry.com

3. Reports of Cases Argued and Determined in the Supreme Court of the State of Louisiana, Vol. XIII, New Orleans, March 1839.

4. *Le Raconteur,* Extracts from the *Lafourche Gazette,* Donaldsonville, Louisiana, 1826.

5. Death certificate of Marie Malvina Vives Reynaud. Funeral certificate, ANO Archives, New Orleans, LA.

6. Laura D. Kelley. "Yellow Fever in Louisiana." https://64parishes.org/entry/yellow-fever-in-louisiana

7. First Settlers of the LA Territory. Orleans Territory Grants from American State Papers Class VIII, Public Lands, Vol. I. Distributed by Ericson Books, Nacogdoches, Texas. Ingmire Publishing, St. Louis, MO.

8. First Settlers of the LA Territory. Orleans Territory Grants from American State Papers Class VIII, Public Lands, Vol. II. Distributed by Ericson Books, Nacogdoches, Texas. Ingmire Publishing, St. Louis, MO.

9. Carl A. Brasseaux. *Acadian to Cajun: Transformation of a People, 1803-1877*, University Press of Mississippi, Jackson, MS, p. 8.

10. Brasseaux, *Acadian to Cajun*, p. 11.

11. Brasseaux, *Acadian to Cajun*, pp.16-19.

12. *Baton Rouge Gazette*, 1845. Quoted in Audisio, "Crisis in Baton Rouge,"p.358.

13. Marius M. Carrière, Jr. "Know Nothing Movement in Louisiana." Ph.D. dissertation, Louisiana State University, 1977, pp.91-115.

14. Brasseaux, *Acadian to Cajun*, p. 99.

15. A. R. Waud. "Acadians of Louisiana," *Harper's Weekly*, October 20, 1866

16. Albert Rhoads. "The Louisiana Creoles," *Galaxy* 14, July 1873.

17. Frederick Law Olmsted. *A Journey in the Seaboard Slave States in the Years 1854-1854*. G. P. Putnam's Sons, 1856.

18. *New Orleans Bee*, Nov. 20, 1861; *The New Orleans Daily True Delta*, Nov. 20, 1861.

19. Notre Dame Archives, Sisters of Charity of Nazareth, KY.

20. 1830 U.S. Census, St. John the Baptist Parish, Louisiana.

21. 1860 Census: 21 July 1860, Bonnet Carré Post Office, St. John the Baptist Parish, LA.

22. *Le Méschacébé*, December 5, 1868, St. John News. *Les Voyageurs*, Vol. XVII, No. 3, September 1996, p.159.

23. 1860 Census: St. John the Baptist Parish Federal Census, LA. June 12-July 21, 1860.

24. Charley Richard. "200 Years of Progress in the Louisiana Sugar Industry: A Brief History." American Sugar Cane League. www.asset.org›louisiana›progress

25. Engineer and Inventor Norbert Rillieux. https://aaregistry.org/story/engineer-and-inventor-norbert-rillieux/born

26. "The 1724 Code Noir of Louisiana." http://64parishes.org/entry/code-noir-of-louisiana

27. "Plaçage." Wikipedia, https://en.wikipedia.org/wiki/Plaçage

28. John M. Sacher. "Antebellum Louisiana: 64 Parishes." https://64parishes.org Encyclopedia of Louisiana. Ed. David Johnson, Louisiana Endowment for the Humanities, July 28, 2011.

29. Richard, "200 Years of Progress."
30. Deborah Gray White, Mia Bay, and Waldo E. Martin, Jr., Freedom on My Mind: A History of African Americans, St. Martin's Press, New York: Bedford, 2013, p.325.
31. Willie Malvin Caskey. *Secession and Restoration of Louisiana.* Louisiana State University Press, Baton Rouge, 1938.
32. U.S. War Department. *The War of the Rebellion: A Compilation of the Official Records of the Union and Confederate Armies.* U.S. Government Printing Office, Washington, D.C. Ser.4, vol.1, p.475.
33. Brasseaux, *Acadian to Cajun*, p.62.
34. Service Records of Confederate Soldiers, National Park Service. https://nps.gov/civilwar/soldiers-and-sailors-database
35. John D. Winters. *The Civil War in Louisiana.* Louisiana State University Press, Baton Rouge, 1963, p.83.
36. Brasseaux, *Acadian to Cajun,* pp.72-73.
37. St. Emma Plantation. Explore the History and Culture of Southeastern Louisiana. National Park Service-U.S. Department of the Interior. https://www.nps.gov/nr/travel/louisiana/stem.htm
38. Don Frazier. "Fort Butler Memorial," archived Oct. 19, 2013 at the Wayback Machine, Donaldsonville Chief, July 16, 2008. https://en.wikipedia.org/wiki/Donaldsonville
39. Charles P. Roland. *Louisiana Sugar Plantations During the Civil War.* Louisiana State University Press, Baton Rouge, 1997, p.56.
40. Brasseaux, *Acadian to Cajun,* p. 73.
41. American Civil War. Wikipedia: https://en.wikipedia.org/wiki/American_Civil_War
42. Brasseaux, *Acadian to Cajun*, Tables 1-14.
43. 1870 Census: Vol. 1. The Statistics of the Population of the United States, U.S. Census Bureau, 1872.
44. Brasseaux. *Acadian to Cajun,* p.151.

Chapter 9

1. Charles P. Roland. *Louisiana Sugar Plantations During the Civil War.* Louisiana State University Press, Baton Rouge, 1997, p.56.
2. New Orleans *Daily Picayune,* December 4, 1862.
3. Henry E. Yoes III. *Louisiana's German Coast: A History of St. Charles Parish.* Racing Pigeon Digest Publishing Company, Lake Charles, 2005, pp.187-191.
4. Yoes, *Louisiana's German Coast: A History of St. Charles Parish,* p.190.
5. St. Charles Parish Conveyance Books, Book D, page 110, February 14, 1870.
6. Yoes, *Louisiana's German Coast: A History of St. Charles Parish,* pp.138-141.
7. Yoes, *Louisiana's German Coast: A History of St. Charles Parish,* pp.119-128.
8. Roland, *Louisiana Sugar Plantations During the Civil War,* p.3, 90.
9. "Reconstruction: A State Divided." Louisiana State Museum, Online Exhibits, www.crt.state.la.us
10. 1870 U.S. Census, St. John the Baptist Parish Federal Census.
11. Will LeBlanc. *Images of America: Donaldsonville,* Arcadia Publishing, Charleston, South Carolina, pp.28-29.
12. *Donaldsonville Chief,* March 13, 1872. In LeBlanc, *Images of America: Donaldsonville,* p.94.
13. St. Charles Borromeo Church, Destrehan, LA. Wikipedia. https://en.wikipedia.org/wiki/St._Charles_Borromeo_Church.
14. Gerald J. Keller, Lisa Keller-Watson, Darroch Watson. *Precious Gems from Faded Memories: A Pictorial History of St. John the Baptist Parish.* Thompson Shore Publishing, Dexter, MI 2007.
15. Wayne Charles Vial. "Charles François Leon Vial and Marie Magdeleine Richard." http://freepages.genealogy.rootsweb.com, 2001.
16. Joseph-Étienne Richard. Wikipedia. https://en.wikipedia.org/wiki/Joseph_Etienne_Richard.
17. Letter by Ella Vial Baudouin. Received copy from Wayne Vial, January 21, 2021.
18. Wayne Charles Vial. "The Vial Family of St. Charles and St. John the Baptist Parishes." Mt. Pleasant, SC, 2002. wcvial@awod.com (current: wvial@comcast.net) Baptism registers, Mexico City, Ascension and St. Michael the Archangel Parishes.

19. Passenger Lists of Vessels arriving at New Orleans, 1820-1802; M259, Roll 18, February 1-July 31, 1839, lists 59-303.

20. 1840 U.S. Census, Louisiana, Orleans Parish, p.123.

21. New Orleans City Directory, NOPL 917.631.

22. 1850 U.S. Census, M432, Roll 239.

23. L'Avant Coureur, Feb. 5, 1859. Wayne Charles Vial. "The Vial Family of St. Charles and St. John the Baptist Parishes." Mt. Pleasant, SC, 2002. wcvial@awod.com (current: wvial@comcast.net)

24. 1860 U.S. Census, M653, Roll 424.

25. Wayne Charles Vial. Personal communication. Letter received by email January 28, 2021.

26. St. John the Baptist Parish conveyances, recorded February 19, 1872.

27. Obituary Charles François Leon Vial. *Le Meschacébé,* August 16, 1873, p.2.

28. Wayne Charles Vial. "The Vial Family of St. Charles and St. John the Baptist Parishes." Mt. Pleasant, SC, 2002. wcvial@awod.com (current: wvial@comcast.net)

29. Leon C. Vial III. Personal communication. Letter received copy January 2020.

30. Yoes, *Louisiana's German Coast*, p.288.

31. Wayne Charles Vial. Personal communication. Letter received by email January 28, 2021.

32. U.S. Census 1880, 1900, 1910, St Charles Parish, ED 150, 49, 63.

33. Goodspeed Publishing Company. *Biographical and Historical Memoirs of Louisiana, Vol. II*. Chicago, 1892.

34. Goodspeed Publishing Company. *Biographical and Historical Memoirs of Louisiana, Vol. II*. Chicago, 1892.

35. Yoes, *Louisiana's German Coast,* p.248.

36. Yoes, *Louisiana's German Coast,* pp.209-210.

37. Death Certificate Louise C. Vial, Parish of Orleans, Board of Health, 15 April 1907.

38. Obituary Louis Adolphe Vial. *New Orleans Daily Picayune*, April 29, 1910, p.6.

Chapter 10

1. Jim Bryant, "St. Charles Parish, Louisiana." Unpublished paper, Study of the City, Garvin, 5/1/81. St. Charles Parish Library, 1981.
2. Hahnville Town History, Courtesy of *L'Observateur*. St. Charles Parish, LA website, www.stcharlesparish-la.gov, 2021.
3. Elizabeth Mullener, "Edgard/Portrait of a Louisiana country town." *Dixie Magazine, The Times-Picayune*, April 18, 1982.
4. Elizabeth Mullener, "Edgard."
5. Henry E. Yoes III. *Louisiana's German Coast: A History of St. Charles Parish*. Racing Pigeon Digest Publishing Company, Lake Charles, 2005.
6. Henry E. Yoes, *The Pursuit of Academic Excellence*. Marlo, St. Charles Parish, 1991, p.18.
7. Charles P. Roland. *Louisiana Sugar Plantations During the Civil War*. Louisiana State University Press, Baton Rouge. 1957.
8. Elizabeth Mullener, "Edgard."
9. *New Orleans Times Picayune*, Oct. 13, 1924; Jan. 14, 1932.
10. *Louisiana Today* (New Orleans Public Library, pp.338-397.
11. The Historic New Orleans Collection. The Collins C. Diboll Vieux Carré Digital Survey. https://www.hnoc.org/vcs/property_info.php?lot=18629.
12. St. Charles Parish Virtual Museum, "Fashion, Labranche, Other Plantations Destroyed," "Labranche-Esperanza." https://scphistory.org/labranche/, accessed Feb. 2021.
13. Leonard Gray, "The Making of a Political Patriarch." *L'Observateur*, Feb. 11, 2000.
14. "First Parish Newspaper," Oct. 16, 2012, St. Charles Parish History, scphistory.org.
15. Yoes. *The Pursuit of Academic Excellence*.
16. "Gumbo," Yearbook Louisiana State University, Vol. II, 1901.
17. Yoes, *The Pursuit of Academic Excellence*.
18. Nancy Robinson, "Golden Wedding Nears For Martins of Hahnville." *New Orleans States-Item*, Sept. 19, 1953, p. 10.

19. Henry E. Yoes III. "A Spunky Little Lady," *River Parish Focus*, January 1979. St. Charles Parish Virtual Museum. https://www.scphistory.org/Paradis.

20. "Tante Keet's Orchestra," *River Parish Focus*. St. Charles Parish Virtual Museum. https://www.scphistory.org/Paradis.

21. Public School System in St. Charles Parish. St. Charles Parish Virtual Museum https://www.scphistory.org/public-education.

22. J.B. Martin. *Diary* as Secretary of the St. Charles Parish School Board. 1911-1944. August 7, 1911.

23. "Supt. Martin of St. Charles Fetes Jubilee," *New Orleans Times Picayune,* April 28, 1938.

24. "Veteran School Chiefs Honored," *New Orleans Times Picayune,* c.1950.

25. Yoes, *Louisiana's German Coast."*

26. Yoes, *Louisiana's German Coast.*

27. Wikipedia.org/wiki/Papa_Celestin.

28. Yoes, *Louisiana's German Coast.*

29. *Times Picayune*. New Orleans, January 14, 1932, January 19, 1932.

30. "Hahnville Town History" courtesy of *L'Observateur*. https://www.stcharlesparish-la.gov.

31. "What's the Role of an Effective School Board?" Council for A Better Louisiana (CABL) https://cabl.org/public-policy/education/school-board-initiative.

32. J.B. Martin. *Diary* as Secretary of the St. Charles Parish School Board. 1911-1944. August 22, 1929: A special meeting was called to review the work of Supt. Martin. Three members attended, and no action was taken.

33. *Good Hope News*. "Hahnville School Has Splendid Record," Sept. 28, 1929. Reprint by St. Charles Parish Virtual Museum. https://www.scphistory.org/education-expansion.

34. State Department of Education of Louisiana, Baton Rouge, Circular No. 344. Letter from T.H. Harris, State Superintendent. St. Charles Parish Virtual Museum. https://www.scphistory.org/education-expansion.

35. J.B. Martin. *Diary* as Secretary of the St. Charles Parish School Board. 1911-1944. June 7, 1938; July 5, 1938.

36. Yoes, *The Pursuit of Academic Excellence*, p.116.
37. "Death Ends 22 Years of Service," *New Orleans Item*, Feb. 7, 1939.
38. "Vial Era." St. Charles Parish Virtual Museum. https://www.scphistory.org/vial-era.
39. Yoes, *The Pursuit of Academic Excellence*, p.117.
40. J.B. Martin. *Diary* as Secretary of the St. Charles Parish School Board. 1911-1944. April 4, 1944; April 7, 1944.
41. Yoes, *Louisiana's German Coast: A History of St. Charles Parish*, p. 311.
42. Yoes, *The Pursuit of Academic Excellence*, p.131.
43. Yoes, *Louisiana's German Coast: A History of St. Charles Parish*, p. 315.
44. Leonard Gray, "Taking Part in the History of St. Charles Parish." *L'Observateur*, June 27, 2001. www.lobservateur.com/2001/06/27.
45. Nancy Robinson. "Golden Wedding Nears For Martins of Hahnville." *New Orleans States-Item*, Sept. 19, 1953, p. 10.

Epilogue

1. Carl A. Brasseaux. *Acadian to Cajun: Transformation of a People, 1803-1877*. University Press of Mississippi, Jackson, 1992. Appendix Tables 1-4, pp.155-157.
2. Lauren C. Post. *Cajun Sketches: From the Prairies of Southwest Louisiana*. Louisiana State University Press, 1990, p.162.
3. Shane K. Bernard. *The Cajuns: Americanization of a People*. University Press of Mississippi, Jackson, 2003, p. 6.
4. Bernard, p.42.
5. Bernard, p.34.
6. Douglas E. Kneeland. "Young in Cajun Country Don't Dig French Language," *New York Times*, May 9, 1968, p.14.
7. Bernard, p.148.
8. CODOFIL. "Réunion annuelle du CODOFIL." October 16, 1999.
9. Bernard, p.81.
10. Bernard, p.118.

11. Bernard, p.137.
12. Barnard, p.147.
13. Manifesto of Action Cadienne.
14. Herbert J. Gans. "Symbolic Ethnicity: The Future of Ethnic Groups and Cultures in America," *Ethnic and Racial Studies*, January 1979, pp.1-20.
15. Barnard, pp.149-150.
16. Warren A. Perrin. *Acadian Redemption: From Beausoleil Broussard to the Queen's Royal Proclamation.* Chapter 11 – The Petition, pp.105-109. Andrepont Publishing, Opelousas, LA, 2004.
17. Perrin, Chapter 14 – The Royal Proclamation, pp. 119-125.
18. Perrin. p.125.

Made in the USA
Middletown, DE
06 October 2022